To James G. March
From Scandinavian friends and colleagues

Original sources

The CHAPTERS 2–14 in this volume have previously appeared as follows:

CHAPTER 2: Reprinted from G. Grabher (ed.), *The Embedded Firm. The Socio-Economics of Industrial Networks,* pp. 35–51, 1993. London: Routledge.

CHAPTER 3: Reprinted from *Studies in Cultures, Organizations and Societies.* Vol. 1: 63–81, 1995. Harwood Academic Publishers GmbH.

CHAPTER 4: Reprinted from *Scandinavian Housing and Planning Research.* Vol. 9: 65–78, 1992. Scandinavian University Press.

CHAPTER 5: Reprinted from *Governance: An International Journal of Policy and Administration.* Vol. 7, no. 3 : 284–306, 1994. Cambridge Mass.: Basil Blackwell.

CHAPTER 6: Reprinted from *International Review of Administrative Sciences.* Vol. 61, no. 4 : 565–576, 1995. London: Sage.

CHAPTER 7: Partly based on "Sentral-forvaltning og offentlig politikk", *Norsk Statsvitenskapelig Tidsskrift.* Vol. 13, no. 3 : 255–278, 1997. Universitetsforlaget.

CHAPTER 8: Reprinted from W.R. Scott and S. Christensen (eds.): *The Institutional Construction of Organizations. International and Longitudinal Studies*, pp. 67–90, 1995. Thousand Oaks, Calif.: Sage.

CHAPTER 9: Reprinted from *Research in the Sociology of Organization.* Vol. 13: 171–209, 1995. Greenwich, CT: JAI Press.

CHAPTER 10: Reprinted from: B. Czarniawska and G. Sevón (eds.), *Translating Organizational Change*, pp. 49–67, 1996. Berlin: de Gruyter.

CHAPTER 11: Revised version of "The Standardization of Organizational Reforms as a Cropping-up Process", *Scandinavian Journal of Management*. Vol. 13, no. 3: 307–320, 1997. Pergamon Press.

CHAPTER 12: Reprinted from *Scandinavian Journal of Management.* Vol. 11, no. 1: 25–41, 1995. Pergamon Press.

CHAPTER 13: Reprinted from G. Morgan and D. Knights (eds.), *Regulation and Deregulation in European Financial Services,* pp. 201–215, 1997. Houndmills, Basingstoke: Macmillan.

CHAPTER 14: Reprinted from *Journal of Political Philosophy*. Vol. 5, no. 3: 203–229, 1997. Blackwell Publishers.

Contents

Original sources 4
Preface 9

I. Introduction
Chapter 1
Organization Theory: Thirty Years of Dismantling, and then...? 13
Nils Brunsson and Johan P. Olsen

II. The Organizational Mosaic: Beyond Markets and Hierarchies
Chapter 2
The Network as a Governance Structure:
Interfirm Cooperation Beyond Markets and Hierarchies 47
Håkan Håkansson and Jan Johanson

Chapter 3
Soft Cultures: The Symbolism of Cross-Border Organizing 65
Kristian Kreiner and Majken Schultz

Chapter 4
The Social Construction of Projects.
A Case Study of Organizing of an Extraordinary Building
Project – the Stockholm Globe Arena 89
Kerstin Sahlin-Andersson

Chapter 5
The Concept of Subsidiarity and the Debate on European
Cooperation: Pitfalls and Possibilities. 107
Lars C. Blichner and Linda Sangolt

Chapter 6
The Policy-administration Dichotomy Revisited:
the Case of Transport Infrastructure Planning in Norway 133
Morten Egeberg

Chapter 7
Public Administration in a Democratic Context –
A Review of Norwegian Research 147
Tom Christensen and Per Lœgreid

**III. Organizing: Beyond Environmental Dictates and
Rational Design**
Chapter 8
Origin and Transformation of Organizations.
Institutional Analysis of the Danish Red Cross 173
Søren Christensen and Jan Molin

Chapter 9
Winds of Organizational Change: How Ideas Translate into
Objects and Actions 197
Barbara Czarniawska and Bernward Joerges

Chapter 10
Organizational Imitation in Identity Transformation 237
Guje Sevón

Chapter 11
Homogeneity and Heterogeneity in Organizational Forms
as the Result of Cropping-up Processes 259
Nils Brunsson

Chapter 12
Institutionalization of Municipal Accounting –
A Comparative Study Between Sweden and Norway 279
Lars-Eric Bergevärn, Frode Mellemvik and Olov Olson

Chapter 13
Changing Managerial Competitive Practices in the
Context of Growth and Decline in the Finnish Banking Sector..... 303
Risto Tainio, Kari Lilja and Timo Santalainen

Chapter 14
Institutional Design in Democratic Contexts 319
Johan P. Olsen

Contributors 351

Preface

This book is meant first and foremost to honour Professor James G. March. Knowing Jim, we have aimed at making a book for everyday use rather than an old-fashioned *Festschrift*. We have wanted to show some of the variety of organizational research going on in the Scandinavian countries over the last decade. At the same time we have tried to focus on a few key issues when it comes to organizational structures and dynamics in contemporary societies.

There is much to celebrate in 1998. Jim is turning 70, and «*Organizations*», the seminal work he co-authored with Herbert A. Simon, is turning 40. Furthermore, 30 years have passed since the first contacts were established between Jim and Scandinavian students of organizations. And 1998 marks 10 years since the cooperation between Scandinavian academics and Jim and his Stanford colleagues was institutionalized. This happened when the Scandinavian Center of Organizational Research (SCANCOR) was established at Stanford University with Jim as the director, a position he still holds.

James March's outstanding contributions to the international literature over more than 40 years is well known. Here we want to emphasize the decisive role he has played for the development of organizational studies in Scandinavia. Given Jim's special position, many of his Scandinavian friends, colleagues and students would have liked to contribute to this book. Only 23 could be given the chance to do so. Yet, this book expresses a warm thanks from the whole Scandinavian community of organizational researchers.

Oslo July 1 1998

Nils Brunsson   *Johan P. Olsen*

I.
Introduction

Chapter 1
Organization Theory: Thirty Years of Dismantling, and then...?

Nils Brunsson and Johan P. Olsen[1]

A student of organizations entering the field during the 1960s could easily become enchanted. Within the span of a decade there was an outpouring of seminal books.[2] The (formal, modern, complex) organization was portrayed as a special type of collectivity, different from all other social forms. The significance of the individual organization as a sociological unit was compared to that of the individual organism in biology (March and Simon 1958:4). Understanding how formal organizations were structured, how they worked and were governed, and how they

---

1   We want to thank Martha Snodgrass and Tor Paulson and his colleagues at Fagbokforlaget for help and advice.
2   March and Simon 1958, Blau and Scott 1962, Crozier 1963, Cyert and March 1963, Jacobsen 1964, Etzioni 1964, March 1965a, Katz and Kahn 1966, Lawrence and Lorsch 1967, Thompson 1967.

were maintained or changed over time, was seen as a key to understanding political, economic and social life in modern societies.

Aspirations were high among leading scholars and attempts were made to pull the emerging field of organizational research together. For instance, the ambition of the 1965 *Handbook of Organizations* was "to summarize and report the present state of knowledge about human organizations" and "to describe the present state of organizational research and organization theory" (March 1965b:ix). Thirty years later, the picture looks more complex and visions of the future development of organization theory are tempered with some elements of disillusion.

We relate to this development by starting out with a brief description of Max Weber's conception of "the organization" (*Verband*). This ideal model, portraying organizations as rational and efficient instruments (Weber 1978), has both inspired and provoked students of organizations. One consequence has been that all its basic assumptions have been challenged over the last three decades. Then, we attend to alternative interpretations of these challenges, interpretations more or less pessimistic with regard to the future of organization theory as a discipline of some significance.

Joining the more optimistic camp, we focus upon two themes: How to describe the ways in which organizations organize their interactions and how such patterns of organized interaction evolve and change. One conclusion is that students of organizational structures have to go beyond describing stable patterns of organized cooperation in terms of hierarchies and markets. Another is that analyses of organizational dynamics must go beyond models of environmental dictates and rational design. An elaboration of these observations will follow in the next chapters.

"The Organization"

"Organization" is derived from the Greek word *organon*, i.e. tool or instrument, and organizations have often been understood as the embodiment of purposeful efforts to coordinate, influence and control human behavior in order to reach some preferred outcome. Organizations, then, are seen to reflect aspirations of rationality, effectiveness and efficiency in the control of social life as well as of nature.

Many discussions of the constitutive characteristics of organizations have been variations on a theme of Max Weber. In his ideal type Weber defined the features and dimensions he saw as basic for all organizations, distinguishing them from other social collectivities (Weber 1978: 48–50, also pp. 34, 212, 1404), to wit:

The organization has clear and definite boundaries. It signifies a social unit which is either closed or limits the admission of outsiders. It has a collective identity of its own and there is a strong differentiation between the personnel and resources that belong to the organization and those that do not.

The organization has a central coordination system. There is one locus of final authority and power able to make and enforce binding collective decisions and to sanction non-compliance. Leaders at the center control the concerted efforts of the organization, making it a unitary, hierarchical actor.

The organization is differentiated internally. Internal organizational roles are sharply differentiated and codified in rationally established formal rules. Decisions are implemented by a disciplined, specialized, continuously and rationally operating staff. The official, recruited on the basis of merit and given a life-long career in the organization, can be expected to work "dutifully and honorably according to rules and instructions" (p. 1404). The staff will execute general policies as well as specific commands and bring about compliance or sanction violations.

The organization is legitimate. The organizational order, including the distribution of authority, power and responsibilities, is legitimate. That is, discipline is based on a belief that actors holding certain positions have the authority to impose orders and rules and others have a duty to obey.[3]

The organization's characteristics determine what is achieved. There is a high degree of consistency between organizational goals, structures, processes, behavior and outcomes. The quality of achievements depends directly on organizational structures and processes.

The organization is malleable. Organizations are rationally designed tools, and are deliberately structured and restructured in order to improve their problem-solving capacity and their ability to realize predetermined goals.

The organization is part of a societal transformation. While organizations are seen as rationally designed instruments, their growth, increased significance and acceptance in society also reflect a changing societal context, i.e. the large-scale transformation from traditional to modern society, with its strong belief in, and pursuit of, rationality and social control.

Many later efforts to understand organizations have dealt with the dimensions suggested by Weber's ideal model. In particular, the significance of the organization as a social institution has been linked to the high specificity of structure and coordination processes within organizations, a feature that differentiated organizations from "the diffuse and variable relations *among* organizations and among unorganized individuals" (March and Simon 1958:4). Organizations have been seen both as facilitating rational calculation and as primary sites for studying

---

3   Yet discipline is also based on the incentives and rewards linked to a life-long career. For Weber, discipline signifies «the consistently rationalized, methodically prepared and exact execution of the received order, in which all personal criticism is unconditionally suspended and the actor is unswervingly and exclusively set for carrying out the command». In addition, disciplined conduct under orders is uniform, impersonal and neutral (Weber 1978: 1149).

two basic prerequisites to rational action: calculation of the ways in which pre-determined goals may be attained and the ability to control others whose action is needed to bring about a desired state of affairs (Dahl and Lindblom 1953: 57).

During the 1960s few formulated more clearly the rational-instrumental creed of organizations, with its emphasis on the role of human will, rationality and power in the development of society, than Etzioni:

> In contrast to earlier societies, modern society has placed a high moral value on rationality, effectiveness, and efficiency. Modern civilization depends largely on organizations as the most rational and efficient form of social grouping known. By coordinating a large number of human actions, the organization creates a powerful social tool. It combines its personnel with its resources, weaving together leaders, experts, workers, machines, and raw materials. At the same time it continually evaluates how well it is performing and tries to adjust itself accordingly in order to achieve its goals. As we shall see, all this allows organizations to serve the various needs of society and its citizens more efficiently than smaller and more natural human groupings, such as families, friendship groups, and communities (Etzioni 1964:1).

Dismantling "the organization"

Predicting the victory of the rational and efficient machine-like organization that would place man in an "iron cage", Weber was concerned whether future forms of organization would allow any remnants of individualist freedom (Weber 1978: 1404). The same fear was reflected in Kafka's *Der Prozess* and Chaplin's *Modern Times*. "The organization" was viewed a rational tool, but also as coercive, inhuman, inhumane, and a threat to civilized society.

Many studies of how organizations make decisions and how they change have, however, taken another route the last thirty years.[4] Students of organizations have formulated an analytical-empirical rather than a normative critique of "the organi-zation". On the basis of empirical studies of how organizations actually work they have challenged the assumption that the ideal model of "the organization" provides the best, or even an adequate, interpretation of contemporary organizations.

Organizational boundaries have been described as unclear and permeable. Organizations have been portrayed as "organized anarchies" with participants, problems, and solutions wandering in and out (Cohen, March and Olsen 1972, March and Olsen 1976). Organized cooperation with outsiders has been found to flourish. Insiders and outsiders are connected in a variety of networks, sectors and fields, and influence and control do not coincide with organizational boundaries.[5]

---

4   As will become obvious, we focus on one strand of development in organizational studies, and the references cited will indicate which part of the field we have in mind.

5   DiMaggio and Powell 1983, Scott and Meyer 1991, Marin and Mayntz 1991, Grandori 1997, Mayntz 1997, Rhodes 1997.

reflect more than an ongoing functional competition between forms of organization. Organizations adapt to their normative, as well as their functional environments, and functional efficiency and normative conformity with the environment often suggest different organizational solutions (Meyer and Rowan 1977). Second, adaptations to external environments are not instanteneous, costless, frictionless or unique. Rather, this matching is often inefficient and crude (March and C' 1989: 15–16, March and Simon 1993:16). Typically, ideal m^d presentations of organization travel more easily than ^ zations actually work (Czarniawska and S^

For those who have shared Weber .   .. umental organization, these challenges might give some comfort. . ui others, the challenges might represent a possible threat to a rational and efficient order. However, the criticism has not weakened the general appeal of viewing organizations as rational tools. The idea that organizations are instruments of governance and that an organizational arrangement is, and should be, the result of leadership, rationality and control, is among the most powerful contemporary norms (Scott 1992, Brunsson and Olsen 1993:12).

In practical life the rational-instrumental model is the one most used when organizations and reorganizations are presented, prescribed and justified. For instance, authority and leadership is legitimated by the democratic creed that elected leaders should control public agencies, and the liberal creed that owners should control firms.

Rational-instrumental models also appeal to many students of organizations. For instance, Williamson sees "an incipient science of organization" in the interface of law, economics and organization theory (Williamson 1990:172). Mayntz and Scharpf have developed an rational actor-centered institutionalism (Mayntz and Scharpf 1995, Scharpf 1997). And in a comment to the new institutionalism in sociology, Stinchcombe has suggested a return to the basic idea that organizations and institutions are created and run by purposeful people. Legitimacy is based on beliefs about what organizations and institutions are for, knowledge about their past actions and accomplishments, and predictions of their future commitment, integrity, competence and comparative performance (Stinchcombe 1997).

... and then?

The criticism over the last three decades has challenged the basic assumptions underlying the ideal model of "the organization". It has provided many interesting insights, yet, it has hardly produced a new coherent, theoretically oriented and empirically based research program. In a way, little seems to have changed since

James March in 1965 observed that the study of organizations had a history but not a pedigree (March 1965b:ix). For example, thirty years later the editors of *Handbook of Organization Studies*, rejecting the idea of a single "organization theory", concluded that the two handbooks in most respects were too different to make a comparison worthwhile (Clegg, Hardy and Nord 1996: xxiii, Clegg and Hardy 1996: 24–25).

Still, the nature of the challenges can be seen in different ways. One interpretation is that the criticism has produced more fragmentation of both the concept of organization and the field of organizational studies. Focus then is on "the deconstruction of a reified and instrumentalist conception of organization and on its progressive replacement by a hazier, more anarchic, and less concrete or materialized notion" (Friedberg 1997:65).

For some, this is a story of a discipline that has lost its coherence and self-confidence. It has been asked to what extent it makes sense to consider organization studies a separate subject of inquiry and whether unclear boundaries makes integration of knowledge too problematic (Pfeffer 1997: 4). Furthermore, recognizing the post-modernist deconstructions of the epistemological and ontological assumptions held by students of organizations, two of the editors of *Handbook of Organization Studies* conclude: "Gone is the certainty, if it ever existed, about what organizations are; gone, too, is the certainty about how they should be studied, the place of the researcher, the role of methodology, the nature of theory" (Clegg and Hardy 1996:3). Uncertainty also prevails regarding the fragmentary dynamic itself. Will disintegration of the concept and the field continue, or will this tendency be counteracted by a regrouping around some new core research program? (Reed 1996: 50.)

An alternative is to interpret the criticism of "the organization" as supplementing more than contradicting the Weberian ideal model. Then, observations over the last thirty years are seen as enriching the field of organizational research by expanding the range of variation in organizational phenomena and therefore opening up new and exciting directions.

The fact that "the organization" in many cases fails to illuminate how organizations are structured and governed, and how they work and change, does not mean that the model never captures important aspects of contemporary organizational reality. Organizational boundaries, hierarchies and power, differentiation, legitimacy, organizational impacts, design and societal embeddedness are by no means insignificant phenomena in contemporary societies. Therefore, the spirit here is to view "the organization" as an ideal model with a limited rather than universal application.

Organized cooperative efforts may have, in different combinations, some but not all of the constitutive characteristics and instruments of "the organization"

20

(Grandori 1997, Brunsson and Sahlin-Anderson 1997). Students of organizations cannot expect a single, dominant organizing principle or logic of action. Instead, there is a need to understand the competing ordering principles, the institutional complexity and the co-existence of different partial orders, each possibly considered legitimate in its sphere, that have become a constitutive feature of national and international orders (Mayer, Rittberger and Zürn 1995: 401,405). Consequently, there is a need for a better understanding of how different institutional spheres regulate, legitimate, promote or forbid various kinds of cooperation among organizations such as cartels in a market context and the "capture" of public agencies by private interests in a democratic context. Likewise, we need to understand how different institutions allow, or counteract, the peaceful destruction of whole populations of organizations when better alternatives become available (Stinchcombe 1997: 13).

This perspective is more consistent with Weber the empiricist than Weber the builder of ideal models. Despite "the organization", Weber observed an empirical world of mixed properties, gradual differences and varying conditions. For instance, according to Weber it was an empirical question for what purposes, within what limits, or under what conditions members of an organization would submit to hierarchical leadership. People were seen to act on the basis of a variety of motives: habits and non-reflected customs, emotion and faith, coercion by staffs, a calculus of self-interest and expected utility, and a belief in authority and a legitimate order deserving of compliance. There were contradictory systems of order, and contradictory interpretations of the meaning of an order. Every system tried to establish and cultivate the belief in its legitimacy, yet some were more successful than others (Weber 1978: XXXV, 31, 32, 36, 50–51, 213). Consequently, Weber defined the constitution of an organization as "the empirically existing probability, varying in extent, kind and conditions, that rules imposed by the leadership will be acceded to" (Weber 1978: 50).

By and large, we agree with the more optimistic perspective, combining an interest in the organizational-structural basis of social life with a focus on individual and collective actors. Modern people tend to be actors. They think of themselves as having purposes, identities and interests, as being rational, and as having some control over resources and capabilities (Meyer and Jepperson 1997). Often they use such faculties for organized collective efforts. As best they can, and with varying results, they act intelligently to order their lives in a complex world not easily comprehended or controlled. They organize for armed protection against outside attack, to secure justice and internal order, to improve their own or others' health, education and social welfare, and to gain prosperity. They create organizations that are supposed to be purposeful and rational actors, able to solve individual and collective problems. Of course, some of these problems are created by existing organizations, either because they do not work as adequate instruments for the purposes of their founders, or precisely because they do.

More than in any previous time society is dominated by organizations. There are more of them and they are more powerful. Organizations focus and hold attention. They provide behavioral rules of appropriateness. They own, control and mobilize resources representing inequalities in wealth and power without presedence in history. They create a durable capability and capacity for action, problem-solving and conflict resolution. In sum, organizations are the main building blocks of social life and it is difficult to understand contemporary societies without understanding the conditions under which organizations evolve, how they work and are governed, their impacts, and how they are maintained and changed.

The challenge, then, is to understand the diversity, complexity and dynamics of contemporary "organizational society". We need better descriptions and analyses of the variety of ways in which individuals and organizations cooperate in a more or less purposeful, unitary, and sustained way. We need better interpretations and explanations of the dynamics of organizational change. Likewise, contemporary societies need normative theories and debates about the alternative ways in which cooperative efforts within or across national borders should be ordered (Føllesdal 1998).

Observing organizations and organizing

To borrow a favorite line of James March: the agenda is tall, our aspirations very modest. This book reflects the belief that the field of organization studies now more than anything else needs detailed empirical descriptions of how cooperative efforts are organized, and how they work and change in practice. Such descriptions are needed across a variety of particular organizational, historical, political and social contexts (also March 1997: 694).

We are less optimistic about attaining progress through meta-debates of the epistemological and ontological foundations of organizational research, or through axiomatic theories that start out with strong (and usually rational) assumptions about organizations, organizing and organizers. In general, the possibility of developing universal, law-like theories may be rather limited. It is unlikely that students of organizations ever will be able to capture the variety and complexity of contemporary organizational society in a single grand theory. An organization theory that covers prisons, armies, courts of law, ministries, universities, firms, trade unions, political parties and others, in different historical periods and cultural contexts, would most likely be too abstract to be very useful. The best we can do is, probably, to locate mechanisms or causal patterns that are frequent, and to point to some conditions that make them more or less likely. We can demonstrate patterns and possibilities and provide posteriori interpretations rather than generate predictions (Mayntz 1997, Elster 1998).

The question, then, is: Where should we look for data in order to get a better comprehension of the organizational mosaic of current societies? Here, we make three suggestions. *First*, it is important to go beyond studies of what is called "organizations" in ordinary language. We need to observe the larger variety of more or less stable patterns of interaction among individual and collective actors, involving to varying degrees and in different combinations the elements of a Weberian organization.[7] That is, we should attend to the actual mechanisms and conditions of organized, cooperative action, whether these are called "organizations" or not (Friedberg 1997:61, 114–115).

Secondly, there is a need to go beyond studies of single organizations and how peoples' thinking and behavior are affected by the fact that they are, or see themselves as, working within a formal organization, and to inquire how interrelations between organizations are organized. In the 1960s Etzioni observed that the interaction among organizations had not been systematically explored and that surprisingly little was known about it (Etzioni 1964:110). During the 1970s a turning point in organization theory was predicted based on the increasing interest in interorganizational networks and processes.[8] However, the development of concepts and data gathering methods appropriate to the interorganizational level has turned out to be remarkably slow (Aldrich and Whetten 1981). Therefore, our motivation is not the belief that an interorganizational focus will revolutionize theories of organizations. Rather, it is the belief that studying how organizations organize their interrelations may provide an opportunity to see more clearly some of the phenomena illuminated by the last decades of criticism.

Thirdly, in addition to studying organizations within a national framework, we might benefit from analyzing their increasing cooperation across national borders. For most students of organizations this is an unexploited source of insights. Yet, students of international affairs have concluded that during this century, and in

---

7   In this chapter we make a distinction between (a) «the organization» as a Weberian ideal model, (b) «organizations» as used in everyday life to identify specific social units like a university, a political party or a business firm, and (c) «organization» as signifying the wider category of more or less stable patterns of organized interaction suggested above. When we refer to the first meaning, we use the term «the organization» or «a Weberian organization». The second meaning is not much used in this chapter and is unlikely to create problems. It is probably more difficult to avoid terminological confusion when we use «organization» in the third meaning, as we do in the rest of the chapter.

8   Evan 1976, also Negandhi 1975, Jørgensen 1977, Nystrom and Starbuck 1981: 385–530, Rogers and Whetten 1982, Sørensen 1998.

particular during the post World War II-period, international institutions, laws, regimes, organizations and networks have become more numerous and more important. The growth in organized, international cooperation has been portrayed as remarkable and unprecedented,[9] and governance is observed to be possible without a world government, a state-like organization or any other source of final authority, power and responsibility (Rosenau and Czempiel 1992, Risse-Kappen 1995). Better insights into international organizations and dynamics are also likely to contribute to a better understanding of organized cooperation in general. One reason is simply that domestic organizations and systems of governance increasingly tend to take on characteristics of international organizations and become less like the Weberian ideal model (Marin and Mayntz 1991, Jachtenfuchs and Kohler-Koch 1996, Rhodes 1997).

These suggestions are pursued and elaborated in the following chapters, presenting a sample of Scandinavian studies published over the last decade. In the context of thirty years of challenges to the rational-instrumental concept of organization, Scandinavian studies may be of interest. This is because, to a large extent, the Scandinavian prescriptive model of governance, organization and welfare has been consistent with the rational-instrumental ethos. Governance has been built on a widespread belief in achieving political purposes and creating a better society by deliberately building and reforming organizational structures (Brunsson and Olsen 1993). At the same time, it is far from obvious that the prescriptive model has coincided with Scandinavian practice, or that it will do so in a period of increasing European integration.

First, however, we go a little further to place these chapters in context by arguing that organizational structures cannot be understood solely in terms of markets and hierarchies, and that organizational change cannot be understood as merely resulting from rational design and environmental dictates.

Organization: Structures beyond hierarchies and markets

Relations among organizations may be diffuse and variable (March and Simon 1958:4), or they may include all the characteristics of "the organization". Then they are based on the same characteristics as intra-organizational relations. They are based on hierarchical authority, shared rules, common conceptions and norms, clear boundaries and identity, common resources and a division of labor and responsibilities. Often, however, only a selection of these organizational characteristics are involved and then in different mixes.

---

9   For a brief summary, see March and Olsen 1998, as well as the literature referred to there.

Sometimes the interaction among organizations follows patterns that are close to the ideal types of markets and hierarchies (Williamson 1975). Organizations may limit their interaction to the spot exchange of resources with whichever partner for the moment provides the best exchange conditions. Or, they can merge into a new organization, in which case those interacting are no longer separate organizations, but individuals belonging to the same organization.

These forms of interaction can be regarded as the extremes on a scale of degrees of organization. Interactions on the (ideal-type) market are organized to a very limited extent; they presuppose only a few common rules. Likewise, relations among states are often seen as "anarchic" (Grieco 1988, Lake 1996). At the other end of the scale, a formal organization can involve all the Weberian organizational characteristics.

In practice, there are many other forms than these extremes. Among the concepts used to capture such forms of interaction are organizational field (Di Maggio and Powell 1983), societal sector (Scott and Meyer 1991), network and multilevel governance.[10] These concepts are used to describe a group of organizations that maintain certain relations to each other. The group may include suppliers and consumers of certain goods and services, state agencies, other regulatory bodies, professional associations and interest groups.

We want to amplify such analyses with a few examples of how organizations that have organizations rather than individuals as members may involve different combinations of the organizational characteristics. Such organized cooperation may take place within a formal organization of organizations or among formally independent organizations.

In either case, the degree of organization can vary substantially in terms of structure, permanence and agenda. Some organizations may just be aware of each other and adapt independently and marginally. Others may develop patterns of interaction based on an elaborate division of labor and authority. Some interactions may occur just once and during a short period of time, as is typical for projects (Jacobsson 1987, Sahlin-Andersson 1989, Lundin and Söderholm 1995). Other interactions may extend over decades (Håkansson 1987). Likewise, agendas vary. Organizations may deal with and affect the activities of their members to varying degrees. For instance, the European Union has a broader agenda, more instruments and more impact on member-states than the OECD has in relations with its members. The industrial branch organization may fight for the members' interests vis-á-vis the state. Still, the members' main activity is to produce and sell and their main environment is likely to be that of their customers, suppliers and competitors.

---

10 Marin and Mayntz 1991, Kreiner and Schultz 1993, Jachtenfuchs and Kohler-Koch 1996, Mayntz 1997, Rhodes 1997.

When the common organization is strong there is less room for "local" autonomy and member organizations take on fewer organizational characteristics. For instance, centralization tends to reduce the need and opportunity for an elaborate "local" administration and task diversity and there is less room for discretion for managers and members (Scott and Meyer 1991). Common rules or goals also constrain the variety of "local" goals and rules. At the same time membership may provide or reinforce an identity for the members. Becoming a member of the United Nations is a sign of being a real state. For states in Central and Eastern Europe becoming a member of the European Union is a sign of being a modern, democratic and market-oriented European state. Being a member of a branch organization may demonstrate that the company is serious and established, and a club that is a member of the national football association is certified as a real club playing real football.

Organizations can be members of organizations on a roughly equal basis, as in many associations. Or there can be huge differences in status and power, as when one organization owns one or several other organizations. In joint ventures two or more companies create a new jointly owned company. A parent company ownde its subsidiaries. In federative corporations the participating companies own a common coordinating company.

Ownership gives the formal authority to impose organizational characteristics. For instance, when one company owns a certain share of another, it has a legal right to influence the selection of the latter's management. Within company groups, the parent company can influence the transfer of resources among the subsidiary companies. More important, the authority of owners can be used to enforce common rules among companies within the group, impose a certain division of labor among them, introduce common goals, and create or reinforce common beliefs and norms. In some combines many of these instruments are used actively, making the difference small between the top management's relation to subsidiary companies and its relations to departments within the parent company. In other cases the parent company cannot, or is not willing to, use such instruments, allowing the subsidiaries more independence.

Interorganizational interactions sometimes involve parts of organizations rather than whole organizations. For instance, one department of one organization may cooperate closely with a department of another organization. Such organizing makes organizational boundaries unclear and makes it difficult for the management of the cooperating organizations to uphold its authority, enforce organizational rules and control organizational resources.

This illustrates that it is not always obvious what should count as an organization with individuals as members and what should be considered an organization of organizations. An organization with individuals as members that by law is one judicial person may sometimes for analytical purposes more fruitfully be viewed as an organization of organizations. This is the case when its various parts are highly independent, which is not uncommon in large, decentralized organizations. The top management has then lost or abdicated authority, and strong internal boundaries have evolved. Parts of a large corporation, being one judicial person, may enjoy a higher degree of autonomy than the subsidiaries in the same company group. Likewise, departments of a large university may have characteristics which makes it reasonable to see them as independent organizations, together forming a common organization of organizations. Furthermore, the public sector in many countries can be analyzed as a large organization consisting of a number of smaller organizations (Ahrne 1998).

Partial organization

Complexity increases because organizations cooperate in many different ways on the basis of some, but not all the organizational characteristics (Grandori 1997). Participants may agree on common rules for how to interact or act towards others. They may have partly the same identity, or work towards the same goals. They may create common external centers with authority to decide on aspects of their activities. They may jointly own resources, or have common members or board members.

International agreements among states, for instance on trade or security, constitute examples of common rules. In some cases, otherwise competing companies agree on common goals when lobbying for better political conditions for their industry. Selling and buying companies cooperate closely on a long term basis in developing products and production processes (Grabher 1993). Companies and trade unions agree on the distribution of surplus and on work rules. Company cooperation within the distribution chain from producer via wholesaler to retailer also involves agreements on common rules (Stern et al. 1997). Such chains sometimes also develop a common identity. Most consumers probably think of the local McDonald's restaurant as part of a single corporation rather than as a franchise owned by a local businessman. In some distribution chains authority is concentrated and participating companies must allow for directives and rules decided centrally by the wholesale company or some other central authority. In other chains the companies jointly own common resources. In construction projects it is common to appoint a third party with the authority to mediate between the participants. Many corporations appoint joint board members (Grandori 1997). Sometimes the terms of cooperation are specified in legally binding contracts. Sometimes they are not, for instance because it may be more difficult to enforce formal contracts if interaction is based on common goals rather than common rules. Cooperation may also be illegal or illegitimate, which makes the parties avoid formal contracts or makes such contracts less useful. Illegal cartel cooperation is one example.

27

In projects common action may be an incentive for organizing rather than its result – a project may attract organizations rather than the other way round. It may provide meaning and identity, and time limits may create rules that facilitate coordinated action (Sahlin-Andersson 1989, Lundin and Söderholm 1995).

Obviously, in some cases cooperation between independent organizations may not be all that different from the formal organization of organizations. The former may even include more organizational properties than the latter.

Additional complexity comes about because interorganizational relations are often influenced by outsiders, like states and standardizing agencies. States use a number of instruments to regulate the relations between other organizations, including hierarchical authority, bargaining, diffusion of information, and appeals to national goals, identities and solidarity. For instance, states exert influence over organizational resources via taxation. They formulate rules for how organizations shall be constructed and work (Olsen 1989). They regulate organizational activities across national boundaries and they facilitate market-building by removing barriers to trade, for example, via laws concerning ownership, associational forms and conditions of employment and pension rights.

Recently many states have lost some of their regulating and structuring powers. In an age of economic globalization and mass migration it has become more difficult to control national borders. State intervention has also fallen into some disrepute, with deregulation and privatization as one result. However, state deregulation does not necessarily mean that the total number of rules structuring inter-organizational relations is reduced. There are many other kinds of rules than those issued by states and one such set is standards (Brunsson and Jacobsson 1998, Vad 1998). Standards are rules offered to many. They are not backed by hierarchical authority, hence compliance is voluntary, at least in a formal sense.

Standards are abundant in modern society and there are many producers of standards. Some of them are established organizations such as ISO (International Organization for Standardization) or CEN (Comité Européen de Normalisation) with standardization as their explicit purpose. Yet a large number of other international and national organizations issue standards. There are standards for terminology, statistics and accounting; for how contracts should be written and products and production processes be designed. There are also standards for how organizations should be structured and managed. For example, the OECD, the World Bank and the European Union issue standards for how public sectors should be organized and managed and how national economies should be run (Olsen 1998, Sahlin-Andersson 1998).

The lack of hierarchical authority may make it hard to implement and enforce standards. This notwithstanding, standards may be powerful instruments of coordination. When many organizations follow common standards their interaction is facilitated. Products and production processes become compatible and communication needed for coordination becomes more efficient. The knowledge or expectation that others are following a certain standard makes it unnecessary to spend time and resources gathering detailed information about the likely behavior of others.

Standardization is a form of inter-organizational coordination that requires few organizational characteristics. It does not imply hierarchical authority. Organizations do not have to share goals or causal beliefs. And there are no boundaries – anyone can choose to follow a standard. Therefore organizations following standards are modestly constrained. They do not have to compromise existing authority relations, goals, causal beliefs and boundaries. In sum, standardization in its pure form is a form of coordination among highly independent organizations. It is a form most likely found in situations where participating organizations value their autonomy highly and where they can not be forced to give up their identities and constitutive characteristics.

By itself standardization is a simple form of coordination. Still it adds complexity to the organizational mosaic of current societies. One reason is that standards often compete, like statistical standards suggested by the United Nations, European institutions and national agencies (Sangolt 1997). Another reason is that standards are often combined with other forms of authority or power. The agency issuing standards may not have the authority or power to impose a standard, yet other institutions and organizations, buyers and consumers, media and public opinion may have the capability to do so.

A reasonable conclusion is that contemporary societies have developed a complexity of inter-organizational structures that are not easily captured by ideal models of hierarchies or markets. It is clearly unsatisfactory to portray the many degrees and combinations of organizational characteristics as deviations or imperfections of these two ideal models. It is equally obvious that concepts like organizational field, societal sector, network and multilevel governance currently are not precise enough to unravel the tangle. The problems of understanding organizational structures are matched by those of comprehending the dynamics of change – as we shall se in the next section.

Organizing: Change beyond environmental dictates and rational design

It is commonly assumed that organizations (to some degree) are controlled and managed by internal leaders who design and reform structures in order to achieve improved results. Likewise, it is commonplace to assume that organizations (to some degree) adapt to their changing environments (Nystrom and Starbuck 1981).

In their purified form these two approaches suggest that organizational dynamics can be understood either in terms of the changing will and power of a leader group, or in terms of macro-changes in the environments of organizations (Olsen 1992, Czarniawska and Sevón 1996). The two purified versions share the assumption that we do not need to know anything about the internal structure, culture, history and dynamics of an organized cooperative effort in order to understand how it changes.

In contrast, we suggest that it is necessary to go beyond micro-theories of rational design, focussing on the will and resources of an identifiable group of actors, and macro-theories of environmental determinism, focussing on environmental changes that "dictate", "require" or "force" organizational changes. In conjunction with the criticism summarized in the beginning of this chapter, it is assumed that we need to know more about internal features of a cooperative effort in order to make sense of the processes by which cooperation emerges, is maintained, develops over time and disappears.

A first step towards understanding organizational dynamics is to make a distinction between the processes and mechanisms that establish, maintain and change actual interaction patterns and relationships between organizations, and those that affect organizational charts, presentations and images. Actors who try to design and reform organizations often operate in an ideal "model-world" of schematic charts, abstract principles and simplified goals and success indicators. In contrast, real organizations operate in a complex world of everyday practices, historically developed on the basis of local experience and codified in a local culture. This is a world which only those directly involved know and understand in any detail, and from the insiders' perspective the model-world of reformers often looks thoroughly simple, naive and distorted. It is therefore no surprise that reforms based on simple prescriptive models seldom succeed in achieving their aims. Neither is it a surprise that such reforms often increase rather than decrease the felt need for, and probability of, new reforms. Finally, from this perspective it is often observed that organizations work well precisely because naive reforms have **not** been implemented (Brunsson and Olsen 1993).

Another step is to observe that change is sometimes the result of shifts in causal and normative beliefs, not of variations in material incentives and powers. Typically such re-definitions include not only shifts in societal belief systems but also organization specific changes. They include changes through a new focus of attention, modifications of key concepts and assumptions, the diffusion and translation of ideas, the redefinitions of issues, problems and possibilities and the construction of new accounts of the past (March and Olsen 1995, 1998, Czarniawska and Sevón 1996). A recent example of such processes can be found in the public sector reforms labeled "the new public management" across a large number of countries. Here public agencies traditionally seen as embedded in a democratic system of governance have been redefined as firms embedded in competitive markets. Bureaucrats have been redefined as managers, and citizens redefined as customers (Røvik 1992, Brunsson 1994, Olsen and Peters 1996, Olsen 1998).

Recognizing these aspects of the dynamics of organizational change, in the following we focus on the integration and disintegration of organized cooperative efforts. We suggest that understanding organizational dynamics implies insight into how single cooperative efforts as well as whole systems of organized action – nation states and international orders included – tend to integrate and disintegrate over time (March and Olsen 1998). At some periods and in some contexts, organizational borders, the degree of central coordination, internal differentiation, legitimacy, performance, the degree of malleability and autonomy from the environment are strengthened. At other periods and in other contexts they are weakened, for example, as an organization becomes part of a larger system.

Integration and disintegration

As mentioned above, the integration of an organized unit into a larger unit is likely to have implications for patterns of behavior and control. "Cosmopolitans" interact differently than "locals" (Gouldner 1957). That is, behavior is strongly differentiated as a function of the degree to which actors are involved with larger systems or embedded in a local system (Stinchcombe 1974:53). In particular, it has been suggested that, as relatively autonomous and independent units become integrated into a larger unit of organized activity, the internal dynamics of the original group tend to change. The effectiveness of internal leadership control is reduced with decreasing organizational autonomy, and the organization loses coherence and unity (March 1953).

Likewise, it may be assumed that disintegration of a unit, where smaller units wrench themselves free and become more autonomous, will have significant effects. For instance, many reforms in European public sectors during the last twenty years can be interpreted as attempts to create more complete organizations at the "local" level and at the same time weakening the relations between them (Brunsson and Sahlin-Andersson 1997). Various authorities that used to be considered agencies and instruments for the higher political levels, with few organizational characteristics of their own, have been given clearer goals and boundaries, more authority and discretion, and more responsibility for their results. Sometimes they have also become separate units in the legal sense.

Consequently, they have formulated their own rules and identity and they have tended to relate to each other in less organized ways. They sell to and buy from each other and they negotiate with or disregard each other. They have probably also become more difficult to control by orders, directives and rules from above. During the same period, similar solutions have also become popular in the private sector.

31

Separate companies have been created for what was previously handled by corporate departments. As "back to basics" and "outsourcing" have become catchwords, corporate departments have been sold or shut down and their services have been bought from other companies.

Just like organizations of individuals, organizations of organizations have to strike a balance between, on the one hand, developing a common identity or a capability for joint action and, on the other hand, protecting the identity and autonomy of the members. Usually, it is difficult to introduce many and strong elements of common organization (e.g. authority, rules, goals, boundaries) and at the same time maintain or increase the autonomy, discretion and variety of member organizations.

One implication is that expected impacts on one's own autonomy affect the support of, or resistance against, processes of integration. Actors inclined to defend the identity, unity and power distribution of the original unit will tend to be against integration into a larger unit. Those who want to modify or change the original unit are more likely to favor integration.

If it is assumed that integration into a larger organized system competes with the desire for autonomy among individual system members (Aldrich and Whetten 1981:401), a major question then becomes which factors affect the degree to which the dilemma becomes acute and the different trajectories of change that actually result. Here we attend to variations caused by (a) how organizations are constituted in the first place, i.e. the basis of an organized effort and (b) the kind of integration and interaction taking place among organizations.

We need to know how change may depend on the nature of the relationships and bonds that constitute and stabilize a pattern of interaction and hold the cooperative effort together. Again, a line may be drawn back to Weber. He argued that an order which is adhered to from motives of pure expediency is generally less stable than one upheld on a purely customary (habitual) basis, which again is less stable than a legitimate order regarded by the actors as obligatory or exemplary, and therefore binding (Weber 1978: 31,33).[11]

If participation is based solely on calculated expected utility, changes will be simple and depend on the varying comparative effectiveness and efficiency of available organizational alternatives. Cycles of integration and disintegration will

---

11 For Weber, in a communal relationship interaction is based on a feeling of belonging together, whether affectual or traditional, i.e. a sense of shared identity that transcends utilitarian concerns and the pursuit of immediate common ends. Associative relationships rest on rationally motivated adjustments of interests. Examples are rational free market exchange, voluntary association based on self-interest, and orientation towards common interest insofar as it seeks only to serve a «cause» (Weber 1978: 40–41)

follow shifts in the comparative efficiency of larger and smaller units. If a unit is held together by coercive means, relative resources and changing alliances will determine the degree and form of change. If the main glue of the system is unreflected tradition, changing patterns of attention and new information may have dramatic and possibly unplanned effects.

The dilemma of keeping an original identity and becoming part of a larger entity will in particular be problematic in organizations held together by a strong shared sense of identity, loyalty and legitimacy. Yet, whether organizations, or parts of organizations, will have to give up constitutive characteristics when entering a larger social unit depends on how well the organizational identities of the larger and smaller units "match".

Such variations can, for instance, be observed in the relationship among the European Union, its member states, and states wanting membership. The dilemma is also observed in the intersection between European integration and Nordic (Scandinavian) cooperation. The fact that 80% of the population in the Nordic countries now are citizens of the European Union provides a potential challenge to the traditional Nordic cooperation. The outcome is likely to depend on the degree to which the Nordic cooperation, to different groups of participants, has been a purely instrumental and pragmatic one based on calculation of comparative efficiency, and the degree to which it has been based on feelings of brotherhood and community among the Nordic countries. The outcome is also likely to depend on the changing "match" between a European order with a competitive market as the institutional center-piece and a Nordic order with the welfare state as a key institution (Olsen and Sverdrup 1998). Predicting such outcomes, however, is extremely difficult. The European Union and national systems have their own internal dynamics. They are at the same time affecting each other in a process of interaction and co-evolution, and they are influenced by external processes of globalization and internationalization.

One implication is that the form of integration taking place is of importance for how members and potential members will respond. Different forms and degrees of integration between organizations have different effects on intra-organizational characteristics such as a shared identity and internal patterns of control. For example, an ideal-type market requires strong organizations. Actors in perfect competitive markets have to be coherent units with clear preferences, authority-relations and boundaries (Brunsson 1999). Standardization is, as we have observed, compatible with member organizations claiming a high degree of independence, as illustrated by the extensive use of standardization within the European Union (Vad 1998). The use of standardization within the EU may reflect claims of national independence and power, together with ambitions on behalf of the European Union to coordinate and control, while lacking adequate authority and resources to issue orders. In contrast, integration taking the form of a merging of organizations will, as we have indicated, usually imply a loss of at least some organizational characteristics. Therefore, this kind of integration demands either a high commitment to a shared vision or a "match" of organizational identities and interests, or extreme power asymmetries among the participants.

Little is known about the precise impacts of the many forms of integration and interaction between full mergers and markets and coordination by standards. If, however, different parts of an organization become integrated into different external networks, e.g. functional networks in their different task environments, internal implications are likely to be considerable. As mentioned above, hierarchical authority and leadership is likely to be challenged, organizational goals and identity tend to be questioned or transformed, organizational boundaries become ambiguous, and internal cohesion can easily be strained. In contrast, when an organization as a whole becomes part of a larger unit, leaders and others with extended external contacts might strengthen their position (Moravcsik 1991, 1993 1997). This would, for instance, be the case when different degrees of external network contacts create increased asymmetrical information among non-participants and participants in the larger system.

The degree to which such considerations are relevant for organizational dynamics may again be studied in the context of the European Union. For instance, the highly specialized participation of bureaucrats, experts and representatives of organized interests in the well developed system of functional committees under the European Commission (Egeberg 1996, Trondalen 1996, Joerges, Ladeur and Vos 1997) is more likely to have a fragmenting effect on nation-states than participation in the Council, where governments are representing member states as territorial wholes.

The studies in this book

These issues are pursued in the following chapters. Here, we make no attempt to summarize each chapter. Rather, the intention is to indicate briefly how these chapters may illustrate aspects of organizational structure (Part II) and organizational dynamics (Part III). We are well aware that several chapters have something to say about both themes.

The theme of the next chapter is well reflected in its title: "The network as a governance structure: Inter firm cooperation beyond markets and hierarchies". Important characteristics of industrial networks, their actors, activities, resources and processes are identified. Activities and resources are analyzed as emergent and enacted phenomena that form webs of interdependencies extending far beyond the horizon of the single actor. The specific features of networks as governance structures are compared to other forms.

Chapter 3 focusses on cross-border organizing, with a study of cooperative efforts in basic research aiming at new products and processes. Here, symbols and a "soft culture" create the identity of a loosely structured research community. They do so by serving as labels defining cooperative efforts as a single project, organization, or network with specific boundaries. This attracts new participants and facilitates the presentation of the cooperation to outsiders, such as financers. At the same time the symbols are ambiguous enough to permit a great variation of non-uniform actions, which may be advantageous for project success.

One large construction project illustrates another form of organization (Chapter 4). Actors did not agree on any purpose, meaning or expected results. Instead, a strict time limit and a well defined site for the building facilitated a concerted action. In many respects the project was ambiguous and changing. Many actors tried to define its meaning and influence its direction. These properties had a similar effect to the ambiguity of symbols: it attracted organizations and resources to the project and facilitated rather than hindered its completion.

Organizational structures capable of balancing membership in a new organization with a desire to keep basic characteristics of the member organizations are discussed in Chapter 5. The focus is on the European Union, where the dilemma has been discussed under the heading subsidiarity. This organizational principle, regulating the authority between levels of governance, suggests that a higher level of authority shall only be involved if an issue cannot be handled adequately by lower levels. In this chapter, as in several others, the positive implications of ambiguity are stressed. The authors argue that the principle of subsidiarity will best serve as a basis for discussing the further evolution of the Union if one can avoid prematurely fixed and detailed interpretations of the principle.

As illustrated by Chapter 6, organizational complexity is by no means limited to loosely organized research and construction projects. Across the OECD area the old doctrine of maintaining a clear distinction between policy-making and administration is still vital. This case study of transport infrastructure planning in Norway portrays organizational reality differently. Interaction is not governed by clear hierarchical authority relations. Enduring institutions, formal organizations, procedures, routines and personnel at the sub-national, national and trans-national levels interact in complex ways, reflecting a variety of competing values, norms, interests and causal beliefs.

Chapter 7 is different from the others. It summarizes a variety of empirical studies and gives a broad overview of Norwegian research on public administration over the last 40 years. The main picture that emerges is that a public administration, historically built primarily on Weberian principles, has lost some but not all of these properties. Public administration is described as integrated into a complex network of domestic political institutions, public agencies, organized interests and clients, as well as extensive European and international networks.

The chapters in *Part III* illustrate a variety of change processes. This section starts out with a chapter emphasizing the importance of environmental features as explanatory factors and ends up with a focus on institutional design. Yet, most chapters document the need for supplementing environmental determinism and rational design as ways of understanding the dynamics of change.

Chapter 8 examines the origin and transformation of the Danish Red Cross. The analysis covers a 12-year foundation period and a more than 125-year history of adaptation and change. The authors primarily emphasize the importance of macro-sociological factors. The origin of the Danish Red Cross is seen as a dramatization of its social environment, and its history as a response to changing normative environments. A Danish felt need to be accepted as a civilized and democratic country and efforts to look good on the international stage are presented as the major explanatory factors.

The next two chapters supplement each other. Chapter 9 is an ambitious, general attempt to move theories of organizational change beyond the received wisdom of understanding change as strategic choice or something environmentally determined. The focus is on how ideas travel in time and space and how they continuously are rejected, transformed and institutionalized in new settings. In order to understand the dynamics of change, it is argued, we have to take into account institutional factors, stochastic events, fashions and intentions, combining in different and changing ways and producing various combinations of change and continuity.

Chapter 10 deals with a specific type of change process – imitation – and argues for its centrality in organizational transformations. Imitation is defined as learning from others and portrayed as part of a process of organizational identity construction. As ideas travel, and as they are interpreted, borrowed selectively, translated and institutionalized in new contexts, whatever is diffused and imitated also changes in the process. One implication is that the traditional dichotomy imitation-innovation becomes unclear and has to be transcended.

The element of local innovation is even more strongly underlined in Chapter 11. Analyzing how homogeneity and heterogeneity arise in the forms adopted by organizations, it is argued that traditional diffusion models are not very useful under modern conditions. One reason is precisely that there is a significant degree of local innovation. Sometimes an organizational form emerges simultaneously in various organizational contexts, without any contact between the organizations and without any exposure to a common transmitter of standard forms. What form a particular organization introduces is highly dependent on the (random) timing of its reform cycles. To capture such processes a "cropping-up" model of homogeneity is presented.

A comparative and historical study of the institutionalization and change of municipal accounting in Norway and Sweden also shows that there are degrees of variation and internal discretion in such processes (Chapter 12). The authors make a distinction between accounting as a norm system and as an action system, and documents how the interrelations between the two vary over time and between countries. Two modes of learning are observed, one ideological and one hierarchical. Even in two countries that in many respects are similar, different historical traditions and structures contribute to different dynamics and outcomes in Norway and Sweden.

Identifiable actors, with an important impact on processes of change, become even more visible in Chapter 13. This is a study of the Finnish banking sector facing a period of deregulation during the 1980s and 1990s, and covers a whole cycle of boom and recession. One conclusion is that even in a period where the banks had to cope with highly turbulent and competitive environments, interpretations of change trajectories have to take into account internal structures, processes and behavior. Changes in competitive practices were to a considerable degree initiated from within the banks. Still, the intentions and goals of the main actors were not necessarily fulfilled.

In the final chapter, the main focus moves all the way from environmental influences to organizational design. Chapter 14 considers the design and redesign of political institutions. Specifically it explores how the possibilities and limitations of change through deliberate design may be affected by the institutional features of contemporary democratic societies. Core questions are: To what degree do democratic contexts create a viable space for institutional design – making design necessary, politically possible and legitimate? What kind of processes tend to make designers able to exploit the available space of design?

References

Ahrne, G. (1998) "Stater och andra organisationer", in G. Ahrne (ed.) *Stater som organisationer*. Stockholm: Nerenius & Santérus.

Aldrich, H. and Whetten, D.A. (1981) "Organization-sets, action-sets, and networks: making the most out of simplicity", in P.C. Nystrom and W.H. Starbuck (eds.) *Handbook of Organizational Design*. Volume 1: pp. 385–408. Oxford: Oxford University Press.

Alvesson, M. and Berg, P.O. (1992) *Corporate Culture and Organizational Symbolism*. Berlin: de Gruyter.

Blau, P.M. and Scott, W.R. (1962) *Formal Organizations*. San Francisco: Chandler.

Brunsson, N. (1985) *The Irrational Organization*. Chichester: Wiley.

_____. (1989) *The Organisation of Hypocrisy*. Chichester: Wiley.

_____. (1994) "Politicization and "company-ization" – on institutional affiliation and confusion in the organizational world", *Management Accounting Research* 5: 323–335.

_____. (1999) "Institutionalized beliefs and practices – the case of markets and organizations", in M. Miller (ed.) *Power and Organization*. London: Sage (forthcoming).

Brunsson, N. and Jacobsson, B. (eds.) (1998) *Standardisering*. Stockholm: Nerenius & Santérus.

Brunsson, N. and Olsen, J.P. (1993) *The Reforming Organization*. London: Routledge. New edition 1997, Bergen: Fagbokforlaget.

Brunsson, N. and Sahlin-Anderson, K. (1997) *Constructing organizations*. Stockholm: SCORE/Stockholm School of Economics and Stockholm University: Working paper 97:8.

Chandler, A.D. Jr. (1962) *Strategy and Structure*. Cambridge Mass.: MIT University Press.

Clegg, S.R. and Hardy, C. (1996) "Introduction: Organizations, Organization and Organizing", in S.R. Clegg, C. Hardy and W.R. Nord (eds.) *Handbook of Organization Studies*, pp.1–28. London: Sage.

Clegg, S.R., Hardy, C. and Nord, W.R. (eds.) (1996) *Handbook of Organization Studies*. London: Sage.

Cohen, M.D., March, J.G. and Olsen, J.P. (1972) "A garbage can model of organizational choice", *Administrative Science Quarterly* 17: 1–25.

Cohen, M.D. and Sproull, L.S. (eds.) (1996) *Organizational Learning*. Thousand Oaks, CA: Sage.

Crozier, M. (1963) *Le Phénomène Bureaucratique*. Paris: Editions du Seuil.

Cyert, R.M. and March, J.G. (1963) *A Behavioral Theory of the Firm*. Englewood Cliffs, N.J.: Prentice-Hall. Second edition 1992, Oxford: Blackwell.

Czarniawska, B. and Sevón, G. (eds.) (1996) *Translating Organizational Change*. Berlin: de Gruyter.

Dahl, R.A. and Lindblom, C.E. (1953) *Politics, Economics, and Welfare*. New York: Harper and Row.

DiMaggio, P.J. and Powell, W.W. (1983) "The Iron Cage revisited: Institutional isomorphism and collective rationality in organizational fields", *American Sociological Review* 48: 147–60.

Egeberg, M. (1987) "Designing public organizations", in J. Kooiman and K.A. Eliassen (eds.) *Managing Public Organizations* , pp.142–157. London: Sage.

_____. (1996) "Organization and nationality in the European Commission Services", *Public Administration* 74: 721–735.

Elster, J. (1998) "A plea for mechanisms", in P. Hedström and R. Swedberg (eds.) *Social Mechanisms: An Analytical Approach to Social Theory*, pp. 45–73. Cambridge: Cambridge University Press.

Eriksen, E.O. and Weigård, J. (1997) "Conceptualizing politics: Strategic or communicative action?", *Scandinavian Political Studies* 20: 219–241.

Etzioni, A. (1964) *Modern Organizations*. Englewood Cliffs N.J.: Prentice-Hall.

Evan, W.M. (ed.) (1976) *Inter-Organizational Relations*. Harmondsworth: Penguin.

Føllesdal, A. (1998) "Survey article: Subsidiarity", *The Journal of Political Philosophy* 6: 190–218.

Friedberg, E. (1997) *Local Orders. Dynamics of Organized Action*. London: JAI Press.

Gouldner, A.W. (1957) "Cosmopolitans and locals: Toward an analysis of latent social roles", *Administrative Science Quarterly* 3: 281–292.

Grabher, G. (ed.) (1993) *The Embedded Firm. On the Socioeconomics of Industrial Networks*. London: Routledge.

Grandori, A. (1997) "An organizational assessment of interfirm coordination modes", *Organizational Studies* 18: 897–923.

Grieco, J.M. (1988) "Anarchy and the limits of cooperation: A realist's critique of the newest liberal institutionalism", *International Organization* 42: 485–507.

Habermas, J. (1992) *Faktizität und Geltung: Beiträge zur Diskurstheorie des Rechts und des democratischen Rechtsstaats*. Frankfurt am Main: Suhrkamp.

Håkansson, H. (ed.) (1987) *Industrial Technological Development*. London: Croom Helm.

Jachtenfuchs, M. and Kohler-Koch, B. (eds.) (1996) *Europäische Integration*. Opladen: Leske and Budrich.

Jacobsen, K.D. (1964) *Teknisk hjelp og politisk struktur*. Oslo: Universitetsforlaget.

Jacobsson, B. (1987) *Kraftsamlingen*. Lund: Doxa.

Jørgensen, T.B. (1977) *Samspil og konflikt mellem organisationer*. København: Nyt fra samfundsvidenskaberne.

Joerges, C., Ladeur, K.-H. and Vos, E. (eds.) (1997) *Integrating Scientific Expertise into Regulatory Decision-Making. National Traditions and European Innovations*. Baden-Baden: Nomos.

Katz, D. and Kahn, R.L. (1966) *The Social Psychology of Organizations*. New York: Wiley.

Kreiner, K. and Schultz, M. (1993) "Networking in biotechnology: Crossing the institutional divide", *Organizational Studies* 14: 189–209.

Lake, D.A. (1996) "Anarchy, hierarchy, and the variety of international relations", *International Organization* 1: 1–33.

Lawrence, P. and Lorsch, J. (1967) *Organization and Environment: Managing Differentiation and Integration*. Cambridge Ma.: Harvard University Press.

Lundin, R.A. and Söderholm, A. (1995) "A theory of the temporary organization", *Scandinavian Journal of Management* 11: 437–455.

March, J.G. (1953) *Autonomy as a Factor in Group Organization. A Study in Politics.* PhD dissertation, Yale University. Reprinted, New York: Arno Press 1980.

_____. (1962) "The business firm as a political coalition", *Journal of Politics* 24: 662–678.

_____. (1965a) *Handbook of Organizations.* Chicago Ill: Rand McNally.

_____. (1965b) "Introduction", in J.G. March (ed.) *Handbook of Organizations*: IX–XVI. Chicago Ill: Rand McNally.

_____. (1981) "Footnotes to organizational change", *Administrative Science Quarterly* 26: 563–577.

_____. (1988) *Decisions and Organizations.* Oxford: Blackwell.

_____. (1991) "Exploration and exploitation in organizational learning", *Organizational Science* 2: 71–87.

_____. (1994a) *A Primer on Decision Making.* New York: Free Press.

_____. (1994b) "The evolution of evolution", in J. Baum and J. Singh (eds.) *Evolutionary Dynamics of Organizations.* New York: Oxford University Press.

_____. (1997) "Administrative practice, organization theory, and political philosophy. Ruminations on the *Reflections* of John M. Gaus", *PS Political Science & Politics* XXX (4): 689–698.

_____. (1999) (forthcoming), *The Pursuit of Organizational Intelligence: Decisions and Learning in Organizations.* Oxford: Blackwell.

March, J.G. and Olsen, J.P. (1976) *Ambiguity and Choice in Organizations.* Oslo: Universitetsforlaget.

_____. (1983) "Organizing Political Life: What Administrative Reorganization Tells Us About Government", *American Political Science Review* 77: 281–297.

_____. (1984) "The new institutionalism: Organizational factors in political life", *American Political Science Review* 78: 734–749.

_____. (1989) *Rediscovering Institutions.* New York: Free Press.

_____. (1995) *Democratic Governance.* New York: Free Press.

_____. (1998) "The institutional dynamics of international political orders", *International Organization* (forthcoming fall 1998).

March, J.G. and Simon, H.A. (1958) *Organizations.* New York: Wiley. Second edition 1993, Oxford: Blackwell.

Marin, B. and Mayntz, R. (eds.) (1991) *Policy Networks.* Frankfurt am Main: Campus.

Martin, J. (1992) *Cultures in Organizations. Three Perspectives.* New York: Oxford University Press.

Mayer, P., Rittberger, V. and Zürn, M. (1995) "Regime theory. State of the art and perspectives", in V. Rittberger, assisted by P. Mayer (ed.) *Regime Theory and International Relations*, pp. 392–430. Oxford: Oxford University Press.

Mayntz, R. (1997) *Soziale Dynamik und Politische Steuerung. Theoretische und methodologische Überlegungen*. Frankfurt am Main: Campus.

Mayntz, R. and Scharpf, F.W. (eds.) (1995) *Steuerung und Selbstorganisation in staatsnahen Sektoren*. Frankfurt am Main: Campus.

Meyer, J.W. and Jepperson, R.L. (1997) *The "actors" of modern society: The cultural construction of social agency*. Stanford CA: Stanford University: unpublished manuscript.

Meyer, J.W. and Rowan, B (1977) "Institutionalized organizations: Formal structure as myth and ceremony", *American Journal of Sociology* 83: 340–363.

Moravcsik, A. (1991) "Negotiating the Single European Act: national interests and conventional statecraft in the European Community", *International Organization* 45 (1): 19–56.

_____. (1993) "Preferences and Power in the European Community: A Liberal Intergovernmentalist Approach", *Journal of Common Market Studies* 4: 473–524.

_____. (1997) "Taking preferences seriously: A Liberal theory of international politics", *International Organization* 51 (4): 513–53.

Negandhi, A.R. (1975) *Interorganization Theory*. Kent: Kent University Press.

Nystrom, P.C. and Starbuck,W.H. (eds.) (1981) *Handbook of Organizational Design*. Volume 1: Adapting Organizations to Their Environments. Oxford: Oxford University Press.

Olsen, J.P. (1989) *Petroleum og politikk*. Oslo: Tano.

_____. (1992) "Analyzing institutional dynamics", *Staatswissen-schaften und Staatspraxis* 3 (2): 247–271.

_____. (1998) "Civil service in transition: Dilemmas and lessons learned", in J.J. Hesse and T.A.J. Toonen (eds.) *The European Yearbook of Comparative Government and Public Administration* . Vol. III, pp. 389–406. Baden-Baden and Boulder Co.: Nomos and Westview.

Olsen, J.P. and Peters, B.G. (eds.) (1996) *Lessons from Experience. Experiential Learning in Administrative Reforms in Eight Democracies*. Oslo: Scandinavian University Press.

Olsen, J.P. and Sverdrup, B.O. (eds.) (1998) *Europa i Norden. Europeisering av nordisk samarbeid*. Oslo: Tano.

Pfeffer, J. (1997) *New Directions for Organization Theory*. New York: Oxford University Press.

Reed, M. (1996) "Organizational theorizing: A historically contested terrain", in S.R. Clegg, C. Hardy and W.R. Nord (eds.) *Handbook of Organization Studies*, pp. 31–56. London: Sage.

Rhodes, R.A.W. (1997) *Understanding Governance. Policy Networks, Governance, Reflexivity and Accountability*. Buckingham: Open University Press.

41

Risse, T. (1997) *"Let"s talk!" Insights from the German debate on communicative behavior and international relations*. Florence: European University Institute: manuscript.

Risse-Kappen, T. (ed.) (1995) *Bringing Transnational Relations Back In. Non-state Actors, Domestic Structures and International Institutions*. Cambridge: Cambridge University Press.

Rogers, D.L. and Whetten, D.A. and associates (1982) *Interorganizational Coordination. Theory, Research and Implementation*. Ames: The Iowa State University Press.

Rosenau, J.N. and Czempiel, E.-O. (eds.) (1992) *Governance without Government. Order and Change in World Politics*. Cambridge: Cambridge University Press.

Røvik, K.A. (1992) *Den "syke" stat*. Oslo: Universitetsforlaget.

Sahlin-Andersson, K. (1989) *Oklarhetens strategi*. Lund: Studentlitteratur.

_____. (1998) "Mötesplatser som standardiserare", in N. Brunsson and B. Jacobsson (eds.) *Standardisering*, pp. 117–132. Stockholm: Nerenius & Santérus.

Sangolt, L. (1997) *The Politics of Counting: Producing official statistics on the North Sea oil industry in Norway and Great Britain, 1966–1986*. Bergen: Doctoral thesis, Department of Administration and Organization Theory, University of Bergen: Report 55:1997.

Scharpf, F.W. (1997) *Games Real Actors Play. Actor-Centered Institutionalism in Policy Research*. Boulder Co.: Westview.

Scott, W.R. (1992, Third edition) *Organizations. Rational, Natural and Open Systems*. Englewood Cliffs, New Jersey: Prentice Hall.

_____. (1995) *Institutions and Organizations*. Thousand Oaks: Sage.

Scott, W.R. and Meyer, J.W. (1991) "The organization of societal sectors: Propositions and early evidence", in W.W. Powell and P.J. DiMaggio (eds.) *The New Institutionalism in Organizational Analysis*, pp. 108–140. Chicago: University of Chicago Press.

Selznick, P. (1949) *TVA and the Grass Roots*. Berkeley: University of California Press.

Simon, H.A. (1945/1957) *Administrative Behavior* (2nd edition). New York: Macmillan.

Sørensen, H. (1998) "Special issue on The 4th Nordic Workshop on Interorganizational Research", *Scandinavian Journal of Management* 14(5).

Stern, L.W., El-Anzari, A. and Coughlon, A.T. (1996) *Marketing Channels*. Upper Saddle River: Prentice Hall.

Stinchcombe A.L. (1974) *Creating Efficient Industrial Administration*. New York: Academic Press.

_____. (1997) "On the virtues of the old institutionalism", in *Annual Review of Sociology* 23: 1–18.

Thompson, J. D. (1967) *Organizations in Action*. New York: McGraw-Hill.

Trondal, J. (1996) *Tilknytningsformer til EU og nasjonale samordningsprosesser. En studie av norske og danske departementer*. Oslo: University of Oslo, Department of Political Science: Thesis and ARENA Working Paper no. 15/96.

Vad, T.B.P. (1998) *Europeanization of Standardization. European Institution Building and National Persistence in the Area of Technical Standardization*. Copenhagen: Doctoral thesis, The Institute of Political Science, University of Copenhagen.

Weber, M. (1978) *Economy and Society*. Berkeley CA: University of California Press.

Williamson, O.E. (1975) *Markets and Hierarchies: Analysis and Antitrust Implications*. New York: Free Press.

_____. (1990) "Chester Barnard and the Incipient Science of Organization", in O.E. Williamson (ed.) *Organization Theory. From Chester Barnard to the Present and Beyond*, pp. 172–206. New York: Oxford University Press.

II.
The Organizational Mosaic:
Beyond Markets and Hierarhies

Chapter 2

The Network as a Governance Structure: Interfirm Cooperation Beyond Markets and Hierarchies

Håkan Håkansson and Jan Johanson

A number of empirical studies have demonstrated the existence and importance of lasting business relationships between industrial suppliers and customers (Carlton, 1986; Gadde & Mattsson, 1987; Håkansson, ed., 1982; Turnbull & Valla, eds., 1986; Håkansson, 1989; Anderson & Narus, 1990). Although such relationships have received little attention in economic and business literature they have been noted in writings about transaction-cost theory (Williamson, 1979, 1985), about industrial policy (Dertouzos et al., 1989) and business strategy (Porter, 1980, 1985).

Based on the studies of business relationships the notion of industrial networks has been developed (Hägg & Johanson, 1982; Håkansson, 1987; Axelsson & Easton,1992; Forsgren & Johanson, 1992). This has in turn given rise to the idea that industrial networks are governance modes with interesting implications for industrial efficiency, industrial development, and control over industrial operations. The first part of this chapter identifies important characteristics of industrial networks, their actors, the activities they perform and the resources they use.

Important processes within the networks are analysed. This characterization of the network is the base for a discussion in the second part of networks as a type of governance mode, which is compared with other modes.

Industrial Networks

Networks of social actors can be defined as sets of connected exchange relationships (Cook & Emerson, 1978). Most of the research about networks have dealt with social networks (Burt, 1982; Cook & Emerson, 1978, 1984; Willer & Andersson, eds., 1981; Iacobucci & Hopkins, 1991). There is an important difference between these social networks and the industrial networks we are interested in. Social networks are dominated by the actors and their social exchange relations. Activities, in which they are engaged and resources they use are basically seen as secondary attributes of the actors. This is not the case in the industrial network model we discuss. Evidently, the reason for placing attention not only on actors but also on activities and resources is the strong interdependencies between all those three elements in the real-world industrial setting. There, the activities are complex and binding in nature and are conditioned by more or less fixed and heavy resource structures. A consequence is that the activities and resources in themselves are important factors determining the behaviour both in terms of "constraints" and "opportunities". The industrial network, as a consequence, consists of the actors and the relationships between them but also of certain activities/resources and the dependencies between them (see Figure 2.1). Each actor controls certain activities and resources directly, but as the dependencies to some extent mean control, the actor has an indirect control over the counterparts' activities and resources.

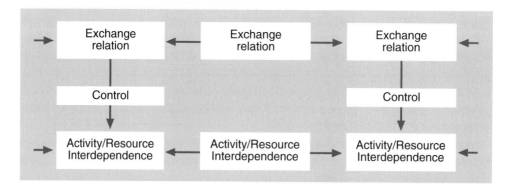

Figure 2.1

An industrial network comprises, then, both an actor dimension and an activity/resource dimension. However, these two are related to each other in a very specific way as will be shown by the two next sections focusing on each of the dimensions respectively.

Industrial Activities and Resources

In an industrial network a number of more or less interrelated industrial activities are performed. Each activity is more or less dependent on the performance of other activities, which have to be done before or are expected to follow after. Every activity is a link in a chain of activities. Such activity chains should, however, not be confused with generic value chains (Porter, 1985). The activity chains and structures we discuss are enacted, they are emergent phenomena that are formed and modified through interaction between the actors (Weick, 1969). Many different kinds of industrial activities can be distinguished. Some of them are basically technical, others are social, still others are financial and legal. Some activities are mainly mental, while others are primarily physical. Some of the activities are mainly related to production, others to exchange. In all, the variations are innumerable. Consider all the activities performed in the chain originating in iron ore mined in Brazil, converted into a band of steel in Germany, further processed by a band saw producer in Italy and finally used by a saw mill in Canada. No activity can be definitely delimited. It can always be partitioned into smaller activities, which in turn can be partitioned into still smaller activities. Correspondingly, every activity can be merged with other activities thus forming new and larger activities. Thus, there is no evident smallest or largest delimitation of activities. Every activity is in some sense discretionarily identified and delimited. The boundaries are, in the specific situation, determined by how the involved actors have chosen to delimit each activity. This means that we do not consider activity structures as determined by some intrinsic technical imperatives. They are rather formed by the views of the involved actors as to how the activities should be delimited, and how they are related to each other. The structures are, in other words, constructed by the actors (cf. Berger & Luckmann, 1967). The structuring of the activities has important effects on how the resources are put together. A certain activity structure leads to a specific resource structure. And this resource structure is costly to change.

Every single activity within a network is dependent on other activities in the sense that the outcome of an activity is dependent on how other activities are performed. Each activity dependence implies that at least one dimension – and usually several – of a specific activity is related to one and often several dimensions of other activities. New activity dependences may give rise to identifying new activity dimensions (and vice versa). Generally, it can be assumed that only a limited number of potentially relevant activity dimensions are known by the actors, and, furthermore, only some of the known activity dimensions influence how the activities are performed. The same is true for the resources. Thus some kind of selection of relevant activity and resource dimensions is made. This selection is based on the actor's cognitive model of the situation. Over time, this selection can change as the cognitive model changes due to experience. Evidently, such changes may lead to adjustments of the activities and/or resources. All activities are more or less repetitive and more or less unique. Together this gives possibilities for learning and conscious change. The unique element in the activities creates variations over time which is an important base for learning. The repetitive element gives possibilities for using the learning by adapting and changing activities, i.e. two interdependent activities can always be performed more productively through adaptation over time. Industrial activities are human constructions in two senses. On a practical level – whether praxis is mental or physical – activities are performed by human actors. On a cognitive level the identification and delimitation of activities is made by human actors. The two levels are related. To some extent activity structuring on the cognitive level is based on praxis. Vice versa, practical activity structuring is a consequence of cognitive activity structuring. In fact, cognitive activity structuring is an important organizing activity. Cognitive activity structuring is also a consequence of exchange. To sum up this section about activities and resources we can conclude that in an industrial network there is a web of more or less interdependent activities performed based on the use of a certain constellation of resources. The web in itself as well as the connections between activities and resources are interpreted in different ways by different actors due either to differences in knowledge or intentions. The web is continuously changing due to learning, changes in resources or in the intentions of the actors.

Industrial Actors

In any industrial network a number of different actors are engaged. We consider actor as a theoretical construct in the sense that the specific actor or actors in a network can be an individual, a department in a company, a business unit in a company, a whole company, or even a group of companies. We do, however, assume that all industrial actors have some basic properties. First, they control certain resources/activities. Second, they are purposeful in their action and they act in order to make economic gain in a general sense. Third, they have bounded knowledge and they are well aware of this. Thus, much of their action and interaction aims at gaining knowledge. The limited knowledge implies that not only their means may change but also their ends (Snehota, 1990). Figure 2.1 shows how each actor is characterized by controlling certain resources/activities and by being linked to some specific other actors through exchange relationships

(Håkansson & Snehota, 1989). The exchange relationships between actors are basic elements in industrial networks. The exchange implies some kind of mutuality (Ford et al., 1986), that is the involved actors give to and receive from each other. It is assumed that the exchange is a network necessity, which furthermore influences the individual actor's perception of its own interests. Thus, and due to the basic properties of the actors, the exchange has not only an economic dimension but also knowledge and value dimensions.

The concept of exchange relationships presupposes time. The relationship can be viewed as a set of more or less implicit rules, which are related to the exchange in the same way as language is related to communication. The rules are formed, reinforced, and modified through exchange at the same time as they constitute the framework of subsequent exchange (cf. Giddens, 1979). These rules are closely related to the cognitive activity structuring model referred to above. A basic assumption of the industrial network model is that those rules imply a mutual orientation of the actors to each other. They view each other as specific counterparts, they have some knowledge about each other, they have some trust in each other, and they are aware of and may even share each other's interests. Thus, the relationships link the actors to each other in a dynamic way. They are also an indicator of preparedness to make exchange with each other, meaning that they can be used for other types of exchange than they were used for before. Obviously, this view of relationships implies that the exchange can be more or less regular and that the relationships can be sleeping for long periods of time (Hadjikhani, 1992).

It is sometimes argued that lasting relationships are mainly a result of inertia and, therefore, are some kind of obstacles and in principal irrational. We mean, however, that, in a complex, interdependent, and dynamic setting they are, or at least can be, very rational. They have important positive effects on the actors' productivity, on their innovative capacity as well as on controlling their environment. The main reason for this is the interdependencies, which exist in the activity/resource dimension discussed in the previous section. Partly, this is possible because the exchange relationships can absorb some of the strong dynamic forces that the actors are exposed to due to their multitude of activity dependencies. Partly, it is the result of the possibilities to transmit subtle and complex messages within the framework of a relationship. In fact, as Figure 2.1 demonstrates, we posit that lasting exchange relationships are modes of governing industrial activities and resources.

Exchange relationships shall not be viewed as entirely cooperative. In every relationship there are both common and conflicting interests between the actors (Laage-Hellman, 1989). Thus, relationships can be viewed as a cooperative mode of handling conflicts (cf. Axelrod, 1984).

Network Characteristics

Let us return to our definition of industrial networks as sets of connected exchange relationships between actors performing industrial activities. A number of basic, and to a large extent interrelated, characteristics of such industrial networks can be identified. We start by pointing at an elementary dynamic feature of networks. Second, we consider how this structures the networks both via the activity interdependencies in the networks and via connections between exchange relationships. Third, we point at and stress the basic opaque and unbounded nature of industrial networks. This leads to a discussion of a second kind of dynamic and how it is influenced by power in the network. When two actors perceive their activities as being interdependent they are inclined to start exchange with each other. When exchanging they learn about each other's capabilities and needs. As they do this they utilize and strengthen the interdependencies between their activities. Thus, there is a circular causal relation between activity interdependencies and exchange relationships (Figure 2.2). Evidently, unless no external factors influence the circle, it implies some kind of automatic mechanism strengthening the relationship and the interdependence. We return below to external factors that necessarily influence and frequently break the circle.

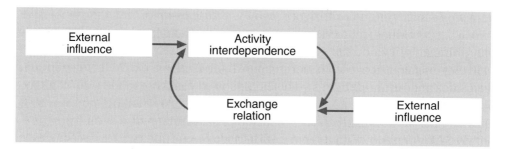

Figure 2.2

No actor's activities are performed in isolation. Instead each actor's activities are more or less embedded in the wider web of industrial activities performed in the network. Activities of one are always dependent on a number of activities performed by other actors. The activities of one actor are, over time, through learning modified and adapted to activities of other actors so that their joint productivity is increased. At the same time, however, the specific interdependence, that is the dependence between the activities of the specific actors, between the activities is strengthened. In this way chains of interdependent and at least quasi-integrated activities are created (cf. Blois, 1972). Thus, every activity is a link in one or several more or less extensive, and closely linked, activity chains engaging a number of different actors. When two activities get closer linked to each other they usually become less closely linked to some of the other activities. Change in the performance of one activity may lead to adjustments through activity chains with consequent increasing interdependence and productivity in one activity chain and decreasing interdependence and productivity in at least some other chain.

Every actor is engaged in a number of different activity chains extending the interdependence of the actor in a number of different directions. And over time, the actor becomes more strongly engaged in one, or some, activity chains while the engagement is lowered in some other. With such developments the activity structuring changes, new activity dimensions become relevant and new activity interdependencies are exploited. The network notion presupposes that the exchange relationships are connected, that is exchange in one relationship is conditioned by exchange in another. Connections may be positive, negative or mixed (Cook & Emerson, 1984). A positive connection means that exchange in one relationship is facilitated or supported by exchange in the other. A negative connection means correspondingly that – exchange in one relationship is hindering exchange in the other. Typically, relationships along activity chains are positively connected while a customer's relationships with competing suppliers generally are negatively connected.

Two different kinds of connection can be distinguished. One operates via the activities. There is some kind of functional logic of activity interdependencies, which has implications for the connections between exchange relationships. In the simple case an actor has input and output relationships, which are connected through the production activity of the actor. Those relationships are positively connected due to activity relations. The actor may also choose between mutually exclusive inputs. The exchange relationships with those input sources are negatively connected. The second type of connection operates via the actors. The actors' network perceptions or "theories", which may not only comprise the present relations between actors and activities but also expectations and intentions regarding the future relations have a bearing on the connections. Two input sources of an actor, which from the activity interdependence point of view are negatively connected, may be considered complementary from a long run supplier development point of view and thus handled so that they become positively connected. Obviously, connections can also be mixed. Generally it can be assumed that the activity connections are relatively more important in the short run. They operate as some kind of short term constraint. With increasing time perspective, those activity constraints become less important and the actors' network "theories" gain importance (Johanson & Mattsson, 1991). The relationships with other actors are especially important in a long term perspective as they relate the network perceptions of different actors to each other. It can also be assumed that the importance of activity connections is related to the type of technology in the field. The more heavy the investments in the activities are, the stronger are the activity constraints on the relationships. Thus, activity based connections will be especially important in process industries, in mature industries and where the production is the major activity, while the actor based connections are particularly important in emergent technology industries.

The patterns and character of the connections between the relationships constitute the structure of the industrial network. To some extent such structures are conditioned by technical and cultural factors, but, primarily, they are interacted, that is they are formed and modified through interaction between the actors. The network structure is a result of history. An important aspect of the network structure is the control structure, that is the control different actors can exert over the activities in the field. The actors have some, although incomplete, direct control over their own activities. They have also some indirect control over other activities via the relationships with other actors. The overall indirect control over other actors' activities in the network is based on the position within the network, the strength of the relationships and on the relative importance of the actors to each other. The control in the network is more or less concentrated to some of the actors. The control structure has consequences for the returns to the actors. But it has also strong consequences for the future development and structure of the network as actors with control can influence other actors to carry through certain investments and to choose certain technical solutions. Consequently, in order to promote their interests, whatever they are, the actors struggle to gain control over the activities in the network.

In the struggle two circumstances are important. The industrial networks are opaque and unbounded. Concerning the opacity, all actors have rather clear views of their own relationships with other actors, albeit the views of interacting actors are not necessarily consistent. Different individuals in an actor may also have inconsistent views of the relationships with other actors. Generally the actors' cognitive models are less differentiated and clear about more distant relations in the network and the cognitive models of distant actors may differ widely.

An actor who is not engaged in a certain network, for instance a network in a foreign country, or with a different technology, cannot get but a very superficial comprehension of the network with its invisible relationships, connections and dependencies. Most are, however, aware of their existence and much industrial action can best be understood as attempts to gain a comprehension, to build a cognitive model, of the network structure. Network entry is very much a cognitive modeling process. The opacity, evidently, implies that the different actors have unclear and different views of the control structure in the network and their success in influencing the development is very much a matter of their cognitive models.

The industrial networks are in principle unbounded, they extend without limits. Extension rather than limitation is one of the basic network features. One way of delimiting a network is to draw boundaries on the basis of the industrial field, for instance technology, country, product type, or a focal actor. But all such boundaries are, in principle, arbitrary. They are a result of perspectives, intentions, and interpretations, or in the case of the actor the cognitive network model. It can be assumed that different actors will do more or less different network limitations. The more the cognitive models of the different actors differ the more the actors will tend to search for solutions in different directions – different combinations of activities, actors, and resources – and the less stable the network structure will be. The network delimitations will have implications for the control structure and consequently, for the possibilities of different actors to influence its development.

Against this background it can be assumed that as a counterpoint to the elementary structuring dynamic outlined as an introduction to this section, the power struggle between actors with different network perceptions results in strong destructuring forces. As the structuring of activities and relationships proceeds openings are created. Due to different network perceptions and delimitations by the dominant actors, other actors can exploit such openings by developing activity and resource structures competing with the dominant structure. The other actors can also form alliances with actors who are not included in the network perceptions of the dominant actors, thus restructuring the network, breaking it up or extending it in new directions.

Network as a Governance Structure

Important characteristics of the industrial networks, as we have found them, have now been identified and described. With a start in a separation between an actor and an activity/resource dimension we have characterized the industrial network setting, as it can be perceived by the participating actors. The description has hopefully shown how the network is directing and controlling the activities performed. Thus, considering governance as the organizational forms and processes through which activities are directed in a field the industrial network can be seen as a specific governance structure or mode (Campbell, Hollingsworth & Lindberg, eds., 1991).

Basically the direction of activities has two different sources; on the one hand it is the consequence of the characteristics of the actors performing or directing the activities, on the other they are a result of external forces giving the conditions on which the actors base their activities. With regard to those two sources a network can be characterized in the following way. Firstly, as our discussion has shown, networks consist of several actors with different interests and different views. The differences exist due to differences in the actors background and history, in their positions, in their knowledge and in their ambitions. Secondly. the actors are linked to specific other actors through exchange relationships, which means that each of them is influenced directly by some specific counterparts; i.e. the external forces influencing the firm are channelled through exchange relationships with specific others and do not operate as some kind of general environmental or market force.

Let us now take these two characteristics as a starting point for a comparison of networks with some other types of governance structures.

The internal forces driving the individual network actor were characterized by the concept interest. The actors are assumed to pursue their own interests when acting. This indicates the existence of variation and multidimensionality. Different actors have different interests and the interests vary depending on situations. Alternatively actors can be assumed to act on the basis of norms. As norms are more closely linked to behaviour this implies a certain standardization. The norms can either be prescribed by some authority or be agreed upon by different actors. The main difference between interest-driven and norm-driven action is that the norms imply a certain action and are more shared by the actors giving them a stable and common direction lacking in the interest case.

The external forces that influence the actors, and in the network case came through the exchange relationships, can alternatively be seen as general in the sense that they are a consequence of the total interplay between all actors. In that case they are not influenced by any other specific actor and are influencing all actors in more or less the same way. Thus the external forces are in this case not related to any other specific actor but to some kind of general conditions which may be stable or changing in some general way. By combining the two internal and external sources we can attain a classification of governance structures demonstrating the specific attributes of networks as governance structures (Figure 2.3).

		Internal force is based on	
		Interesis	**Norms**
External force is based on	Specific relations	1 Network	2 Hierarchy
	General relations	3 Market	4 Culture profession

Figure 2.3

The classification distinguishes four different types of governance structure or mode. Let us start with cell number one. This is, as we already noted, network governance. Activities are governed by the individual and varying interests of a number of different actors, who are related to each other in specific ways meaning that the major external forces operating on each specific actor are channelled via some other specific actors.

Cell number two differs from one as interests are replaced by norms. This is the case in the hierarchy, which is governed by a common overall norm decided by central authority, from which are deduced specific norms that are imposed on the individual actors within the hierarchy. The actors within the hierarchy are specifically related to each other and to the external world so that the various activities performed are related to each other in an optimal way given the overall norm. The similarity in comparison with network governance lies in the possibilities to systematically relate specific activities to each other, to take advantage of specific dependencies. Thus, like network governance hierarchical governance can exploit possible activity interdependencies and in this way attain coordinated productivity. The main difference is that this structure looses the dynamic ingredient, which lies in the confrontation between varying interests.

When the network is compared with cell number three the difference is found in the way the external forces influence the actors. We get units that are pursuing their own interests and hence are freer in relation to each other. At the same time, however, the advantages regarding handling the specific dependencies are lost. This type is close to the traditional models of competitive markets, where the actors are assumed to act in their own interest. Competition is based on the actors' efforts in pursuing their own interests. The external forces driving the actors are here general market relations – demand and supply – without reference to specific other actors. Thus, due to the assumed generality of the external forces this type does not imply possibilities to exploit productivity gains through different combinations of specific actors and activities.

Type four, finally, implies that actors are governed by norms and that external forces are general in the sense that no specific influences are not channelled via any specific actors. One rather general example of a type four governance is culture which by many organization researchers is considered a very important factor governing business behaviour. Culture is often viewed as sets of more or less implicit norms. A more distinctive third type of case four governance is the profession. The profession usually has – strong norms regulating the behaviour of individual actors. The limited access to professions is based on a general trust that the actor will act in accordance with the specific profession's code of conduct. The norms are agreed upon by the members of the profession and are expected to give members a power position in relation to non-members (Collins, 1979; Larson, 1977). A basic feature of this type of governance is stability and uniformity.

As the discussion of the four cells has indicated we do not mean that any of the above forms can be found in a pure form in the reality. They should be considered as theoretical types. In the real world we will find different mixes. The important conclusion from our point of view is that the typology implies that network governance should not be viewed as some kind of intermediate governance mode on a unidimensional scale between market and hierarchy but as a unique type. Let us now look closer into some issues concerning networks as governance structures.

The first issue concerns the circumstances, under which network governance is a viable mode of governing industrial fields. The second issue concerns the basic economic problems the network structure takes care of and/or gives rise to.

In any real-world industrial field we can expect a blend of different governance modes existing more or less side by side or rather penetrating each other. Thus, in any specific industry or industrial field at all we expect to find industrial networks directing activities in some ways, hierarchical organizations directing them in others, market competition in still others, and profession-like structures in still others. To some extent they are complementary, as is demonstrated by the idea of hierarchical firms competing in the market. Similarly, as has been discussed recently in organization analysis, hierarchical organizations are often to a large extent, governed by their culture (Ouchi, 1980; Schein, 1985). In the same way, we can expect that networks in the real-world setting will coexist with and interpenetrate both hierarchies, markets and cultures. In fact, it can be assumed that there is an ongoing competition between the governance modes, where their relative viabilities have a bearing on their existence under different circumstances. This does, however, not mean a competition leading to the most efficient governance structure. Structures may be dominant so that other structures are hindered from taking over. Power is an important factor behind the viability of the governance structures.

Network governance is an effective and viable governance structure, we posit, if there are many, changing, strong specific activity interdependencies. Consequently, when technological change and multiple technological dimensions are important the network type is effective. If there are no possibilities to exploit specific activity interdependencies market governance is probably more efficient. Correspondingly, if the changes in the field or a sub-field are small norm- based governance can be expected to be more competitive. This is also the case if there is only one or a dominating specific interdependencies.

In a situation with strong specific activitiy interdependencies existing together in a certain stable way hierarchical governance can be expected to be competitive. The culture or profession can be assumed to be competitive when there are no specific activity interdependencies and the situation requires stability, vis. as long as the norms are relevant for handling upcoming situations.

As there is an inherent dynamic in network governance a more or less continuous reorganizing of the network structure takes place, which as effect has that network governance on the surface does not look as stable as the market or hierarchy. although it remains intact its structure changes and cannot easily be recognized. In contrast the market looks the same irrespective of changes, and the hierarchy is the same until it is changed radically.

Considering the dynamic aspects of networks it is worth noting the special relation between stability and change in networks. A network combines stability and change in an interesting way. In general, the stability is high in some dimensions for a certain period of time, while quite dramatic changes take place in other dimensions. Furthermore, there is a connection in so far as stability in some dimensions is required in order to bring about the needed mobilization behind the changes in other dimensions. The network does not, in other words, only make the combination of stability and change possible, it makes use of the combination too. From an industrial point of view this is of critical importance as it makes it possible to combine efficient production methods requiring stability with changing demand and business conditions.

Concerning the viability of network governance two other comments can be made. While it is generally assumed that competitive markets in equilibrium lead to Pareto-optimal allocation of resources to different activities, no such optimality can be assumed regarding networks. First, no equilibrium can be expected. The networks are, by their very nature, in imbalance. Second, as the activities, at least partly, are performed on the basis of power relations what is good for one actor may be bad for the other. In contrast to the market model, in which power is seen as some kind of imperfection, the network model views power as a necessary ingredient in exploiting activity interdependencies. Evaluations of network efficiency have to be conducted from a specific perspective.

For example, as the networks function across country boundaries the power relations have obvious international implications. A section of a country's economy can, through the network be controlled by actors situated in other countries. An important aspect of such power relations is that they have consequences not only for the returns to different actors but also for the future network structure. This issue has been investigated in some studies but the whole complex of dependence, control and power within industrial networks should receive much more research interest in the future. Some theoretical starting points can be found in studies of social network structures (Patton & Willer, 1990) but they have to be modified so as to accommodate the special dynamic characteristics of industrial networks (Forsgren, 1989).

In the comparison between different governance structures we suggested that structural conditions affect the viability of the governance modes differentially. But, given the way we have characterized industrial networks, structural conditions shall not be viewed as external constraints but as enacted structures, in which the perceptions and experiences of the actors are important. Hence, activity interdependencies are enacted and they are based on cognitive models of the interdependencies. Similarly, the network structure is enacted and the actors base their action on their network perceptions. Thus, the network viability in a certain industrial field is largely dependent on the network perceptions of the actors involved and in their ability to mobilize other actors in realizing network structures rather than on any external structural conditions. To the extent that actors have network perceptions that in some way can replace received market or hierarchical perceptions they may be able to change the governance structure in the field so that network governance gains in viability. In such processes imitation can be an important element (DiMaggio & Powell, 1983).

Summary

This chapter has outlined a model of industrial network, in which actors, activities and resources are important interrelated elements. In a discussion of industrial activities and resources we have viewed activity and resource structures as emergent and enacted phenomena that form webs of interdependencies extending far beyond the horizon of the single actor. In a section about industrial actors we have described how actors control activities and resources and how the exchange relationships between actors are important modes of handling the interdependencies. Based on these assumptions about actors, activities and resources a number of network characteristics have been discussed. In particular, we have stressed the special dynamics of industrial networks, both the elementary structuring dynamics and the power struggle leading to restructuring dynamics. The specific features of networks as governance structures have been elaborated and compared to other types of governance. This comparison has been based on a classification of the internal and external forces operating on the specific actors. The classification was used in a discussion of the viability of network governance.

References

Anderson, J.C. and Narus, J.A. (1984) "A Model of Distributor Firm and Manufacturer Firm Working Partnership", *Journal of Marketing* 48(4): 62–74.

Axelrod, R. (1984) *The Evolution of Cooperation*. New York: Basic Books.

Axelsson, B. and Easton, G. (eds.) (1992) *Industrial Networks: A New View of Reality*. London: Routledge.

Berger, P.L. and Luckmann, T. (1967) *The Social Construction of Reality: A Treatise in the Sociology of Knowledge*. New York: Anchor Books.

Blois, K.J. (1972) "Verical Ouasi-Integration", *Journal of Industrial Economics* 20(3): 253–272.

Burt, R.S. (1982) *Toward a Structural Theory of Action. Network Models of Social Structure, Perception and Action*. New York: Academic Press.

Campbell, J., Hollingsworth, J.R. and Lindberg, L.N. (eds.) (1991) *Governance of the American Economy*. New York: Cambridge University Press.

Carlton, D.W. (1986) "The Rigidity of Prices", *American Economic Review* 76(4): 637–658.

Collins, R. (1979) *The Credential Society: An Historical Sociology of Education and Stratification*. New York: Academic Press.

Cook, K.S. and Emerson, R.M. (1978) "Power, Equity and Commitment in Exchange Networks", *American Sociological Review* 43(5): 721–739.

_____. (1984) "Exchange Networks and the Analysis of Complex Organizations", in S.B. Bacharach and E.J. Lawler (eds.) *Research in the Sociology of Organizations*, pp. 1–30. Greenwich, CT: JAI Press.

Dertouzos, M.L. et al. (1989) *Made in America: Regaining the Productive Edge*. Cambridge, Mass.: MIT Press.

DiMaggio, P.J. and Powell, W.W. (1983) "The Iron Cage Revisited: Institutional Isomorphism and Collective Rationality in Organizational Fields", *American Sociological Review* 48(2): 147–160.

Ford, D., Håkansson, H. and Johanson, J. (1986) "How Do Companies Interact?", *Industrial Marketing and Purchasing* 1(1): 26–41.

Forsgren, M. (1989) *Managing the Internationalization Process. The Swedish Case*. London: Routledge.

Forsgren, M. and Johanson, J. (eds.) (1992) *Managing Networks in International Business*. Philadelphia: Gordon and Breach.

Gadde, L.-E. and Mattsson, L.-G. (1987) "Stability and Change in Network Relationships", *International Journal of Research in Marketing* 4(1): 29–41.

Giddens, A. (1979) *Central Problems in Social Theory: Action, Structure and Contradiction in Social Analysis*. London: Macmillan.

Hadjikhani, A. (1992) "Managing International Package Deal Projects", in M. Forsgren and J. Johanson (eds.) *Managing Networks in International Business*, pp. 138–150. Philadelphia: Gordon & Breach.

Hägg, I. and Johanson, J. (eds.) (1982) *Företag i nätverk – ny syn på konkurrens-kraft (Firms in Networks – A New View of Competitiveness)*. Stockholm: SNS Förlag.

Håkansson, H. (ed.) 1982) *International Marketing and Purchasing of Industrial Goods: An Interaction Approach*. Chichester: John Wiley & Sons.

_____. (ed.) (1987) *Industrial Technological Development: A Network Approach*. London: Croom Holm.

_____. (1989) *Corporate Technological Behavior: Cooperation and Networks*. London: Routledge.

Håkansson, H. and Snehota, I. (1989) "No Business is an Island: The Network Concept of Business Strategy", *Scandinavian Journal of Managment* 5(3): 187–200.

Iacobucci, D. and Hopkins, N. (1992) "Modeling Dyadic Interactions and Networks in Marketing", *Journal of Marketing Research* 29(1): 5–17.

Johanson, J. and Mattsson, L.-G. (1991) "Strategic Adaption of Firms to the European Single Market: A Network Approach", in L.-G. Mattsson and B. Stymne (eds.) *Corporate and Industry Strategies for Europe. Adaption to the European Single Market in a Global Industrial Environment*, pp. 263–281. Amsterdam: North-Holland.

Laage-Hellman, J. (1989) *Technological Development in Industrial Networks*. Comprehensive Summaries of Uppsala Dissertations from the Faculty of Social Sciences No. 16. Uppsala: Uppsala University.

Larson, M.S. (1977) *The Rise of Professionalism: A Sociological Analysis*. Berkeley, Calif.: University of California Press.

Newcomb, T.M., Turner, R.H. and Converse, P.E. (1952) *Social Psychology: The Study of Human Interaction*. London: Tavistock Publications.

Ouchi, W.G. (1980) "Markets, Bureaucracies and Clans", *Administrative Science Quarterly* 25(1): 129–141.

Patton, T. and Willer, D. (1990) "Connection and Power in Centralized Exchange Networks", *Journal of Mathematical Sociology* 16: 31–49.

Porter, M.E. (1980) *Competitive Strategy: Techniques for Analyzing Industries and Competitors*. New York: The Free Press.

_____. (1985) *Competitive Advantage. Creating and Sustaining Superior Performance*. New York: The Free Press.

Schein, E.H. (1985) *Organizational Culture and Leadership: A Dynamic View*. San Francisco, Calif.: Jossey-Bass.

Snehota, I. (1990) *Notes on a Theory of Business Enterprise* (dissertation). Uppsala: Uppsala University.

Turnbull, J.P. and Valla, J.-P. (eds.) (1986) *Strategies for International Industrial Marketing: The Managment of Customer Relationships in European Industrial Markets*. London: Croom Holm.

Weick, K.E. (1969) *The Social Psychology of Organizing*. Reading, Mass.: Addison-Wesley.

Willer, D. and Andresson, B. (eds.) (1981) *Networks, Exchange and Coercion*. New York: Elsevier.

Williamson, O.E. (1979) "Transaction-Cost Economics: The Governance of Contractual Relations", *Journal of Law and Economics* 22(2): 233–261.

_____. (1985) *The Economic Institutions of Capitalism: Firms, Markets, Relational Contracting*. New York: The Free Press.

Chapter 3
Soft Cultures: The Symbolism of Cross-Border Organizing
Kristian Kreiner and Majken Schultz

This chapter provides a picture of cross-border collaborative ventures as *"soft cultures"*. Such ventures are *cultures,* in the sense that action undertaken by the venture partners is judged against criteria of meaning and legitimacy. However, such ventures are *soft* cultures, in the sense that only vague and ambiguous criteria are available for such judgment. As a result, different renderings of reality may be acceptable and convincing.

The "reality" that is culturally rendered consists of action taken by the organizationally and geographically dispersed actors of the venture. That action is culturally rendered does not mean that action is also culturally controlled or determined. Common sense might suggest that action is chosen with a view to an inescapable reading of the deeds in the community. However, if the premises for such readings are vague and ambiguous, the ensuing meaning will be as much a result of the process of readings as the action in itself. Meaning and legitimacy may be developed *ad hoc,* and could be considered an outcome of, more than a premise for, action (Feldman 1991; Swidler 1986; Cohen 1985). For the actor, any action provides a *sense-making opportunity.* Here "opportunity" is used with the common double connotation of option *and* obligation.

While behavioral constraints and institutionalized meanings are not presumed for soft cultures, aspects of the processes by which diversity is produced may be identified with regularity. In fact, soft cultures are characterized by the sharing of symbols as sense-making "tools" (Cohen 1985). The concept "tools" will appear in quotation marks to warn against a too functionalist reading. They may be of different kinds. In this chapter, the "tools" for sense-making opportunities are the labels of the collaborative venture that invoke a specific surplus meaning (Ricoeur, discussed in Hatch 1993) and stimulate prospective interpretation. We specifically focus on the *categorizing, magnetizing, and licensing* outcomes of the symbolic labeling. While the "reality" constructed by such "tools" is somewhat arbitrary, it is nonetheless real to the participants and seldom questioned.

The spark to develop the concept "soft culture" came during a field study that was conducted in the framework of EUREKA, the pan-European programme for the promotion of cross-border and cross-institutional collaboration on technological development. Such a field is less common in cultural studies, but the field of technology itself is well researched from other perspectives. In *Science in Action,* Latour (1987) gives a lively account of the rhetoric and inscription practices of science and technology. Our chapter originates from a similar context, i.e., scientists and researchers actively drawing and redrawing the front-line separating fact from artifact. But we capture the scientists in a different position than Latour did. His "technoscience" is inhabited with strong-minded individuals with pronounced interests and arrays of inscription devices that they employ in the battle over truth and reputation. Our actors are less strong-minded and less certain about their own interests. If they are spokespersons (Latour, 1987: p. 71,), they are spokespersons looking for something to say and represent. If they are proponents of some idea, value, or solution, they are so tentatively, for brief moments and in *sotto voce.* Our researchers struggle to persuade others to believe in their work, its results and commercial significance. However, they struggle no less to persuade themselves of the fact that their endeavours are intelligent and have a rationale.

Furthermore, we approach "science in action" with a different research interest than Latour did. While legitimacy and meaning are implicit premises for Latour's account, his interests are probably better described as the "politics" of science in action, while we will be preoccupied with the "culture" of science in action. We will study and discuss the ways in which actual behaviour in cross-national collaborative ventures come to be seen as a realisation (or betrayal) of the explicit agreements and implicit values on which the collaboration rests. In doing so, we will search for the symbolic labeling involved in the construction of meaning and legitimacy.

The observation period lasted in some cases more than four years. Since the volume of data is overwhelming, only a small part of it will be described below in the form of a case-study. BIOPHARMA is the code name of one particular EUREKA project that operated on the intersection between biotechnology and pharmaceuticals. The study involved data collection in the different countries represented in BIOPHARMA, and employed a qualitative research methodology.

In the pages to follow we will first further develop the notion of soft culture that allows for weak phenomena of community and strong behavioral variety. Second, we will describe BIOPHARMA and the symbolism surrounding EUREKA as a European programme. Third, we analyze the ways in which meaning and legitimacy are constructed by applying various symbolic "tools". Finally, we conclude by drawing the implications for the culture concept of loosely structured communities and geographically dispersed projects.

Cultures of Variety

Studying culture means ". . . study[ing] social significance - how things, events, and interaction come to be meaningful" (Smircich 1985: p. 63). The "social" in "social significance" implies that studying culture also means studying *community*, that is, some collective of individuals that produces meanings in relation to "things, events, and interaction" (Louis 1985: p. 28). By common consent the meaning that the individuals of a community ascribe to phenomena in their world is learned and non-negotiable. These meanings represent what could be called the sediments of historical processes by which arbitrary connections between "signifier" and "signified" have been developed, adjusted and, finally, taken for granted. Such sediments picture in the body of literature on organizational culture as, e.g. "basic assumptions" (Schein 1985, 1992), "beliefs and expectations" (Martin and Siehl 1983), and "symbols and interpretations" (Smircich 1983, 1985: Pondy et al. 1983). Like the sediments in the natural world channel the flow of a river, the historical sediments that we call culture are believed to channel interpretations and action in the community in question.

Meaning and Action

In the version of cultural studies mentioned above, "action" and "meaning" keep each other in place. Things, events, and interaction are interpreted, i.e., the world is made meaningful. Furthermore, things, events, and interaction must make legitimate sense, i.e., the interpretation must be attractive, valuable, and sensible. If action would pass un-interpreted, it would not exist, at least not in a cultural study. If action did not make attractive sense, it would be discontinued after being met with sanctions. Perhaps in response to the dominating instrumental rationality in organization studies, the invocation of culture also develops into causality claims: that is, things exist, events take place, and interactions unfold *because* they make sense and have social significance (Swidler 1986). Cultural or community boundaries are drawn around a group of people who "live by" such specific causalities, socialize new members into them, and use them to define deviance (Van Maanen and Barley 1984).

From an action point of view, the cultural causality seems to be but a slight revision of an ordinary instrumental logic. Instead of acting in order to produce desired outcomes, the motif seems to be the desire to do right things in terms of meaning and legitimacy. Action is calculated and planned on the premise that it should not embarrass the actor by suggesting an illegitimate purpose and/or ignorance about taken-for-granted means ends relations. Of course, this does not rule out the possibility that locally specific "versions" of cultural causality may co-exist within a community (Martin 1992; Young 1989; Rosen 1985; Schultz 1991; Kunda 1992).

Culture and Community

Parallel to the assumed relationship between "action" and "meaning", most culture studies assume that "culture" and "community" keep each other in place (Martin 1992; Schein 1992). Culture develops within fairly tightly coupled collectives that share experiences and problems, and it often defines the demarcation between the community and its environment. Although the cultural causality, as stated above, has been fragmented, this fragmentation has been rooted in fairly traditional notions of existing and coherent communities, typically formal organizations occupations or branches (Phillips; Martin 1992; Borum 1989; Van Maanen and Barley 1984; Schein 1992).

Such notions of community become untenable, however, when organizing efforts are separated in time and space. The temporary venture of a cross-border collaborative EUREKA project is a case in point. Here, organizational actors are located in different independent local environments, forming a loose structure, where connections are constructed by infrequent and discrete meetings, exchanges and communications. Although they all participate in the same organizational venture, no shared organizational frame of reference exists. Rather, what is shared is the very tacit, flexible and expressive idea of being partners in a EUREKA project.

We claim that such as absence of a strong community foundation for culture allows us to expect realities with even more equivocal properties. As Weick (1990: p. 2) says: "An equivoque is something that admits of several possible or plausible interpretations and therefore can be esoteric, subject to misunderstandings, uncertain, complex and recondite." What Weick claims to be true of technology as equivoque is equally true of cross-border ventures. "[They] make both limited sense and many different kinds of sense." As a result, ongoing interpretation and sense-making is required. The process of sense-making becomes much more important to understanding than the resulting meaning for any particular thing, event, or interaction Thus, instead of mapping the culture (s) of a community, cultural studies become focused on how sense-making processes occur within confusing and ephemeral realities.

Soft Culture

At the present stage of the argument it might be argued that an equivocal reality is made real by the culture: that ambiguous events are given specific meaning, and that order and predictability are achieved due to a trained capacity to read reality in a specific way amongst the members of a culture. With the notion of *soft culture* we try to suggest that cultures need not function that way. Allowing members of a culture to recognize reality as an equivoque need not be seen as a weakness, even if doing so undermines predictability and control. To the extent that sense-making opportunities are exploited to their fullest, equivocality could also be seen as a strength.

The argument so far has suggested that (1) the emergence of sense-making opportunities are haphazard and neither culturally determined nor intentionally planned, and (2) the exploitation of any such opportunity is not determined solely by the nature of the opportunity. Thus, instead of forming consistent and integrated patterns, meaning is situated, improvised to fit a specific, ambiguous and uncertain context (Dubinskas 1988). Furthermore, ambiguity and uncertainty do not simply disappear with increased experience:

> [t]hese situated meanings, one at a time, do not "add up to" some summary, general meaning..... Rather, in our studies, they "point to" or, better, evoke some larger context in which they are situated and where they become meaningful. (Dubinskas 1988: p. 24)

We are far from the notion of culture as historically sedimented meaning universes that channel current interpretation and action. What is left is something "softer", a notion of culture and symbols that recognizes equivocal realities, and one that seeks insights into the on-going community *processes* of sense-making. Such insights cannot depend on predicted or produced outcomes, and the gains from increased insight in the processes of soft cultures are not better control over outcomes. Such outcomes will remain contextually determined, improvised and/ or idiosyncratic. The gains from the soft culture processes come in the form of a better understanding of the *opportunities for sense-making* and the *symbolic "tools "for their exploitation.

Symbols are no longer seen as specific and reliable (if arbitrary) pointers to given meanings and significance, but rather as "tools" applied in an interactive process of interpretation (Cohen 1985; Swidler 1986). The application of "tools" and the patterning of processes may rest on shared "orientations" to issues, without implying that issues draw dependable and similar reactions across the community:

> *Indeed quite different values may be displayed by people of the same culture. In such an instance, what is it that holds together the members of the organization? I suggest that we look to the existence of a common frame of reference or a shared recognition of relevant issues. There may not be agreement about whether these issues should be relevant or about whether they are positively or negatively valued.... but whether positively or negatively they are all oriented to it (Feldman 1991: 154).*

The common use of similar symbolic tool-kits (Swidler 1986) for defining and interpreting a select set of issues is what constructs and delineates the community that is analyzed as a soft culture. Defined in this way, actors are no longer seen as merely reenacting and reinforcing pre-existing meanings residing in their "mental programming" (Hofstede 1991). Neither is culture characterized by rigid and dependable behavioral patterns. Within a soft culture, meaning does not in any causal sense pre-exist action, and therefore cannot "tame" or channel performances. Instead, we would expect soft cultures to allow a healthy non-uniformity on action, expression, appearance, belief and sentiment. Within a soft culture, social significance emerges in the course of action and as a result of, rather than a premise for, organizational action.

Thus, the notion of culture that we will pursue here is *soft* because it does not eradicate equivocal realities. It is softer than most conventional notions of culture because it focuses on sense-making *opportunities* rather than control and constraints of sense-making. It is softer because it offers *insights* rather than making strong *explanatory claims*. Figure 1 illustrates how we conceptualize the process of soft culture.

Figure 1 suggests that action gives rise to sense-making opportunities. Such opportunities may be any event, activity, situation, performance, managerial intervention, experimental victory, disappointment, etc., which calls for interpretation of meaning and judgment of legitimacy. In the construction of meaning, initiated by sense-making opportunities, symbols are readily available for members of the culture. Symbols do not substitute the actors' effort in the process of interpretation; they aid actors in making sense of an event or action in just the same way as any analytical "tool" would assist decision makers. Neither symbolic nor analytical "tools" can be held accountable for the results of their use. The outcome of this sense-making is the construction of meaning which, however, has no necessary implication for future actions,

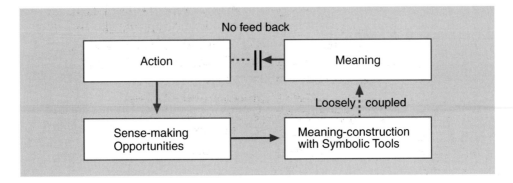

Figure 3.1 Sense-making in soft culture.

When processes of sense-making are idiosyncratic and/or situationally conditioned, community action is not culturally controlled, and action may risk to become totally *non-uniform*. Our claim is that such non-uniformity in terms of action is not antithetical to the notion of organizational culture. In fact, organizational cultures may be important precisely because they allow or spur non-uniform action. As such, they may enable communities to explore unknown opportunities and experiment with different values and beliefs (March 1988). Cultures may thus have a licensing as well as disciplinary function. The latter function has been extensively studied. The notion of *soft culture* implies an investigation into the licensing function of organizational culture.

The Empirical Field

The EUREKA programme the empirical field of our study, has proven very successful. It was launched in 1985 with the purpose of promoting scientific and commercial collaboration across the many national and institutional borders in Europe. By mid 1993, 817 collaborative projects has been announced, representing a total value of some 15 billion ECU, and involving some 5,000 participants from 20 member states and the European Commission (EUREKA Annual Report 1993).

Under the *EUREKA Management Research Initiative* (or EMRI) a longitudinal study of 34 projects was made. In the following section, a single EUREKA project with the code-name, BIOPHARMA, will be introduced. All names are fictional. This project forms the empirical foundation for the development of the concept of "soft culture".

71

Data and Methods

BIOPHARMA was one of the 34 EUREKA projects studied under the *EUREKA Management Research Initiative.* Over a period of more than four years, data on the progression of the EUREKA projects were collected in biannual, semi-structured interviews.

EUREKA projects are cross-national ventures characterized by a strong market-focus and a component of technological innovation. Compared to the majority of EUREKA projects, BIOPHARMA has perhaps a weaker commercial focus. In fact, to most of the participants, BIOPHARMA was mostly about conducting basic research on the frontier of the field of biotechnology, a field characterized by strong competition, high hopes and pervasive uncertainty.

BIOPHARMA received formal notification as a EUREKA project in the late 1980s and operated for five years on a combined budget of 12,000 KECU. Data were collected in repeated interviews with several (primarily, but not exclusively Danish) participants with various responsibilities in the host-companies and in BIOPHARMA. On average, the 25 interviews lasted for two hours and the majority of them were taped. Taped interviews with two foreign partners produced another eight hours of recorded data. In connection with interactive feedback sessions with the Danish partner and with programme evaluation exercises, additional privileged access to the realities of BIOPHARMA was achieved.

Due to the long period of observation, substantial changes were experienced over time in staffing and the distribution of responsibilities in and around BIOPHARMA. Therefore, for example, the term "project coordinator" is a more ambiguous identification than may be apparent in the quotations below. It covers three different informants, all of whom acted as project coordinator at some point in time, or in some context. We have not found reasons to distinguish between the informants personally. They are all quoted in their capacity of project coordinators.

The Partnership

BIOPHARMA involved two industrial partners and two academic partners in a collaborative venture. PHARMA was a large pharmaceutical company, whereas BIO was a small biotech company recently established as a spin off from a university. Both academic partners were distinguished professors in their fields. In addition to the partners, two important "suppliers" of biological material were integrated into the collaboration in various parts of the process. BIOPHARMA spanned Europe from North to South. The partners and suppliers were located in Denmark, the UK, France, Italy, and Spain.

In many respects BIOPHARMA was established in direct response to the creation of the EUREKA programme. The original initiative came from the academic partners, both of whom had collaborated with PHARMA on earlier occasions. Learning about the EUREKA programme they approached PHARMA with a fairly open-ended proposition to collaborate. BIO were identified much later and were accepted in the partnership only after serious negotiations on terms of research and agendas. Thus, instead of forming their collaboration on the basis of strategic calculations, the industrial partners were brought together in the process of forming the EUREKA project. Notification as a EUREKA project made the partners eligible for EUREKA funding. Apart from the requirements on which the public funding was conditioned, the partners in BIOPHARMA were free to manage and organize themselves in any way they found suitable.

EUREKA Project as a Loosely Organized Community

In line with what was true for the whole population of EUREKA projects, BIOPHARMA organized itself loosely, avoiding any central authority in the project and specifying only modest commitments concerning integrated collaborative efforts and development targets (Kreiner 1993 a,b,c). Each partner was represented by a project-coordinator, but these were not given much authority to decide over resources and priorities. Rather, all activities in BIOPHARMA remained highly integrated into the work of the host organizations. That was true for all partners. This is not to say that there was no collaboration envisioned, but any such collaboration was organized in ways that did not require integrating the work of the various partners. A considerable sharing of information, ideas, results, biological material, etc., occurred. But such sharing happened on the basis of voluntary coordination of efforts and contributions, rather than according to any planned coordination of work activities and resources.

Instead of formal coordination and authority, the partnership was held together by strong personal ties between individual actors (as also shown by Sevón 1993) and by semi-annual conference-like meetings for everybody associated with BIOPHARMA (i.e., including bench scientists and suppliers). Furthermore, all partners in BIOPHARMA were fully fledged members of an international research community through which ideas, organic material, services and partners are exchanged rather freely. This is claimed to be a normal pattern "where science is really at its edge" (Kreiner and Schultz 1993; Sapienza 1990, 1988; Wroblewski 1985:1 Wigand and Frankwick 1989; Perides 1990).

Entering into collaboration in BIOPHARMA did not cut off the partners' access to previous networks and research communities. Thus, not only did the partners come together, in a sense, but their respective networks were also drawn together by BIOPHARMA. That provided new contacts and relationships in excess of what was originally envisioned. Furthermore, each partner continued a seemingly unrestrained search for scientific leads and new partners. Several of these relationships were external to the partnership and emerged from haphazard opportunities. Participation in BIOPHARMA did not tempt the various partners to turn their back on the rest of the international research community. However, only a few of these network relationships lasted throughout the duration of BIOPHARMA. The majority of the international network relationships were terminated as the partners had explored their potential. Thus, the total number of new relationships associated with BIOPHARMA increased dramatically over time.

Furthermore, BIOPHARMA was characterized by a surprising amount of change in research agendas during the whole project period. While the general ideas and visions survived the turbulence, the research strategies, the sub-themes and planned experiments of BIOPHARMA did not. The exploratory mode of basic research, and the complexities and uncertainties involved, demanded a step-wise learning process that was not conducive to long-term commitments and strategies. In this sense, the realignment of networks and the emergence of research agendas may easily be rationalized. They reflected a continuous adaptation to experience and to new information about competitor behaviour and scientific break-throughs.

We will claim that BIOPHARMA can be conceived as a loosely structured community (Orton and Weick 1990; Weick 1976). All partners are linked in formal arrangements, yet they maintain their own identity. While to a large extent independent, they are nevertheless mutually responsive, not by obligation, but by opportunity. The organizational framework consists of active networks that are brought together by the formation of a project. The project is by definition exclusive, but in practice the boundaries between project and networks are only temporarily and inconsistently reinforced. The content of collaboration emerges over time, less as a matter of agreement and planning than as a matter of discovery and learning.

The Project as a Symbolic "Tool"

If it is true, as described above, that different participants in BIOPHARMA kept project activities well integrated in the host organization's operations, that partnerships also outside the project were explored, and that research agendas seemed to shift radically over time, the name BIOPHARMA must have denoted quite different things to the different partners, and even to the same partner at different points in time. Paradoxically, much also seems to indicate that the significance and meaning of BIOPHARMA was never seriously questioned or doubted. Without the slightest hesitation partners would refer to the project *as if* it represented something definite. Or in the words of one of our informants: "Everybody knows now what EUREKA is, so everybody is working on the EUREKA idea now."

EUREKA as a Symbol

In the above quotation, EUREKA is not only a reference to the particular project under study, BIOPHARMA. It is also a reference to the European programme for cross-national collaborative ventures, as described in the introduction. "EUREKA" is obviously more than merely a name, it is a symbol in the traditional sense of that word, i.e., a "sign which denotes something much greater than itself, and which calls for the association of conscious and unconscious ideas, in order for it to be endowed with its full meaning and significance" (Pondy *et al.* 1983: p. 5). The name itself, being accompanied by a logo consisting of the Greek letter epsilon and an exclamation mark (X!) makes an unmistakable reference to Archimedes' "heureka", thus alluding to the triumph of scientific discovery in general. It further alludes to the cultural heritage of Europeans which might be claimed to unite otherwise divided countries in their race for competitiveness on the world market against the US and Japan. Allowing for some differences in national style, the symbolic message seems nowhere to have been lost: EUREKA elicits responses from politicians and partners alike expressing a fair amount of reverence and pride.

Thus, part of the symbolic potency of BIOPHARMA stems from EUREKA as an *idea* (Cohen 1985: p. 18). Neither the specific work plans, nor the formally designated set of partners, the written business contracts, nor even the Hanover Declaration laying the legal and ideological ground for the programme as a whole, could function as a sign with symbolic powers. The symbol is the pertinent idea of collaborating across boundaries, of pooling resources and competencies in new and non-conventional ways to the mutual benefit of the partners. Apparently, the elusiveness and vagueness of such a symbol does not make it a less effective "tool" for assessing social significance. We claim that the partners regularly interpreted and justified their tumultuous experiences with reference to this potent symbol, thereby creating a sense of order and structure, however rudimentary, idiosyncratic and unfounded. As expressed by some of our informants:

> *Everybody is feeling that Europe is coming by, so if he can play a role there [Project Coordinator, tape transcript].*
>
> *It is easier to develop a scientific project and you get more liberty of moving around if you can say, well this research project is done by EUREKA [Project Coordinator, tape transcript].*
>
> *People are seeing EUREKA as a very important project and they are very proud to co-operate with it [Project Coordinator, tape transcript].*

The above citations illustrate the importance and legitimacy that actors involved in collaboration ascribe to EUREKA. Thus, EUREKA does seem to offer a shared orientation of being European. of being proud of contributing to the development of Europe and of being where the action is. It may now be suggested that the

EUREKA symbol, when applied as a "tool" for sense-making, may somehow turn the mundane turmoil and inconsistencies of BIOPHARMA into something quite significant and sensible. Partners may be engaged and disengaged, research agendas may be completely redefined, and collaborative ambitions may rise and fall. But no matter the specific content at any particular moment in time, such activities would remain EUREKA and thus signal an important boundary-crossing venture and its innovative pooling of dispersed resources and competencies. What BIOPHARMA lacked in terms of organizational robustness it could be claimed to possess in overall symbolic robustness.

To be specific, the symbolic robustness of the cross-national collaborative venture stemmed from the fact that the EUREKA label would stick on almost any phenomenon, action, expense, etc., and thus provide a symbolic distinction between EUREKA and non-EUREKA. This distinction between EUREKA and non-EUREKA was required *culturally,* i.e., as almost the only general orientation that unites the dispersed partners of the EUREKA project (Feldman 1991). The arbitrariness of the labeling was not due to lack of competence or ill will, but to the equivocal nature of the realities in which the project operated.

Amongst the symbols used as sense-making "tools", EUREKA was arguably the most important and most generally understood one. But there were others that were more particular to BIOPHARMA.

However, the importance of the EUREKA program as context for BIOPHARMA should be emphasized. It provided the venture with a ready-made and widely recognized symbolism that may easily have prolonged the life of the collaboration under highly tumultuous and unpredictable conditions in the respective host organizations. In daily reference the EUREKA label was used rather than the BIOPHARMA one. This added the above mentioned special significance to this particular project. It may be confusing to outsiders when reference is made to EUREKA in the quotations below. It should be kept in mind that it is the BIOPHARMA project that is referred to, not the overall EUREKA program as such.

The Symbol as a Categorizing "Tool"

The use of symbols as a categorizing "tool" refers to the way in which symbols facilitate the recognition and labeling of project activities. As a result of the categorization, the partners are able to make distinctions between project and non-project activities. Such distinctions provided history with a certain degree of order and legitimacy.

The application of symbolic "tools" for categorization must be seen on the backdrop of life in organized anarchies. Life in these research-intensive organized anarchies is lived in an organizational landscape with few natural or given contours.

Many tasks have neither clear beginnings nor absolute endings; most employees work simultaneously on many different jobs and tasks; the relevance of any one activity for one or the other task may often only be established after a breakthrough or significant findings. In this contourless landscape, "tools" for making distinctions help everyone to regain a sense of order and organization. The EUREKA label introduced such "tools" for scientists, managers and outsiders alike.

Asking whether something is EUREKA or not is much more important in this respect than the eventual answers. Its effectiveness in categorizing, and thus recognizing activities and events, does not depend on the appropriateness of the categories or the reliability of their uses. It only depends on the legitimacy of the distinction between EUREKA and non-EUREKA. The symbolic pervasiveness and salience of EUREKA made it such a highly legitimate "tool" for categorization.

In most respects, categorizing phenomena, things, activities, and resources is a fairly trivial task. Consider for example the following statements as illustrations of the symbol as a categorizing "tool":

> If we send them the [materials] we always write EUREKA so that they will know that it's part of the EUREKA project [Project Coordinator, tape transcript].

The partners in BIOPHARMA were, as already mentioned, active participants in the biotechnological "barter economy" (Kreiner and Schultz 1993). The actual practice did not change with the emergence of BIOPHARMA, but the labeling of biological materials, ideas, services, etc., as EUREKA or non-EUREKA presumably gave it an additional and partly different meaning.

> We have a code for that: EUREKA Research 'ER.' And then everybody knows that's a code so everything which is carrying that mark gets into the EUREKA Research [Project Coordinator, tape transcript].

The implications for the financial bookkeeping of coding things in this way are quite apparent, but in terms of other dimensions of significance we are left to speculate, as are the participants themselves. There is no authorized interpretation of the significance of the labeling that everybody should respect and enact. It is not even certain that inclusion under the EUREKA label is always considered as a privilege or advantage. But when such labeling opens access to new resources and scientific results, the EUREKA label seems valuable, and strategic considerations may easily enter into the categorization:

> Interviewer: Is it to provide access to the project of the EUREKA partners that you categorize it under EUREKA? As such the project takes place in California and has nothing to do with EUREKA?

Informant: *The project has nothing to do with EUREKA. You could easily conduct those activities outside EUREKA. But it is easier to turn it into EUREKA. It is a strong motivation to the partners [Manager, Section Head, tape transcript]*

The use of the symbol as a "tool" for categorization takes more elaborate forms as well. There is a strong interweaving of organizational activities and project activities. Most managers may probably long for a clearer distinction and the labeling itself may inspire the restructuring of the host-organization:

... so that's a project in which we have ideas in that direction and we made them individual points. Just thinking about it and talking about it, have structured groups at [the company] [Project Coordinator, tape transcript].

So, if EUREKA comes in, EUREKA takes over the structure [Partner, tape transcript].

These new structures seem to materialize not by conscious design nor by managerial fiat; rather they materialize as a result of a concomitant change in people's orientation in different parts of the organization occasioned by the formation of the EUREKA project. The potential impact on the structure of the host-organizations may be pervasive, even if achieved through informal means.

He [i.e., one of the project coordinators] puts an enormous emphasis on all the positive aspects of the EUREKA collaboration. In a way it makes collaboration easier, because then there is a common framework, if nothing else a visible framework, which we can all relate to [Manager, Division Head, Tape transcript].

To have everybody define themselves in relation to the shared visible framework may indeed provide a kind of order, no matter how valid and how consequential any actual definition may be. The order lies in the uniformity of orientation, not in the uniformity of the outcomes of such orientated efforts.

The Symbol as a Magnetizing "Tool"

The use of symbols as a magnetizing "tool" refers to the way in which symbols may mobilize actors external to the EUREKA project and thus occasion new and redefined collaborative relations for the project. Thus the boundaries and the scope of the project are emergent properties that are ascertained in ongoing processes of "partnering". This is true in relation to both the host organizations and the external networks of the various project partners.

One of our informants observed the tendency of his EUREKA project to attract a lot of (unexpected) people, ideas and energy. In his own words:

It's a kind of a magnet function; so people start co-operating with our people. That has been very successful [Project Coordinator, Tape transcript].

It's working like a magnet. If a project is successful things are attracting successful researchers, so for the [X-part of the EUREKA project] I think it's going to be our most important. Maybe one day it will swallow up everything [Project Coordinator, Tape transcript].

Obviously, a project known to be rich on resources and prestige may attract people of opportunistic motives. However, in the highly competitive climate of this kind of R&D, few can afford to go for the easy resources and few are likely to offer them. Attention is more likely to be stimulated by the opportunity of collaboration as such (Kreiner and Schultz 1993). The magnetizing effect of the project may emerge simply when researchers inside and outside the organization (re-)interpret their own activities and ideas in the light of the EUREKA project:

Interviewer: *So they would like to be partners'.'*
Informant: *They would love to be partners, but we have only met them once. I was down there with [the other industrial partner], but we are still in the beginning of this negotiation [Project Coordinator. Tape transcript].*

In the process of making sense of one's own activities and ideas in the light of EUREKA, actors may come to discover and develop non-obvious linkages, unknown kinship of research ideas and synergetic relationships. Such discoveries often carry high rewards on the R&D frontier, but never materialize without proper effort, trust and opportunity. The EUREKA project provided one such opportunity to which a number of actors responded.

On this background, several new people and activities got involved in the project. As would be expected, this inclusion certainly fueled the dynamic progression of the collaboration. However, in a paradoxical way, this magnetizing device may also have segmented the project. It added to the fragmentation of activities by engaging the individual partners in external collaboration that was occasioned by the BIOPHARMA project, but not fully integrated into it.

The Symbol as a Licensing "Tool"

The role of EUREKA as a licensing "tool" may explain why the fragmentation of activities within BIOPHARMA did not imperil the collaboration significantly. The concept of licensing refers to the ways in which symbolic "tools" legitimated the local exploration of new opportunities as they arose during the project, which often seemed to refocus attention in new and unforeseen directions. It is true that, to a certain extent, each partner followed his own trajectory in response to new opportunities, and thus produced fragmentation in the project activities; but these individual trajectories were not random nor seen as intentionally disintegrative.

79

Rather, they were construed as "normal" search behaviour on the frontier of biotechnology. The behavioral fragmentation of the project was a perhaps regrettable aspect of the R&D work but not an irrational response to the immense uncertainty under which they operated. Some informants did indeed express regrets over the way things were developing. That they did not meet local diversions from original plans and scopes with sanctions reinforces the postulate that fragmentation was construed as a side-effect of an earnest pursuit of opportunities in an unpredictable, unplanned, uncontrolled and highly competitive R&D context of the EUREKA project. Even when the participants allowed themselves to pursue new and upcoming opportunities for collaboration, this in no way questioned the existence or legitimacy of the EUREKA project. This is expressed by several informants as follows:

> Informant: ... *We were not loyal to them as partners, we had also other relations outside the company which gave us more advantages in the same field. So our EUREKA partners were not only [the two academic partners], but also [Professor X in California and Y in Washington]. We did not think of the field in terms of limitations* [Manager, Section Head, Tape transcript.
> Interviewer: *You make it sound as if it is a breakthrough for the EUREKA project although it is achieved through a contact outside [the partnership].*
> Informant: *But that is how it is. At once I must emphasize: We must escalate our work on [the new field], and with whom should we then do it? Then I go somewhere else [because the academic EUREKA partners lack expertise in this field].* [Project Coordinator, tape transcript].

Thus, the EUREKA symbols allow the partners to rationalize and legitimize the fact that their BIOPHARMA activities take them outside the group of official partners. Although one informant raises the issue of loyalty to the EUREKA project, the need to "go somewhere else" is constructed within the notion of the EUREKA partnership. Explicitly or implicitly labeled EUREKA, these explorations outside the project remain part of the collaborative effort.

Along with the labeling and licensing, the implicit expectation emerged that eventual exploits from the explorations would be offered to the partnership. Only on a few brief occasion during the lifetime of BIOPHARMA was this expectation actually tested, followed by mildly disruptive uneasiness. But between these few rifts, the exploration and pursuit of external opportunities continued as legitimated and rationalized BIOPHARMA performance. It did not undermine the identity of the EUREKA project. Instead, what in formal projects might easily be seen as disintegrative behaviour, here came to reaffirm the collaborative venture by symbolizing initiative and determination to the expected benefit of the project as a whole.

The EUREKA symbol granted legitimacy to a surprisingly wide range of behaviour. It did so by legitimizing exploration *per se*. In a world of many R&D ventures riddled with uncertainty, exploration promises high pay-offs, but with very small probabilities. In most cases, granting license to the pursuit of opportunities outside the EUREKA partnership carried no costs, because nothing would come of it in the end. The way in which the partners would "waste their time and effort" on such ventures was of no concern to the other partners. Only rarely, when the pursuit turned out to look promising, would the issue of legitimacy of external linkages be aired. In this sense, the use of the symbol as a licensing "tool" was made conditional on the outcomes of the behaviour. One could argue that judgments of legitimacy were not really waived. They were only temporarily suspended, that is, suspended until the outcomes of the licensed behaviour could be determined.

Overview of Symbolic "Tools"

We have described and discussed the ways in which the very idea of the EUREKA project BIOPHARMA as a cross-national collaborative venture (i.e., the symbol) enabled the partners to categorize, magnetize and license activities in and around the project. Several times we have pointed out that this symbolic "tool" is not a reliable "tool" in a traditional sense. We make no presumption that the categorization is consistent across partners and situations. Nor do we claim that the scope and the boundaries are redrawn predictably, visibly and in full agreement, or that the partners will exploit the license in similar ways. All we claim is that activities do get categorized, that environments of researchers and ideas do get mobilized, and that fragmentary activities do get reintegrated as a legitimate part of the EUREKA project.

Table 3.1 Conceptualization of Symbolic Tools within a Soft Culture.

Concepts	Categorizing	Magnetizing	Licensing
General Definition	Facilitates recognition and labeling of project activities	Facilitates attraction of actors and their collaborative networks	Facilitates legitimization of explorative activities in relation to emergent opportunities
Relation to Internal Project	Distinction between project and non-project activities	Mobilization of formal and informal partners	Freedom to pursue locally defined agendas independent of collective project framework
Relation to External Environments	Legitimacy and funding of project activities	Construction of the boundaries and scope of the project	Non-exclusiveness of project ventures
Primary Organizational Context	Local host organization National funding agency	Research Community	Project partners

In Table 1 we summarize the ideas about the symbolic "tools" that unite the BIOPHARMA partners in their pursuit in making sense of an uncertain and equivocal reality.

The categorizing "tool" allows actors to recognize and label activities as part of or external to the project. The magnetizing "tool" allows them to mobilize, evaluate and integrate external ideas and collaborators. The licensing "tool" allows them to explore new opportunities and test ideas that are foreign to the original partnership. Respectively, the three "tools" provide us with order or contours, variety, and freedom to explore. They are "tools" that are most relevant in relation to different organizational contexts: the local host organization, the wider research community, and the project partners, respectively.

Soft Cultures and Ephemeral Communities

The previous discussion has established a picture of BIOPHARMA that has two distinct features. On the one hand, BIOPHARMA was portrayed as a loosely organized community. Instead of well-structured, preconceived, and coordinated efforts across the partners, this project could more easily be recognized as a dynamic realignment of separate networks. As an action set (Aldrich and Whetten 1981), BIOPHARMA shared only vague visions about where the collaborative efforts might lead. On the other hand, BIOPHARMA was also portrayed as sharing a common ground for sense-making. The significance of being a EUREKA project was recognized widely. and the very idea of being together in BIOPHARMA provided opportunities for sense-making. The project itself was a symbol that became commonly and publicly applied to situations, events, performances, managerial interventions, experimental victories and disappointments, etc. Few structural limitations existed on the applicability of this label, and it enabled the partners to ascertain which activities, external parties, and experimental results belonged to the partnership process.

From a narrow BIOPHARMA perspective, action tended to proceed in a rather haphazard manner. It responded locally to the leads, opportunities and inspirations that float around on any research frontier. If a certain degree of behavioral discipline and coordination is most commonly assumed in cultural perspectives, our observations seem to deviate. Four reasons for this, are easily available.

(1) Above we compared our field of investigation with the technoscience depicted in Latour (1987). In this comparison, the participants in BIOPHARMA seemed much less certain about and committed to specific pieces of knowledge. The uncertainty was enormous, in respect to the scientific as well as the commercial aspects of the venture. The frame of mind was one of exploration, not exploitation (March 1991). Individually and collectively, BIOPHARMA seemed to invest few resources in as many tracks as possible, rather than risking all the efforts and resources on one or a few tracks.

(2) The symbolic "tools" available to the parties in BIOPHARMA were quite equivocal. The idea of a collaborative venture might be used to argue convincingly for inclusion as well as exclusion in any particular case. The resolution of such conflicts was not predestined by the symbolism itself; it was determined contextually and by the skillfulness of the actors applying the "tools".

(3) Although the various actors developed their own local, symbolic framework during the collaborative process, the EUREKA framework did offer a set of ready-made symbolic "tools" to the actors, involved in BIOPHARMA. The prior existence of such symbolic "tools" may facilitate and intensify the processes of soft culture.

(4) The retrospective construction of meaning, and thus the weak cultural Control or determination of behaviour, was facilitated by the fact that the project organization in our case was geographically dispersed over most of Europe. Thus, face-to-face encounters occurred only occasionally.

We recognize that these particular features about our empirical field of study may explain why we have observed the kind of behaviour that we have. However, we are not convinced that the notion of "soft culture" for that reason might not have significance in other contexts. After all, occasionally realities appear ephemeral in most organizations; most symbols emerge as more equivocal than we normally like to admit; and performance requires retrospective sense-making as events become increasingly abstract, stochastic, and continuous (Weick 1990).

To the extent that realities are increasingly portrayed as ephemeral, symbols lose their denotative and referential character. But as we have shown above, thereby they have not lost their significance. The symbols of European unity and cross-border collaborative ventures would become unintelligible if we depended on them to refer to some existing state of reality. But symbols may be less important as signifiers of realities than as images of rea*lities yet, to be created*. In the latter sense, they contain a promised future, evoke the will to realize it, and inspire the efforts to do so. The efforts thus inspired may easily depart from the originally agreed plans and current conventional wisdom, and yet be seen to be culturally intelligible and legitimate.

There is no point in ignoring the fact that in many organizational contexts behaviour is tightly controlled and determined by cultural means. However, it need not necessarily be so. The emergence of new organizational forms, promoted under labels like business process re-engineering and learning organizations, is generally orchestrated with efforts to empower employees, deploy responsibility for policy, and change management roles from control to coaching. Thus, an organization acquires a less tangible character and its emergent processes leave an image of virtual organization.

If "reality" demands flexibility in organizational production processes, it would be natural to expect that such flexibility was also required in the organizational sense-making processes. Control and constraints on sense-making would become inadequate, just like hierarchy and functional structures have become in many respects. Having escaped the hierarchical and departmental containment, it is time to escape the cultural containment of organizational effort and performance. We have attempted to illustrate a "soft culture" that enabled continuous sense-making in a highly ephemeral reality. Equivocal symbols were not a weakness, but a strength, since they allowed the partners to construct futures and inspire the pursuit thereof. In other contexts, "soft cultures" may similarly be a competitive strength if the equivocal symbols can be exploited to spur rather than restrict sense-making.

References

Aldrich, H. and Whetten, D. (1981) "Organization-Sets, Action-Sets and Networks: Making the Most of Simplicity", in P.C. Nystrom and W.H. Starbuck (eds.) *Handbook of Organizational Design*. New York: Oxford University Press.

Borum, F. (1989) "Divergence and Convergence: A Community Analysis of the Structuring of the Danish IT Field", in F. Borum and P. Hull Kristensen (eds.) *Technological Innovation and Organizational Change*, pp. 219–249. Copenhagen: New Social Science Monographs.

Cohen, A. (1985) *The Symbolic Construction of Community*. Chichester: Ellis Horwood Limited; London: Tavistock Publications.

Cohen, M.D., March, J.G. and Olsen, J.P. (1972) "A Garbage Can Model of Organizational Choice", *Administrative Science Quarterly* 17(1): 1–25.

Dubinskas, F.A. (1988) "Cultural Constructions: The Many Faces of Time", in F.A. Dubinskas (ed.) *Making Time. Ethnographies of High-Technology Organizations*. Philadelphia: Temple University Press.

EUREKA, Annual Report (1993).

Feldman, M. (1991) "The Meanings of Ambiguity: Learning from Stories and Metaphors", in P. Frost et al. (eds.) *Reframing Organizational Culture*, pp. 145–157. London: Sage.

Hatch, M.J. (1993) "The Dynamics of Organizational Culture", *Academy of Management* 18: 657–693.

Hofstede, G. (1991) *Cultures and Organizations. Software of the Mind*. London: McGraw-Hill.

Kreiner, K. (1993a) *EUREKA – på dansk*. Copenhagen: Samfundslitteratur.

_____. (1993b) *Managing the Internationalization of R & D: The European Experience*, paper presented at the Academy of Management Meeting, August 9. Atlanta, Georgia, U.S.A.

_____. (1993c) *Eureka Projects and Contextual Turbulence. The Impact on Managerial and Organizational Strategy*, paper presented at the Oxford Conference on Management of Collaborative European Programmes and Projects in Research and Training, April. Oxford University, UK.

Kreiner, K. and Schultz, M. (1993) "Networking in Biotechnology: Crossing the Institutional Divide", *Organization Studies* 14(2): 189–209.

Kunda, G. (1992) *Engineering Culture. Culture and Control in a High-Tech Organization*. Philadelphia: Temple University Press.

Latour, B. (1987) *Science In Action. How to Follow Scientists and Engineers through Society*. Milton Keynes: Open University Press.

Louis, M.R. (1985) "Perspectives on Organizational Culture", in P. Frost et al. (eds.) *Organizational Culture*, pp. 27–29. Calif.: Sage.

March, J.G. (1980) "Science, Politics and Mrs. Gruenberg", in *National Research Council in 1979*, US National Academy of Sciences.

_____. (1988) *Decisions and Organizations*. Oxford: Blackwell.

_____. (1991) "Exploration and Exploitation in Organizational Learning", *Organizational Science* 2(l): 71–87.

March, J.G. and Olsen, J.P. (1976) *Ambiguity and Choice in Organizations*. Bergen: Universitetsforlaget.

Martin, J. (1992) *Cultures in Organizations. Three Perspectives*. New York: Oxford University Press.

Martin, J. and Siehl, C. (1983) "Organizational Culture and Counter Culture: An Uneasy Symbiosis", *Organizational Dynamics*, 12: 52–64.

Meyerson, D. (1991) "On Acknowledging and Uncovering Ambiguities in Cultures", in P. Frost et al. (eds.) *Reframing Organizational Culture*, pp. 131–145. Calif.: Sage.

Orton, D.J. and Weick, K.E. (1990) "Loosely Coupled Systems: A Reconceptualization", *Academy of Management Review* 15(2): 203–223.

Perides, T. (1990) *Strategic Alliances for Smaller Firms*, paper presented at the 10th International Conference of Strategic Management Society, Stockholm, September 24–27.

Pondy, L. et al. (eds.) (1983) *Organizational Symbolism*. Greenwich: JAI Press.

Rosen, M. (1985) "Breakfast at Spiro's: Dramaturgy and Dominance", *Journal of Management Studies* 11(2): 31–84.

Sapienza, A. (1988) *Technology Transfer: Pharmaceutical Industry Research Relations with American Universities*, Research Rapport. Cambridge, Mass.: Harvard University School of Public Health.

_____. (1990) "Strategic Alliances in Biotechnology. Problems at the University-Industry Research Interface", Research Paper. Cambridge, Massachusetts: Harvard University School of Public Health.

Schein, E. (1985) *Organizational Culture and Leadership*. San Francisco: Jossey-Bass.

_____. (1992) *Organizational Culture and Leadership*. (Second edition.) San Francisco: Jossey-Bass.

Schultz, M. (1991) "Transitions between Symbolic Domains in Organizations", *Organization Studies* 12(4): 489–506.

Sevón, G. (1993) *The Joints in Joint R & D Ventures*, paper presented at the conference Cross-border Ventures in Innovation, Copenhagen, March.

Smircich, L. (1983) "Organizations as Shared Meanings", in L. Pondy et al. (eds.) *Organizational Symbolism*: pp. 55–69. London: JAI Press.

_____. (1985) "Is the Concept of Culture a Paradigm for Understanding Organizations and Ourselves?", in P. Frost et al. (eds.) *Organizational Culture*, pp. 55–73. Calif.: Sage.

Smircich, L. and Morgan, G. (1982) "Leadership: The Management of Meaning", *The Journal of Applied Behavioral Science* 18(3): 257–273.

Swidler, A. (1986) "Culture in Action: Symbols and Strategies", *American Sociological Review* 51: 273–286.

Van Maanen, J. and Barley, S. (1985) "Cultural Organization: Fragments of a Theory", in P. Frost et al. (eds.) *Organizational Culture*, pp. 31–55. Calif.: Sage.

_____. (1984) "Occupational Communities: Culture and Control in Organizations", in B. Staw and L. Cummings (eds.) *Research in Organizational Behavior* 6: 287–366.

Weick, K.E. (1976) "Educational Organizations as Loosely Coupled Systems", *Administrative Science Quarterly* 21: 1–19.

_____. (1990) "Technology as Equivoque: Sense-making in New Technologies", in P.S. Goodman, L.S. Sproull and Associates *Technology and Organizations*, pp. 1–44. San Francisco: Jossey-Bass.

Wigand, R. and Frankwick, G. (1989) "Inter-Organizational Communication and Technology Transfer: Industry-Government-University Linkages", *International Journal of Technology Management* 4(1): 63–76.

Wroblewski, R. (1985) "The Pharmaceutical Industry and Academic Medicine in Collaboration", *Circulation*, Part II, 72: 13–17.

Young, E. (1989) "On the Naming of the Rose: Interest and Multiple Meanings as Elements of Organizational Culture", *Organization Studies* 10(2): 187–206.

Chapter 4

The Social Construction of Projects. A Case Study of Organizing of an Extraordinary Building Project – the Stockholm Globe Arena

Kerstin Sahlin-Andersson

The modernization of western cities and societies is often pursued in the form of big projects. Such projects are seldom realized the way they were initially intended (cf. for example Hall, 1980; Ross and Staw, 1986). A number of big projects have been carried through in spite of seemingly impossible conditions. Other projects have not been realized although they seemed highly needed and met favourable conditions. The fact that some projects are realized and not others, and that some parts or aspects of cities are renewed and not others cannot be explained by the importance of the problem. In this chapter it is argued that part of the explanation of why some projects are realized and not others is to be found in the processes of project organizing.

In the field of project management certain problems are usually attributed to big projects (Morris, 1900, Morris and Hough, 1907, Hall, 1900). They are often characterized as complex, ambiguous, uncertain and demanding long term commitments. Big projects often concern new tasks or new inventions. This usually adds to their complexity, uncertainty and ambiguity. In particular those city building projects which involve both public and private interests exhibit great complexities. It is often claimed that the many actors involved and the diverse interests pursued lead to a complexity which hinders realization.

The great number of books published about problems associated with big projects indicate that they seem more difficult to realize than smaller or less extreme projects. It is assumed that this difficulty follows from the complexity and ambiguity characterizing big projects. Out of this way of problematizing big projects, the natural recommendation given is to reduce the complexity, to clarify the ambiguity and to play down the uniqueness.

One important finding from studies of big projects is that they hardly ever seem to be carried through in accordance with "the handbook". Some of the more famous projects realized in the last decades have also been termed "Planning disasters" (Hall, 1980). In some cases the complexity and the big and unique character are turned into favourable circumstances for the project at hand (Brunsson, 1989; Jacobsson, 1987; Sahlin-Andersson, 1989). The normative recommendations to clarify the ambiguity, to reduce complexity and to play down the uniqueness have in other studies been shown to be most efficient for those who want to obstruct or stop a project realization (Brunsson, 1985; Sahlin-Andersson, 1986).

In this chapter, I will describe and analyze how one case of a complex city building project was pursued. This project marks a new way of accomplishing city planning in Sweden. The case illustrates two different strategies for pursuing big projects. One is the clarity strategy. This is the kind of strategy often outlined in the normative literature referred to above. Problems, possible solutions, intentions, preferences and conditions are clearly mapped and stated from the start. The assumption is that differences, ambiguity and uncertainty have to be eliminated in order to facilitate a collaboration between the participants taking part in the project. Clarity is seen as the way to get things done. This strategy is based on the idea that intentions, preferences and conditions may be stable during the process and will steer the outcome of it. The case analyzed here illustrates how the differing and changing intentions, preferences and conditions presented difficulties in pursuing the clarity strategy. However, the formulation and definition of the project as new and different and the characterization of it as complex and ambiguous was used by the major actors involved as a means to realize the project. This way of pursuing the project is a sharp contrast to the clarity strategy and is summarized as the ambiguity strategy. In the ambiguity strategy, the complexity, ambiguity and the changing conditions are not seen as problematic but are emphasized and made use of in realizing the project.

The Stockholm Globe Arena – a descriptive account

The construction of a sports and culture complex – a spherical building with a diameter of 110 meters and a roof height of 85 meters, in the Johanneshov area of southern Stockholm, was finished in 1989. This complex, which is known as the Stockholm Globe Arena, has been described as the world's largest spherical building. Another building complex, with shopping centre, hotel and offices, is also being constructed around the arena as part of the same project. Few Swedish projects have attracted as much public attention as this one.

The aim of the study reported here was to understand what strategies were used in the pursuing of big projects, the possibilities and prerequisites for using these strategies and how the using of various strategies affected the outcome of the project. One crucial aspect of such strategies proved to be how the project was formulated and perceived as ordinary or extraordinary and what such classifications entailed. For this purpose, it was important to understand the various actors' interests, expectations, positions, interrelations and interactions. Therefore I followed the project for three years. The study includes tape-recorded in-depth interviews with the major actors in the project: politicians, city planners, architects, and representatives of consulting, construction and real estate companies. The interviews lasted one to four hours. Several of the persons interviewed have also given me their personal notes and documents. During the three years I have had continual contact, and done repeated interviews with representatives of the architects' bureau who designed the Arena building. Apart from this material all official documents, decision reports, programs and plans, have been analyzed. During these years I have also followed what has been written in the newspapers. A first draft of the case was distributed to the interviewees and on the basis of this, further interviews were carried out with all participants (for a more complete analysis of this case, see Sahlin-Andersson, 1989).

The project initiation

Before 1989, there was no arena in the city of Stockholm big enough to house for example an ice-hockey world championship. For many years politicans and administrators in the City Leisure Department, representatives of the National Hockey Association and private companies discussed the alternative possibilities of either modernizing and expanding an old arena or constructing a new one. The possibility for Stockholm to arrange the ice-hockey world championship added to the importance given this matter in the beginning of the 1980s. The City Government, however, did not find it possible to build a new arena at public expense.

91

At this time, another public project just being planned in Stockholm was being financed by way of a deal between the City Government and the private construction companies involved. Private companies were here given the opportunity to construct commmercial office buildings on the publicly-owned land in return for the rebuilding of the railway station. This project provided a model for financial solution that could also be applied to the new sports arena.

The City thus intended to get a new arena without using any tax money, or at least no more than a small share of what it would cost to build such a complex. In the railway station project, the financial solution was made possible because of the attractive location for office buildings in central Stockholm. The land surrounding the planned sports arena, however, was not at that time estimated to be of such high value. Therefore, at the same time as this model presented an attractive alternative, there were considerable doubts among the city planners, as to whether such a financial solution could be applied to the sports-arena project. Either the planners had to assess the value of the land quite optimistically – too optimistically to be realistic many thought – or the suggested deal would not be possible. The leading politicians and planners chose the former alternative.

The suggested deal was motivated in financial terms. The politicians, however, had additional motives for this way of designing the project as well. A rise of unemployment among construction workers was expected. Furthermore, a widely discussed topic in the city at this time was how to handle an increasing unbalance between the northern and southern parts of Stockholm. Most offices and higher education facilities were placed in the northern part. To offer private companies the opportunity to build offices in the southern part of Stockholm, where the new sports arena was planned to be located, was a way to finance the arena and in addition contributed to easing the regional unbalance as well as the expected unemployment[1].

The plans for such a new arena to be financed in a deal with private companies started. However, the project was not generally regarded as being of vital strategic value. "Most of the politicians and managers in the city just saw it as building one more sports arena," said one of the planners. Thus the planning of the project was assigned to rather low levels in the city administration. The planners working on the project were afraid that the whole matter would be forgotten as it seemed to be difficult to argue for its importance. And as the economic base of the project seemed weak, the only way they thought this project would attract enough attention, so it would not be stopped, was to make it bigger, both in terms of the

---

1   A few years later, when the construction of the project started, the situation was reversed. So many commercial buildnings were built in Stockholm, that a temporary stop for construction projects was introduced.

planned square meters of business facilities, and in terms of formulating the project as "world class" and extraordinary.

In July 1984 the City Government sent an inquiry to about 30 big companies in the Stockholm area, asking them if they were interested in entering a project competition concerning the design and financing of a sports arena and commercial buildings. Companies that wanted to take part in the competition had to form groups in order to combine financing, real estate, construction, architectural and other necessary competence. The arena was supposed to be ready for the world ice-hockey championship in 1987.

Even though the leading politicans and planners in the leisure department, as well as a few politicans and planners in other departments took an active hand in starting the project, the initiation was not controlled by any single person or the result of any single interest. The expected event – the World Championship in Ice-hockey – offered an opportunity to assemble various problems, solutions and actors (cf. Cohen *et al* ., 1972). Thus, the project came to be motivated out of many problems and perspectives. It is a well known observation that expected events breed projects. Joerges (1990) has showed how the coming bimillennium as well as a variety of other epoch-making expected events guide action and become the context for big new projects.

The competition directives given by the City Government were in parts quite specific and detailed. Location and deadline, for example, were fixed. In addition, the number of square meters to be built for offices, shopping centre, hotel and recreation areas were specified. However, as described above, behind this there were quite ambiguous and unspecified motives, prerequisites and assumptions. Also the competing groups were encouraged to interpret the program freely, and to come up with new ideas. The purposes of the project were many and unclear. One reason for this was that the whole venture concerned tasks which the involved actors had not encountered before. Thus, to a great extent the participating actors had to assume or guess the other participants' intentions, preferences and actions.

A political debate concerning how much of the project should be directly financed with tax money delayed the competition somewhat. As a result of these discussions a political agreement was reached, where much less tax money was allocated to the project than planned initially[2]. The changes did not affect the size and scope of the planned project. The political discussions as well as the planned

---

2 In the initial plans 80 Miljon SEK were planned to be allocated to the project in the budget. This sum was seen by the leading polticians as the lowest amount possible in order to be able to finance the project by the designed deal modelled on the railway station project. The reached political agreement resultet in 28 million SEK being allocated to the project in the budget.

financial model were thus loosely coupled to the size and scope of the project as well as to the more or less taken for granted idea about the relevance of the whole venture[3].

A multi-purpose arena develops

Only a few groups of companies responded to the city government's inquiry. Several groups were quite doubtful about the whole project. Their hesitation was partly due to the location of the edifice in the south of Stockholm. The southern part of Stockholm was perceived as less prosperous than the north. The companies also considered that political support for the project was doubtful as the financial solution was unclear. As the amount of tax money being allocated to the project had been decreased without any other changes being made in the plans the proposed financial deal seemed even less realistic than before. Thus the groups found it difficult to follow the City Councils' competition directives which they found to be partly unrealistic, inconsistent and vague.

One group was formed on the initiative of one of the leading technical consulting companies in Stockholm. This group, however, had difficulties in getting support from the leaders of some of the participating companies. Financial support and commitment were lacking. After having met a few times, the group dissolved.

The architects who had participated in the group, however, found the project attractive for several reasons. They saw designing a big project as a challenging and interesting task. The architects also saw the possibility to use the project as "an arena" in metaphorical terms: to establish new contacts, to change their position *vis-à-vis* other professional groups, to exhibit a new image, to develop a professional competence in new areas, to learn new things, etc.

A smaller group working at the architects' office met a few times in the early spring of 1985, and came up with an idea which was later to be of central importance for the whole project, the spherical design of the arena building. The architects were not planning for the building of the project. They started working on the project and tried to get as much out of it as possible, irrespective of whether

---

3   In a study of the decision making and realization of big building projects Sahlin-Andersson (1986) could conclude that financial considerations, political debate and the design of the project are often carried through in three parallel loosely coupled subprocesses. This obsevation was explained by the fact that the realization of a big project depends on the possibility to build, to finance and to create commitment for the project. Different and to some extent conflicting demands make claims on these subprocesses in terms of openness and narrowness as well as the stableness and the flexibility of the definition and planning of the planned building. The different and conflicting demands can be met by separating the subprocesses.

or not the project would be implemented later. To them, at that time, what happened after the competition deadline in October 1985 remained uncertain and almost uninteresting. As they were not tied to a group when developing their idea, they could work independently, without having to compromise their ideas. Having formed the idea about the spherical globe, the architects started to seek external contacts in the late spring of 1985.

Due to the time pressure, and because of the way the architects contacted possible partners for the competition, the new group (here called the "Globe Group")[4] came to consist of several companies who had not worked together before and who had quite diverse ideas and interests concerning these kinds of projects and competitions. Representatives of the companies which joined the "Globe Group" were mainly attracted[5] by the basic architectural idea as well as by the big project as such, despite its ambiguity and uncertainty. Generally, the persons I have interviewed have to a large extent motivated their participation in the project as a personal treat, rather than a benefit for the company they represent. The group included established construction and real estate companies, some of them who, like the architects earlier, had taken part in groups in the competition which had been dissolved. The "Globe Group" also included companies who had not worked on bigger projects in the Stockholm area before and there were also some smaller companies who had not worked on these kinds of big projects earlier. Furthermore, the expected world championship put a deadline for the venture which meant that the project attracted a lot of attention (cf. March and Olsen, 1976) at the same time as the participating actors did not have time to discuss all aspects of the project in detail or to clarify the differences in interests, intentions or experiences. The different actors could support the project without having to agree on any specified meaning of it. Thus, none of the participants in the group could control the whole group and much of what was done was done in a way unusual for such project competitions.

The "Globe Group" made some important deviations from the competition program as their alternative was based on the architects' idea about the circular

---

4   I here term the group the Globe-group. However, the term Globe was not used for the spherical arena nor for the group at that time. The arena was not named the Globe until much later, after the competition was due and the arena was being built.

5   "Attracted" is here largely used in an emotional sense. When I interviewed the actors who had taken part in the project, they described and explained their actions and decisions very much in emotional terms. Terms such as "dare", "challenge", "fright", "exiting" and "fun" were frequently used by these men. An alternative title of this whole case could thus be "Men and their dreams" since the participants were almost entirely men and their "emotional" stands towards the project were very much expressed in masculine terms.

arena. The "globe idea" took over the competition-directives' role as a basis for the groups' forming of an alternative.

Negotiation and choice between alternatives

A parliamentary jury was to assess and choose between the alternatives. A group of planners worked as experts for the jury. As the competition deadline was due, these planners and politicians started to scrutinize the four competing alternatives supplied. The jury's ambition was to make the alternatives comparable, and to evaluate them in relation to earlier formulated criteria. This proved to be a difficult task. As mentioned above, even though the competition directives were in some parts detailed, they were in other parts unclear and inconsistent. The groups interpreted the competition directives in different ways, and they all deviated from the program. Parts of the alternatives were incomplete and vaguely presented. Not only the competing groups, but also the politicians and planners diverged from their initial intentions when they saw the alternatives presented. With what should the alternatives then be compared?

As the competition concerned the entire design, financing and construction of the project and because of the tight deadline, the city planners could not, as is sometimes done in architectural competitions, use the ideas provided and combine them into a new alternative. Instead, the jury had to accept one alternative or to postpone the whole project.

The Globe alternative was incomplete, in parts vaguely presented and diverged in some aspects considerably from the directives given for the competition. The alternative centred around the spectacular arena. And this is what later has attracted the most attention. The deviations from the competition directives, however, mainly concerned the quantity of commercial space in the area and the financial deal. The City owned the land where the new building complex was to be built. In the directives for the competition, the private companies were offered to rent the land around the arena without paying for it (or paying very little). In their alternative, the "Globe Group" suggested that the City Government should pay for the arena by giving away the land surrounding the arena to the group. This was against the governing Social Democrats' policy. This policy stated that city-owned property should not be sold out. Also, the "Globe Group" had exploited the area for commercial use about twice as much as the 75,000 square meter stated in the competition directives.

One reason why the "Globe Group" presented an incomplete and ambiguous proposeal was simply that they had not had time to clarify it before the competition deadline at the end of October 1985. The group did not form until July that year. However, the "Globe Group" also produced ambiguity intentionally, in order to keep the initiative and prevent the city jury from being able to easily compare their alternative with the announced directives, and with the other alternatives.

The proposed deal as well as the enlarged commercial space meant that the city could get the new arena without using a lot of tax money. Therefore the financial aspects of the project no longer seemed to be unrealistic, and the deal was positively received by the jury. It was now clear that the jury no longer could keep the competing groups at a distance. When preferences as well as evaluation criteria changed endogenously as the project developed the chairman of the jury, assisted by some of the planners, had to start negotiating with the groups, asking the groups to reformulate their alternatives in accordance with ideas and intentions developed out of the other alternatives. For the most part, the other competing groups were asked to change their proposed alternatives in accordance with the changed financial deal and the enlarged commmercial space suggested in the "Globe alternative".

At that time, there was not enough time to take up the matter for debate in the political bodies. In addition an open debate would have destroyed the City Government's possibilities to negotiate successfully with the groups. The detailed competition directives, which had been so hotly debated in the political bodies initially proved to be of little value in the end. And the wider group of politicians had no opportunities to take part in the decisions about which deviations to make. These were formed and reformed in the negotiations.

Towards the end of the negotiations the "Globe alternative" and another alternative were regarded as the most promising. The other group presented an alternative which followed the competiton directives very closely and was more traditional and less spectacular than the "Globe alternative".

The "Globe alternative" was however declared winner of the competition at the end of April 1986. One result of the negotiations was that the City-owned land was exchanged for having the arena built. The Social Democrats thus made an exception to their policy which they had considered of great political importance. No-one wanted to upset the project for the sake of a few principles. The chairman of the jury went almost directly from the negotiation table to Moscow, where he presented the planned arena for the international ice-hockey association, and Stockholm was then appointed to host the world ice-hockey championship in 1989[6]. The Globe Arena was opened for the hockey championship in February 1989.

---

6 Due to the political discussions concerning the financing of the arena the original aim to have the arena built for the 1987 Ice Hockey World Championship had been postponed two years.

The architects used a snowball metaphor to describe the development of the project. Starting with the group of planners in the City administration, who made the project bigger than previously planned, continuing with the architects and their spectacular idea, the project continued to grow in size, cost and "quality-image".

Two different modes for project development

Projects are intentionally designed formations, deliberately established extraneous to the routine activities of organizations. Projects are often created with an expressed aim. When activities are defined as projects, they are regarded as unique or new. A project is also a temporal group organized around a stated aim. In the case described above, the project attracted participants from various organizations who did not work together regularly. These actors came from various traditions and organizational cultures. Projects therefore display complexity and ambiguity. The pursuing of a project involves ways of handling complexity and ambiguity.

The case described above illustrates two ways of pursuing a project. I term them "the clarity strategy" and "the ambiguity strategy"[7]. I will now analyze how these alternative strategies treat the complexity and ambiguity of projects in different ways. When a project is pursued according to the clarity strategy, complexity and ambiguity are seen as problems. Thus, the ambition is to simplify, conform and clarify. When a project is handled in terms of the ambiguity strategy, the complexity and ambiguity are instead emphasised and utilized in order to attract attention, mobilize support and pursue the project.

The clarity strategy

In established organizations, a pattern of taken-for-granted meanings, routines, rules and roles evolve from common experiences. A joint frame of reference is formed, which reduces differences in views between actors, stabilizes activities and reduces uncertainty (cf. Weick, 1979). One conclusion often drawn from this is thus that purposeful actions are stimulated in such organization-like settings.

---

7   Of course the development and realization of the Globe-project can be described and explained in various ways. Often referred to during the last decade is the diffusion of big projects all over Europe in the 1980s. This diffusion process is sometimes understood as a kind of fad or resulting form the "time-sprit" of the 1980s. In order to find support for such explanations one cannot rely on a single case, but need empirical data which can map the possible diffusion process as well as the "time-spirit". In this chapter the aim is however not to go through all explanations which may be relevant for understanding how and why this particular project came about. Instead, the aim is to use the case to illustrate two different models for pursuing projects.

Complexity and ambiguity that stem from the lack of a common frame of reference are seen as problematic.

Models have been developed where clarity, coherence and simplicity are considered to be superior to complexity and ambiguity. In the normative literature, advice is given on how to attain conformity and simplicity in order to breed action and development. Because organizations are the standard forms for reducing complexity and uncertainty, it follows that activities should be formed in as "organization-like" settings as possible. The motto is: Organize first, then act; First clarify, then take action.

This way of handling a project were reflected in those parts of the Globe project which concerned the formal decision process, the design of the competition and also in the way those groups who sought to follow the detailed directives tried to find out what the city government really wanted. Accoring to the clarity model, the intentions should be established early in the process and they are assumed to remain unchanged. Thus in the political discussions and in the planners' initial work the ambition was to form as clear and detailed directives and decision criteria as possible. From this perspective the inconsistencies in the competition directives as well as the deviations from the declared intentions made in the project were problematic.

In line with the kind of reasoning above, the common reaction to the City Council's inquiry about taking part in a project competition was "Let us form a group". The project group assembled and clarified the basis for their work, before they started to form an alternative. They saw the project as a task to implement ideas formulated by someone else. The project group was seen as an instrument for someone else's interests. The competition program was the starting point for the groups who treated their formulation of an alternative as such a task. They formulated their alternatives as refinements of the directives given. Some problems, however, became apparent for the groups who worked in this way because the directives were incomplete, unclear and to some extent unrealistic. The groups had difficulties in finding out what the politicians really wanted. The groups therefore asked for clarifications from the city planners and politicians, without getting very many. The groups then interpreted the lack of clear and complete directives as a sign that the City Council's decision to build a new arena might not have been realistic.

When projects are managed according to the clarity model, the process is perceived as a set of choices. The idea is first to settle the basic intentions and restrictions and then to derive fitting means out of them. A tight coupling between intentions and expressions is assumed. It is further assumed that the best alterantive can be chosen based on an assessment of how well the proposed alternatives will fulfill the stated (and assumably unchanged) ends. Thus according to this model, control over the project is attained by stating the ends initially and by making the choice between the assessed alternatives.

In the Globe Arena case the assessment of alternatives proved to be problematic. The jury tried to make the alternatives comparable but the competing groups had interpreted the ambiguous directives differently. Furthermore, the jury changed its intentions and preferences after having seen the alternatives presented.

In studies of organizing and decision-making, the distinction between programmed and un-programmed decisions has been emphasized (Cyert *et al* ., 1956; Mintzberg *et al* .,1976; Soelberg, 1967) but also questioned (March and Simon, 1958; Cohen *et al* ., 1972). Unprogrammed decisions are described as unstructured, strategic, novel and complex. When projects are treated according to the clarity model, the ambition is to reduce the unprogrammed character of the process and manage it as if it could be programmed in any case. With this view projects should be formed as extensions of existing facilities (cf. Hirschman, 1967). Too much attention is believed to add to the complexity. The uniqueness of the project is played down. By referring to similar projects the suggested solutions are clarified.

Based on the the characteristics found in the Globe project, we could, from this view, predict that it would be an almost impossible project to realize. Political support was initially not very strong. There was little response to the City Council's inquiry. The project was located in the "wrong part" of Stockholm. The financing of the project seemed unclear and far from realistic. The directives given were in part incomplete, in part imperfect. Yet, as we have seen, the project was successfully carried through! Is something then wrong with the clarity model for pursuing big projects?

The problems in following the clarity model followed from the difficulties in simplifying and clarifying. The clarity model tends to ignore that many complexities and ambiguities cannot be solved. March and Olsen (1976), Brunsson (1989) and Sahlin-Andersson (1986), among others, have emphasized that complexity and ambiguity cannot be organized away, but have to be handled! Also, the problems followed from the fact that initially stated and mapped intentions, preferences and conditions did not remain stable but changed as a result of the what happened in the environment of the project, but also that the participating actors changed their intentions and preferences as a result of working with the project.

The ambiguity strategy

The Globe arena case also illustrates the ambiguity model for pusuing projects. When pursued in this way the unprogrammed character of the process is emphasized and made use of. A project may then be considered as an arena for several objectives, activities and possibilities: for example to solve problems, implement solutions, form and strengthen relations, exhibit a new image, collect and test power, learn new things, develop professional competence, have a nice time, to develop an understanding of the situation as well as one's history (cf. March and Olsen, 1976). The participation as well as the object of the project is here ambiguous.

The many meanings of the project as well as the relevance of the process, were obvious in the case described above. The winning architects utilized the project for education, marketing, to convey a professional image, etc. All these aims were not dependent upon the end product of the project, but were parts of the process. The same was true for most actors who joined the "Globe Group". They had various purposes for joining the Globe Group. The end product was not the only, or not even the most important aspect of the project. Thus, we can see that actors may be attracted by projects that are phrased in such a way as to allow this arena function. The ambiguity characterizing many inter-organizational projects can in such a way give room for actors who want to pursue different purposes and interests. Hence, the project is handled as an arena for a number of loosely coupled actors and activities. The separate parts of the projects to some extent correspond to each other, but they are also clearly separated and preserve their own identity (Weick, 1976; March and Olsen, 1976; Sahlin-Andersson, 1986).

In the case described here, the differences between the participants were not clarified since the actors had no time to do this. Time pressure thus gave no room for discussions about the basic assumptions from which the various actors worked, and instead the ambiguity and complexity of the project was emphasized and used as a basis for forming commitments and expectations as explained below. Thus the ambiguity strategy points to the importance of time-pressure and timing for the pursuing of projects.

Many inter-organizational projects don't follow the logic where actors first organize and then act. Instead, the project is formed in response to an expected event. It is around this expected event, not out of common interests, the actors gather. In this case the world championship in hockey formed an opportunity to gather various problems, solutions, actors and activities. The actors did not have to agree exactly on how and why the arena and the area around it was to be exploited. Various meanings could and were ascribed to the project. The various actors related the project to their interests and contexts.

Another basis for such projects formed by the temporary association of actors with various interests is a single expression or design to which various meanings can be ascribed. The spherical building presented by the winning architects was such a distinct expression which attracted attention and interests, but at the same time gave room for various interpretations[8]. The assumptions and conditions were not clarified but were presented in highly vague terms. The expression in the form

---

8 Interestingly enough, during the spring of 1989, several articles were found in the press where journalists tried to find out what the meaning of this special design was- what it really had symbolized. My reaction to that is that there is no true or single answer to this question. The arena does not symbolize any true meaning, but many, or none.

of a spherical building was not changed after the group formed. But, the way to construct such a building, the way to finance and build it, the conditions under which to construct it, etc were changed in the following process. Also, meanings ascribed to the form of the arena changed. The arena was first designed to create a pleasent indoor atmosphere. Later discussions and argumentation for this alternative were almost entirely focused around the exterior of the arena. New meanings were thus ascribed to the same expression. Declared intentions and directive do not then steer the development of the project but are endogenously formed in the process. What drives a project to realization is then not the initially declared ends and means, but commitments, dependencies and expectations developing in the process of interaction (cf. Brunsson, 1985).

Ambiguously formulated ideas, expressions or events, which give room for various meanings, interests and implications for future action, can hold the actors of the project together just because they allow various meanings to be ascribed to the project. The actors can ascribe their own preferences or their own interests to the expression. Thus, it is a process where commitment is easily obtained. However, in such a project it is difficult to predict and control the end product.

In the competition directives the diverse motives and purposes behind the project were not expressed, but kept unarticulated. A group may according to the clarity model take this as the (only) formulation of the project. The "Globe Group" made deviations from the competition directives as they formed their proposed alternative based on the spherical arena idea. But when presenting their alternative they referred to implicit motives and interests. Even motives that the group did not refer to, were actually ascribed to the project because the city jury interpreted this ambigous alternative in line with their own expectations and prospects.

What is more, initatially vaguely presented ends and assumptions are not problematic, but a possibility according to the ambiguity model. The partly vague and inconsistent competition directives were not treated as a problem by the "Globe Group", but as a possibility since they gave room for changed intentions and preferences during the process. Plans which are unclear from the start carry a kind of promise of being clarified in the future. They encourage the actors involved to fill in their own expectations. This also has implications for potential critics' possibilities to react.

Although it was a very big project attracting considerable attention, the Globe project quite remarkably received almost no criticism. Everyone was taken by surprise. The project had been defined as being so extraordinary and different that potential opponents did not know how to react. Those who were doubtful tended to postpone their critique until they had a clear proposal to react to. It is difficult to question vague ideas, since they give so much room for expectations and interpretations. Actors may thus use ambiguity for tactical purposes (Eisenberg, 1984).

102

This way of handling the project in tems of the ambiguity model was contradictory to the formal decision process and the design of the competition. I have shown above that the extraordinary character of the project was stressed initially as the planners in the city government were afraid that it would not attract enough attention. In stressing the extraordinary it attracted attention and it became more difficult to compare this venture with other ones. When stressing the extraordinary character of a project it is implied that it cannot follow any regular program, the project is something beyond the ordinary which needs to be pursued in an unprogrammed way. Thus a way for actors with an interest in pursuing a project according to the ambiguity model is to launch the project in extraordinary terms.

The social construction of a project definition

I have shown how the pursuing of a project by the actors involved follows from the extraordinary character of the project. Can we then conclude that the case analyzed here is so special that no general conclusions could be drawn from it?

When such classifications, as the distinctions between the extraordinary and the ordinary, are taken for granted, projects tend to be treated as fixed entities with specific features. However, several studies show that there are no "given" or inherent properties of any tasks or issues. Instead they are classified as big or small, as important or trivial, or as ordinary or extraordinary (Edelman, 1988; Hilgartner and Bosk, 1988). A project is best described as a social construction made up by a whole set of actors and activities. The formulation of the project and the meaning ascribed to it are important and often neglected in explanations of projects and decisions. The alternative formulations result from the meanings that various actors ascribe to the project. These meanings are influenced by earlier experiences and by interests concerning the project (Dutton and Jackson, 1987) and moulded by activities taken by the actors, their interrelations and contextual dependencies. Defining a project as extraordinary follows from the actors' disregard of earlier experiences. Thus, the formulation of the project as extraordinary may be used, and was in this case used by the actors as a strategic device in order to facilitate commitment, to keep potential opponents away and to argue for the appropriateness of the considerable deviations from established policies and practices.

Extraordinary, dramatic appeals, have often proved to attract attention and interest (Edelman, 1988; Conolly, 1984; Hilgartner and Bosk, 1988). Also, the extraordinary character of the analyzed project justified that the presentation of the alternative was incomplete, and that the project was to be handled in a specific way. What was new and different from everything that had been before could not be presented in clear terms, but had to be clarified later on. The deviations made from decided policies and directives were referred to as logical consequences of the extraordinary character of the project.

103

Conclusion

I have in this chapter contrasted two ways of pursuing a big project. Both could be illustrated with the Globe Arena case. First I described how a project may be handled according to the clarity model. The aim is then to clarify the project and to manage it in a programmed way. The basis for and the frame within which the project is to be pursued is settled from start. The ambition is then to keep the project within this settled frame. It was argued that many big projects do not seem to follow this model. Big projects tend to expand and they often end up as something entirely different from what was intended in the beginning. The difficulties in following the clarity model were ilustrated by the Globe project. When pursuing big projects it is not only the case that the clarity model proves to be difficult to follow because of difficulties in clearly stating means and ends initially and also to keep these from changing as a result of the process. Conditions as well as intentions change both external to the project and as a result of the handling of the project. Instead of aiming at reducing or defining away these complexities and changes, another strategy is to base the pursuing of the project in these complexities and changes. Here conditions, assumptions or meaning are not initially being settled. Instead diverse meanings, assumptions, expectations and interests are being ascribed to the project. The extraordinary character of the project is then emphasized. In such a process commitment is easily obtained, critics are kept away and it is easy to handle changed conditions or intentions.

This second strategy, here named the ambiguity strategy can, as was illustrated with the Globe arena case, be a successful one in pursuing a big project. However, as long as normative recommendations as well as formal procedures for undertaking big projects are based on the same assumptions as the clarity strategy, the ambiguity strategy is pursued behind the facade of the clarity model. The normative recommendations to follow the clarity model may also lead to unrealistic expectations both as to the possibilities for those initiating big projects to control the content of the outcome and to the fruitfulness of settling detailed plans and instructions from the start.

In the project management literature, as well as in the normative literature on decision making, to manage a project is seen as both being able to realize and to control a project. These two aspects are treated more or less as being the same thing that can be accomplished in the the same way. In this chapter I have shown that to pursue a project according to the ambiguity model is a way to realize big projects. But it is a way of realizing that is done partly at the cost of losing control of the outcome.

References

Brunsson, N. (1985) *The irrational organization*. Chichester: Wiley.

_____. (1989) *The organization of hypocrisy*. Chichester: Wiley.

Cohen, M.D., March, J.G. and Olsen, J.P. (1972) "A garbage can model of organizational choice", *Administrative Science Quarterly* 17: 1–25.

Conolly, W. (1984) *Legitimacy and the state*. Oxford: Basil and Blackwell.

Cyert, R.M., Simon, H.A. and Trow, D.B. (1956) "Observations of a business decision", *Journal of Business* 29: 237–248.

Dutton, J.E. and Jackson, S.E. (1987) "Categorizing strategic issues", *Academy of Management Review* 12(1): 76–90.

Edelman, M. (1988) *Constructing the political spectacle*. Chicago: University Press.

Eisenberg, E.M. (1984) "Ambiguity as strategy in organizational communication", *Communication monographs* 51: 227–242.

Hall, P. (1980) *Great planning disasters*. London: Wiedenfeld and Nicholson.

Hilgartner, S. and Bosk, C.L.(1988) "The rise and fall of social problems", *American Journal of Sociology* 94: 53–78.

Hirschman, A.O. (1967) *Development projects observed*. Washington DC: The Brooking inst.

Jacobsson, B. (1987) *Kraftsamlingen (The accumulation of power)*. Lund: Doxa.

Joerges, B. (1990) "Global 2000", *Futures* January/February: 3–20.

March, J.G. and Olsen, J.P. (1976) *Ambiguity and choice in organizations*. Oslo: Universitetsforlaget.

March, J.G. and Simon, H.A. (1958) *Organizations*. New York: Wiley.

Mintzberg, H., Raisinghani, D. and Théorêt, A. (1976) "The structure of "unstructured" decision processes", *Administrative Science Quarterly* 21: 246–275.

Morris, P.W.G. (1988) "Lessons in managing major projects successfully in a european context", *Technology in Society* 10: 71–98.

Morris, P.W.G. and Hough, G.H. (1987) *The anatomy of major projects*. Chichester: Wiley.

Ross, J. and Staw, B.M. (1986) "Expo 86: An escalation prototype", *Administrative Science Quarterly* 31: 274–297.

Sahlin-Andersson, K. (1986) *Beslutsprocessens komplexitet (The complexity of decision processes)*. Lund: Studentlitteratur.

_____. (1989) *Oklarhetens strategi (The strategy of ambiguity)*. Lund: Studentlitteratur.

Soelberg, P.O. (1967) "Unprogrammed decision making", *Industrial Management Review* 7: 19–29.

Weick, K.E. (1976) "Educational organizations as loosely coupled systems", *Administrative Science Quarterly* 21: 1–19.

_____. (1979) *The social psychology of organizing*. Reading, Mass.: Addison-Wesley.

Chapter 5

The Concept of Subsidiarity and the Debate on European Cooperation: Pitfalls and Possibilities[1]

Lars C. Blichner and Linda Sangolt

This chapter explores whether and how subsidiarity can serve as an instructive aid to discussion and clarification of the current and future structure and functioning of the European Union. We argue that the debate over the principle of subsidiarity may be undermined or cut off prematurely in at least three ways. First, if the debate is conducted with a view to arriving at a fairly fixed, detailed and instrumental understanding of the allocation of responsibilities and tasks between different levels of government. Second, if the principle of subsidiarity is mainly used as an instrument of political expediency and opportunism to further organizational- or self-interests. Third, if the principle is linked to and interpreted as an endorsement

1   We thank Johan P. Olsen for helpful comments and Erik O. Eriksen for inspiring discussions on topics related to the ones addressed in this chapter.

and justification of existing (entrenched) political and social doctrines. In a concluding last section we consider how the principle of subsidiarity may contribute to constructive discussion.

The launching of the word subsidiarity into the current debate on the European Union[2] has shown it to be both a politically potent and highly ambiguous concept. Subsidiarity is controversial because it strikes not only at the heart of the most pressing, intricate and interrelated issues and dilemmas of cooperation between political and administrative institutions of local, national and supra-national governments, but also pertains to perceptions of the relationship between political authority and civil society.[3] As a common reference-point the principle of subsidiarity may serve to stimulate and sustain a reasoned and balanced debate on the desirability and feasibility of present institutional arrangements and proposals for change (Denton 1992).

The European Union is a novel, exploratory exercise in political cooperation calling for a degree of experimentation that in itself is unsettling and confusing. If subsidiarity is used as a way of relinquishing or abdicating political power by leaving its definition and application to the market, to courts and legal experts, or to bureaucrats this can be seen as political impotence. If politicians cannot give substance to political goals and the means of attaining them they have failed the raison d'être of their mission. The perception of such a failing could be seriously damaging in a situation in which both the effectiveness and the accountability of political leaders of most European countries are increasingly called into question.

This chapter starts from the premise that the principle of subsidiarity will make a positive contribution to the debate on European cooperation to the degree that it helps to establish a common framework for further discussion. The basic argument presented departs from an instrumental view of politics as a struggle over who gets what and how, following a different tradition that views politics as interpretation of existing or emerging practices and ideas. Through an integrative political process, the meaning of fundamental principles are developed and elaborated on. Common goals develop and change over time through common experience and interaction. Conflicts of interest are seen as the basis for reasoned deliberation in order to reach a common understanding, not necessarily agreement in a more narrow sense (March and Olsen 1984:126).

In light of this "Europeification" may be seen as a process generating a common discourse that in turn will affect how national practices are evaluated (Soysal 1993:179–80). Debate in itself does not assure the quality of political decisions or

---

2 The European Union as of 1.11.1993.
3 At the borderline between public and private spheres and individual and collective responsibilities.

the effectiveness of action. Still, we believe that debate is necessary if we want to increase understanding through an integrative process involving reasoned contestation of views which is not solely focused on short term output. The political, economic and cultural diversity of the EU countries and the unprecedented nature of the Union as a political organization stands in need of concepts and frames of reference that acknowledge and facilitate the ability to deal with this uniqueness and heterogeneity.

Following this line of reasoning our aim is not to try to discover the "true" intentions of those responsible for introducing the principle of subsidiarity into a EU context, or to establish the "true" meaning of the word by reference to its historical origin. The principle of subsidiarity may serve a purpose, not by removing all ambiguity, and making discussion sterile if not superfluous, or by increasing ambiguity to a level where discussion becomes unintelligible and meaningless, but by furthering and focusing debate.

In the next section we briefly outline the evolution of the concept in social and political thought and indicate some key factors in its (re)emergence in the current debate on the European Union in order to arrive at what we consider three core proposals linked to the principle of subsidiarity. In the following three sections we argue that the debate linked to the principle of subsidiarity may be undermined, or cut off prematurely, in at least three ways. First, if the debate is conducted with a view to arriving at a fairly fixed, detailed and instrumental understanding of the allocation of responsibilities and tasks between different levels of government. Second, if the principle of subsidiarity is mainly used as an instrument of political expediency and opportunism to further organizational- or self-interests. Third, if the principle is linked to and interpreted as an endorsement and justification of existing political and social doctrines. In a concluding last section we consider how the principle of subsidiarity may contribute to constructive discussion. As an evolving principle, subsidiarity offers an alternative to the often one-sided discussion of integration as an end in itself. Still, proposals for change in the existing division of competencies and tasks in the EU will have to be argued and justified in light of practical experiences and achievements.

Career of a Concept

Until recently the word subsidiarity has not been frequently used or widely discussed, at least not in the English-speaking part of the world. It has even been argued that it is a word without meaning in English.[4] Even so the concept has been

---

4   Doogan (1992:171) cites the Select Committee on European Communities (House of Commons 1990–91).

around for some time and the considerations it raises are much older still.[5] The concept of subsidiarity is linked to important debates in political theory dealing with the relationship between the state and the individual, between different levels of government and between state and society. It is difficult to find a political thinker who has not touched on these questions.[6]

Prior to the present discussion within the EU the concept has been used in three main settings. First, the principle of subsidiarity has been a part of Catholic social doctrine at least since the early 1930s, regulating the relationship between the society as a whole and the individual[7]. Support and help, the etymology of the word subsidiarity, should not deprive the individual of responsibilities or inhibit the development of his/her abilities. A main idea is that "the state should not deal with those matters which can be handled by individual or small units" (Kühnhardt 1992:83). The principle of subsidiarity aims to promote the priority of smaller units and prohibit their repression. The pivotal question is whether human association "is of assistance to its members or is only an annoyance".[8] The function of

---

5   Oswald von Nell-Breuningen (1962:826): "Die Sache ist Uralt, nur der Name Subsidiaritätsprinzip... ist neu."

6   A broad range of earlier writers are cited in connection with the subsidiarity concept. One of those referred to is Thomas Aquinas:"This whole, such as a civil society (civilis multitudo) or domestic family, has only unity of order, so as not to be one simpliciter. Therefore, the part of this whole can have a task (operatio) which is not that of the whole, just as a soldier in an army has a task which is not that of the whole army. None the less, the whole itself also has a task which is proper to the whole but not to any of its parts, such as the charge of the whole army." As cited in Black (1988:600). Another is Abraham Lincoln: "The legitimate object of government is to do for a community of people whatever they need to have done but cannot do at all, or cannot so well do for themselves in their separate and individual capacities. In all that the people can individually do as well for themselves, government ought not to interfere". As cited in Nell-Breuningen (1962:828). John Stuart Mill and Pierre-Joseph Proudhon are also frequently referred to.

7   Pope Pius XI (1931) frequently cited statement in one translation reads: ".. it is an injustice, a grave evil and disturbance of the right order for a larger and higher organization to arrogate to itself functions which can be performed efficiently by smaller and lower bodies. This is a fundamental principle of social philosophy, unshaken and unchangeable and it retains its full truth today". Oswald von Nell-Breuning's (1932) influential commentary on the Quadragesimo Anno emphasized the principle of subsidiarity and denied that the document could be used in support of state intervention in economic and social affairs. His interpretations were however disputed by some Austrian and German Catholics (Diamant 1960:184, 185). The words "subsidiarii officii principium" was used in the "Quadragesimo Anno" (Nell-Breuningen 1962:826). Gustav Gundlach is sometimes mentioned as the one who coined the term.

8   Oswald von Nell-Breuning (1990) as cited in Kühnhardt (1992:83).

authority is subsidiary to the freedom of the individual and smaller communities (Kelly 1982:203; Burgess 1990:152). Still, the concept of subsidiarity has not only been used to argue for non-intervention and non-centralization, but also for increased central authority.[9] The focal question is when it is appropriate for a central authority to intervene.

Emphasis on the principle in Catholic social philosophy was a reaction to mass society and the totalitarian tendencies in Europe in the interwar period (Kühnhart 1992). However, as early as the 1890s Leo XIII had given the first indications of a Catholic approach to subsidiarity, against the background of both a "threatening socialism and rampant economic liberalism" (Kelly 1982). Gustav Gundlach espouses the same position when he argues that "though social philosophy and natural law both condemn as false these basic principles of liberalism, this should not lead us into the opposite error of defining society as part of the state and letting the state engulf society".[10] In Catholic doctrine the principle of subsidiarity has played a critical role in both individualistic and collectivistic ideologies (Kaufmann 1988:281).[11]

After the Second World War, the important role of government in an increasingly complex society was emphasized by Pope John XXIII (Higgins 1980:93). In the early 1960s, Pope John, following Pius XI, embraced the idea of subsidiarity, but broadened its scope to include the relationship between nations. It was argued that the world community had to solve problems that could not be adequately dealt with by the nation-states acting alone (Leaper 1975:83). Kossel (1984) has argued that the use of the principle of subsidiarity will result in a single complete society made up of lesser societies with different identities, functions and ends. The smaller units should not, however, be reduced to mere agencies for a higher unit. This would lead

---

9 "See for example Higgins (1980): "To say that "small is beautiful" is not to say, without a carload of qualifications, that that government is best which governs least or that so-called big government is by definition a violation of the principle of subsidiarity." (p.88). "the principle of subsidiarity, as we understand it today, does not mean that that government is best which governs least" (p.92).

10 Gustav Gundlach, "Fragen um die berufsständishe Ordnung", Stimmen der Zeit, CXXV (1933) pp. 217–226, as cited in Diamant (1960:183).

11 The concept of subsidiarity in Catholic social doctrine does not in principle make a clear-cut choice between individualism and collectivism, between private and state solutions, or between centralization and decentralization. Still, there is a bias towards non-centralization since any move to centralize will have to be argued and any existing centralized solution should be defended by argument. There is a distinction, however, between the "essential hierarchical functions of the Church, which arise from its sacramental order, and those which are only accidentally hierarchical and arise from its administrative order" and it is the latter that "lends itself to decentralization" (Kaufmann 1988:289,291).

to totalitarianism, and according to Kossel (1984:46) "it makes little difference whether this totalitarianism be that of a dictator, a party or the "will of the majority", it is the death of a free society".

Second, and related to the first, the principle of subsidiarity has been linked to the discussion of federalism. Again, the core of the argument is that at any level of government, centralization should only take place if a task cannot be accomplished as well or better by a lower level (Kühnhardt 1992:84). Nell-Breuningen (1990:132) saw federalism as "the realization of the principle of subsidiarity in political life".[7] Pinder (1992:7) holds that the choice of a federal system of government "has always reflected the will to retain for the constituent states those powers which there is no compelling reason to allocate to the centre". Third, the concept of subsidiarity has been incorporated into basic features of Germany's federal structure and basic law. Neo-conservatives have used it in their critique of the welfare state in Germany (Richter 1987). From this perspective the concept of subsidiarity is related to liberal philosophy stressing individual freedom and minimal state intervention. The state should only act in situations where the market fails (See Lorenz 1991). In Germany, the debate over subsidiarity was activated in the 1950s, and the principle was incorporated in all relevant social legislation passed between 1950 and 1975 (Anheier 1992:37). It was reactivated in 1982 when the Conservative-Liberal government of Federal Chancellor Helmut Kohl took over and presented its program for change. Still, in the German debate the concept was also used by the opposition, the Social Democrats (SPD) as well as by the "green alternative", to argue their case (Richter 1987:293).

In the context of the European Union the principle of subsidiarity was formally defined for the first time in 1984[12]:

> "The Union shall only act to carry out those tasks which may be undertaken more effectively in common than by the Member States acting separately, in particular those whose execution requires action by the Union because their dimension or effects extend beyond national frontiers"

Still, it has been argued, with reference to the Treaty of Rome, that the principle of subsidiarity has been an integral part of Community discussions from the start (Gretschmann 1992:54). The first Community Action Programs on the Environment (1973) state that "in each different category of pollution, it is necessary to establish the level of action (local, regional, national, Community, international) that befits the type of pollution and the geographical zone to be protected". The

---

12 Article 12, European Parliament Draft Treaty on European Union, 1984. See Laffan (1992:8).

effectiveness of an action was considered a key criterion for choosing the appropriate level of government.

Over the last couple of years the principle of subsidiarity has increasingly been taken into account in discussions dealing with the question of European integration (Laffan 1992:216). The principle is presented in Article 3B of The Treaty on European Union which states that decisions should be made at the lowest possible level of government in order to reach EU goals. All else being equal one should prefer non-centralized decision making. If decisions can be made with as good effects and on an appropriate scale without EU intrusion this should be done. The EU should react only when lower level solutions are demonstrably inadequate (Kaufman 1988). The solutions chosen should interfere as little as possible with the established structures of the Member States, and private solutions should be given preference over state solutions (DGIII[13] working paper 7.5.1992).

The concept of subsidiarity is often presented as ambiguous, confusing and difficult to define. The multiple definitions and interpretations that are linked to the concept of subsidiarity according to different political and social philosophies have so far made for a muddled discussion of its perceived merits and shortcomings as a principle of governance. While some regard the concept as so loose and impracticable as to hinder a clear-cut and reasoned debate on the sharing of sovereignty and responsibilities between institutions and levels of government (e.g. Schaefer 1991a:690), others consider its "richness" (Delors 1992:18) and multiple meanings to be its major strength. In any case with its insertion in the Treaty on European Union[14], the concept has taken on the status of a formal normative standard and a pre-constitutional principle of Community law (Emiliou 1992:383; Kühnhardt 1992:84). Mackenzie-Stuart (1992:38) notes that however vague the concept of subsidiarity may seem, it cannot be written off as a topic :"It is on the agenda and once the thing is printed in the Community it stays there." Still, the term's ability to stir up and sustain widespread discussion and multiple interpretations of the EU's aims and institutional arrangements, clearly demonstrates that although formally recognized as a guideline for delineating powers and competence among EU institutions and different levels of government, subsidiarity has not yet become institutionalized. It has not attained the character of a routinized, self-activating principle with a relatively fixed, taken-for-granted meaning and rationale.

So far there seems to be relatively broad agreement on and endorsement of subsidiarity applied generally (Mackenzie-Stuart 1992:38). The Maastricht Treaty, for example, states that the Community should act only where the objectives

---

13 The EU bureaucracy is divided into 23 Directorates-General, usually referred to by number.
14 Article A(2) and B and Article 3(b)(2)EEC

cannot be sufficiently achieved by member states. The relationship between the member states and the Community is singled out in article 3D, while the preamble stresses the relationship between the individual and the state, namely that decisions should be taken "as close as possible to the citizen in accordance with the principle of subsidiarity." Subsidiarity has also been applied to a range of more confined policy areas. Generally we would expect the level of conflict to vary with the degree to which the area of application is specified. When subsidiarity is presented as a way to further the "common good", enhance efficiency or make up for the "democratic deficit", it is difficult not to agree. In general, we expect more conflict when the objectives are more narrowly stated, for example, who should decide on drinking water standards, industry subsidies or commercial whaling. In each of these policy areas one will have to establish more specific criteria and in each case the basic question is where centralized regulation should stop. If drinking water is dirty but not hazardous, subsidies are used to curb local depopulation and unemployment, and whaling does not threaten any of the whale species, reaching agreement on common objectives may be more difficult.

With reference to these four settings in which the principle of subsidiarity has played a role, we formulate three propositions that make up the core of what we see as the principle of subsidiarity. All three focus on the need for deliberation and debate. The first is linked to the idea of inviolate and inalienable rights. Not only individuals but also communities have such rights. There are some rights a higher level under no circumstances can revoke, or a lower level give away. Still, rights may change over time through interpretation (March and Olsen 1989:126). This means that rights that are considered inviolate and inalienable today may not have that status in the future and new rights may be added to the existing ones. The principle of subsidiarity should at least guarantee a lower level the opportunity to participate in the process by which collective interpretation of rights is formed.

The second proposition is that a higher level has a duty to support a lower level to the degree that this helps the lower level to fulfil its true potential. The right amount of help, neither too little nor too much, is important for the achievements and autonomy of the lower level, but also for the larger community that will benefit in the long run. The ambiguity concerning the degree to which help is necessary in each particular case, again focus attention on continuous deliberation and debate.

The third proposition is that "the principle of subsidiarity governs the burden of proof" (Kaufmann 1988:288)[15]. The higher level is obliged, through arguments, to make it clear why a decision should be taken at a higher level. This view is

---

15 This corresponds to an interpretation made early on (1957) by Oswald Nell- Breuning.

reflected in an EC Working paper on subsidiarity for the Directorate General III (Internal Market and Industrial Affairs): "From now on, more than in the past, the burden of proof that a particular action needs to be pursued on Community level will lie with the Commission and other Community institutions" (DGIII 7.5.1992, p.1).

These propositions constitute what may be seen as a three-pronged test of subsidiarity. The basic argument is that in order to conduct this test, deliberation and debate is necessary. In the next sections we present in turn what we consider three main pitfalls if the principle of subsidiarity is to further a focused and informed debate over European cooperation.

The Pursuit of a Clear, Stable and Applicable Definition

Much of the energy that has been invested in attempts to make subsidiarity work is premised on the perceived need for a constitutional blueprint for the European Union and the desirability of an unambiguous operationalization of the concept (Toonen 1992:114). As such the introduction of the principle in the EU context represents a quest for a complexity-reducing standard under conditions of rapid political, economic and social change. In the House of Commons debate prior to Maastricht, a number of MPs requested that subsidiarity be clearly defined as a legal constitutional principle if it was to have any use-value.[16] Prevailing opinion is that as long as its political substance remains uncertain, subsidiarity is not ripe for legal adjudication by the European Court of Justice (Commission meeting 24.06.1992; Mackenzie-Stuart 1992; Toonen 1992:114). Use of the principle in practical politics presupposes agreement on a clear-cut and applicable definition. This can be seen as the planners' road to subsidiarity. Following this line of reasoning the debate on subsidiarity is seen as a catch-all opportunity to establish

---

16 This seems contradictory to a British/British Conservative political and legal tradition based on an uncodified constitution, empiricist law based on the gradual accumulation of rules and precedents through belief in the evolutionary character of political change in general (Burgess 1990:155–8). Foreign Minister Douglas Hurd characterized the British as "the craftsmen rather than the visionaries of Europe" (Hansard 1991:447). British Conservatives generally are anti-federalist and anti-legalist and wary of the alleged need to spell out rules and principles of government: "The Community – the Commission- does not need competence in order for an initiative to work. Let us concentrate on the substance. (..) In any case, given our differing legal traditions and judicial systems, the case is not made for generalized supranational enforcement" (Hansard 1991:442).

a division of work between different levels of government and between different governmental institutions.

The current discussion on subsidiarity is important because it helps us to establish some general criteria for the use of the principle. However, if the criteria become increasingly narrowly defined there will be less and less room for debate. The principle of subsidiarity will no longer guide debate, but rather serve to legitimate the end of debate. This also seems to be the explicit goal of some of those taking part in the discussions. Pappas (1992), for example, argues that thanks to the principle of subsidiarity "we may be able to avoid in the future this endless debate about national sovereign rights and the supranational structure of the Community" and he thinks that it should be "up to the lawyers… to give this still vague principle some real substance and make it a tool of management".

The idea of an unambiguous and applicable definition of subsidiarity fits well in with the wording of Article 3B in the Maastricht treaty. Implicitly it seems to build on at least three presumptions. The first is that decisions within the EU are based on clearly defined and relatively stable goals. The second presumption is that it is possible to know before the decision is taken what alternative action will give the best effect. The third presumption is that it is possible to reach an agreement on goals, choice of the best alternative and on the expected effect of alternative actions. These presumptions are questionable to say the least. Goals are often contradictory, unstable and ambiguous. We would also expect there to be disagreement on what the goals are or should be, what alternatives should be chosen and on the effect of the different alternatives. Further, it is often difficult to know in advance what result will follow from the implementation of one alternative over another, particularly in cases where there is little previous experience. Lastly, as has been observed, while goals may lead actions, actions may lead to change in goals. Goals may change if the results of some actions are not as positive as expected (reduced aspirations) or when actions lead to unexpected, but positive results which then are turned into official goals (March 1978).

The Commission argues that the sharing of sovereignty and competence between EU institutions and national executives and parliaments must be clear-cut and not allow for "grey areas" which fuel accusations of bureaucracy and technocracy. The Commission has sought to establish a hierarchy of objectives by drawing clear distinctions between what it must do, what it can do and what it cannot do.[17] The notion of an "undefined European interest" has also been criticized (Douglas Hurd, Hansard 1991:443). These and other statements concerning the necessity of establishing not only some main overarching objectives,

---

17 "La Subsidiarité. Principes et applications", EC Working Paper, 22.6.1992, p.1.

116

but also a system of relatively detailed goals at several nested levels, indicate that such a detailed system does not as yet exist.

That it is difficult to establish a clear-cut division of responsibilities and a detailed hierarchy of goals is not surprising. In a situation where countries with different languages, cultural backgrounds, economic interests and institutional traditions are asked to cooperate we should not expect ready made or fixed solutions. To expect quick agreement on a "hard", cut-and-dried definition of subsidiarity is not only premature, but counter-productive and divisive unless there is a fair measure of convergence on political preferences and values beyond what is spelled out in written agreements. Ambitious goal-setting exposes implementation lags and difficulties and management deficits at both local and central levels (Raadschelder and Toonen 1992; Sutherland 1992). An instrumentalist approach to subsidiarity risks overemphasizing matters of procedure, rule-making and constitutionalization of the Union.[18] This increases the likelihood that means will subvert ends and detract attention and energies from objectives and policy-implementation.

The only way to establish a clear-cut definition of subsidiarity may be to exclude certain issues or policy-areas from the sphere of European cooperation, not because these areas may do as well without European cooperation, but because it is more difficult to come up with a clear definition of subsidiarity that would include these areas. Important issues, currently on the European agenda, may thus be taken out with reference to the principle of subsidiarity. The Commission could use the principle to reduce its involvement in for example environmental policy in order to ward off criticism that its policies are ineffectual and inconsistent. As an instrument of rational decision-making, subsidiarity is likely to hold most promise in policy-areas in which there is substantial agreement and which have higher priority than others, notably economic and fiscal policies related to the realization of the internal market and the "four freedoms". This is borne out by the Commission's follow-up report to the Maastricht treaty entitled "Finding the means to match ambitions" which states that: "In areas so vital to society as the environment, social policy, health, education, culture and consumer protection, the new Treaty contains provisions that are fully consonant with the principle of subsidiarity. These are the most obvious areas where national diversity has to be respected." (Commission of the European Communities, February 11, 1992, p.28).

As a means of securing optimal allocation of competence, tasks and resources, subsidiarity presupposes clear and stable goals and a fairly high degree of

---

18 Jacques Delors (1992) notes that the complexity of EU texts threatens the ability to implement objectives and "damages the quality of the democratic debate".

consensus on the desired end-states of political cooperation. In the absence of clear and stable political objectives, efforts to define the criteria – for example determining which policy-fields should be "subsidiarised", will be exercises in form rather than content. The quest for a "sesame" solution thus risks short-circuiting political deliberations on how subsidiarity should be applied.

A serious effort to construct a clear and unambiguous definition of subsidiarity will tend to undermine constructive debate whether the effort fails or not. If it fails, the likely conclusion would be that the concept is too ambiguous and impossible to use. If successful, the matter would then be left to an established authority, like the courts, to decide. This would limit debate and seems counteractive to the very idea inherent in the principle of subsidiarity.[19]

The relationship between different levels of government cannot, and should not, even if it were possible, be settled once and for all. It is difficult to argue with those who say that action should be taken at the most suitable level. However, like Brinkhorst (1991a:4) we believe that boundaries should not be fixed once and for all: "The more it is attempted to be precise the greater the difficulties there will be in achieving either Community or national action".[20] Moreover, in a democracy we should accept and even encourage "endless debates" concerning the ways in which we organize society. The debate inspired by the principle of subsidiarity over whether action most appropriately, effectively or with necessity should be taken at a local or central level would in most cases be political rather than legal matter (Mackenzie Stuart 1992:40). Thus, an alternative interpretation of subsidiarity, more radical than the one discussed in this section, is that subsidiarity implies the possibility for anyone at any time, by arguments, to challenge the established order with reference to this principle.

---

19 It has also been argued that if the Court is left this task, for which it is not fitted, it may destroy the credibility of "what is undoubtedly the Community's most effective institution" (MacKenzie-Stuart 1992:41). Charging the European Court of Justice with resolving disputes on a case by case basis is not reassuring to Eurosceptics given its record of defending the supremacy of EU legislation (Shapiro 1992). It would imply the abdication of political will. Opinion is strongly divided on whether subsidiarity can be or should be narrowed down to a legal principle, leaving its application and clarification to the Court of Justice of the European Communities. A "government by judges" scenario is unacceptable to the European Parliament (Roumeliotis 1992:35). A House of Lords Scrutiny committee concluded that subsidiarity cannot be used as a precise measure against which to judge legislation (1992:41) and that leaving its interpretation with the European court would create "immense confusion in Community law".

20 See also Schaefer (1992:104): "Environmental policy is precisely an area where a rigid division of competencies would not be practical.".

The Politics of Subsidiarity

The idea of subsidiarity as an unambiguous, stable and easily applicable principle may be linked to what March and Olsen (1989:74ff.) have referred to as the "rhetoric of administration", which "proclaims that explicit, comprehensive planning of administrative structures is possible and necessary." Administration is seen as a neutral instrument and through reorganization the efficiency of this instrument is improved. An alternative model may be linked to what they refer to as the "rhetoric of realpolitik". This rhetoric describes the world as an arena for struggling interests where the strong win and the weak lose. The stronger will try to influence developments directly, while the weaker will have to enter into coalitions, make compromises, mobilize resources and act strategically in an effort to fulfill their goals. For many critics this model reflects much of what is happening within the Union not only at a rhetorical level. Redistribution of power and reallocation of tasks and responsibilities opens the door to strategic action, or inaction. The ambiguity of the wording of the clause on subsidiarity in the Maastricht Treaty left ample scope for political manoeuvreing.

In this section we argue that the debate over subsidiarity is undermined to the degree that the "rhetoric of realpolitik" dominates. There will easily be a deadlock if the name of the game is to point out what strategic reasons any participant has for arguing about subsidiarity in a particular way. Intentions will be questioned and reasonable arguments in favour of a system that will benefit all will be seen as "leitmotifs" for some other purpose. In a system where power dominates it will be hard to see the difference between justified claims and worries, and manipulating tactics. In such a climate it will be difficult to get a reasoned debate. Important distinctions will be blurred by limited short-term claims presented as basic principles. If a decision is reached it will be a solution that either some member states or institutions of the EU do not accept or a compromise that may not satisfy anyone.

Accordingly, what we would expect is that those who anticipate loss of influence by the establishment of the principle of subsidiarity will oppose it. To the degree that the establishment of the principle is seen as unavoidable they will tend to either keep the concept as unclear and ambiguous as possible, or to define subsidiarity within a context and in ways which protect their own interests. Those positive to the idea of subsidiarity will in the same way be seen as strategically trying to further their own interests.[21]

---

21 The main problem with a model that explains everything by reference to self serving individuals is that almost any action with hindsight may be interpreted as being self-serving. In light of this it is not difficult to understand the popularity of the simple "cui bono" interpretations of actions.

In much of the literature on the EU and in the current discussion this seems to be an at least implicit assumption,[22] and is often reflected in the debate on subsidiarity. Introducing subsidiarity into the debate on the responsibilities of the EU institutions and national/regional centres has been interpreted as a strategic ploy by the Union's institutions, notably the Commission. It is suspected of employing subsidiarity disingenuously, under the pretext of concern for the Union's "democratic deficit", in order to offset criticism of its alleged centralism and interventionism.[23] The Commission's prime motivation would be to determine the parameters under which it can lessen its own overload, allowing it to hive off those tasks and responsibilities which are unprestigious or with which it has had little success[24]. "Some critics even hold that subsidiarity is mostly used as a disguise whenever the Commission is trying to extend its powers" (Gretschmann 1992:56). Nigel Lawson,[25] when asked to comment on the principle of subsidiarity states: "What the Brussels Commission wants to do is to destroy the nation state – both ways. Not just through taking far more powers to the centre, to Brussels. But also by devolving powers, and they decide which powers it will be, to the lowest levels."

The outcome of the Maastricht negotiations was not compellingly gratifying either to those favoring a more decisive push towards a federal framework or those opposed to it. Embodying ideas like "small is beautiful" and self-determination, subsidiarity is hard to reject on principle. The inclusion of the subsidiarity clause (3B) in the Treaty can be seen as a consensual mechanism, a guiding principle for further negotiations on institutional reform and as a measure to reassure opponents

---

22 See for example Majone 1991. Even though he criticizes a simple conflict model he does not replace this with a basically different model, but rather by a more complex conflict model. The basic theoretical presumptions remain the same. Interests are the driving force behind the developments he seeks to explain. The challenge is to show what interest groups are activivated and what their interests are. Certain outcomes are the result of mobilizing force behind a given alternative, but it is unclear if this arrangement of forces happens by chance or if it is due to deliberate cooperation, bargaining or coalition building. Integration for example would be explained by adding up all the resources of the interests that are positive to integration, and ideally this would be held up against the resources of the interests that are against integration.

23 A Commission working paper (22.6.1992 p.1) describes subsidiarity as a "common-sense" and "democracy-enhancing" principle ("principe de bon sense" and "facteur de démocratie").

24 Nigel Lawson, interview in The Guardian Nov. 7, 1992; Philippe Seguin, The European June 5, 1992.

25 Lord Lawson, former British Chancellor under Mrs Thatcher, in an interview with Terry Coleman, The Guardian (7.11.1992), in connection with his new book; "The view from No. 11".

of fast-track federalism. It has been argued that the reason why former European Commission President Jacques Delors embraced the concept of subsidiarity was to calm the sceptics within the EU, most notably the German Länder, who saw the internal market as a threat to their sovereignty in certain areas (Schaefer 1991a:689). According to Gretschmann (1992:54) the German Länder are not simply fighting a defensive "war", but are actually fighting for co-determination on the European level.

Through the creation of a common understanding and culture of subsidiarity the Commission will be able to assert its rightful role more effectively inter alia by enabling it to withstand amendments to proposals forwarded by both the European Parliament and the Council which, in the Commission's view are often in breach of its tenets (DGIII working paper 1992:7). Commissioners have noted that subsidiarity has been seized on as a "weapon" to attack the Commission at every opportunity and make it a scapegoat for unsatisfactory compromises or concessions made by national executives in the Council. Jacques Delors observed that if "incorrectly" used, subsidiarity camouflages vicarious motives:

"(F)requently I have the impression that subsidiarity is a fig-leaf used to conceal unwillingness to honor the commitments which have already been endorsed." (Delors 1992:13).

If one starts from the premise that national governments will do what they can to maintain and increase their influence,[26] the use of the principle of subsidiarity by national governments will easily be interpreted as strategically motivated. Each level of government will argue that subsidiarity means that tasks are best performed at the level where they are responsible (Doogan 1992:171). But the argument can be turned around. In some situations local units will be better off if there are common rules. In such cases they may argue for centralized solutions.

Subsidiarity has also been seen as a way of securing European integration by avoiding or blurring some of the most critical issues. The definition of terms by evoking shared or partisan symbols is a key element of political persuasion and rhetoric. In the House of Commons debate[27], Foreign Minister Douglas Hurd stressed the importance of "using a style and language that make it possible to persuade others of the value of our ideas for the future of Europe". Still, most terms in the political vocabulary leave considerable scope for exaggeration, evasion or

---

26 "It would be an interesting question to find out what arouses the reticence of national authorities more – the idea of giving powers to those lower down or of surrendering powers to those higher up?" (Gretschmann 1992:52).

27 Debate on the draft Maastricht Treaty in November, 1991. (Hansard 1991:442).

partisan attacks. Politically, unspecified formulas often carry considerable political advantage in situations where it is important to reach an agreement. Thus the concept of subsidiarity can be "a useful tool for paving the way to European integration by smoothing over and concealing political differences" (Gretschmann 1992:49). At one point subsidiarity was seen as a way of solving "the Danish problem". In Norway, prior to the referendum on EU membership, the sudden emphasis on the principle of subsidiarity within the EU was seen as a strategy to mislead the people (St.tid. 1992-93, p.1302, 1305).[28] Some Norwegian Euro-sceptics regarded the concept as an instrument for liberalist political movements that want to undermine the welfare state. Others, however, have argued that the principle may help Norway to retain control of the management of national resources (St.tid. 1992–93, p.1338).

The British government has employed the notion of subsidiarity as a protective shield by linking it to a particular Conservative view of the proper role of the unitary nation-state and parliamentary sovereignty in order to ward off criticism within its own ranks.[29] Mackenzie-Stuart (1992:38) asserts that the British Government on the one hand uses the principle of subsidiarity to argue that in Community affairs "things should as far as possible be kept at a national level". At the same time the government is "trying to take large chunks of education away from the regions." Mackenzie-Stuart indicates that there is a discrepancy between the two policies. As should be clear from our previous discussion this need not be the case. The principle of subsidiarity can be used to argue for centralization as well as non-centralization. In order to decide how a proposed British policy in the educational sector relates to the principle of subsidiarity we have to know much more about this policy. What is it that may be achieved by centralization that may not be achieved by leaving matters at a regional level? By focussing on the possible strategic motives of the actors involved, it is possible to avoid discussion of the content of government policy and instead center on the strategies that governments may have.

So far, arguments both pro et contra subsidiarity have been used, or are perceived as being exploited in support of different political interests and groups and as bolstering the ambitions of different institutions in relation to their relative stakes in EU policy-making. If the use of subsidiarity is interpreted as strategically motivated, the hope that the principle will encourage debate on what is efficient, sufficient, appropriate or adequate policy performance (Gretschmann 1992:56),

---

28 St.tid. refers to the proceedings of the Norwegian Parliament.
29 "On issues of Community competence concentrate the development of action on those issues which cannot be handled more effectively at the national level." (Minutes of Evidence taken before the Foreign Affairs Committee on 19th November 1991, House of Commons paper 35–i.).

will be lost. In struggles between levels of government the strongest contender and not the best arguments, will win.

The Pavlovian Response to Subsidiarity

There exists no universally accepted, once and for all definition of democracy, federalism, popular sovereignty – nor of subsidiarity. If subsidiarity is defined by "each according to his own creed" the result may be a sterile and predictable regurgitation of existing opinions. It may be associated or disassociated with different conceptions of political and cultural identity which are (still) largely rooted in and identified with national histories. Subsidiarity in the EU is difficult because it exposes the basic difficulty of uprooting oneself from received opinions. What words mean to people will almost by definition be linked to how they have been used in the past. Still, the meaning of words may be more or less ambiguous, unstable and unclear. When a concept is revitalized after a period of non-use or little use, its link to the past may be more or less forgotten. It may be important to how a concept is understood and valued, and eventually what impact it will have, to what degree and in what way such links to the past are activated. The risk, from our point of view, is that subsidiarity is automatically, positively or negatively, linked up with different doctrines or ideas according to habitual conceptions or beliefs (See Millon-Delsol 1992:191). Consequently one gets indirect declarations of support for different doctrines or ideas, without an informed debate over what the principle could and should comprise in a new context.[30]

The link to the past may not be made at all. The chance that a link is not made should increase to the degree that the concept or similar concepts have not been used before. Yet, even if one invents a totally new concept that has no previous meaning, the link to the past may still be made by way of what is currently understood by the concept. The concept may simply be translated or used as a synonym or as a word representing something familiar, as when Lord Mackenzie-Stuart (1992:38) argues that "there is nothing new about subsidiarity, ... it is simply an elementary principle of good government".

Linked to established and contentious doctrines such as Catholicism, federalism and neo-conservatism, the concept carries varying connotations and evokes different responses. We expect that the nature of the linkage will influence how the concept

---

30 Delors similarly argues that subsidiarity must not be perceived as an (exclusive) attribute of any political or economic doctrine. "It must not be allowed to become the weapon of dissuasion used by the integrationist of "tout marché" or of "tout laisser faire"" (Delors 1992:17).

of subsidiarity is conceived by the different parties involved, and it may also lead to reinterpretations of established doctrines. Our concern here, however, is whether and how such linkages may have an adverse effect on the debate over subsidiarity.

We have not found much evidence that non-Catholics have difficulties in accepting the principle of subsidiarity simply because it is linked to Catholicism.[31] In a wider European usage the concept has been "deconfessionalized" (See Toonen 1992:114). For example, given the longstanding history of the concept of subsidiarity in continental European federalism, particularly in Germany, and its affinity to Catholic theology and social philosophy, it is somewhat surprising that the term was included in the Draft Treaty on European Union of 1984 (Article 12,2) on the insistence of a British Conservative member of the European Parliament[32] Christopher Jackson (Burgess 1990:166).

In Britain much of the debate over the European Union has turned around the concept of federalism. While the idea of federalism in Germany is linked to decentralization, in Great Britain the word has come to mean centralization at the European level (Shell 1993:8). While the German Länder see subsidiarity in connection with a notion of federalism that gives them certain rights vis-à-vis the centre, British Conservatives worry that subsidiarity will come to be defined and applied in accordance with federalist ambitions. Conservative MP Nigel Lawson claimed that the Maastricht Treaty granted powers to Brussels exceeding those of the United States constitution and with insufficient protection of member states' rights. The doctrine of subsidiarity was feeble and inadequate, implying a "federal vocation" without offering the constitutional safeguards of a truly federal system (Hansard 1991:469–70).[33]

---

31 In the Norwegian debate on Europe, however, Steinar Stjernø has warned against an understanding of subsidiarity that does not take its close relation to the Catholic social doctrine into consideration. He sees subsidiarity as a key concept in a continental and Catholic model of the welfare state, a model which he claims, is at odds with a Scandinavian conception of the welfare state. See Dagbladet 11.6.92, 16.6.92, 18.6.92, 25.6.92.

32 MEP Christopher Jackson was a member of the Committee on Institutional Affairs. According to Burgess (1990:166) Altiero Spinelli was personally indifferent to the use of the term.

33 "Who is to decide and how are they to decide what it is appropriate for the former(sic) nations to have within their responsibility? Who is to decide what is to be determined centrally? The idea is that issues should be decided at the appropriate level and, presumably the Commission will make the proposal as to which that level is. That is nothing like the protection contained in the constitution of the United States where there are clearly defined and written responsibilities for the federal Government and everything that is not clearly written down. There is no such protection here."(MP Nigel Lawson, Hansard 1991:469–70).

The possible problems with the close historical association between federalism and subsidiarity has been noted by main participants in the debate. An EU paper argues that the express mention of this principle in the Treaty on European Union "acknowledges the move towards a federal structure, at least in certain areas." (DGIII working paper 7.5.1992). Former Commission President Jacques Delors (1992) is mindful of the sensitive nature of this relationship when he urges a distinction between federalism and a "federal approach" to the term to prevent subsidiarity from being exclusively tied to well-established political and philosophical traditions. In the same manner, EU Commissioner Leon Brittan generally cautions against the way words are used: "For some continental politicians, federalism means subsidiarity. It has different connotations for the UK. For Scandinavians the word union means something quite different. It brings echoes of the days when union was imposed on them. It is better too to avoid such words as federalism. The EC is unique."[34]

If the word subsidiarity is linked to liberalism and neo-conservative ideas it may make the principle of subsidiarity more acceptable to the conservatives that want a common market, but do not want a strong, centralized EU with wide regulatory powers. Euro-sceptics among the British Conservatives have seen subsidiarity as a way of avoiding detailed and unnecessary EU regulations. One of the main theoretical propositions of Chile's military junta under Pinochet, building their economic policies on a neo-liberal economic model, stressed the principle of subsidiarity.[35] If subsidiarity is linked to a neo-conservative doctrine and with a right-wing authoritarian regime, the principle would quickly lose legitimacy.

When devoted integrationalists argue for subsidiarity this may discourage support from Euro-sceptics. The principle of subsidiarity has been linked to the renewed effort at further integration in Europe in the last five or six years. For those not familiar with the concept this will be the most likely connection they will make. In Norway this link seems to have been made more or less automatically. The word subsidiarity[36] was first mentioned in the news bulletins from the major press agency in February 1991. In the next two years the word was mentioned in 46 bulletins. To the degree that politicians and officials referred to in the bulletins

---

34 The European, 30 Dec. 1992– 3 Jan. 1993.

35 See Chossudovsky (1975:37) who cites the Junta's "Declaración de Principios del Gobierno Chileno" (paragraph II.4). "The common good requires abiding by the principle of subsidiarity (subsidiaridad)...Man is the end of all societies... The State should perform only those tasks which cannot be adequately fulfilled by intermediate or private entities...The principle of subsidiarity is the cornerstone of an authentically free society".

36 Translated into Norwegian as "nœrhetsprinsippet", the "nearness principle".

revealed their opinion, those opposed to Norwegian EU membership were also critical of the principle of subsidiarity. Those positive to Norwegian membership were also positive to the principle of subsidiarity. The same tendency was apparent in a parliamentary debate on Norway's application for EU membership in November 1992 (S.tid.1992–93, p.1275–1370).

In this section we have indicated that the automatic links made between subsidiarity and other more or less accepted doctrines or ideas may serve to undermine the European debate over subsidiarity. This is not to argue for a precise and value-free definition of subsidiarity. On the contrary, ambiguity concerning what a concept means can in some cases open up a debate for new arguments and insights. Still, we believe that it is a very different matter to let the doctrine associated with a concept automatically decide how the concept should be perceived. One could also argue that it is meaningless to use a concept detached from it historical roots and that this means running the risk of emptying the concept of any real content. We have not argued that open-minded historical reference should not be made. What we warn against is the more or less automatic acceptance or rejection of something with reference to its links to an established doctrine or idea. Subsidiarity will not facilitate or enlighten the European debate if it is equated with existing political views, concepts and preferences. Ambiguities concerning the real meaning of a concept may stimulate discussion, whereas generalized slogans, as Titmuss (1967)[37] notes, may "prevent us from asking significant questions about reality".

Conclusion: Can Subsidiarity Guide Debate?

Is there an alternative to the three propositions on the pitfalls of subsidiarity presented, an alternative that will increase the possibility of a balanced and informed debate? A different perspective sees the content of the principle of subsidiarity as evolving over time based on experience on a case by case basis, with each case setting a precedent for similar cases in the future. When a new and deviant case comes up a discussion based on the principle of subsidiarity will take place. When a case that is identical to earlier cases is presented, special reasons would have to be given to treat it differently. Given that the process is hardly perfect[38] and that perceptions change, it may be argued that the principle of subsidiarity has not been appropriately applied in the past. Over time, the practical

---

37 As cited in Leaper (1975:84).
38 It is for example unlikely that all matters of concern to a case will be dealt with and it is also difficult to keep track of all relevant cases.

interpretation of subsidiarity will become part of routine decision-making, and the debate will be kept alive only as long as new and deviant cases are presented or perceptions of the old order change.

Initially we would expect many new cases and discussions with reference to subsidiarity to be common. Over time, as more and more cases are tested against this principle we will expect less discussion. This may have a long-term effect as standard interpretations of subsidiarity may come to dominate at the expense of open debate. To avoid this it is important to leave open the possibility that existing and accepted solutions as well as newly proposed solutions may be tested against the principle of subsidiarity. The principle of subsidiarity as presented in the Maastricht Treaty builds on the opposite premise when stating that the Community shall take action in accordance with the principle only in areas that "do not fall within its exclusive competence" (Article 3b).

As noted earlier, the principle of subsidiarity places the burden of proof on the higher authority when competencies are to be moved from a lower to a higher level. But this also implies that if, for example, it is shown that one level is not able to perform certain tasks, and it is convincingly argued that a higher level can do so better, then the lower level cannot refuse to cede competencies to a higher level simply by claiming autonomy. Each level of government will also have to show in practice that they are able to perform the tasks associated with their competencies. If it is decided that some competencies are to be taken over by a higher level, this higher level will in turn have to show, not only by arguments, but also in practice, that the tasks are better performed there. If this cannot be demonstrated then competencies should be taken away from this level and either referred to a higher level or be given back to the lower level. Accordingly, any level of government will constantly have to be prepared to defend its competencies, where the ultimate test should be linked to experience. There are, however, some difficulties linked to this line of reasoning. The important role of arguments has to be stressed. Anyone can claim that they are able to perform a task better than a lower or higher level. Such claims must be backed by arguments referring both to relevant experience and thought. Morover, if higher levels are systematically more prosperous than the lower levels and performance is dependent on resources, the result may be a long term tendency towards centralisation.[39] This problem underscores the importance of the original idea, inherent in the principle of subsidiarity, that higher levels of government should not automatically take over tasks that lower levels cannot

---

39 The line of reasoning pursued here is inspired by Roemheld's discussion of integral federalism (1990: 322–).

adequately deal with, but should respect and support their autonomy, if necessary in terms of additional resources.

The general perspective indicated here is echoed in many comments on the development of the EU. It has been argued that it is difficult to delineate the principle of subsidiarity because the EU is a "dynamic, constantly evolving project".[40] Just as the distinction between the private and the public sphere is part of an ongoing political discussion in most Western democracies, political discussions concerning the content and use of the principle of subsidiarity will be part of an evolving European polity (Laffan 1992:217). Schaefer (1991b:104) argues that environmental problems change rapidly and that a "once and for all" separation of competencies would hamper the required response once they arise. Brinkhorst[41] (1991b:17) similarly states that "it is necessary to examine each case individually before deciding whether it is appropriate to take environmental measures at Community or Member State levels." If one takes the view that governments "are not made, but grow" (Mill 1962:2), the principle of subsidiarity may be seen as an aid to the gardeners of political life rather than its architects.

Cultural and political differences make the quest for a common political ground and culture more urgent. Rather than viewing political and cultural heterogeneity as an insurmountable obstacle to cooperation, it may be perceived as providing extra impetus and a challenging dialectical framework to the problems of developing European integration. Diversity enhances the need to search for common ground and to (re)affirm fundamental, universal principles – guidelines that acquire the status of "self-evident truths". As a formalized norm with far-reaching implications, the principle of subsidiarity has stimulated debate on the institutional structures of the EU. As an evolving doctrine it might prove a catalyst, a slippery yet beneficial focal point in developing a common supranational political culture that must simultaneously overarch and accommodate national traditions and particularisms: "(T)he political culture must serve as the common denominator for a constitutional patriotism which simultaneously sharpens an awareness of the multiplicity and integrity of the different forms of life which coexist in a multicultural society. One's own national tradition (..) must be connected with the overlapping consensus of a common, supranationally shared political culture of the European Community." (Habermas 1992:7). National sovereignty is a question of how the relationship with other nation-states is organised.

---

40 European Parliamentary Report, The d'Estaing Report on "Subsidiarity", En/DT/83354, 5 April 1990. See Laffan (1992:217).
41 Laurens Jan Brinkhorst, Director General for the Environment, Nuclear Safety and Civil Protection Commission of the European Communities.

We believe that the current debate on subsidiarity may represent an alternative to the often one-sided discussion of integration and instead highlight the real issue; why should there be further integration? According to this line of reasoning subsidiarity as a principle may not only represent an alternative alongside the concept of integration, but may well have the potential to replace it. While the concept of integration may serve as a political slogan that gives direction to the devotees, the concept of subsidiarity has more to offer as a base for deliberations and discussions. Once established it may undermine the institutionalized idea of one-sided integration. Policies implying further integration will to a greater extent than before have to be defended by arguments, without the help of the idea of integration as a value in itself. In a situation where the EU moves from a discussion on the practical questions of economic cooperation to the more ideological questions of further political integration, issues concerning how to limit and control the supranational international institutions are bound to emerge. This debate will echo classical democratic theory dealing with questions of representation, accountability and sovereignty.

Perhaps the paradoxical strength of the term lies in its negotiable meaning and in its ability to evoke and inspire diverse interpretations and foster serious and ongoing deliberation on the fundamental aims and policies of the European Union both at the supra-, national and subnational level. When an obscure word, absent from most standard English dictionaries, calls forth such intense headwork and discussion it has served a purpose, regardless of whether it proves "workable" or not. Its political, symbolic and rhetorical potency is not a shortcoming if it serves to transcend the pitfalls of instrumentalism, partisan politics and institutionalized meanings. By evoking reflection on, rather than reinforcing diverging interpretations, standpoints and identities, the concept may have a pedagogic effect that will raise consciousness of the futility of trying to come up with easy answers and solutions to complex and unprecedented questions. In such a context subsidiarity could be useful precisely because it is so evocative and does not push out of view the complexity of the challenge.

References

Black, A. (1988) "The Individual and Society", in J.H. Burns (ed.) *The Cambridge History of Medival Political Thought c.350–c.1450*. Cambridge: Cambridge University Press.

Brinkhorst, L.J. (1991a) *Subsidiarity and European Environment Policy*. Presentation at the First Jacques Delors Colloquium. Paper, EC.

————. (1991b) "Subsidiarity and European Environmental Policy", in *Subsidiarity: The Challenge of Change*, Proceedings of the Jacques Delors Colloquium, Maastricht, 21–22 March 1991. Maastricht: European Institute of Public Administration.

Burgess, M. (1990) *Federalism and European Union*. London: Routledge.

Chossudovsky, M. (1975) "The Neo-Liberal model and the Mechanisms of Economic Repression – The Chilean Case", *Co-Existence* 12: 34–57.

Cunningham, S. (1992) "The Development of Equal Opportunities. Theory and Practice in the European Community", *Policy and Politics* 20 (3): 177–189.

Delors, J. (1991) "The Principle of Subsidiarity: Contribution to the Debate", in *Subsidiarity: The Challenge of Change*, Proceedings of the Jacques Delors Colloquium, Maastricht, 21–22 March 1991. Maastricht: European Institute of Public Administration.

Denton, G. (1992) *Federalism, "Subsidiarity" and the European Community: How can common decision-making be combined with democratic control in the community and its member states*. Background Note, Wilson Park Conference 384: 6–10 July 1992.

DG III, 1992, 7. May, *Some Reflections on the Role of the Subsidiarity Principle for DG III*. Paper, Working Group on Subsidiarity, EC.

Diamant, A. (1960) *Austrian Catholics and the First Republic. Democracy, Capitalism, and the Social Order, 1918–1934*. New Jersey: Princeton University Press.

Doogan, K. (1992) "The Social Charter and the Europeanisation of Employment and Social Policy", *Policy and Politics* 20(3): 167–176.

Emiliou, N. (1992) "Subsidiarity: An Effective Barrier Against "the Enterprises of Ambition", *European Law Review*, 17: 383-407.

Gretschmann, K. (1991) "The Subsidiarity Principle: Who Is to Do What in an Integrated Europe?", in *Subsidiarity: The Challenge of Change*, Proceedings of the Jacques Delors Colloquium, Maastricht, 21–22 March 1991. Maastricht: European Institute of Public Administration.

Habermas, J. (1992) "Citizenship and National Identity: Some Reflections on the Future of Europe", *Praxis International* 12(1): 1–19.

Higgins, G.G. (1980) "Religion and National Economic Policy: A Catholic Perspective", in E.J. Fisher and D.F. Polish (eds.) *The Formation of Social*

Policy in the Catholic and Jewish Traditions. Indiana: University of Notre Dame Press.

Kaufman, F.-X. (1988) "The Principle of Subsidiarity Viewed by the Sociology of Organizations", in H. Legrand, J. Manzanares and A.G.Y. Garcia (eds.) *The Nature and Future of Episcopal Conferences*. Washington, D.C.: The Catholic University of America Press.

Kelly, J. (1982) "Subsidiarity and Social Renewal", *Afer* 24: 200–208.

Kossel, C. (1981) "Global community and subsidiarity", *Communio* 8: 37–50.

Kühnhardt, L. (1992) "Federalism and Subsidiarity", *Telos* 91: 77–86.

Laffan, B. (1992) *Integration and Cooperation in Europe*. London: Routledge.

Leaper, R.A.B. (1975) "Subsidiarity and the Welfare State", *Social and Economic Administration* 9(2): 82–97.

Lorenz, W. (1991) "The New German Children and Young People Act", *British Journal of Social Work* 21(4): 329–339.

Macenzie-Stuart, L. (1991) "Assessment of the Views Expressed and Introduction to a Panel Discussion", in *Subsidiarity: The Challenge of Change*, Proceedings of the Jacques Delors Colloquium, Maastricht, 21–22 March 1991. Maastricht: European Institute of Public Administration.

Majone, G. (1991) *Regulatory Federalism in the European Community*. Paper.

Manno, B.V. (1978) "Subsidiarity and Pluralism: A Social Philosophical Perspective", in D. Tracy, H. Küng and J.B. Metz (eds.) *Toward Vatican III*. New York: The Seabury Press.

March, J.G. and Olsen. J.P. (1989) *Rediscovering Institutions, The Organizational Basis of Politics*. New York: The Free Press.

Mill, J.S. (1861/1962) *Consideration on Representative Government*. Indiana: Gateway Editions.

Millon-Delsol, C. (1992) *L'Etat Subsidiaire*. Paris: Presses Universitaires de France.

Nell-Breuningen, O. von (1962) *Subsidiaritätsprinzip. Staatslexikon*. Vol. 7, pp. 826. Freiburg: Herder Verlag.

_____. (1990) *Baugestze der Gesellshaft: Solidarität und Subsidiarität*. Freiburg: Herder Verlag.

Olsen, J.P. (1992) "Analyzing Institutional Dynamics", *Staatswissenshaften und Staatspraxis* 3: 247–271.

Pappas, S.A. (1991) "The Legal Basis for Action to be Taken by the EC in the Field of Envionmental Policy", in *Subsidiarity: The Challenge of Change*, Proceedings of the Jacques Delors Colloquium, Maastricht, 21-22 March 1991. Maastricht: European Institute of Public Administration.

_____. (1992) "Towards a European Public Service", EIPASCOPE, no. 3, European Institute of Public Administration. Conference on "Effective and Efficient Management in the New Europe".

Pinder, J. (1992) "The Community after Maastricht: How Federal?" *New european* 5.3.

Raadschelders, J.C.N. and T.A.J. Toonen (1992) *Adjustments of the Dutch Public Administration to European Demands: Coordination without a Coordinator?* Paper submitted to the Conference on Administrative Modernization in Europe, Perugia, June 12–13, Manuscript.

Richter, E. (1987) "Subsidiarität und Neokonservatismus. Die Trennung von politischer Herrschaftsbegründung und gesellschatlichem Stufenbau",*Politische Vierteljahress* 28(3): 293-314.

Roemheld, L. (1990) *Integral Federalism*. Frankfurt am Mein: Verlag Peter Lang.

Roumeliotis, P. (1991) "The Subsidiarity Principle: The View of the European Parliament", in *Subsidiarity: The Challenge of Change*, Proceedings of the Jacques Delors Colloquium, Maastricht, 21–22 March 1991. Maastricht: European Institute of Public Administration.

Schaefer, G.F. (1991a) "Institutional Choices. The rise and fall of subsidiarity", *Futures* 23(7): 681–694.

_____. (1991b) "The Subsidiarity Principle and European Environmental Policy", in *Subsidiarity: The Challenge of Change*, Proceedings from the Jacques Delors Colloquium, Maastricht, 21–22 March, 1991. Maastricht: European Institute of Public Administration.

Shapiro, M. (1992) "The European Court of Justice", in A.M. Sbragia (ed.) *Europolitics. Institutions and Policymaking in the "New" European Community*, pp. 123–156. Washington, D.C.: The Brookings Institution.

Shell, D. (1993) *The British Constitution 1991–2*. Parliamentary Affairs.

Sutherland, P. (1992) "Progress to European Union. A Challenge for the Public Service." EIPASCOPE, no 3. European Institute of Public Administration. Conference on "Effective and Efficient Public Management in the New Europe".

Toonen, T.A.J. (1992) "Europe of the Administrations: The Challenge of '92 (and Beyond)", *Public Administration Review* 52(2): 108–115.

Wilke, M. and Wallace, H. (1990) *Subsidiarity: Approaches to Power-sharing in the European Community*. The Royal Institute of International Affairs.

Chapter 6

The Policy-administration Dichotomy Revisited: the Case of Transport Infrastructure Planning in Norway

Morten Egeberg

Introduction

In this chapter I want to investigate to what extent the intended division of work between a comparatively small department and relatively large agencies actually takes place. To what extent do we find a core department focusing on policy-making on the one hand and agencies concentrating on execution and implementation on the other? In the chapter it is argued that, ideally, the separation of policy-making and administration presupposes a neutrally functioning institutional framework at all levels. However, all institutions are, by necessity, biased in one way or another. Therefore, in the chapter, much attention is devoted to the way institutional factors intervene in the policy process.

The empirical focus will be on two parallel national planning processes in Norway: one dealing with road construction and maintenance, the other with the construction and maintenance of rail infrastructure. To assess the importance of institutional factors, I will be looking for the differences they might have caused as regards the investment levels and profiles of the plans. The analysis will not encompass the parliamentary stage. (The parliament passed the two plans without noteworthy alterations.)

An old, but still vital, administrative doctrine

The idea that good administration requires specialization along the lines of "policy" and "execution" is an old and venerable doctrine of Public Administration. Policy units should concentrate on clarifying values, goals, policy guide-lines and overall control frameworks. Executive units should concentrate on implementation or keeping the machinery running (Hood and Jackson 1991, 115). As a doctrine, this "policy-administration dichotomy" had been adopted by several European administrations long before it was presented to the U.S. administrative milieu by Woodrow Wilson in the 1880s (Wilson 1887). A hundred years later, the doctrine appears as part of the so-called "modernization programs" of governments across the OECD area (Olsen 1991). Countries like the U.K. and the Netherlands, until then characterized by large and integrated ministries, started to implement the norm on a broad scale by "hiving off" departmental tasks to newly established agencies (Hogwood 1993; Kickert 1993). In Norway, the idea is an old one, both in theory and in practice. However, only since the end of WW II has the doctrine been contended consistently across reports on administrative policy (Christensen og Egeberg 1989).

Dynamic Policy-Making and Enduring Institutions

The administrative doctrine outlined above fits well into a standard interpretation of how a representative democracy should work: The citizens' opinions and preferences are supposed to be articulated and aggregated by parties and other organizations, elections are supposed to bring the winning party or coalition into the leading positions of the state, and the holders of these positions are authorized to translate their program into public policies. In such an interpretation, a ministry is a flexible, adaptive secretariat of shifting ministers. Agencies are neutral executors of the policy programs of those in position. In this perspective, institutions, like departments and agencies, are needed to convert inputs into outputs, but the content of public policies does not reflect characteristics of the institutions themselves. Institutions are necessary means, but their forms, procedures, routines and personnel composition are not that important. It is an indeterminate relationship between organizational structures and programs (Rose 1993, 123).

Opening the "black box", and focusing on institutional factors, means to modify considerably the open system model outlined above. By "institutional factors" I mean normative structures, both in the form of formal organizational structures and decision rules and in the form of informal procedures and routines, and organizational cultures. In addition, the demography and physical structure of institutions are included. These factors focus the decicion-maker's attention on certain problems and solutions, while others are excluded from consideration. They thereby simplify decisions that might have been complex. The selection of decision premises is, however, systematic, and contributes to stability by making the decisions relatively predictable (Simon 1965; 1993; Sharkansky 1970, March and Olsen 1989). "Incrementalism" (Lindblom 1959) is an example of an informal routine or decision rule that is supposed to contribute substantially to the continuity of expenditure decisions (Wildavsky 1964; Peters 1989, 218–28). Thus, from an institutionalist's point of view, policy-makers are embedded in institutional frameworks that furnish them with action capacity for certain purposes, but not for others. Institutions can not work "neutrally"; they have to influence the choices that are made via the structures (Hammond 1986). The extent to which formal policy-makers may be able to act as real policy-makers therefore depends heavily on such factors as the distribution of organizational and professional capacity between the department level and the agency level, the way the apparatus is formally specialized, and the prevailing cultures and routines.

Method and data

The data applied in this study resulted from the author's stay in the Norwegian Ministry of Transport and Communications as a non-participant observer during the period January – June 1993. I focused mainly on two sections that were of special interest for the topic of the study (more about these sections later on). I was allowed to attend all meetings at all levels, including the level of the minister, and also meetings between the ministry and other ministries and agencies. No formal interviews were made, but I had informal talks with the officials on a regular basis, i.e. in their offices, in corridors and during lunch time. Further, no restrictions were imposed on my access to written material. This type of data, however, served primarily to check the information obtained through observation and talks. Therefore, in the chapter no references are made to concrete written documents.

The study was financed by my university, and I was not expected to report to anybody. The presentation of my role as that of an independent researcher, having only a long-term, scholarly interest to look after, may have contributed to the officials behaving more "normally" than they might have done if my role had been defined otherwise, e.g. as that of an evaluation researcher. At the end of my stay

I was informed from different sources that my attendance did not seem to have affected the processes in any significant way. This, however, is hard to determine definitely of course.

I also had talks in the Directorate of Roads and in the Norwegian State Railways (cf. the attached organizational chart). In addition, I visited the ministries of transport in Stockholm and den Haag.

How much can be accounted for by institutional factors?

The planning processes focused on in this chapter started "automatically" according to an established routine: four-year-plans are worked out regularly for both roads and railways. The road planning process was by far the more comprehensive one. It involved all the regional offices of the Directorate of Roads (DR) (one in each of the 19 counties), and also the elected bodies of the county governments. Historically, most state grants for road-construction had been distributed among the counties, and the counties themselves were allowed to develop and to give priority to projects. Since 1970, the pattern of allocation among the counties had been rather stable in relative terms. During spring 1991, the DR, after consultation with the Ministry of Transport and Communications (MTC), announced how the economic resources were to be distributed among the counties for the period 1994–97. As expected, this preliminary allocation also appeared to be largely a prolongation of the last plan (1990–93). At the same time, guidelines that pointed out aspects to be elaborated in the planning process were communicated to the regional offices of the RD.

From April 1991 to March 1992, the regional offices of the RD worked out their investment program proposals in detail. Thereafter, the elected bodies of the county governments were consulted. If they disagreed, the RD and the MTC had the final word. However, in most cases, the elected bodies approved the proposals. Since the jurisdictions of the regional offices of the RD coincided with those of the county governments, the observed consensus between the two is understandable: they shared their geographical perspective, and they had a common interest in maximizing the investment resources made available from the central government to the respective counties.

The road planning capacity was mainly located in the regional offices of the RD. This fact, in combination with the procedures and routines discussed above, makes it understandable that the sub-national level of government turned out to be rather influential in the planning process. The RD's investment program proposal then appeared to be close to a "national summary" of the nineteen county plans. It was handed over to the MTC in October 1992 (cf. table 6.2).

The railway planning process was, in comparison to the road planning process, a centralized decision process. The state railway company (NSB), the actions of which the Minister of Transport and Communications was ultimately responsible for, had reorganized its local apparatus into only four regions. Steps had recently been taken to increase the capacity for infrastructure planning, and this organizational growth occurred primarily in the regions. However, preliminary budgetary frames for the period 1994–97, within which the regions were supposed to give priority to certain projects (like in the road planning process), were not announced. All important decisions concerning the profile of the plan were taken at the central level of the company, without any institutionalized consultation with the county governments. On this background, it is understandable that the infrastructure plan proposal from NSB concentrated very much of the activity to come on the south-eastern part of the country, where most passenger traffic took place, and where the greatest potential for increased traffic was expected.

The road plan proposal from the RD was taken care of by the Road Transport Department (headed by a director general) within the MTC (cf. the attached organizational chart). The process involved several sections in that department, but the Road Infrastructure Section had been assigned responsibility for the coordination of the work. This unit was composed of nine economists and one jurist. The Road Transport Department was headed by two economists. The department approved the RD's four years budget (cf. table 6.2), and also, at large, the investment projects given priority to by the directorate. However, because of the comprehensive process that had already taken place at the subnational level of government, the department felt it had little real leeway to make any substantial changes. In fact, the RD had informed the department that substantial alterations of the budgetary frames could necessitate a new process at the county level. In that case, the whole schedule could be jeopardized. In a couple of cases, however, the department expressed a divergent view on the ranking of investment projects made by the directorate. In the department's view, more weight should be assigned to the results of cost-benefit-analyses. According to these analyses, some other projects should be given a higher priority than those pointed out by the RD. At this stage of the process, the political leadership of the MTC was still not involved in profiling the plan in detail. The standpoint of the department, therefore, is probably best explained by considering the professional background of its personnel. To be sure, the cabinet, in its long-term program, had stressed the importance of cost-benefit-analyses as an instrument in transport infrastructure planning. But other considerations, like regional balance and environmental protection, were also pointed out as both legitimate and necessary concerns. Cost-benefit-analyses of new projects were routinely worked out in the RD. But, as the departmental economists saw it, the directotate's engineers, who made the analyses, were not really interested in applying the results. From the economists' point of view, the engineers primarily focused on technical challenges, like bridges and tunnels. The economists realized, however, that the main reason why the cost-benefit-analyses were not that important, was the road planning system itself, with its relatively stable geographical distribution of state investment resources.

The railway plan proposal from NSB was dealt with by the Railway Section, which was a part of the MTC's Air and Rail Transport Department (cf. the attached organizational chart). Five economists and two jurists worked in the section. The director general of this department was also an economist. The NSB proposal concerning rail infrastructure investments for the next period deviated very much from earlier budgetary decisions (cf. tables 6.3 and 6.4). Since political signals that could support such a radical policy change were lacking at this moment, the Railway Section found no grounds on which it could legitimately endorse the proposal. Thus, the section recommended that the level of investments might be somewhat above the 1993 level multiplied by four. The priority given to the different projects by NSB was mainly approved by the department.

It was the intention of the cabinet to tightly coordinate infrastructure investment decisions across means of transportation. However, the sectorially organized ministry (cf. the attached organizational chart) channeled the two planning processes relatively independently of each other. The physical arrangement of the MTC, in which "our" two departments were located in different parts of the building, strengthened the effects of the formal structure. To some extent, then, the departments became committed to support "their" plans. For instance, immidiately after the cabinet had decided on the budgetary frames for the two plans, the Air and Rail Transport Department tried to "reopen" the process, aiming at an internal redistribution within the ministry. The Road Transport Department defended "their" share, and the minister made no changes in the road budget. However, by furnishing the minister with good arguments, the Railway Section contributed to expanding the rail budget considerably without doing "harm" to the road plan.

Even if a sectorial orientation may be traced in the way the departments behaved, it would be wrong to describe them as mere spokesmen of their respective agencies. They were, at the same time, organizations in their own rights. Their perspectives deviated on several occasions from those of the agencies. It has already been shown that the Railway Section found it impossible to approve the expansive proposal from the railway company. And the Road Transport Department informed the minister that further investments in new roads probably would show decreasing economic utility since most gains (e.g. reduced costs of transportation) had already been realized. Such somewhat divergent and critical views taken by the departments are understandable when we take into account *their* institutional characteristics: As units in the same ministry, they were, after all, both subordinated to the same administrative and political leadership. As units in a ministry, they were also closely related to coordination ministries, like the Ministry of Finance. The career pattern of the MTC had also been characterized by interdepartmental exchange. Together, these conditions provided the officials in the ministry with a somewhat broader view than that of their counterparts in the agencies.

The cabinet's final decision on the budgetary frames of the two plans for the period 1994–97, resulted in expenditure levels that were rather close to the 1993 level multiplied by four (cf. tables 6.1 and 6.3). The priority given to particular investment projects by the cabinet reflected by and large the plan profiles worked out by the agencies. The actions and opinions of the different actors may, to a great extent, be interpreted as reflective of established routines, procedures, and organizational and professional affiliations.

The role of the political leadership

What room, if any, was left then for manoeuvring by the political leadership in this system? Let us start by looking once more at the budgetary frames of the two plans. As mentioned, the planned expenditure levels appeared to be rather close to the 1993 level multiplied by four. However, the relatively high 1993 level was a consequence of an extraordinary program for increased employment and infrastructure development that was initiated in 1991. Thus, the Ministry of Finance stressed the temporary nature of the existing level, and found it quite unacceptable to continue at the same level in the next period. For this reason, it was far from obvious that a prolongation of the 1993 level would take place. To secure the continuation of the established level therefore, the Minister of Transport proposed considerably higher expenditure levels for both plans. As regards the railway plan, the minister in fact adopted the expansive proposal of the rail company. (NSB had been allowed to work out its plan within three alternative budgetary frames, but the company chose to present only the most expensive alternative (cf. table 6.4).) The minister's initiative in the cabinet *may* have contributed substantially to the actual prolongation of the 1993 level.

Nor can the priority given to particular investment projects be understood completely without taking into account the role of the political leadership of the MTC. At least when considering the road sector, this seems to be true: the minister transferred resources from maintenance to investments (compare tables 6.1 and 6.2), and also, though smaller amounts, from central parts of the country to more peripheral parts. Thus, the minister made alterations equivalent to about five per cent of the budgetary frame.

So far then, the processes, in which the budgetary frames of the two plans were determined, may be interpreted in at least two ways: one focusing on incrementalism,

139

and one focusing on political bargaining in the cabinet. In both interpretations, however, the 1993 level turns out as an important premise. Therefore, to explain the economic frame decisions for the period 1994–97, it seems crucial to grasp the escalation that took place during the years 1991–93 (cf. tables 6.1 and 6.3). The considerable growth in infrastructure investments in this period was primarily a by-product of a governmental effort to fight unemployment by spending more money on different public works. To achieve this purpose, resources were redistributed among ministries. A political initiative was of course necessary to formulate such a policy, but this was probably a cabinet initiative more than an initiative of the Transport Minister. Apparently, the minister himself, without involving his officials, allocated the "fresh" money between the two relevant departments in his ministry. However, this allocation was very severely constrained by the fact that investment projects made ready for implementation were only available in the road sector. In the rail sector, the so-called "plan reserve" was almost non-existing at the time due to low investment activity during the preceding decades, and a corresponding lack of organizational capacity for infrastructure planning. *This* explains, in fact, why the road sector got 665 million NOK from the employment program in the first year (1991), while the rail sector received only 50 million NOK. Thus, the distribution of resources between road and rail infrastructure that took place during the period 1991–93, and which became so crucial for the 1994–97 allocation, was to a great extent an unintended consequence of the institutional context within which the decision process unfolded.

Transnational arenas for policy-making

So far we have, in a conventional way, sought to understand the results of the decision processes within a national context alone. It may be objected, however, that such a perspective is rather unrealistic in systems as internationalized as western nations today. Like many other policy sectors, the decision system of the transport sector has for long made up a transnational policy community, consisting of national administrative units, intergovernmental organizations (like the EC and the European Conference of Transport Ministers), interest groups and parliamentarians. Within and around EC institutions, particularly the Commission, networks had no doubt become intensified considerably (cf. for instance Dang-Nguyen et al. 1993). The Norwegian MTC participated in parts of this committee system, and also had, for shorter periods, officials placed in the Commission's Directorate General of Transport (DG VII). Senior officials in the MTC were personally acquainted with their counterparts in several European administrations.

Transport had naturally an important role to play in developing a frictionless "internal market" in the EC. In 1990, the Commission received the report "Transport 2000". In January 1991, the Commission launched its program "Trans-european Nets". Escalating road and rail infrastructure investments was thereby put on the European agenda. However, single countries had long before that started to pay more attention to this issue area. In 1988, for instance, the governments of the Netherlands and Sweden had both made important transport policy decisions. They both launched expansive investment programs, and the railways became better off in relative terms.

Parallel with this growth of investment resources, several railway companies were reorganized according to the so-called "road traffic model". The idea was that the government should be responsible for rail infrastructure in the same way as it was for road construction and maintenance. The users of the infrastructure, in this case the rail companies, were supposed to pay the government for their use. The reform, which was a Swedish innovation from 1988 (Brunsson *et al.* 1989, 68), became soon "institutionalized" (Meyer and Rowan 1977). Thus, it was implemented in Norway in 1990, and adopted by the EC in 1991 and made part of its railway directive. The reform may have contributed substantially to legitimating the escalation of rail investments: disturbing deficits in the companies' accounts were reduced considerably, and competitors in the transport market were pleased to observe that governmental grants no longer were transferred to the operating parts of the companies to the same degree as before. In addition, since the new arrangement, at least in principle, made competition between *different* rail companies possible, rail transport also came to look more acceptable from a market ideological point of view.

Given these circumstances, it is hard to imagine that the Norwegian policy choices discussed could be unconnected to the policy trends found on a broader European scene. The actual policy harmonization that took place may be interpreted as a transnational process of diffusion, imitation and learning. It may also be interpreted as a process in which a policy solution (expansive transport infrastructure programs), developed in a transnational policy community, became coupled to an urgent policy problem, or to a "political stream", as a function of their simultaneity (Cohen et al. 1972; Kingdon 1984; 1992). In Norway, unemployment was the politically defined problem to which infrastructure investments of a large scale represented a possible solution. In other countries, however, the same program might be welcomed as a solution to other problems high on the agenda, like traffic congestion or air pollution.

Conclusion

Our initial question about the actual division of work between the ministry and the subordinated agencies may now be answered. The main impression seems to be that real policy-making took place to a great extent at the agency level. The ministry provided the agencies with few initial guidelines, and those formulated appeared to be rather indefinite. One may say that the ministry only marginally altered the profiles of the plans as these were presented to it by the directorate and the company. And, the important resource escalation that happened during the period 1991–93, can probably better be understood as a by-product of processes external to the transport sector than as a result of active policy-making in the ministry itself. In addition, transnational policy networks may have contributed substantially to the policy processes in focus.

Ideally, the so-called "policy-administration dichotomy" presupposes, as mentioned, a neutrally functioning institutional framework. Public policies are not supposed to reflect characteristics of the institutions themselves. In its pure form, at least, the idea has to be a naive one. This study reveals how institutional factors did have an impact at all stages of the policy process: the planning took off almost automatically according to established routines. In the road sector, investment resources were distributed among the counties in the same proportion as before. The profile of the plan reflected the geographical specialization of the road administration. Correspondingly, the profile of the railway plan is understandable given the more centralized procedures and apparatus that we found in this branch. Our two departments in the ministry recommended an incremental prolongation of the expenditure levels reached in the 1993 budget. Due to the sectorial specialization and modest organizational capacity of the ministry, investment decisions concerning the two means of transportation were not coordinated to the extent the cabinet wanted them to be. Regarding the few projects in which the Road Transport Department's view deviated from that of the directorate, the deviation may be accounted for by the professional background of the officials in the department. The weight they assigned to the results of cost-benefit-analyses did not in any respect reflect the wishes of the minister, on the contrary. The precedent-setting allocation of resources between the two sectors that materialized during the period 1991–93 appeared to be very much an unintended consequence of the organizational capacity for planning in the two agencies. Last, but not least, the institutional framework of an emerging transnational transport policy community had routinized policy learning across national boundaries.

So far, the institutional framework has been taken for given. However, organizational structures, personnel composition, procedures and routines are intended or unintended consequences of previous decisions. Thus, at least in the long run, the framework may be subject to deliberate change efforts. Still, one has to accept and live with an inherent tension in the relationship between dynamic policy-making and its institutional context.

The organizational problem raised by the "policy-administration dichotomy" is, no doubt, an intricate one. So far, however, research seems to indicate that political direction, or steering, of the administrative apparatus is, after all, better served by integrated ministries than by ministries split into so-called "core departments" and executive agencies (Egeberg 1994). On the other hand, vertical specialization of the kind we have dealt with in this chapter, seems to facilitate the possibility for policy continuity and predictability across election periods, and for institutional and professional autonomy. Good government presupposes that sufficient attention is paid to these values too.

Table 6.1

State grants to the road sector (1993 prices. Million NOK)				
	Plan 90–93	Actually granted 90–93	1993 budget x 4	Plan 94–97
Investments	16 245	17 806	18 950	17 200
Maintenance	13 018	14 634	15 022	15 550
County roads	753	1 028	1 030	1 050
Administration	5 775	5 847	6 114	5 800
Total	35 791	39 315	41 116	39 600

Table 6.2

The Road Directorate's budget proposal for the road plan 94–97 (Million NOK)	
Investments	17 000
Maintenance	17 200
County roads	1 420
Administration	6 000
Total	41 620

Table 6.3

State grants and loans to the rail sector (1993-prices. Million NOK)				
	Plan 90–93	Actually granted 90–93	1993 budget x 4	Plan 94–97
Infrastructure (grants)				
Investments	1 515	2 583	3 800	3 705 *
Maintenance	6 019	6 123	6 400	6 664
Traffic				
Operation **	4 156	4 500	4 520	3 228
Investments ***	2 774	3 111	4 480	4 000
Refinancing				2 203
Total	14 464	16 317	19 200	19 800

*:   In addition 2 741 on state loan
**: Subsidies, incl. state purchase of passenger services
***: State loans for rolling stock

Table 6.4

The railway company's proposal (state grants/loans) for the railway plan 94–97
(Million NOK)

Infrastructure

Investments (grants)	7 600
Maintenance (grants)	7 075

Traffic

Operation (grants)	4 520
Investments (loans)	6 165
Total	25 360

Organizational chart

The Ministry of Transport and Communications
and subordinated ("independent") agencies, 1993 (simplified)

Minister
Under Secretary of State

Secretary General

Administration department 4 sections	Postal and Telecom. Serv. dept., 2 sect.	Air and Transp. dept. 2 sect.,incl. Railw. Sect.	Rail Road Transport dept., 5 sect., incl. Road Infra- structure Section

Postal Services	Telecom. Services	Telecom. Regulat. Agency	Aviation Authori- ties	Railway company	Road Directorate

Regional Offices				(4)	(19)

References

Brunsson, N., Forssell, A. and Winberg, H. (1989) *Reform som tradition. Administrative reformer i Statens Järnväger*. Stockholm: EFI, Handelshögskolan i Stockholm.

Christensen, T. and Egeberg, M. (1989) "Norske departementer 1976–86: Noen trekk ved formell struktur, personell og beslutningsatferd", in M. Egeberg (ed.) *Institusjonspolitikk og forvaltningsutvikling. Bidrag til en anvendt statsvitenskap*. Oslo: Tano.

Cohen, M.D., March, J.G. and Olsen, J.P. (1972) "A Garbage Can Model of Organizational Choice", *Administrative Science Quarterly* 17: 1–25.

Dang-Nguyen, G., Schneider, V. and Werle, R. (1993) "Networks in European Policy-making: Europeification of Telecommunications Policy", in S.S. Andersen and K.A. Eliassen (eds.) *Making Policy in Europe. The Europeification of National Policy-Making*. London: Sage.

Egeberg, M. (1994) "Bridging the Gap between Theory and Practice: The Case of Administrative Policy", *Governance* 7: 83–98.

Hammond, T.H. (1986) "Agenda Control, Organizational Structure and Bureaucratic Politics", *American Journal of Political Science* 30: 379–420.

Hogwood, B.W. (1993) "Restructuring Central Government: The "Next Steps" Initiative in Britain", in K.A. Eliassen and J. Kooiman (eds.) *Managing Public Organizations*. London: Sage.

Hood, C. and Jackson, M.(1991) *Administrative Argument*. Aldershot: Dartmouth.

Kickert, W.J.M. (1993) *Administrative Reform in British, Dutch and Danish Civil Service. Towards Policy-making Core Departments and Autonomous Executive Agencies*, Working paper. Rotterdam: Erasmus University.

Kingdon, J.W. (1984) *Agendas, Alternatives and Public Policies*. Boston: Little, Brown and Company.

_____. (1992) *Agendas, Ideas and Policy Change*, Working paper. University of Michigan.

Lindblom, C. (1959) "The science of "muddling through"", *Public Administration Review* 19: 79–88.

March, J.G. and Olsen, J.P. (1989) *Rediscovering Institutions. The Organizational Basis of Politics*. New York: The Free Press.

Meyer, J.W. and Rowan, B. (1977) "Institutionalized Organizations: Formal Structure as Myth and Ceremony", *American Journal of Sociology* 83: 340–363.

Olsen, J.P. (1991) "Modernization Programs in Perspective: Institutional Analysis of Organizational Change", *Governance* 4: 125–149.

Peters, B.G. (1989) *The Politics of Bureaucracy*. New York: Longman.

Rose, R. (1993) *Lesson-Drawing in Public Policy*. Chatham, New Jersey: Chatham House Publishers.

Sharkansky, I. (1970) *The Routines of Politics*. New York: Van Nostrand.

Simon, H.A. (1965) *Administrative Behavior*. New York: The Free Press.

_____. (1993) "The State of American Political Science", *PS Political Science and Politics* 26: 49–51.

Wildavsky, A. (1964) *The Politics of the Budgetary Process*. Boston: Little, Brown and Company.

Wilson, W. (1887) "The Study of Administration", *Political Science Quarterly* 2: 197–222.

Chapter 7

Public Administration in a Democratic Context – A Review of Norwegian Research[1]

Tom Christensen and Per Lægreid

The Weberian ideal model of a public bureaucracy has often been used as a point of departure for describing, analyzing and assessing public administration. This model combines a fairly simple notion of the public administration's external relations with a fairly simple notion of its internal structure. The external organization is dominated by the administration's subordination to the political leadership, a relation primarily regulated by law. Its internal organization is dominated by strict hierarchy and rules. The assumed result is that the civil service can be portrayed as a rational and efficient instrument for its political masters.

In modern democracies this ideal has limited relevance. The reason is not that hierarchy, law and rule-bound behavior do not exist. They certainly do. Yet, they

---

1   We would like to thank Kerstin Sahlin-Andersson, Morten Egeberg, Tore Grønlie, Knut H. Mikalsen, Johan P. Olsen, and Paul G. Roness for help and comments. This chapter was mainly written while the authors were visiting scholars at Scancor, Stanford University in 1996/97. A slightly revised version has been published in Norwegian (Christensen and Lægreid 1997).

147

have been supplemented with a variety of other features, changing somewhat the nature of both the external and the internal organization of the public administration (Christensen and Lægreid 1998).

This chapter traces this development by reviewing 40 years of Norwegian research on public administration. It describes a research tradition based on organization theory and democratic theory (March 1997), and it paints a picture of a public administration integrated into complex political and societal networks of organized interests and clients. It is a story of a complex interplay between competing logics, loyalties and influences, demanding more elaborated models of decision-making and change than assumed by the Weberian ideal model. It shows how a strong theoretical tradition based on bounded rationality is supplemented by an arsenal of theories of anarchic processes and different types of institutional theories, and that recent developments in a way have reactivated some of the Weberian notions in the form of «logic of appropriateness» and its tensions with a logic of consequentiality (March and Simon 1958, March and Olsen 1976, 1989, 1995, March 1994).

Three periods may be distinguished in public administration research in Norway[2]. The first – the pioneer period – lasted from 1955 until 1971; the second was the breakthrough period from 1972 until 1986; and the third, from 1987 until today, has been characterized by continuity, growth and variation[3]. The first period can be associated with Knut Dahl Jacobsen's work, and the other two with Johan P. Olsen's professional leadership and comprehensive studies. These two scholars have had a decisive influence on the study of the civil service and public policy in

---

2   The periods are delimited by the two major research programmes in this field. The first was the Study of the Distribution of Power in Norway (the Power Study) which was a research program initiated by the government of Norway. It lasted from 1972 until around 1980. Its main purpose was to describe "the real power relations in Norwegian society", and it concentrated on studies of public administration, political bodies, markets and interest groups. The second was the research program in organization and management (LOS) from 1987 until 1997.

3   This chronology is not followed systematically through the whole chapter. In the interest of conherence we have chosen to discuss certain types of studies together, even though they were published in different time periods. This makes the discussion of the second period somewhat overarching, as certain themes, for example the relationship to interest groups and to the Storting and reorganization studies, are treated here. However, their connections to both the first and third periods are also discussed. A disadvantage of this approach is that continuity between the second and third period is deemphasized. On the other hand, it is makes clearer that the third period produced some new theoretical and empirical trends.

Norway. Together with James G. March, Olsen has made a major contribution to the development of the theoretical basis of public administration research in Norway. We will account for international influences on this approach, its contribution, both theoretical and empirical, to the development of this field of study and compare Norway's tradition to that of other countries.

The pioneer period

Political science in Norway is rooted in the disciplines of law and history, but gradually the field gained more independent features throughout the 1950s and 60s. This development occurred in all areas of the discipline. What was special about public administration research was that organization theory gained a central position, and that a transition occurred from constitution analysis to organization analysis.

Jacobsen founded the basis for public administration research in Norway through an explicit combination of theories of decision-making in organizations and political science theory. This was an important professional innovation when modern public administration research became established in Norway. This combination was, and still is, unusual even in an international perspective, but has emerged as a fruitful integration which has made its mark on the development of this research area. The theoretical focus was on *bounded rationality*, suggesting that organization structure is important for channeling decision making behavior, while simultaneously allowing discretion within the formal framework. Jacobsen was also concerned with the development of the value basis and cultural norms in public administration. He emphasized variety, complexity and conflicting loyalties in the administrative role, but also general mechanisms, norms and values in the relationship between politicians and civil servants, i.e. he put public bureaucracy in an explicit political-democratic context (Eckhoff and Jacobsen 1960, Jacobsen 1960, 1966).

The traditional focus on the internal structure within organization theory was extended to include the significance of the environment for administrative behaviour and development. The central public administration was regarded as a political actor with dynamic relations to the political leadership and actors in the civil society (Jacobsen 1964). The relationship between politics and administration was a central theme, and was explicitly associated with Simon's (1947) distinction between value premises and factual premises. Politics was regarded as an activity preoccupied with the formulation of problems, attempts to have these definitions of problems accepted as binding and to organize a continuous problem-solving activity around them. Political organization implies systematic and routine-based selection. Through the establishment of participation rights and obligations, rules

149

of the game, decision-making procedures and routines, some of the actors and conflicts are organized out of the public decision-making processes, while others are organized into such processes (Schattschneider 1960).

In his study of the organization of the central agricultural administration, Jacobsen showed how tension and inconsistency between the problem structure and organizational structure, between the demands of the society and the professional administration's answer, created a potential for change. At the same time, he also provided insight into the relations between the internal administrative condition, professions, political leadership and external client interests (Jacobsen 1964). He emphasized the relationship between professionals and clients and the significance of client-oriented professions (Jacobsen 1965), and this was later followed up through the development of the so-called theory of access (Bleiklie, Jacobsen and Thorsvik 1997).

Summing up, Jacobsen showed how specific sector-oriented case studies could be carried out, and at the same time he managed to raise principal questions based on his empirical results. Likewise he formulated theoretical ideas about the complexity of the administrative role in a democratic context. Norwegian public administration research during the pioneer period was built on a tradition of theoretically-oriented and empirically based studies of decision making in formal organizations, which, in general, have shown that rational decision-making models must be elaborated and that their relevance will vary concerning area of application. As a consequence, those models have been modified in many important respects (March and Simon 1958, Olsen 1983a, March 1988). Decision-makers have limited time, attention and analytical capacity in relation to the tasks and problems with which they are confronted, and their attitudes and actions are influenced by the organizational structure within which they work and by the external environment to which they are connected.

Other studies emphasized additional factors which could modify the rational models. One was that public organizations are characterised by *conflicting goals* and *heterogeneity*, reflecting typical features in political-administrative processes (March and Olsen 1983, Olsen 1983a). Organizations do not function as unitary actors and they exist under both tension and dissension. Another factor is the element of *ambiguity* and *unpredictability*. Decision-makers operate in a world where the past, the present and the future are ambiguous and require interpretation, and actors, problems and solutions are selected and linked to decisions in different and unpredictable ways (March and Olsen 1976). A third line of development which has received considerable attention during the last decade is the significance of *institutional factors*, i.e. the constraints which established cultural traditions and socially defined conventions imply for decision-making (March and Olsen 1989, 1995).

The great leap forward[4]

There is a clear continuity between Jacobsen's research program and that part of the *Power Study* which examines central administration and the corporative system. The research-strategic approach to the study of civil service and politics, combining political science and organization theory, was broadened, extended and strengthened. The conception of bounded rationality was combined with basic questions about the working of democracy, and the significance of the administrative apparatus both as a tool for implementation and as a part of a political community was underlined (Olsen 1978:8). This continuity is also seen in the choice of two main areas for empirical studies: the internal organization and decision-making of the civil service and the relationship between the civil service and a crucial set of external actors, the interest groups.

Olsen's research programme was, however, also a theoretical and empirical extension of Jacobsen's work. Theoretically, it was more explicit, regarding both the democratic-theoretical research questions and the organizational-theoretical point of departure. Empirical models subject to testing were also developed. The focus was on actors who represented formal organizations, and how their models for thought and action, their decision premises and decision behaviour are formed by the organization and the organizational context they belong to (Olsen 1978:11, 16).

The Garbage Can model also contributed to the theoretical basis of the *Power Study* (Cohen, March and Olsen 1972). First, the main elements in the decision-making process – the flows of participants, problems, solutions and choice opportunities and their coupling to each other – emerged more clearly and were systematised. This general model or analytical scheme was later widely used (Christensen and Egeberg 1979, Egeberg 1984, Roness 1992). Secondly, the model, as a specific «anarchical» decision-making model, emphasized the ambiguous, unpredictable and contextual elements in decision-making situations, and the temporal sorting and coupling of actors, problems, solutions and decisions. In this second respect, the model has established a basis for the study of open organizational structures and non-routine decision-making situations (March and Olsen 1976, Sætren 1983). This has resulted in a better understanding of public administration and public decision-making processes, not only those characterised by «routine policy», but those containing elements of fragmentation, ambiguous lines of authority, complexity and problems of governance.

---

4   This notion is borrowed from Kuhnle (1986), who characterizes the Power Study as the "big leap forward" in Norwegian political science.

151

Empirically, the *Power Study* focused on the factors that shape administrative structures, changes and effects. A broad empirical program was outlined, and was followed up by case-studies of the public administration and its relations with the environment. Not least, a number of surveys of individual decision-makers in the ministries and the interest organizations were also carried out. In an international perspective, the latter supplied unique material which has contributed to the development of systematic knowledge as to how the Norwegian political-adminis-trative system functions. It is precisely this combination of surveys and case studies which has characterised Norwegian public administration research from the period of the *Power Study* up until now.

The broad survey of the civil service was also the basis of Lægreid and Olsen's (1978) study of the organization of knowledge, beliefs, authority and interests in the ministries. In this book, the relative explanatory power of two analytical models – the responsible and the representative bureaucracy – for the beliefs and the contact and control patterns of the civil servants were analyzed. The main results of the study emphasize the significance of the employees' bureaucratic biography and formal position within this administrative structure. Through socialisation and disciplinary and control mechanisms, political and administra-tive constraints are emphasized and the significance of social background factors on decision-making behaviour is reduced. Civil servants are presented as key actors who are members of different teams, all engaged in the formulation of public policy (Lægreid and Olsen 1984). This study modified the conception of a uniform administrative apparatus and argued that the civil service was characterised by institutional pluralism.

The civil service survey was repeated in 1986 and this time included the directorates[5]. In the main report of this survey (Egeberg 1989a), the continuity with previous studies is clear. A comparison was made over time and between ministries and directorates. Further, reorganization processes were analyzed, as were the effects of formal structures, demography and physical structural aspects on decision-making behaviour. Throughout, the results from this survey support earlier main findings which underlined the structural factors' significance in explaining decision-making. Among aspects of change which are revealed in the later surveys, the increasing degree of collegial organization (Stigen 1991) and 'feminisation' in the central administration (Lægreid 1995a) might be mentioned.

---

5   The directorates are administrative units subordinated to the ministries (Christensen 1997). They are the result of vertical, interorganizational specialization. The most common type of directorate, labled the "Swedish type", is similar to more independent agencies in other countries.

The description applied in the early 1980s, «The State: Women – no admittance» (Hernes 1982), is thus no longer as relevant today.

In 1996, the civil service survey was undertaken for a third time. The first results show continuity in that the administrative structures, demography and decision behavior are described and compared over time (Christensen and Egeberg 1997). On the other hand, also new trends are discussed, for example through studies of the 'europeanisation' of the public administration (Egeberg and Trondal 1997) and of New Public Management reforms in the civil service (Christensen and Lægreid 1998).

The relationship between the cabinet and the political leadership in the ministries on the one hand, and the central administration on the other, is important in administrative studies. Jacobsen showed how the various organizational models of the relation between ministries and directorates have different implications for political governance and professional autonomy. This has been followed up by studies of competing decision-making principles in the civil service (Egeberg 1989b) and by historic analyses of reorganization of the relationship between the political leadership and the civil service (Christensen 1994 and 1997). Jacobsen's (1960) classic article on loyalty, neutrality and professional autonomy analyzed the balance between political and professional premises in the administrative role. His conclusion, that a certain ambiguity in their role enables civil servants to handle complexity and to integrate opposing values in the decision-making process, is confirmed in later studies (Christensen 1991a).

Olsen analyzed how the content of the Cabinet's decision-making was influenced by the organizational frameworks within which it was operating (Olsen 1983c). He argued that the role of the political leadership in relation to the administration could not be understood only on the basis of the traditional hierarchical model of control. The leadership is confronted with problems of capacity, understanding and authority which, to a large extent, are managed through increased specialisation and negotiation, both within the administrative apparatus and with organised interests in society.

With the *Power Study* as the point of departure, an interest in a constructive approach to administrative research emerged, and the question was raised whether political science could be regarded as an architectural discipline (Olsen 1988c). This constructive line has been further developed by Egeberg (1994) in his instrumental model, which elaborates the knowledge base for decision-making and professional working practices and is inspired by the works of Gulick (1937) and Simon (1947), among others. Egeberg has shown how this type of theory can be applied to studies of administrative-political processes and their effects. He emphasizes empirical analyses, but has also focused on normative questions through a discussion of central values in government and how these are used in the organization of the political-administrative apparatus (Egeberg 1997).

Another related trend is found in a number of studies of the reorganization of the civil service. Wetlesen's research (1977) of the activities of the Directorate of Organization and Management, and Roness' (1979) study of the reorganization of ministries are earlier works on the conditions for the reform of the civil service. These have been followed up by a number of broader studies of reorganization and more typically historically oriented case studies (Christensen 1994, Egeberg 1984, Roness 1994). Generally, these reorganization studies have been more preoccupied with process aspects than the effects of the various forms of organization. One main empirical result is the considerable significance of the political and administrative leadership in the processes of reorganization. Leadership participation varies, however, with the political and administrative importance of the reorganization, and the possibility for political control appears to be less in the major and comprehensive reorganization processes than in the reorganization of individual agencies (March and Olsen 1983).

An empirical observation in these studies is that formal organizations seldom adapt to changing political signals or to changes in the environment quickly, optimally or without cost. One example where this is particularly emphasised is Sætren's (1983) study of the implementation of public decisions, in an investigation of the relocation of state agencies. He studied the lack of implementation based on models of symbolic politics and interest politics and as a social by-product. The ambiguity of implementation processes in formal organization was particularly emphasised (Baier, March and Sætren 1986). A later example of an implementation study is Matland's (1991) dissertation on the accomplishment of budget reforms in Norwegian central administration.

A third line of development in the study of public administration, which may also be traced back to the *Power Study,* encompasses the analyses of organizational demography and personnel policies. One study of how demographic and organizational factors influence decision-making in administrative agencies characterised by considerable mobility was conducted in the public petroleum bureaucracies (Lægreid 1988). That study showed that structural position plays a more substantial role than place of origin in explaining decision-making behavior. The research on recruiting and mobility patterns, workplace democracy and other aspects of salary and personnel policy in the public administration has shown that these aspects of administrative policy cannot be reduced to technical/administrative questions, but are political processes (Lægreid 1987, 1995b). Personnel policy is influenced by interests and traditions within the administrative system.

In the wake of the *Power Study,* sector studies were also carried out. An analysis of the encounter between Norwegian representative democracy and the oil age showed that decision-making was a complex interplay of rational planning, institutional routines, interest representation and interpretation of contextual events (Olsen 1989). The conditions of representative government were examined in studies of goal formulation, the formation of knowledge, institutional development, personnel resources, interest representation and the representativeness of public institutions. The governance of the petroleum sector and its relation to other actors was also examined through comparative studies of the authorities' strategies concerning the oil companies (Andersen 1988, Thorsvik 1991).

Another sector study was aimed at the environmental sector (Jansen 1989). Through a case study of the formulation of environmental policy in Norway, Jansen shows how the Ministry of the Environment became a «growth and protection» ministry, and how this was associated with the pattern of influence between various actors and the structure within which they operated. In a broad study of the modernisation of the Norwegian state up to 1970, Gran (1994) draws upon historical knowledge and research methods in his analysis of particular cases.

Administrative-historical studies from the end of the 1970s have also made important contributions to the understanding of the development of the civil service, for example through the analysis of the conflict between central political and administrative actors concerning different organization models for the civil service (Benum 1979). Historical studies of individual sectors of obvious relevance to political science include studies of the Health Directorate (Nordby 1989), the industrial sector (Grønlie 1989), and of the Ministry of Finance (Lie 1995). These show how institutional features and the educational background of the actors make their mark on policy development.

There is, furthermore, an increasing interest among political scientists in studies of administrative changes with an explicit historic dimension. Examples of the latter are inquiries into the development of the professions, such as studies of the development of the health professions and health policy (Berg 1991, Erichsen 1996). They show how a particular type of professional control has emerged over time within the health sector, but languished during the last decade.

Regarding the more specific *external networks* of the central administration, the relation between the civil service and the Storting has not been a consistent focus of research interests. It was, however, a central theme in Jacobsen's (1964) analysis of the organization of the central administration of the agricultural sector, in which the relationship between the Storting and the civil service was interpreted as a transition from a detractive into a contractive phase, from emphasis on political control to growing discretion and autonomy. These ideas were further developed by Olsen, who argued that parliamentary power in relation to the civil service is characterised by cycles and that the power relationship has not necessarily been displaced in disfavour of the Storting (Olsen 1983b). Studies of later periods appear to support this view (Rommetvedt 1995).

155

Olsen (1983b) described the contact between the Storting and the administration as relatively limited, formalised, hierarchical and specialised. Subsequent surveys among ministerial employees in 1986 and 1996 also report that the contact between the civil service and the Storting is not particularly frequent (Christensen and Egeberg 1997). However, Hernes and Nergaard (1990) studied this relationship from the perspective of the individual parliamentary representatives and drew a slightly different picture. They argued that formal contact between the Storting and the civil service is supplemented by a network of close informal contacts, which they refer to as 'power integration'.

The pattern of contact between the civil service and the interest organizations was given considerable attention in the *Power Study* and in subsequent studies. The report's survey of interest organizations and their participation in public decision-making processes provided the basis for a number of studies (Christensen and Egeberg 1979, Egeberg 1981, NOU 1982:3, Olsen 1981). The focus in these studies was particularly on the characteristics of negotiations between the administration and the organizations, and involved analysis of the various organization forms and their selection. These surveys showed that the interest organizations were closely integrated into public policy and that the pattern of participation in the various forms was biased towards large interest groups. Hernes (1978) introduced the term 'mixed administration' to describe this form of public organizing was characterised by an increasing integration of the public and private sectors.

One source of inspiration for these studies was Stein Rokkan's work, i.e. the thesis on numerical democracy and corporative pluralism, and the apt statement «votes count but resources decide» (Rokkan 1966). While Rokkan emphasised that the corporative and the numeric channels were alternative paths for promoting influence, the *Power Study* attached importance to these as supplementary channels (Lægreid and Roness 1996). «The segmented state» was advanced as a concept to account for how the cleavages are not *between* the institutions, but *through* them (Egeberg, Olsen and Sætren 1978). Later studies questioned the relevance of the segmentation theory to the Norwegian administrative system today (Nordby 1994, Rommetvedt 1995).

Another forerunner to these studies was work on 'collegial administration', i.e. the participation of the interest organizations in a large number of public committees and the significance of this integrated participation (Kvavik 1976, Moren 1974). Several sector studies have also been made of the relationship between the civil service and the interest organizations, for example within the fishing sector (Hallenstvedt 1982, Hoel et al. 1996, Jentoft and Mikalsen 1987).

Despite the fact that during the last 10–15 years administrative policy has been aimed at reducing the significance of the corporate channel in policy formulation through a reduction of the number of public committees (Eriksen 1990), the integrated cooperation between the interest organizations and the authorities continues to play an important role (Nordby 1994). Neverthless, the question has been raised of whether a 'decorporation' tendency may be observed in Norwegian society (Fimreite 1997).

Continuity, growth and variety

The last decade has been characterized by continuity, growth and variety in public administration studies in Norway. The growth in the number of administrative studies has been substantial. There is, however, also a tendency toward *theoretical pluralism* and more variety in methods, analytical foci and empirical areas studied.

The article «The New Institutionalism: Organizational Factors in Political Life» (March and Olsen 1984) outlined a broad institutional perspective on analyses of public administration and policies. Here the main research interest is on the institutional frames through which policies are determined and implemented, not the individual decision-making process or individual decision makers (March and Olsen 1989, Olsen 1988a). The broad institutional perspective of March and Olsen is mainly formulated as an alternative to economic perspectives in political science, as outlined, for example, in public choice theory. Institutionally related patterns of thought and action are supposedly more typical of political life than means-ends rational decisions. Traditions, structures and processes have intrinsic value, apart from their instrumental implications. An institutional perspective emphasizes the interaction between institutions and political governance. Institutions promote and impede political behavior, but they also change gradually over time through political initiatives. A central hypothesis according to this perspective is that institutional features have a major impact on how public administration reacts to reforms and attempts at political control (Brunsson and Olsen 1993). The argument is also that both structural features and policy content restrict the possibility of self-interest influencing the decision-making behavior of bureaucrats (Egeberg 1995a).

March and Olsen (1989) emphasize that politics has both an instrumental and a symbolic or «creation of meaning» side, and they stress the important distinction between aggregative and integrative processes in politics. In their latest book, the focus is more on the development of identity and the discretion for democratic governance (March and Olsen 1995). In this regard, they specifically emphasize the development of political capabilities, as well as political accounts and adaptiveness, thereby coming back to some important Weberian elements, but from a different angle.

The development of theory in institutional analysis and public administration research is not only related to a broad institutional perspective, but to the different elements in it. Olsen outlines different models of governance, contrasting an institutional model, which portrays the state as a «moral community», with a sovereign rationality-bounded state model, a corporate-pluralist model, and a model of the state as a supermarket (Olsen 1988b). Institutional analysis can, however, as outlined in major works in organizational sociology, also be said to consist of at least two main theoretical schools (Scott 1995). One of them is related to the cultural, institutional analyses of Selznick (1949, 1957). It focuses on «institutionalized organizations» and has increasingly been used in empirical studies of public administration (Christensen 1994). Another school is more clearly social-constructive and preoccupied with how certain concepts, organizational forms, procedures, knowledge, etc. are gaining a «ideological hegemony», are taken-for-granted and accepted (Meyer and Rowan 1977). These theoretical currents have also inspired Norwegian researchers in their studies of public sector reforms (Christensen 1991b). Often labeled the myth or fashion/fad perspective, these theoretical ideas focus on the «institutional environment», and can be defined either as a natural perspective or as having instrumental elements. Røvik has especially been concerned with developing a fashion perspective on studies of changes in public administration (Røvik 1992, 1996, 1998). Instead of discussing only the adaptation of broad myths from the institutional environment, he emphasizes the possibility that organizations are «multi-standard organizations», combining institutional components from different «organization fields».

The development of theory on political and administrative institutions has increasingly been related to political theory and democratic theory, and March and Olsens' (1995) most recent book is a typical example. Eriksen has also contributed to this development through his interest in communicative rationality, and deliberative and discursive aspects of politics (Eriksen 1993, Eriksen and Loftager 1996). He points out that, as public administration becomes less hierarchical, mechanisms of control less centralized and local autonomy greater, governance will depend more on political consideration and reflection, judgment and ability to interact in new ways (Eriksen 1995). These works are mainly inspired by political philosophy, with Habermas as a central contributor. In relation to this tradition, an increased interest in normative questions in public administration research has appeared, in discussions of the limits of governmental control and regulations and the relation between the state and civil society. This type of theory has not been tightly linked to empirical, administrative research but has inspired it in a more general way.

The increased variety of theoretical perspectives has implied new angles on empirical areas that traditionally have been dominant in public administration research in Norway. Furthermore, it has also opened up new empirical fields of research. The institutional perspective, both as March and Olsen (1983, 1989) have developed it and in other versions, has been applied to the central administrative system in a number of studies. One stronghold has been the LOS program since the late 1980s, which has been concerned with analyzing reform processes in the public sector. Problems of democratic government, the relationship between central control and institutional autonomy, and a number of more specific efforts towards change and reform in the public sector have been studied (Baldersheim et al. 1989, Grønlie and Selle 1998, Lægreid and Olsen 1993). Studies of administrative policies, based on comprehensive programs of modernization and renewal, have analyzed changes in administrative structures, processes and personnel, Management by Objectives (MBO) and increased devolution, wage reforms and public personnel policy (Christensen 1991b, Lægreid 1994, Olsen 1991, 1996a). Studies have been made of the role of the Storting and the employees' organizations in administrative policy processes (Roness 1994, 1995), and historians working with public administration have analyzed the development of different organizational forms more generally (Grøndahl and Grønlie 1995) and the use of the directorate form in central, public administration in particular (Grøndahl 1997).

Studies have also been conducted of the relationship between central institutions and professions in the defence sector (Skauge 1994), of planning processes in the transport sector (Egeberg 1995b) and of the role of the central administration in the foreign aid sector (Gran 1993). A common feature of these studies is that they emphasize how organizational factors influence the processes.

Public administration research has tried to supplement and challenge a one-sided economic analysis of public administration, politics and society. This research can in many ways been seen as a criticism of the management thinking in the 1980s, in which the private sector was uncritically adopted as a model for public sector organizations, and market-orientation, efficiency and consumerorientation were the main elements (Lægreid and Olsen 1993). Instead the functioning of the public administration has been characterized and analyzed on the basis of a democratic-political perspective, in which the value-, interest-, knowledge- and power-basis of the public sector has been emphasized (Olsen 1992). A philosophy of political and administrative control, focusing on internal management, has been challenged by one based on democratic governance and external representativity. Ingraham (1996) distinguishes two research traditions in civil service research – the governance tradition, stressing an political-democratic context and «managerialism» – and Norway belongs obviously to the former one.

Studies of administrative policies and politics have shown that reform processes have often been characterized by compromise and an apolitical rhetoric, creating incremental results (Lægreid and Roness 1998, Olsen 1996a). The link between «talk» and action, and between general attitudes, specific solutions and actual implementation, has not always been very tight (Brunsson 1989). Even though general comprehensive programs of administrative policy have been formulated, a segmented public administration has to a large extent created segmented reforms. Compared to the political-administrative doctrines in effect in the central administration until the 1970s, with strong centralization, standardization and rule-following, there has in the last decade been a development in the direction of relatively more decentralization, increased flexibility and more management by objectives (Christensen and Lægreid 1998, Grønlie and Selle 1998). An organizational and procedural devolution has been instrumental in creating more variety and hetereogeneity in the public administration. While its fundamental and traditional features endure the homogeneous and hierarchical model of control that characterized the building of the welfare state has been supplemented with changes and reforms that create more autonomy for administrative units and civil servants (Fimreite 1997, Roness 1996). This actualizes the question of the balance between autonomy and political control of the administrative apparatus.

In the last decade, more attention has been given to *comparative*, empirical studies, and there has been an increased interest in how the public administration is influenced by internationalization and europeanization processes. Internationalization of political processes, understood as the development of more extensive networks of transactions and organizations among countries, has been a continuous process in the post-war period. This implies that the traditional division or distinction between domestic and foreign policy processes has been blurred and is gradually more problematic in guiding political organization and political science research (Blichner and Sangolt 1993). Traditional studies of foreign policy decision-making processes (Ørvik et al. 1972) have in recent decades been supplemented by transnational policy perspectives and the idea that a fourth system level exists in addition to the traditional three characterizing domestic political processes – the local, county and state levels (Egeberg 1980). A central set of questions analyzed in the new comprehensive research program on the europeanization of the national state (ARENA) includes to what extent and in what ways national institutions of governance in small countries like Norway are influenced by processes of europeanization (Olsen 1996b, 1997a, 1997b, Sverdrup 1998).

The increased realization that it is impossible to understand the development of the Norwegian public administration from an internal, domestic point of view alone, has led to a greater interest in comparative studies between countries. Examples here are studies of agriculture policy in Norway, Sweden and the United Kindom (Steen 1988), studies of producing official statistics in Norway and Great Britain (Sangolt 1997) and studies of environmental policy in the Nordic countries (Jansen and Osland 1996). Lægreid and Pedersen (1994, 1996) have studied administrative policies in the Nordic countries. They show how the Scandinavian welfare model has been challenged by new administrative doctrines related to New Public Management. The Nordic countries share many common features in this development, but there are also differences and national characteristics. The Scandinavian model has been changed, but not dismantled. Olsen and Peters (1996) show that there are clear variations among OECD countries concerning administrative reforms and changes. The development in Norway is more halting and gradual than in Anglo-American countries such as England and Australia, where market- and management-oriented reforms have been implemented to a larger extent.

The Olsen and Peters study also illustrates the interest in *learning processes* in the research of the central administrative system. They show that experiential learning is characterized by ambiguity and uncertainty, and that the learning often is more internal and management-oriented than externally directed and political. The question of organizational learning under ambiguity was first raised by March and Olsen (1975), and was introduced on a Norwegian empirical material by Bratbak and Olsen (1980) in a study of the feedback of information to the ministries regarding effects of public programs. The interest in learning processes is related to an increased focus in the administrative policy field on evaluation and effects, and the analysis of reforms and processes of change (Berg 1995). While the emphasis earlier was on planning and the ability to analyze future consequences of actions (Østerud 1979), today there is increased attention on learning and the ability to look back and learn from one's own mistakes (March and Olsen 1989). An example is Sangolt's study of the politics of counting, in which she discusses the production of statistics as a reality-defining, institutionalised and political activity. In his study of organizational learning, with an empirical focus on technology-agreements in the Norwegian petroleum sector, Blichner analyzes the conditions for radical change (Blichner 1995). The interest in learning processes is closely linked to more emphasis on organizational change (Olsen 1991, Roness 1997), which also to a great extent is influenced by the work of James G. March (1981).

Main features and challenges in the future

A systematic, cumulative and growing research effort has increased the knowledge base regarding the role of public administration in the Norwegian political-administrative system and contributed to clarifying the conditions that influence the actual behavior, effects and changes in public administration. The special mixture of political science and organization theory has given Norwegian public administration research a relatively stronger theoretical profile than comparable research in many other countries. This theoretical basis has been used to formulate and conduct large empirical studies, a feature that underscores the substantial empirical orientation also. March (1997) argues that these are all features that were

161

typical in public administration research in U.S. until the 1960s, a tradition that was later lost.

Lundquist (1985) emphasizes that modern public administration research in political science has been characterized by a development from a classical, Weberian point of departure – stressing rationality, centralization and hierarchy – to an emphasis on anarchy, decentralization and democracy. The focus has changed from the intraorganizational to the interorganizational. Static analyses have been supplemented by dynamic process studies and studies of effects, and there is an increasing interest in normative and constructive problems. Norwegian research on public administration has developmental features like the above, but it also shows a strong continuity through its focus on the democratic context of civil service, on formal structure, bounded rationality and internal processes.

The criticism of «pure» theories of rational choice has gradually expanded, first emphasizing bounded rationality, then temporal logic, and finally the «logic of appropriateness» (March and Olsen 1976, 1989). If we make a distinction between analytical-descriptive studies, where the attention is directed towards how the central administration actually *is* working; constructive studies, which are more preoccupied with how public administration *can* function, and normative studies focusing on how the public administration *should* or *ought to* work; we will conclude that the analytical-decriptive studies have had a dominant position in Norwegian research on public administration. However, the constructive and normative studies have been strengthened over time, especially in the last decade.

Research on public administration in Norway has been instrumental in modifying and elaborating ideal views about the administrative system, such as formulated in the «doctrine of the parliamentary chain» (Olsen 1978). Public administration is substantially influenced by political signals and decision premises, and a division between political and administrative roles, but it does not function entirely as an obedient instrument of the superior political leadership. Civil servants exercise substantial political discretion, and administrative bodies are central political actors in public decision-making processes (Jacobsen 1997). Public administration has certain typical features of hierarchical patterns of control and contact and common norms and values, but it is also interwoven with external networks and characterized by collegial structures, local administrative cultures and negotiation processes that limit the possibilities of hierarchical control. Some of the most important cleavages in public policy are between representatives of different administrative agencies. Increasing specialization and autonomy has contributed to greater heterogeneity and complexity and is creating new challenges of coordination between institutions, sectors and administrative levels.

A central question in the future is what role the central public administration should and can play in the Norwegian political system. The national administrative institutions are being challenged by internationalization, europeanization, regionalization, communalization, devolution, privatization and deregulation. It is possible that public administration will be robust in resisting demands to change rapidly and that externally enacted reforms will be adapted to the existing administrative culture, while it changes gradually. Another possibility is that the central public administration will be functionally preempted. A third possibility is that, for example, increased europeanization will result in a strengthening of the role of public administration in the political-administrative system. A fourth development possibility is that simultaneous decentralization and europeanization will change the structure of public administration, its functioning and its relationship to other actors, without necessarily either weakening or revitalizing it.

To be able to answer these questions, it will probably be necessary to strengthen the comparative dimensions in public administration research, both concerning systematic comparisons over time and between countries, but also with respect to the emphasis on the normative and contructive aspects and studies of effects. Another major challenge to public administration research is to balance the need for continuity and further development of existing theories, methods and empirical fields, on the one hand, against, on the other hand, the need to develop new theory and find new approaches to the study of the functioning of the public administration.

Finally, an important challenge for future public administration research will be to study the civil service in a wider democratic context, which implies that attention will be focused not only on economy and efficiency, but on how public administration attends to many other important considerations and influences values, interests, the knowledge basis and power conditions. A substantial democratic dilemma is how public administration can have enough autonomy to function effectively, but not so much freedom that it will be uncontrollable (Dahl and Lindblom 1953).

Referances

Andersen, S. (1988) *British and Norwegian Offshore Industrial Relations.* Aldershot: Avebury.

Baier, V.E., March, J.G. and Sætren, H. (1986) "Implementation and Ambiguity", *Scandinavian Journal of Management Studies,* 2: 197–212.

Baldersheim, H. et al. (1989) *Sentral styring og institusjonell autonomi.* Bergen: Alma Mater.

Benum, E. (1979) *Sentraladministrasjonens historie 1845–1884.* Oslo: Scandinavian University Press.

Berg, O.T. (1991) "Medikrati, hierarki og marked", in D. Album and G. Midre (eds.) *Mellom idealer og realiteter – Studier i medisinsk sosiologi,* pp. 147–175. Oslo: Ad Notam.

Berg, A.M. (1995) *Vellykket forvaltning.* Oslo: TANO.

Bleikiie, I., Jacobsen, K.D. and Thorsvik, J. (1997) "Forvaltningen og den enkelte", in T. Christensen and M. Egeberg (eds.) *Forvaltningskunnskap,* pp. 301–334. Oslo: Tano.

Blichner, L. (1995) *Radical Change and Experimental Learning,* Dr.philos. thesis. Bergen: Department of administration and organization theory, University of Bergen, Report nr. 37.

Blichner, L. and Sangolt, L. (1993) "Internasjonalisering av offentlig forvaltning", in P. Lægreid and J.P. Olsen, *Organisering av offentlig sektor. Perspektiver – reformer – erfaringer – utfordringer,* pp. 171–200. Oslo: Tano.

Bratbak, B. and Olsen, J.P. (1980) "Departement og opinion: Tilbakeføring av informasjon om virkninger av offentlige tiltak", in J.P. Olsen (ed.) *Meninger og makt,* pp. 86–174. Bergen: Scandinavian University Press.

Brunsson, N. (1989) *The Organization of Hypocrisy. Talk, decisions and actions in organizations.* Chichester: John Wiley.

Brunsson, N. and Olsen, J.P. (1993) *The Reforming Organization.* London: Routledge. New edition 1997 at Fagbokforlaget, Bergen.

Christensen,T. (1991a) "Bureaucratic Roles: Political Loyalty and Professional Autonomy", *Scandinavian Political Studies,* 14(4): 303–320.

_____. (1991b) *Virksomhetsplanlegging. Myteskaping eller instrumentell pro-blemløsning?* Oslo: Tano.

_____. (1994) *Politisk styring og faglig uavhengighet. Reorganisering av den sentrale helseforvaltningen.* Oslo: Tano.

_____. (1997) "Utviklingen av direktoratene – aktører, tenkning og organisa-sjonsformer", in T. Christensen and M. Egeberg (eds.) *Forvaltningskunnskap,* pp. 119–144. Oslo: Tano.

Christensen, T. and Egeberg, M. (1979) "Organized group-government relations in Norway: On the structured selection of participants, problems, solutions and choice opportunities", *Scandinavian Political Studies* 3(2): 239–260.

_____. (1997) "Sentralforvaltningen – en oversikt over trekk ved departemen-ter og direktorater", in T. Christensen and M. Egeberg (eds.) *Forvaltnings-kunnskap,* pp. 85–118. Oslo: Tano.

Christensen, T. and Lægreid, P. (1997) "Sentralforvaltning og offentlig politikk", *Norsk Statsvitenskapelig Tidsskrift,* 13(3): 255–278.

_____. (1998) *Den moderne forvaltning.* Oslo: Tano.

Cohen, M.D., March, J.G. and Olsen, J.P. (1972) "A Garbage Can Model of Organizational Choice", *Administrative Science Quarterly,* 17: 2–15.

Dahl, R.A. and Lindblom, C. (1953) *Politics, Economics and Welfare: Planning and Politics Economic Systems Resolved into Basic Social Processes.* New York: Harper & Row.

Eckhoff, T. and Jacobsen, K.D. (1960) *Rationality and Responsibility in Administrative and Judicial Decisionmaking.* København: Munksgaard

Egeberg, M. (1980) "The Fourth Level of Government: On the Standardization of Public Policy within International Regions", *Scandinavian Political Studies,* 3(3): 235–248.

_____. (1981) *Stat og organisasjoner. Flertallsstyre, partstyre og byråkrati i norsk politikk.* Bergen: Scandinavian University Press.

_____. (1984) *Organisasjonsutforming i offentlig virksomhet.* Oslo: Tano.

_____. (ed.) (1989a) *Institusjonspolitikk og forvaltningsutvikling – bidrag til en anvendt statsvitenskap.* Oslo: Tano.

_____. (1989b) "Om å organisere konkurrerende beslutningsprinsipper inn i myndighetsstrukturer", in M. Egeberg (ed.) *Institusjonspolitikk og forvaltningsutvikling – bidrag til en anvendt statsvitenskap,* pp. 94–113. Oslo: Tano.

_____. (1994) "Bridging the Gap Between Theory and Practise: The Case of Administrative Policy", *Governance* 7: 83–98.

_____. (1995a) "Bureaucrats as public policy-makers and their self-interests", *Journal of Theoretical Politics* 7(2): 157–167.

_____. (1995b) "The policy-administration dichotomy revisited: the case of transport infrastucture planning in Norway", *International Review of Administrative Sciences* 61 : 565–576.

_____. (1997) "Verdier i statsstyre og noen organisatoriske implikasjoner", in T. Christensen and M. Egeberg (eds.) *Forvaltningskunnskap,* pp. 405–422. Oslo: Tano.

Egeberg, M., Olsen, J.P. and Sætren, H. (1978) "Organisasjonssamfunnet og den segmenterte stat", in J.P. Olsen (ed.) *Politisk organisering,* pp.115–142. Bergen: Scandinavian University Press.

Egeberg, M. and Trondal, J. (1997) "Innenriksforvaltningen og den offentlige politikkens internasjonalisering", in T. Christensen and M. Egeberg (eds.) *Forvaltningskunnskap,* pp.335–366. Oslo: Tano.

Erichsen, V. (ed.) (1996) *Profesjonsmakt. På sporet av en norsk helsepolitisk tradisjon.* Oslo: Tano.

Eriksen, E.O. (1990) "Towards the Post-Corporate State?", *Scandinavian Political Studies,* 13(4):345–364.

_____. (ed.) (1993) *Den offentlige dimensjon.* Oslo: Tano.

_____. (ed.) (1995) *Deliberativ politikk.* Oslo: Tano.

Eriksen, E.O. and Loftager, J. (eds.) (1996) *The Rationality of the Welfare State.* Oslo: Scandinavian University Press.

Fimreite, A.L. (ed.) (1997) *Forskerblikk på Norge.* Oslo: Tano.

Gran, T. (1993) *Aid and Entrepreneurship in Tanzania. NORAD's Contribution to Entrepreneurial Mobilization in the Public Sector in Tanzania.* Dar es Salam: University Press.

_____. (1994) *The State in the Modernization Process. The Case of Norway 1850–1970.* Oslo: Ad Notam.

Grøndahl, Ø. (1997) *Fristilling og politisering. Om bruken av direktoratsformen i norsk sentralforvaltning.* Dr.art.thesis. Bergen: The LOS centre. Report 9712.

Grøndahl, Ø. and Grønlie, T. (1995) *Fristillingens grenser.* Bergen: Fagbokforlaget.

Grønlie, T. (1989) *Statsdrift.* Oslo: Tano.

Grønlie, T. and Selle, P. (eds.) (1998) *Ein stat? Fristillingas fire ansikt.* Oslo: Samlaget.

Gulick, L. (1937) "Notes on the Theory on Organizations. With Special Reference to Government", in L. Gulick and L. Urwin (eds.) *Papers on the Science of Administration,* pp. 3–45. New York: A.M. Kelley.

Gaasemyr, J. (1979) *Organisasjonsbyråkrati og korporativisme.* Bergen: Scandinavian University Press.

Hallenstvedt, A. (1982) *Med lov og organisasjon: Organisering av interesser og markeder i norsk fiskerinæring.* Tromsø: Scandinavian University Press.

Hernes, G. (ed.) (1978) *Forhandlingsøkonomi og blandingsadministrasjon.* Bergen: Scandinavian University Press.

Hernes, H. (1982) *Staten – kvinner ingen adgang.* Oslo: Scandinavian University Press.

Hernes, G. and Nergaard, K. (1990) *Oss imellom. Konstitusjonelle former og uformelle kontakter Storting – regjering.* Oslo: FAFO.

Hoel, A.H., Jentoft, S. and Mikalsen, K.H. (1996) "Problems of user-group participation in Norwegian fisheries management", in R.M. Meyers et al. (eds.) *Fisheries Utilization and Policy: Proceedings of the World Fisheries Congress,* pp. 287–303. New Dehli: Oxford & IBH Publishing Co.

Ingraham, P.W. (1996) "The Reform Agenda for National Civil Service Systems: External Stress and Internal Strains", in H.A.G.M. Bekke, J.L. Perry and T.A.J. Toonen *Civil Service Systems in Comparative Perspective,* pp. 247–267. Bloomington and Indianapolis: Indiana University Press.

Jacobsen, D.I. (1997) *Administrasjonens makt.* Bergen: Fagbokforlaget.

Jacobsen, K.D. (1960) "Lojalitet, nøytralitet og faglig uavhengighet i sentraladministrasjonen", *Tidsskrift for Samfunnsforskning* (1): 231 –248.

_____. (1964) *Teknisk hjelp og politisk struktur.* Oslo: Scandinavian University Press.

_____. (1965) "Informasjonstilgang og likebehandling i den offentlige virksomhet", *Tidsskrift for Samfunnsforskning* 6(2): 147– 160.

Jansen, A.-I. (1989) *Makt og Miljø.* Oslo: Universitetsforlaget.

Jansen, A.-I. and Osland, O. (1996) "Norway", in P.M. Christensen (ed.) *Governing the Environment, Politics, Policy and Organization in the Nordic Countries,* pp. 179–256. København: Nord.

Jentoft, S. and Mikalsen, K.H. (1987) "Government Subsidies in Norwegian Fisheries: Regional Development or Political Favourism?" *Marine Policy* 11: 217–228.

Jørgensen, T.B. (1996) "From Continental Law to Anglo-Saxon Behaviorism: Scandinavian Public Administration", *Public Administration Review* 56(1): 94–103.

Kuhnle, S. (1986) "Linjer i norsk statsvitenskap: Institusjonell differensiering og forskningsekspansjon", in S. Kuhnle (ed.) *Det politiske samfunn. Linjer i norsk statsvitenskap,* pp. 47–68. Oslo: Tano.

Kvavik, R.B. (1976) *Interest Groups in Norwegian Politics.* Oslo: Scandinavian University Press.

Lie, E. (1995) *Ambisjon og tradisjon. Finansdepartementet 1945–65.* Oslo: Scandinavian University Press.

Lundquist, L. (1985) "From Order to Chaos: Recent Trends in the Study of Public Administration", in J.-E. Lane (ed.) *State and Market. The Politics of the Public and the Private,* pp. 201–230. London: Sage.

Lægreid, P. (1987) "Styring av personalressurser i statsforvaltningen", *Politica* 19(4):403–419.

_____. (1988) *Oljebyråkratiet.* Oslo: Tano.

_____. (1994) "Going against the Cultural Grain: The case of Norway", in C. Hood and B.G. Peters (eds.) *Rewards at the top,* pp. 133–145. London: Sage.

_____. (1995a) "Feminization of the central public administration", in L. Karvonen and P. Selle (eds.) *Women in Nordic Politics,* pp. 229–248. Aldershot: Darthmouth.

_____. (ed.) (1995b) *Lønnspolitikk i offentlig sektor.* Oslo: Tano.

Lægreid, P. and Olsen, J.P. (1978) *Byråkrati og beslutninger.* Bergen: Scandinavian University Press.

_____. (1984) "Top Civil Servants in Norway. Key Players – on Different Teams", in E.N. Suleiman (ed.) *Bureaucrats and Policy Making,* pp. 206–241. New York: Holmers and Meier.

_____. (eds.) (1993) *Organisering av offentlig sektor.* Oslo: Tano.

Lægreid, P. and Pedersen, O.K. (eds.) (1994) *Forvaltningspolitik i Norden.* København: Jurist- og økonomforbundets forlag.

_____. (eds.) (1996) *Integrasjon og desentralisering.* København: Jurist- og økonomforbundets forlag.

Lægreid, P. and Roness, P.G. (1996) "Political Parties, Bureaucracies and Corporatism", in K. Strøm and L. Svåsand (eds.) *Challenges to Political Parties,* pp. 167–190. Ann Arbor: University of Michigan Press.

_____. (1998) "Frå einskap til mangfald", in T. Grønlie and P. Selle (eds.) *Ein stat? Fristillingas fire ansikt,* pp. 21–65. Oslo: Samlaget.

167

March, J.G. (1981) "Footnotes to organizational change", *Administrative Science Quarterly* 26. 303–77

————. (1988) *Decisions and Organizations.* London: Basil Blackwell.

————. (1994) *A Primer in Decision-Making. How decisions happen.* New York: The Free Press.

————. (1997) "Administrative Practice, Organization Theory, and Political Philosophy: Ruminations on the *Reflections* of John M. Gaus", *PS Political Science* 30(4): 689–698.

March, J.G. and Olsen, J.P. (1975) "The Uncertainty of the Past: Organizational Learning under Ambiguity", *European Journal of Political Research* 3: 147–71.

————. (1976) *Ambiguity and choice in organizations.* Oslo: Scandinavian University Press.

————. (1983) "Organizing Political Life: What Administrative Reorganization Tells Us About Government", *American Political Science Review* 77: 281–297.

————. (1984) "The New Institutionalism: Organizational Factors in Political Life", *American Political Science Review* 78: 734–749.

————. (1989) *Rediscovering Institutions.* New York: The Free Press.

————. (1995) *Democratic Governance.* New York: The Free Press.

March, J.G. and Simon, H.A. (1958) *Organizations.* New York: Wiley.

Matland, R. (1991) *The Implementation of Budgetary Reform,* Ph.D. thesis. Ann Arbor: University of Michigan.

Meyer, J.W. and Rowan, B. (1977) "Institutionalized Organizations: Formal Structure as Myth and Ceremony", *American Journal of Sociology* 83: 340–363.

Moren, J. (ed.) (1974) *Den kollegiale forvaltning.* Oslo: Scandinavian University Press.

Nordby, T. (1989) *Karl Evang – en bibliografi.* Oslo: Aschehoug.

————. (1994) *Korporatisme på norsk 1920–1990.* Oslo: Scandinavian University Press.

NOU 1982:3. *Maktutredningen. Sluttrapport.* The Office of The Prime Minister.

Olsen, J.P. (1978) "Folkestyre, byråkrati og korporativisme", in J.P. Olsen (ed.) *Politisk organisering,* pp. 13–114. Bergen: Scandinavia University Press.

————. (1981) "The Dilemmas of Organizational Integration in Government", in P.G. Nystrom and W. Starbuck (eds.) *Handbook of Organizational Design.* Vol. 2, pp. 492–516. New York: Oxford University Press.

————. (1983a) *Organized Democracy. Political Institutions in a welfare state – the case of Norway.* Bergen: Scandinavian University Press.

————. (1983b) "The ups and downs of Parliament", in J.P. Olsen *Organized Democracy,* pp. 39–76. Oslo: Scandinavian University Press.

_____. (1983c) "The Cabinet and the Limitations of Executive Leadership", in J.P. Olsen *Organized Democracy,* pp. 77–119. Oslo: Scandinavian University Press.

_____. (1988a) *Statsstyre og institusjonsutforming.* Oslo: Scandinavian University Press.

_____. (1988b) "Administrative Reform and Theories of Organization", in C. Campbell and B.G. Peters (eds.) *Organizing Governance: Governing Organizations,* pp. 233–254. Pittsburgh: Pittsburgh University Press.

_____. (1988c) "Reorganisering som politisk virkemiddel og statsvitenskapen som arkitektonisk disiplin", in J.P. Olsen (ed.) *Statsstyre og institusjonsutforming,* pp. 61–76. Oslo: Scandinavian University Press.

_____. (1989) *Petroleum og politikk.* Oslo: Tano.

_____. (1991) "Modernization Programs in Perspective: Institutional Analysis of Organizational Change", *Governance* 4(2): 125–149.

_____. (1992) "Utfordring for offentlig sektor. Noen sentrale spørsmål og problemstillinger", *Norsk Statsvitenskaplig Tidsskrift* 9(1): 3–28.

_____. (1996a) "Norway: Slow Learner – or Another Triumph of the Tortoise?", in J.P. Olsen and B.G. Peters (eds.) *Lessons from Experience,* pp. 180–213. Oslo: Scandinavian University Press.

_____. (1996b) "Europeanization and Nation–State Dynamics", in S. Gustavsson and L. Lewin (eds.) *The Future of the Nation State,* pp.245–285. London: Routledge.

_____. (1997a) "European Challenges to the Nation State", in B. Stevenberg and F. van Vught (eds.) *Political Institutions and Public Policy,* pp.157– 188. Dordrecht: Kluwer Academic Publishers.

_____. (1997b) "Institutional Design in Democratic Contexts", *The Journal of Political Philosophy* 5(3):203–229.

Peters, B.G. and Olsen, J.P. (eds.) (1996) *Lessons from experience.* Oslo: Scandinavian University Press.

Rokkan, S. (1966) "Norway. Numerical Democracy and Corporate Pluralism", in R.A. Dahl (ed.) *Political Oppositions in Western Democracie,* pp. 70–116. New Haven: Yale University Press.

Rommetvedt, H. (1995) "Personellressurser, aktivitetsnivå og innflytelsesmuligheter i et Storting i vekst", *Norsk Statsvitenskapelig Tidsskrift* 11(4): 251–276.

Roness, P.G. (1979) *Reorganisering av departementa – eit politisk styringsmiddel?* Bergen: Scandinavian University Press.

_____. (1992) *Forvaltningspolitikk gjennom organiseringsprosessar,* Dr. philos. thesis. Bergen: The LOS centre. Report 9206.

_____. (1994) "Tenestemannsorganisasjonar og forvaltningsreformer: påverknadsmuligheter og handlingsrom", *Norsk Statsvitenskapelig Tidsskrift* 10(1): 25–39.

(1995) *Stortinget som organisator.* Oslo; Tano.

_____. (1996) "Institusjonell orden – Norge", in P. Lægreid and O.K. Pedersen (eds.) *Integration og Decentralisering,* pp. 59–92. København: Jurist og økonomforbundets forlag.

_____. (1997) *Organisasjonsendringar.* Bergen: Fagbokforlaget.

Røvik, K.A. (1992) *Den "syke" stat: Myter og moter i omstillingsarbeidet.* Oslo: Scandinavian University Press.

_____. (1996) "Deinstitutionalization and the Logic of Fashion", in B. Czarniawska and G. Sevón (eds.) *Translating Organizational Change,* pp. 139–172. Berlin, New York: Walter de Gruyter.

_____. (1998) *Moderne organisasjoner. Trender i organisasjonstenkningen ved tusenårsskiftet.* Bergen: Fagbokforlaget.

Sangolt, L. (1997) *The Politics of Counting: Producing official statistics on the North Sea oil industry in Norway and Great Britain 1966–1986,* Dr.philos. thesis. Bergen: The LOS centre. Report 9710.

Scott, W.R. (1995) *Institutions and Organizations.* Thousand Oaks, Calif.: Sage.

Schattschneider, E.E. (1960) *The Semi-Sovereign People.* New York: Holt, Rinehart and Winston.

Selznick, P. (1949) *TVA and the Grass Roots.* New York: Harper.

_____. (1957) *Leadership in Administration.* New York: Harper & Row.

Simon, H.A. (1947) *Administrative Behavior.* New York: Macmillian.

Skauge, T. (1994) "Contraction and Detraction: Non-Equilibrium Studies of Civil-Military Relations", *Journal of Peace Research* 31(2): 189–203.

Steen, A. (1988) *Landbruket, staten og sosialdemokratene.* Oslo: Scandinavian University Press.

Stigen, I.M. (1991) "Avbyråkratisering og modifisert forhandling? Om bruk av prosjektorganisasjon i norsk sentralforvaltning", *Norsk Statsvitenskaplig Tidsskrift* 7: 173–191.

Sverdrup, U. (1998) "Norway: An Adaptive Non Member", in K. Hauf and B. Soetendoerp (eds.) *Small States in the EU,* pp. 149–166. London: Longman.

Sætren, H. (1983) *Iverksetting av offentlig politikk. En studie av utnytting av statsinstitusjoner fra Oslo 1960–1981.* Bergen: Scandinavian University Press.

Thorsvik, J. (1991) *Politikk og marked.* Oslo: Bedriftsøkonomenes forlag.

Wetlesen, T.S. (1977) *Rasjonalisering og forvaltningspolitikk. Rasjonaliseringsdirektoratets virksomhet 1948–1972.* Oslo: Scandinavian University Press.

Ørvik, N. (ed.) (1972) *Departemental Decision-Making.* Oslo: Scandinavian University Press.

Østerud, Ø. (1979) *Det planlagte samfunn.* Oslo: Gyldendal.

III.
Organizing: Beyond Environmental Dictates and Rational Design

Chapter 8

Origin and Transformation of Organizations[1]
Institutional Analysis of the Danish Red Cross

Søren Christensen and Jan Molin

Our aim in this chapter is to examine the origin and transformation of organizations. The empirical basis for our discussion is a study of the Danish Red Cross (DRC) over a period of more than 125 years. We trace the origin of the organization to 1864, when Denmark (along with other nations) signed the Geneva Treaty and agreed to establish local Red Cross organizations. The founding of the Danish Red Cross organization was, however, not easily achieved. It took 12 years before the local organization was established.

Rather than understanding the creation of the Red Cross organizations as the mobilization of particular interests (Brint & Karabel, 1991), we claim it to be a

---

1   We would like to thank the other for their high spirits during the workshop, and for their constructive comments. Special thanks to Asmund Born, Frank Dobbin, James G. March, W. Richard Scott, and Pamela Vergun for detailed comments on earlier versions of this manuscript.

dramatization by the environment. Scott (1994b, p. 208) talks of such a process as the "enactment of an organization by the environment." The creation of the Danish Red Cross became a symbol of Denmark's status as a civilized nation, and the institutional form of the Red Cross was a sort of celebration of the newly won democratic rights of citizens to participate in public life. The approach of this chapter draws attention to the symbolic aspects of organizations and environments, and to participants as carriers of cultural beliefs created at the societal level (Friedland & Alford, 1991).

From its founding in 1876 to the present day, the Danish Red Cross has undergone substantial changes in tasks, in leadership, and in its member base, adapting to changing demands and opportunities in its environment. In spite of these changes, the basic organizational form a democratic structure-has been retained throughout the history of the organization.

The central thesis of population ecology, "that environments differentially select organizations for survival on the basis of fit between organizational forms and environmental characteristics" (Scott, 1992, p. 113), does not apply to our case. The organizational form has been retained, and, at the same time, the organization has adapted to changing environments. The resilience of this organization makes a case for a key argument of new institutionalism: Organizations that devise structures that conform closely to institutional requirements "maximize their legitimacy and increase their resources and survival capabilities" (Meyer & Rowan, 1977, p. 352).

It has been argued that new institutionalism "is more applicable to the study of institutional form and functioning than to the equally important topics of institutional origin and transformations" (Brint & Karabel, 1991, p. 338), and that the process of creating and transforming organizations is profoundly a political process that "reflects the power of organized interests and the actors that mobilize around them" (DiMaggio, 1988).

In this chapter, we try to demonstrate that the new institutionalism is applicable to origin and transformations of organizations, and that interests should not be conceived as naturally occurring groups with transparent and primordial interests, as pluralist and neo-Marxist theorists tend to conceive them, but rather as institutionally defined and shaped. This calls for "three (nested) levels of analysis-individuals competing and negotiating, organizations in conflict and coordination, and institutions in contradiction and interdependency" (Friedland & Alford, 1991, p. 241).

Models of organizational change often use organizational goals as a key variable. In Powell and Friedkin's (1987) study of change in nonprofit organizations, they discuss change in terms of the achievement, subversion, or supplanting of goals. Rather than postulating the importance of goals, we view the Danish Red

Cross as an "empty vessel" which acts as a recipient of institutionally defined and shaped interests. In our analysis we use the model of an "organized anarchy" (Cohen, March, & Olsen 1972), viewing the organization as an opportunity structure that, through time, accommodates shifting problems, solutions, and participants. The tasks taken on by the Danish Red Cross at a given period in time depend on the mix of the streams of participants, problems to be dealt with, and available solutions that flow past the organization. However, the way the tasks are performed is in part determined by the identity, structure, and activity pattern (Meyer, 1994) that is established in the organization over time.

The approach in this chapter is inductive. We think it is important to separate data from the subsequent theoretical analysis of the data to make it possible for the reader to develop his or her own understanding of the material before we present our interpretation, so we begin by summarizing the history of the DRC, and then we examine the founding and subsequent transformations of the organization, discussing the founding of the organization as a case of dramatization by the environment, and the transformations of the organization as a case of adaptation to changing conditions in the environment. We discuss the loose coupling between the organization form and governance system, and the effects of sediments (or early established ways of doing things). We also treat the impact of symbolism on the origin of the DRC and discuss the impact of participants, problems, and solutions on the organization's transformation.

Our main theoretical points will be summarized in the analysis section. In the conclusion we develop the more general implications of our analysis for organizations in institutionalized environments.

History[2]
1864–1876: The Founding of the Danish Red Cross
In 1876 "The Society for the improvement of the Conditions for the Sick and Wounded during War" was founded in the "King's Club" Restaurant in Copenhagen. General Thomsen, former Minister of War, became president of the society. The other members of the executive committee were men drawn from the nobility and the military establishment. Although the society was formally organized as a voluntary association, with open membership and election of the leadership, the founding members were drawn from very conservative circles in Copenhagen, the capital of Denmark, and the leadership of the society reflected this. The executive

---

2   The history of the Danish Red Cross presented here draws heavily on an unpublished manuscript prepared for a doctoral dissertation by Barbara Zalewski. Her cooperation is acknowledged and greatly appreciated.

committee assumed power and got concessions from the board, allowing it to increase its size and replace members as it saw fit.

Nevertheless, the actual founding of the society took place a full 12 years after Denmark had committed itself to creating a local Red Cross-type organization based on guidelines set out in the Geneva Treaty. In 1864 Denmark, along with 12 other European countries, had responded to the initiative of a committee headed by Henri Dunant to participate in a conference in Geneva on aid to the sick and wounded in war situations. The conference resulted in the signing of the first Geneva Convention.

At this same point in time (1864), Denmark was at war with Prussia. The Geneva Committee sent delegates to the Danish side as well as to the Prussian side. This was not looked upon favorably by the Danish government, which questioned the impartiality of the delegates. Nor did the Danish army view the committee favorably; it felt criticized for not being able to adequately prevent and care for wounded soldiers. Denmark lost the war in 1864.

The military establishment, however, was reluctant to have civilians involved in military affairs. Apart from various measures concerning the treatment of the wounded and the neutrality of Red Cross personnel and materials (e.g., ambulances), the Geneva Treaty stipulated some kind of cooperation between the (civilian) Red Cross Committee and the military establishment. The national governments that signed the treaty were supposed to accept the role of a civilian organization in assisting the army in caring for the sick and wounded on the battlefield.

During the period from 1864 to 1876, the Red Cross Committee in Geneva tried several times to establish contact with Denmark. Its inquiries were not answered. In 1876 the Red Cross Committee once again asked why Denmark – having signed the Geneva Convention – offered no assistance to the wounded in the French-Prussian War taking place at the time. This time Denmark was criticized in public, and the story was published in the International Bulletin of The Red Cross Committee in Geneva.

And so, finally, the pressure on Denmark bore fruit.

1876–1917: Supporting the Danish Army

The charter of the Society – which later changed its name to The Danish Red Cross – was to organize private individuals to provide assistance to the sick and wounded during wartime and, in peacetime, to prepare such help and to encourage interest and skill in voluntary (as distinguished from military) nursing. However, for a long period of time, the goal that was primarily pursued by the society was the more narrow one of supporting the Danish army; this was a reflection of the primary interests of the society's leadership. The society collected money for preparing military sanitary depots and later organized the training of nurses and first aid volunteers.

In 1881 the name was changed to The Red Cross. This reflects the fact that the society wanted to be considered a part of the international movement. Although it was supposed to be part of the International Red Cross, the many appeals in the period from 1876 to 1917 to the Danish Society from other societies and from the International Red Cross Committee were not answered. The society was very reluctant to get involved. Only in three cases did the society respond favorably: during the Turkish-Russian War in 1877–1878, in 1897 when the Red Cross sent 12 nurses to Greece during the war with Turkey, and again in 1912 during the Greek-Turkish War. In all three cases, the Danish royal family had put pressure on the Red Cross to assist, and in all cases there were family ties between the royal family and the courts of Greece and Russia. Not until the outbreak of the First World War in 1914 did the Danish Red Cross engage in major relief work abroad.

From 1886 the society received a small contribution from the government, but the major part of the funding was still membership fees, philanthropic gifts, and voluntary work aimed at supplementing the Danish army. The society was still tightly controlled by the executive committee, which in this period made no attempt to consult the general assembly, nor did it consider trying to transform the Danish Red Cross into a popular movement. On the contrary, during the first 20 years of its history, even though the society had difficulty building its membership and getting donations, it still firmly believed that private initiative and charity were the key to dealing with the sick and wounded in the battlefields.'[3]

To expand the capacity of the society to organize field hospitals, the executive committee decided, in 1899, to introduce "Ladies' Circles," which had been a success for Red Cross societies in other countries. The executive committee used its connections with the best circles in Copenhagen, and a Copenhagen Ladies' Circle was founded. In 1900 the executive committee asked Crown Princess Louise to become the patroness of the Ladies' Circles. She accepted and asked prominent ladies all over the country who numbered among her friends to organize such circles. (These women were drawn primarily from the nobility.) Two years later, some 5,000 ladies recruited from the upper class were busy collecting donations and organizing field hospitals.

Another task of the Red Cross was the training of nurses and first aid volunteers to work in war zones. However, in the years before the First World War, the board, beginning in 1910, tied the need for training in first aid to the issue of workplace safety, which at this time was a growing problem in the major industrial plants in Copenhagen. As a result of this strategy, many young workers were recruited as

---

3   Barbara Zalewski: Hattedamer-Dameafdeiingernes Historie 1899–1948. DRK's ugebrev
    1991.

177

first aid volunteers, but they never came to join the organization as members. Concerns over worker safety caused the trade union movement to establish its own organization to provide first aid training for the workplace. In 1912, with a view to the threat of war, the Trade Union First Aid Organization joined the Red Cross and got a representative on the executive committee. When the war broke out in 1914, Denmark did not become involved. Although the first aid volunteers were not members of the Danish Red Cross, they had organized themselves informally and now wanted to have a say in the decisions of the society. Nevertheless, the issues that concerned them had to do with uniforms, stretchers, and badges, rather than with the policies pursued by the executive committee.

1917–1976: From Military Support to Voluntary Relief

By 1917 it was clear that Denmark would not get involved in the war. The growing pressure from the first aid volunteers resulted in a reorganization of the society. At this point the society consisted of three parts: the society, with some 400 members, the Ladies' Circles, with some 4,000 members, and the first aid volunteers, with some 2,000 members.

The military establishment, which had totally dominated the central committee until 1917, now completely withdrew. At a meeting of the central committee in 1919, it was decided that because the army was now apparently very reluctant to make a contract with the Red Cross for support, maybe, "instead of servicing the army as an appendix, the Red Cross should change to become a voluntary relief organization primarily concerned with civilian tasks."[4]

Although the organization of the society until 1917 had formally included a general assembly, this body had never exercised its formal influence: The executive committee had been in total control. Now the general assembly passed a new constitution that gave the society a federated structure with local branches. According to the new constitution, a central committee would be elected by delegates from the local branches. The central committee appointed an executive committee, and a university professor from the University of Copenhagen was elected as the new president. The executive committee consisted of medical doctors and other prominent citizens. This executive committee, for all practical purposes, took control of the organization. Therefore, although there was a change of formal structure in 1917, the control of the organization was still in the hands of a small group of people at the executive level. Even so, the federated structure – the outcome of the reorganization in 1917 – became a major source of change in the society.

---

4   Minutes from the central committee meeting, 1919.

Because the majority of the members belonged to Ladies' Circles throughout the country, it would have been an obvious move to take these as the starting point for establishing local branches. However, Louise (who had become Queen of Denmark) insisted that she alone, as had been the case since 1900, was to appoint the presidents of the local Ladies' Circles. She also insisted that the Ladies' Circles could not be part of the local branches. Consequently, it became very difficult to establish local branches, partly because of local rivalry and partly because the ladies with the time and resources needed for the task had already been recruited to the circles. It took some 10 years until the society had national coverage with its local branches. Until the Ladies' Circles disappeared in 1948 with the death of Louise, you could still find a local branch and a Ladies' Circle in the same town, although in the 1930s and the 1940s, some of the Ladies' Circles did merge with local branches, in spite of the queen's dictate.

In 1919 the League of Red Cross and Red Crescent Societies was established, and the Danish Red Cross became a member. As a consequence, the name was changed from the Red Cross to the Danish Red Cross.

From an organization originally intended to support the Danish army, the Red Cross became primarily involved after the First World War in helping prisoners of war. It established offices in St. Petersburg, Berlin, Vienna, and Paris. This was its first major international effort, but the effort ended in 1920. From 1920 until the outbreak of the Second World War, its international involvement virtually disappeared. In stead, the efforts of the DRC were concentrated in Denmark, and the tasks engaged in were related to the furthering of health and the prevention of illness and need, in accordance with the league's charter.

In the period from 1920 to 1940, the local branches became very important in the organization. Local initiatives flourished, and the DRC became dependent on its local branches for its activities. The fate of the organization depended on local initiative. The tasks undertaken by the organization during this period can be described as supporting and supplementing the welfare state; these included care and assistance to young mothers, infants, and those in old folks' homes, as well as blood donor services, sanatoriums, first aid training, and so on.

During the Second World War, Denmark was occupied by Germany from 1940 to 1945. During the war and in the years afterward (1939–1951), the activities of the DRC were concentrated on tasks related to the war-relief assistance to Danish prisoners in German concentration camps and to families particularly affected by the war. Following the war, the DRC established and administered some 1,000 war refugee camps and provided assistance to Holland, Belgium, and France. This was done primarily through donations from the government.

The DRC continued its work in international relief and disaster operations throughout the period from 1952 to 1976, for example, providing assistance to victims and cities affected by flooding in the Netherlands in 1956. The financing of these operations came from donations and gifts, as well as funds collected by the local branches through activities such as organizing lotteries. At the same time, the branches continued to develop their local activities as well, organizing first aid guards at local sporting events, providing safety equipment at beaches, and so on. Even so, the activity level of the Danish Red Cross, in the period from 1952 to 1976, was far below that following the Second World War (1945–1951). Also, the number of members dropped dramatically: In 1948, there were 160,000 members; in 1976, the figure was 80,000.

1976–1992: Accommodating the Professionals: Development Aid and Refugee Services

In 1976 a series of meetings of the central committee of the DRC were held to find ways of expanding and revitalizing the organization. The committee decided to professionalize and internationalize the organization; its decision was confirmed by the general assembly in 1978. Two years later, a new secretary general was hired – a civil servant from the Ministry of Foreign Affairs, with a network of contacts in the public sector, international development agencies, and Third World countries. The organization thus shifted from a primarily volunteer-run to a professionally run operation, and with the change came greater access to resources.

Meanwhile, the branches still maintained their local activities, though the activities had changed from previous periods: The welfare state was now well developed; local municipalities had assumed many of the social responsibilities that the local Red Cross branches had previously tried to shoulder. The consequence for the organization was that new members became more difficult to attract.

The society as a whole came to be characterized by growing internationalism. The Danish International Development Agency (DANIDA), which is part of the Ministry of Foreign Affairs, began to look for non-governmental organizations (NGOS) through which to channel the increasing public commitment to disaster relief and development work in the Third World.

Around this time, other NGOs became professionalized as well. The NGOs recruited from the same group of professionals as DANIDA, held regular meetings, and kept in close contact with their colleagues at DANIDA. A number of Danish NGOs became involved in government funded relief and development work in the Third World. The DRC figured prominently among them. Normally, 10% of the project funding is provided by the NGO, and the remaining 90% comes from DANIDA. The government agencies involved required accurate accounting standards and budgeting procedures: During the late 1980s, government consultants conducted studies of the organizational setups of the NGOs to make sure that these organizations were accountable.

The DRC became involved in other types of international relief efforts as well. In 1984 the Ministry of Justice subcontracted with the DRC to establish and run camps for political refugees seeking asylum in Denmark. These developments changed the DRC dramatically. In 1980 the DRC employed 50 persons and had an annual operational budget of some 50 million Danish Kroner (DKK). In 1991 the staff at the head office numbered 150, there were 100 delegates abroad, and 500 people were employed at the refugee centers (a 15-fold growth in personnel). The operational budget in 1991 was 500 million DKK, 10 times that of 1980.

Around 1990 the organization was split between its volunteer part (which now numbered some 75,000 members) and its professional part. The branches operated as self-contained units and were only loosely coupled to the head office, and the refugee operations were decoupled from the rest of the organization. The volunteer part of the Danish Red Cross consisting of 17 regional and 250 local branches-performed activities such as first aid training and visitors' service for elderly, disabled, and lonely people, and for prisoners. Its first aid groups provided services at local sporting events, concerts, and so on. Sewing and needlework groups' made baby and children's clothes for Third World countries. Funds for international disaster and relief operations were generated at the local level through the sale of secondhand clothing and through local fund-raising. But only 8% of the operating budget of the organization was now generated locally. The rest of the operating budget was generated by the DRC professional operations. At the head office, the professional part of the DRC worked with international disaster and aid programs primarily directed toward the Third World. This operation involved a professional staff and was financed primarily through governmental funding; 42% of the DRC's operational budget stemmed from support of these activities. The administration of the refugee programs was financed entirely through a subcontracting arrangement with the Ministry of Justice; this activity generated 50% of the DRC's operating budget.

These different parts were tied together by the formal structure of the organization; this structure had remained unchanged since the reorganization in 1917. The general assembly, composed of delegates from local and regional branches, met biannually and was responsible for electing the regular members of the central committee. The central committee in turn was responsible for electing the executive committee, the president, and the three vice presidents. Although appointed formally by the central committee, another group of individuals who were special members of the committee, called "the King's elect," were chosen by the president and the secretary general. The phrase *the Kings elect* reflects the history of the organization. In practical terms, people who were believed to have special knowledge useful to the central committee were asked to join it.

The executive committee was in control of decision making, a reality that was very much consistent with the history and traditions of the organization. Nevertheless, the secretary general, the president, and the professional staff felt that the elected decision makers were not qualified to deal with the increasingly complicated issues involved in aid and disaster operations. They held the opinion that a more professionalized decision structure was needed.

The idea of modernizing the decision structure had been advocated by the professional staff, and especially by the secretary general during the expansion in the 1980s. In 1986 the general assembly decided to appoint a committee to suggest a new structure for the organization. However, the suggestion offered by the committee was rejected at the assembly meeting in 1988. At the next general assembly, in 1990, the president threatened to resign if a new structure was not devised, and the general assembly decided to ask for an independent analysis by outside consultants. The analysis would address the overall, federated structure of the organization and the quality of decision making at the executive level.

The consultants submitted their report in October of 1991. They did not recommend a single model but suggested that the organization discuss three alternative models. Model one suggested completely separating the voluntary organization from the professional organization, whereas models two and three involved modifications of the existing structure. All three models, however, suggested that the governing structure should be simplified.

In October 1992, after a year during which the report was discussed widely throughout the organization, the general assembly decided to make the changes suggested by the consultants and chose to maintain a simplified democratic structure of the organization (i.e., to not separate the volunteer organization from the professional organization). The biannual general assembly was replaced with an annual council consisting of the chairs of the branch and regional offices.

In April 1993 the newly formulated council met for the first time. It has been given responsibility for electing a slimmed down central committee. now consisting of the president, the vice president for international affairs, the vice president for national affairs, and 12 other members.

Analysis: The Origin of the Danish Red Cross

It took 12 years from the signing of the first Geneva Treaty in 1864 before the Danish Red Cross society was created in 1876. How can we understand the obvious delay in its founding? Why did Denmark sign the Geneva Treaty and commit itself to establish a local society if it was so very reluctant to implement that decision? And why was the DRC eventually founded anyway?

The Symbolic Nature of Environments

In their analysis of the founding of the American community colleges, Brint and Karabel (1991) identify organizational elites ready to take on the creation of a new organization, in order to further their own interests, as well as those that the new organization is overtly designed to serve. The claim is that " . . . the determination of organizational interests can be read with a high degree of probability out of the power structure and opportunity fields faced by new organizations trying to become established" (Brint & Karabel, p. 346). In the case of the Danish Red Cross, powerful interests such as the Danish government and the military establishment were trying to prevent the creation of the organization. As we shall discuss below, there were citizens who wanted Denmark to have a Red Cross Committee. However, the interests of many such citizens in there being a DRC Committee had to do with the symbols involved rather than the substance of such an organization.

It should be kept in mind during the following discussion that Denmark's first democratic constitution came into being in 1849 (only 15 years before the signing of the Geneva Treaty). To understand the process of the founding of the Danish Red Cross, we will look at three levels of analysis: individuals, organizations, and institutions. The founding of the DRC was a highly symbolic event. In important ways it reflected the shaping of a modern, civilized, and democratic society (Friedland & Alford, 1991; Meyer et al., 1987).

In particular, we need to address the question of why the Red Cross Committee was established when it was (in 1876), and why it was established at all, and we need to look at the role of the military and the bourgeoisie in this process. The answer to the question of why the committee was founded at all comes in two parts. First, we need to understand the forces that created the Red Cross Committee, and, second, we need to understand why the military establishment took control of the organization once it was established – and why it was able to do this successfully.

Although the Red Cross may have been full of positive symbolism to those interested in democracy, to the military establishment (and perhaps the ruling class from which the military elite came), it was heavy with foreboding symbolism. In the year that Denmark signed the agreement supporting the founding of the Red Cross, the army lost the war, and Denmark lost part of its territory to Prussia. In consequence, efforts to make good on the promise of Geneva faced a stalemate in the years that followed. The army was especially sensitive to the criticism implied in establishing a Red Cross Committee to care for those injured or made sick by war. Furthermore, the Danish government had questioned the impartiality of the delegates ever since its experience with Red Cross delegates during the Danish-Prussian War. The military establishment had its reservations as well. Would the creation of an organization to cater to the sick and wounded during wartime not question the ability of the military forces to do its job? Establishing a Red Cross

Committee in Denmark to take care of the sick and wounded on the battlefields would bring up the issue of the military. After 1864 the issue of the military had become a political issue in parliament as well. where the up-and-coming Farmers' party tried to use it in a power play with the ruling conservative party.

Nevertheless, the pressure from 1864 to 1876 from the Red Cross Committee in Geneva made the difference-the Danish government gave up its resistance. As we will see further in the next section, the symbolism contained within the social construction of this organization facilitated the enactment of the DRC by its environment. The logic behind the government's giving in to international pressure bad to do with Denmark's quest for international recognition and legitimacy, and a need to demonstrate that Denmark was a modern civilized nation. The structuration of civilization was an ongoing process in Europe at this time, and it resembles what Scott (1987, p. 504) terms "acquisition at the organizational level." Powerful interests in the Danish society and in government chose to "acquire" the Red Cross Committee as a building block to be used in the construction of a civilized nation.

The audiences of this acquisition were other civilized countries, with whom Denmark would like to be compared, as well as the Danish public themselves. Although highly symbolic, the signing of the treaty was an important act. At the founding of the society in 1876, it was argued that "the most important thing is to establish an organization.... it does not look good if our country is the only one among civilized nations that is not part of this movement" (Zalewski, 1992, p. 21). Thus, it was not so much interests in founding such an organization that caused it to come about, but rather it was the environment that pushed (dramatized) the organization within Denmark.

The Dramatization of the Danish Red Cross

It was in 1874, with the visit of Hans Suenson from Copenhagen to Geneva, that the pressure on Denmark began to increase. Suenson learned from Gustave Moynier, the president of the Geneva Red Cross Committee, that Denmark had not replied to the numerous appeals from Geneva, and he started writing about this in Danish newspapers, thus creating pressure to establish a local organization. He succeeded in getting a group of people – primarily officers and medical doctors – to send an invitation to a group of people from all classes of society (among whom were several from the provinces who were in the capital as members of parliament) to discuss establishing a local Red Cross Committee affiliated with the international organization (Zalewski, 1992, p. 12). Thus, pressure from the outside brought about the Danish Red Cross through a process of dramatization-or in Scott's

(1994b, p. 208) terms, there are "multiple ways in which environments operate to enact [to socially construct] organizations."

The organizational structure chosen for the "Society for the improvement of the Conditions for the Sick and Wounded during, War" was that of a voluntary association, with a democratic structure, based upon open membership and the secret election of leadership.

Following the first democratic constitution in Denmark, in 1849, voluntary associations became institutionalized as an organizational form in such disparate fields as political parties, farmers' cooperatives (dairies, slaughter houses, stores), folk high schools, savings banks, and trade unions. The pressure toward structural isomorphism can clearly be seen at the societal level in this period (see DiMaggio & Powell, 1983; Meyer & Rowan, 1977). We suggest that voluntary associations can be understood as symbolic manifestations of the larger project of constituting the individual as an abstract legal entity with rights to assemble and to vote (which was also going on at this time) (Boli, 1987; Friedland & Alford, 1991, p. 240; Thomas & Meyer, 1984). "The wider setting contains prescriptions regarding types of organizational actors that are socially possible and how they conceivably can be structured. Collectivities are thus as much the embodiment of the prescriptions available for constructing cultural forms as they are the aggregation of lower-level units and interests" (Meyer et al., 1987, p. 19).

Voluntary associations were an organizational form that carried important messages of a Political, economic, and cultural nature. They became a symbol of the newly won democratic rights (Gundelach, 1988, p. 94).

Loose Coupling of the Governance System and the Organizational Form

The governance system of the society, however, was far from the democratic structure of its organizational form (that of a voluntary association with free membership and popular control). The governance system resembled that of elite associations, which had been the dominant organizational form prior to the democratic constitution of 1849.

On a formal level, the organization of the DRC was open and was controlled by leaders elected by the members. In fact, an elite composed of prominent citizens took full control of the organization They constituted the governing body, which was headed by the former Minister of War. General C.A.F. Thomsen.

Also, decisions were made and steps were taken by the governing body without consultation with the rank-and-file members. Although, officially membership was open, comparatively high membership fees prevented the ordinary citizen from joining.

Loose coupling between governance systems and organizational forms is repeatedly found in studies of organizations (e.g., March & Olsen, 1976, Orton & Weick, 1990; Weick, 1979). One of the basic assertions in new institutionalize is that formal structures "must be taken for granted as legitimate, apart from evaluations on their impact on work outcomes" (Meyer & Rowan, 1977, p. 344). Organizational forms are important for demonstrating legitimacy, not only to the environment but also to participants, who may sometimes value the procedures themselves more highly than the results they generate, as in the case of a free school committed to direct democracy (one person, one vote). In this school, decision makers strongly supported the organizational form, although they were dissatisfied with the results generated by this organization form (Christensen, 1976).

Sediments

As we have pointed out, the DRC at its founding imported competing values and normative structures. On one hand, the organization was structured on the basis of the ideals of representative democracy. The charter of the organization and the very nature of this civilizing project reflected democratic values and humanitarianism. On the other, its actual governance was based on an elitist model of autocracy and on military principles of discipline, loyalty, authority, and control. To a large extent, these seemingly antagonistic ideals and structures present at its founding became organizational components that were integrated into the organization. Despite the many institutional waves flooding the DRC over the following decades, these components or sediments that were introduced early on are still significant forces in the organization, even 125 years later.

This is in line with Stinchcombe's (1965) classic paper on founding processes, which suggests that the basic features of organizations vary systematically by the time of the organization's founding and remain fairly constant over time.

The Transformation of the Organization

It has been argued that institutional theory tends to defocalize interests and agency in the analysis of organizational transformations (DiMaggio,, 1988; DiMaggio & Powell, 1991). As we noted above, Brint and Karabel (1991) claim similarly that institutional theory is more applicable to the study of organizational form and function than to the study of organizational origin and transformation. These authors take a utilitarian position on interests and argue that actors pursue some form of primordial interests. In the case of the transformation of the American community colleges, an organizational elite is seen to take advantage of the environment to further their own interests as well as those of their organizations (Brint & Karabel, p. 345).

If, as in our analysis, we understand the interests of actors as institutionally defined and shaped (Friedland & Alford, 1991, p. 245), we would want to demonstrate the collective and cultural character of the development of a rationalized environment (Meyer, 1994). This position leads us to also question the concept of organizational goals so prominent in studies of organizations and change. Rather than postulating the importance of goals (e.g., Powell & Friedkin, 1987), we see the organization as a "recipient" of the evolving set of patterns, models, and cultural schemes of its rationalized environment (Meyer & Scott, 1983).

Viewing the organization as a recipient or an empty vessel is similar to the view of decisions as choice opportunities, as put forth in the garbage can model of decision making in organized anarchies (Cohen, March, & Olsen, 1972). In organized anarchies, preferences are seen as inconsistent and ill defined, technologies are unclear, and participation is fluid. In organized anarchies, a choice situation becomes a "meeting place for issues and feelings looking for decision situations in which they may be aired, solutions looking for issues to which they may be an answer, and participants looking for problems or pleasure" (Cohen, March. & Olsen, 1976, p. 25).

In studying the transformation of an organization over a long period of time, as in our case study of the DRC over a period of 125 years, the conditions surrounding an organization are seen as similar to those of an organized anarchy. In important ways, the DRC reflects the development of the Danish nation-state. We want to understand the resilience of this organization, and what allowed it to survive in the face of great changes and challenges. We suggest that the DRC is truly an institutionalized organization, in the sense that keeping old forms and even old names has allowed the organization to survive. We believe that what has happened in this organization is a reflection of changing conditions in the wider society.

We will use a modified version of the garbage can model to understand the transformation of the DRC. In our version, the organization is an opportunity structure that connects problems, solutions, and participants over time. In organized anarchies, the meaning of choice changes over time as a reflection of the participants, problems, and solutions that are connected to the choice opportunity. In our analysis of the DRC, the nature of the organization changes as a reflection of the streams of participants, problems, and solutions that are connected with the organization over time.

The Empty Vessel Model

The view of the organization (or the opportunity structure) as an empty vessel suggests that it is open to all available participants, problems, and solutions. In principle, there are no restrictions on access to the organization as long as participants, problems, or solutions are conceived as legitimate for this type of

187

humanitarian, nonprofit organization. With this broad definition, we see the structure as unsegmented, with respect to both participation and access of problems and solutions (Cohen et al., 1972).

Participants join an organization for different reasons. Their motivation to participate is a reflection of the interests that they bring to the organization. These interests are, as we noted earlier, created and shaped by the institutional environment and may be either symbolic or material. Such individuals may be looking for work or for a professional career, or for the status attached to a leadership position in the organization. They may join for ideal (humanitarian) reasons, or to further particular (material) interests.

Problems are, like the roles and interests of participants. created and shaped in the institutional environment. We see the DRC as a major, although not the only, recent recipient for a number of humanitarian problems that have arisen in Danish society over the years. These problems may be defined in the organization itself (e.g., when the DRC took the initiative of supplementing welfare in the 1930s), or they may be defined in the environment (e.g., in 1984, when the government decided to ask the DRC to establish and handle the camps for political refugees seeking asylum in Denmark). Solutions may be generated in the organization (e.g., when the professional staff wanted to expand from relief and disaster work to development work in Third World countries in the 1980s) or in the environment (e.g., the decision in the 1980s by the government to increase the NGOs' share of the Danish international development budget).

Participants

In 1899 the Executive Committee of the DRC decided to introduce Ladies' Circles to expand the capacity of the organization with respect to organizing field hospitals. This had been done successfully in Red Cross Societies in other countries and is a very early case of international diffusion of models, as discussed by Meyer (1994).

The military bourgeoisie domination of the DRC ended in 1917, when this group withdrew from the organization. Their attempts to protect military interests from civilian intervention were no longer relevant, and the protection of the old institution of autocratic rule was no longer possible. Denmark had come out of the First World War without having been involved, and the old autocratic rule was, from an institutional perspective, outdated. The bourgeoisie were vanishing or finding themselves supporting the democratic movement in society. The process of industrialization had changed the class structure and had given rise to trade unions, the social democratic party, and the liberal Farmers' party. After 1917 the new governing elite of the DRC reflected the modern class structure, and recruitment to the governing elite was based on academic standing rather than social class. We

188

do not mean to suggest, of course, that these are not to some degree correlated. The leadership of the organization was and still is mostly composed of doctors and lawyers.

In 1917 the structure was changed from a unitary to a federated structure, and this made room for new members and new local elites. In the local branches, the governing bodies were recruited from the middle class. Both liberal and conservative individuals joined the DRC through their local social networks. This recruitment pattern is still dominant in the organization. In general, all members take pride in the international work of the DRC while at the same time focusing on local activities. The same type of people can be found in other humanitarian organizations like the Lion's Club, or even the Rotary Club.

The professional employees have, for good reasons, a somewhat shorter history in the DRC. They entered the organization at the time when the DRC expanded as a consequence of the growing Danish commitment to international development aid. Today they constitute a specialized category of NGO professionals. Their careers normally involve working in different NGOs in Denmark, as well as in Third World countries. Their focus is primarily international and professional, with only a little respect for the rank-and-file members of the DRC, and they pay little attention to the work performed at the local level of the organization.

The member base of the organization has changed over time. In general, the issues at hand have had a different appeal to the population at different times. In 1948 there were 160,000 members; in 1976 the figure was only half of that. The difference between the rulers and the ruled that we observed at the founding of the organization is a pattern that not only continued after 1917 but also exists today. In general, members are recruited from the lower classes and are not at all active in the leadership of the organization. Members have different motivations for joining the organization, which vary over time and by social class.

As we have seen, participants have different motives for joining the organization; these include status, work, and professional careers. The number of participants changes with changing conditions in society. The number and composition of participants in the organization have changed over time and across categories. Each of the groups has a profile of interests, which has formed the basis for the involvement in the organization. These institutionalized interests are then applied, transformed, and developed, even as they are employed in the everyday activities of the organization.

Problems and Solutions

It is difficult to separate problems from solutions, but we argue that the changing tasks of the DRC are a reflection of problems and solutions generated in the institutionalized environment, national as well as international, and in the organization itself.

The main point of this analysis is to understand how problems and solutions are generated in the wider environment, thus reflecting the development of society. With the broad humanitarian charter of the DRC, the organization functions as a recipient of a diverse pool of problems and solutions arising in society over time. The following list shows the diversity of tasks taken up by the DRC and suggests how new tasks are added to the list, rather than replacing previous activities:

1876–1917	Support of the army's sanitary corp
1920–1940	Support of welfare development at the local (branch) level
1940–1950	Aid to prisoners of war and war refugees
1950–	International disaster and relief operations
1980–	International development aid to Third World countries
1984–	Refugee centers for political refugees seeking asylum

The basic argument here is that macro-sociological processes occurring in society affect the development of problems and solutions that have become defined as relevant tasks for nonprofit organizations such as the DRC. This is a reflection of the development of the nation-state, of citizens, and of professions.

As we have demonstrated in this analysis, the DRC has been a recipient of developments in the wider environment, leading to a continuous evolution of both the activities carried out and the organization's identity. This organization has changed from having a primary goal of supporting the army to being a humanitarian organization with national as well as international activities. Since the early 1980s, part of the organization has become highly professionalized. However, the formal structure of the organization has not changed, and we have argued that the democratic structure has been a carrier of important values, such as democracy, values which were important to the members and, during the past decade, important to the government as well. Popular control, as it is formalized in the democratic structure, has legitimized the use of the DRC and other NGOs to channel still larger public funds to developing countries.

Loose Coupling

Beginning with the founding of the DRC, we observe that governance was decoupled from the formal democratic structure. The organization has always been dominated by an elite. This pattern has persisted throughout the history of the organization and has also been replicated in the local branches. We also observe a decoupling between structure and activities.

We observe, like Zald and Denton (1963), that the federated structure, occurring through the loose coupling (Orton & Weick, 1990) of the local branches from each other and from the head office, has made room for organizational development through local adaptation, and thus the federated structure is important in explaining the resilience of the organization.

Sediments

Organizations are meaning systems that develop normative rules to define values and activity scripts that are important mechanisms for producing stability (Scott, 1994a). The humanitarian values of the DRC provide a strong basis for organizational resilience. Many of the problems in society (welfare, aid, disasters, refugees, etc.) have been channeled into the organization.

However, we also observe that the discipline and loyalty dominant in the early years of the organization, when the military was in control, still dominate the organization. The authority structure-with officers in command and private soldiers performing the work-is now translated into an elite governing the organization at central and local levels, and the rank-and-file members doing the everyday work. The activity scripts have also been influenced by the early years of military support. The technology of sanitary work developed in military situations was later applied to disaster operations in civilian settings. Early tasks, such as preparing sanitary depots, were transformed into others, such as knitting and other types of handicraft manufacturing in the local branches. The training of first aid volunteers and nurses to assist at the battlefields has likewise evolved. Nurses were used to assist young mothers and the poor in the early years of the welfare state (1920–1940), and the first aid volunteers are now attending sport events, outdoor concerts, and the like. The work with refugees after the Second World War is now being continued in the camps providing asylum for political refugees. Such phenomena are also observed by March and Olsen (1994): "Institutional routines seem to endure far beyond the historical settings in which the developed as plausible responses and after it is forgotten what made them meaningful."

Adaptation

Metaphorically speaking, we have suggested understanding the organization as an empty vessel that was and still is dramatized (or "filled") by the environment. Participants, problems, and solutions have dramatized the organization and the tasks of the DRC; they reflect the interests that have developed in society at different times. These processes are not unlike the findings of Selznick in his study of the TVA (1 949), Zald and Denton's study of the YMCA (1963), and Clark's

191

(1956) study of community colleges. All of these studies emphasize organizations adapting to changing environments. In the early years, supporting the military establishment was the primary task of the DRC; in the period from 1920 to 1950, supplementing the emerging welfare state dominated the Danish Red Cross. Beginning around 1950 the local municipalities gradually took over these welfare tasks, and the DRC adopted a more international perspective. In fact, the DRC continued supporting welfare programs, now in Third World countries rather than in Denmark, moving where the need was greatest.

From around 1980 the Danish Red Cross and similar humanitarian organizations were dramatized by the Danish International Aid Agency (a branch of the Danish Ministry of Foreign Affairs). The Danish government adopted a policy of channeling a growing amount of Danish aid to Third World countries through NGOS. A similar story could be told about the camps for political refugees seeking asylum in Denmark. With the fluctuating number of refugees coming to Denmark, the government decided to employ a private humanitarian organization to take care of this task. The choice was the DRC, whose neutrality and good public image made this choice a feasible one.

The three variables employed in this analysis-decoupling, sediments, and dramatization-help explain how the organization has developed a robustness that has made it possible to accommodate a diversity of tasks and participants-in a reflection of the development of society.

Conclusion

Because our main theoretical points have been summarized in the previous sections, we will now use these insights and discuss the more general implications for organizations in institutionalized environments.

In our analysis of the origin and transformation of the Danish Red Cross, we have stressed the macro-sociological processes in the wider society as the source of the origin and transformation of this organization The development of a modern society has created and transformed the rationalized environment. Stemming from this environment, changing institutional orders have, over time, shaped and defined not only the problems, solutions, and participants, but also the interests that have determined the evolving shape of the organization We have viewed the organization as an empty vessel or a recipient of these macro-sociological streams of change.

Organizational structure is the product of the institutional order at that point in time when the organization was founded. It is important not only for legitimating the organization in the wider environment but also as a meaning system to the participants. Although we have observed decoupling between the structure and the governance of the organization, and between structure and activities, and loose coupling between organizational units, the organizational structure has been maintained since the organization's founding. The DRC has survived and been able to adapt to rather dramatically changing conditions in the environment. As March and Olsen (1994,) have suggested: "Institutional survival depends not only on satisfying current environmental and political conditions but also on an institution's origin and history."

Although in our analysis of the Danish Red Cross we have used a version of new institutionalism rather than old institutionalism as an explanatory frame. We will now use a term of Selznick's (1949) and argue that the resilience of the organization is due to the fact that the structure and identity of the organization have been "infused with value." We want to speculate about the conditions under which organizations show such resilience. In an early formulation of new institutionalism, Meyer and Rowan (1977) argued that organizations that devise structures that conform closely to institutional requirements "maximize their legitimacy and increase their resource and survival capabilities" (p. 352). The democratic structure dramatized at the founding of the Danish Red Cross is a case in point. However, not only structure but also identity and activity scripts add to survival capabilities. In our case, the identity of the organization as a prestigious, humanitarian. nonprofit organization has appealed to shifting groups of participants. These participants have used the organization as a platform for very different activities, within the broad definition of humanitarianism, and for different purposes: status, career, prestige, work. social relationships, and so on. In the long history of the DRC, activity scripts have been sedimented in the organization and have been readily available to participants, as well as to problems and solutions. These scripts have been defined and shaped by society and by the larger cultural environment.

We have argued that the founding of the organization in 1876 was highly symbolic and came about as a dramatization by the environment. The organization came to symbolize Denmark's status both as a civilized nation and as a democracy in which the citizens could exercise their individual rights to elect their leadership. We believe that these values are important cornerstones of the resilience shown by the DRC. They have made it possible for the organization to change with the shifting and even contradicting institutional demands of the wider environment (those of both Danish society and the increasingly important international community). The more central the values are to the institutional demands faced by the organization (i.e.. democracy and humanitarianism in the case of the DRC), the greater the organization's resilience, and the broader these values are, the easier it is for them to be interpreted favorably by different participants. In Danish society, it is difficult if not impossible to be *against* democracy and humanitarianism. In the same way as the federated structure allows the organization to adapt to local environments, the broad values of democracy and humanitarianism allow for local interpretations within the same organizational form.

The main threat to the organization would be if the organizational form (democracy) and core identity (humanitarianism) were seriously questioned. In recent times, there are examples of two such threats, both of which questioned the "central (institutional) logic, i.e., a set of material practices and symbolic con-structions-which constitutes the organizing principles and which is available to organizations and individuals to elaborate" (Friedland & Alford, 1991, p. 248).

The first of these threats was the questioning of whether the organization was truly democratic. In the 1960s the development of grassroots movements led to a questioning of whether the representative democratic structure of organizations like the DRC was truly, democratic. The grassroots movements were organized on a more ad hoc activity basis and subscribed to direct forms of democracy. This did cause some problems for the DRC. The member base decreased, and it was difficult for the organization to recruit young people, in spite of the fact that a separate Young People's Red Cross division was created in 1973.

However. the endorsement of the organization by the government in the 1980s, through the increased use of the DRC (and other NGOS) as partners for govern-ment-financed development work in the Third World, renewed the DRC's legitimacy. This was especially true because the government designated the organizational form of the NGOs (the democratic structure) to be an assurance of popular control.

The other major threat questioned whether the "institutional logic" (Friedland & Alford, 1991, p. 248) of the organization should be participatory and democratic rather than bureaucratic and hierarchical. This attack was launched around 1990 by the professionals in the organization who questioned the feasibility of the democratic structure (although, as we have noted earlier, the governance of the organization is only loosely coupled to the structure), in view of the complicated and highly professionalized work with refugee camps in Denmark and the development and relief work in the Third World countries.

The resilience of an organization is increased if the organizational form conforms closely to institutional requirements, and if its governance and activities are decoupled from the structure. It is further increased if the values of the organization (its identity) are consonant with the institutional logic of the organi-zational form, but are ambiguous enough to allow for a diversity of potential resources (participant, problems, and solutions) to get connected to the organization.

References

Boli, J. (1987) "Human rights or state expansion? Cross-national definitions of constitutional rights", in G.M. Thomas, J.W. Meyer, F.O. Ramirez and J. Boli (eds.) *Institutional structure: Constituting state, society, and the individual*, pp. 133–149. Newbury Park, Calif.: Sage.

Brint, S. and Karabel, J. (1991) "Institutional origins and transformations. The case of American community colleges", in W.W. Powell and P.J. DiMaggio (eds.) *The new institutionalism in organizational analysis*, pp. 337–360. Chicago: University of Chicago Press.

Christensen, S. (1976) "Decision making and socialization", in J.G. March and J.P. Olsen (eds.) *Ambiguity and choice in organizations,* pp. 351–385. Oslo: Universitetsforlaget.

Clark, B.T. (1956) *Adult education in transition.* Berkeley: University of California Press.

Cohen, M.D., March, J.G. and Olsen, J.P. (1972) "A garbage can model of organizational choice", *Administrative Science Quarterly* 17: 1–25.

_____. (1976) "People, problems, solutions and the ambiguity of relevance", in J.G. March and J.P. Olsen (eds.) *Ambiguity and choice in organizations*, pp. 24–37. Oslo: Universitetsforlaget.

DiMaggio, P.J. (1988) "Interest and agency in institutional theory", in L.G. Zucker (ed.) *Institutional patterns and organizations: Culture and environment*, pp. 3–21. Cambridge, Mass.: Ballinger.

DiMaggio, P.J. and Powell, W.W. (1983) "The iron cage revisited. Institutional isomorphism and collective rationality in organizational fields", *American Sociological Review* 48: 147–160.

_____. (1991) "Introduction", in W.W. Powell and P.J. DiMaggio (eds.) *The new institutionalism in organizational analysis*, pp. 1–38. Chicago: The University of Chicago Press.

Friedland, R. and Alford, R.R. (1991) "Bringing society back in. Symbols, practices and institutional contradictions", in W.W. Powell and P.J. DiMaggio (eds.) *The new institutionalism in organizational analysis*, pp. 232–266. Chicago: The University of Chicago Press.

Gundelach, P. (1988) *Sociale Bevægelser og Samfundsændringer (Social movements and societal changes).* Aarhus, Denmark: Politica.

March, J.G. and Olsen, J.P. (1976) *Ambiguity and choice in organizations.* Oslo: Universitetsforlaget.

_____. (1994) "Institutional perspectives on governance", in H.-U. Derlin, U. Gerhardt and F. Scharpf (eds.) *Systemrationalität und Partial interesse: Festschrift für Renate Mayntz (Collective nationality and member interests)*, pp. 249–270. Baden-Baden: Nomos Verlagsgesellschaft.

Meyer, J.W. (1994) "Rationalized environments", in W.R. Scott and J.W. Meyer (eds.) *Institutional environments and organizations. Structural complexity and individualism*, pp. 28–54). Thousand Oaks, Calif.: Sage.

Meyer, J.W., Boli, J. and Thomas, G.M. (1987) "Ontology and rationalization in the western cultural account", in G.M. Thomas, J.W. Meyer, F.O. Ramirez and J. Boli (eds.) *Institutional structure: Constituting state, society, and the individual*, pp. 12–37. Newbury Park, Calif.: Sage.

Meyer, J.W. and Rowan, B. (1977) "Institutionalized organizations: Formal structure as myth and ceremony", *American Journal of Sociology* 87: 340–364.

Meyer, J.W. and Scott, W.R., with Rowan, B. and Deal, T.E. (1983)*Organizational environments: Ritual and rationality*. Beverly Hills, Calif.: Sage. (New edition in 1992).

Orton, J.D. and Weick, K.E. (1990) "Loosely couples systems. A reconceptualization", *Academy of Management Review* 15: 203–223.

Powell, W.W. and Friedkin, R. (1987) "Organizational change in nonprofit organizations", in W.W. Powell (ed.) *The nonprofit sector – A research Handbook*, pp. 180–194. New Haven, CT: Yale University Press.

Scott, W.R. (1987). "The adolescence of institutional theory", *Administrative Science Quarterly* 32: 493–511.

_____. (1992) *Organizations: Rational, natural, and open systems.* Englewood Cliffs, N.J: Prentice Hall. (3rd edition, original work published in 1981).

_____. (1994a) "Institutions and organizations: Toward a theoretical synthesis", in W.R. Scott and J.W. Meyer (eds.) *Institutional environments and organizations: Structural complexity and individualism* , pp. 55–80. Thousand Oaks, Calif.: Sage.

_____. (1994b) "Conceptualizing organizational fields: Linking organizations and societal systems", in H.-U. Derlin, U. Gerhardt, and F. Scharpf (eds.) *Systemrationalität und Partial interesse: Festschrift für Renate Mayntz (Collective nationality and member interests)*, pp. 203–221. Baden-Baden: Nomos Verlagsgesellschaft.

Selznick, P. (1949) *TVA and the grass roots*. Berkeley: University of California Press.

Stinchcombe, A.L. (1965) "Social structure and organizations", in J.G. March (ed.) *Handbook of organizations*, pp. 142–193. Chicago: Rand McNally.

Thomas, G.M. and Meyer, J.W. (1984) "The expansion of the state", *Annual Review of Sociology* 10: 461–482.

Weick, K.E. (1979) *The social psychology of organizing*. Reading, Mass.: Addison-Wesley. (2nd edition, original work published in 1969).

Zald, M.N. and Denton, P. (1963) "From evangelism to general service: The transformation of the YMCA", *Administrative Science Quarterly* 8: 214–234.

Zalewski, B. (1992) *The history of the Danish Red Cross*. Unpublished manuscript for a doctoral dissertation. Copenhagen Business School.

Chapter 9

Winds of Organizational Change: How Ideas Translate into Objects and Actions[1]

Barbara Czarniawska and Bernward Joerges

How does an idea – reality conceived – become materialized – reality practiced? Where and when do ideas cease to float freely in organizational thought worlds and turn into entrenched institutional patterns? In many long accepted traditions in the social sciences, from Marx to Maslow, these questions are discredited; instead, social change is pictured as emerging from some material base to some post-material superstructure. On the other hand, particularly in the history and philosophy of science, the enlightenment belief in the possibility of establishing truth and value without taking into account material circumstance, has held considerable

1 The first version of this essay was published by the Study of Power and Democracy in Sweden, Uppsala, January 1990, under the title "Organizational Change as Materialization of Ideas". We thank Eric Abrahamson, Bryan Mundell, Anders Forssell, Pasquale Gagliardi, John Meyer, Richard Rottenburg, Kerstin Sahlin-Andersson, Guje Sevón and Tony Spybey for their comments which helped us prepare the present version of the essay.

influence in the social sciences. As a consequence, an uneasy opposition has developed between "materialist" and "idealist" preconceptions.

We hope to go beyond the characteristically modernist opposition of materialism and idealism and the dichotomies which follow from it: social/technical, intentional/deterministic, subjective/objective. By presenting organizational change (the crux of organizational life), as a story of ideas which turn into actions in ever new localities, we hope to approach the question of how local action emerges and becomes institutionalized on a more global scale in a way which goes beyond received models of change. Having espoused the idea of non-antagonistic science, we refrain from a detailed critique of other theories of change. Rather we begin by charcterizing the intellectual landscape from which we come ourselves and which, we hope, is familiar to our readers. Next we present a sample of puzzling phenomena which attracted our attention but about which we failed to find an explanation within this landscape. We continue with the presentation of the roadposts which lead us beyond its borders: the notions of idea, localized and globalized time and space, and translation. Having done this we proceed in recontextualizing the phenomenon of organizational change.

Received Images of Change

The modernist dichotomies mentioned above find their reflection in two dominating images of organizational change: as a planned innovation and as an environmental adaptation. Under the first label are grouped approaches such as strategic choice, decision-making and organizational learning; under the second, contingency theory, population ecology and, certain variations of institutional theory.

Yet the image of organizational change as presented by these two schools of thought is constantly contradicted by organizational practice. Yes, we can see actors and groups learning and making conscious choices, carefully designing programs of change, but those very programs leave us (and them) with a heap of "unintended consequences" and "unexpected results" that are supposed to be disposed of in the next approach, but somehow never are. As a result of a constant critique from the environmentalists,we have received more sophisticated rational models and concepts like "bounded rationality" and "opportunism" were advanced.

There are similar problems with adaptive approaches, whether the mechanistic or organic type. Practical and political problems are involved: if everything is determined from outside, what can researchers contribute to managers' attempts to deal with practice-induced problems? Shall we recommend a Hindu-type of fatalism, or shall we try to sell what McCloskey (1990) calls the snake-oil story,that is, present ourselves as possessors of a secret that will help the chosen few to control the world? There are also serious problems concerning theoretical developments: what are the social mechanisms which are commensurate to biological mechanisms? We know (or at least we think we know) what kind of phenonmenon isomorphism is when it comes to crystals, but what exactly does its equivalent in an organization field look like? Another contentious issue is which evolutionary perspective to adopt: Lamarckian ideas of functional evolution, largely rejected in biology but still very attractive to social scientists, or some geneticist version, resorting to something as fanciful as "organizational genes"?

There is a certain comfort in the fact that the two schools criticize each other, leading to improvements and achieving a kind of balance. But this balance seems to have been static for a while now, resembling more a stalemate than anything else. We are not the first to seek a way out from this stalemate: it is enough to mention the enormously impressive and, at the time of its emergence, revolutionary "garbage-can model" (Cohen and March, 1974; March and Olsen, 1976; March, 1988) which moved in the direction of accepting both contingency and control as elements shaping the process of change. In this sense our attempt is close to the garbage-can, but we differ in at least two respects from this perspective.

The first difference is that we do not go along with the model's behaviorist distance towards the actors involved, the distance which results in largely disregarding their intentions and attempts to make sense. We hasten to add that such readings of others' texts are, of course, very risky. In fact, Cohen and March's (1974) recommendations on how to influence a garbage-can decision-making process seem to suggest that the authors give priority to intentional action – even in the face of randomness. However, the fact that intentions fail does not prove that they are irrelevant for understanding the outcomes. Thus our stance is one at the same level as organizational actors: we sit inside, or in any event within listening range to the garbage-can, in order to follow how the actors try to put together ideas and actions that come to them, in their never ending activity of sense-making.

This leads to the second difference. Garbage-can and related theories, even when they allow for reflexivity, still aim at establishing a meta-level explanatory discourse, not readily accessible for the actors studied. They know better – –and different.

We begin with listening to the actors, not because they know best, but because they know:

> [It is] a mistake to think of somebody's own account of his behavior or culture as epistemically privileged. He might have a good account of what he's doing or he might not. But it is not a mistake to think of it as morally privileged. We have a duty to listen to his account, not because he has privileged access to his own motives but because he is a human being like ourselves (Rorty, 1982, p. 202).

Rorty continues by saying that social scientists should act as interpreters – in order to facilitate a conversation between groups who do not have the same language. Thus, if we seem to know more than a specific actor does, it is not because we are omniscient, but because we have had the chance to look at many garbage-cans, have had the leisure to see them in a sequence, and to produce serialized accounts of what we saw. If we see things in a different light than actors do, it is because our *Sitz-im-Leben* is different. Their duty is to act, ours is to reflect and interpret, although it would be silly to attempt to draw a strict line between the two, as everybody acts and (almost) everybody reflects. Nevertheless, there is a social division of labor between managers and researchers, where both sides gain from perfecting their respective specialties and then engaging in a dialogue about them.

In other words, we have no intention to tell managers what to do in the face of change or stagnation. We want to tell everybody who wants to listen a complex story of how changes come about and leave the actors to decide which conclusions to draw, fully expecting that managers might come to different conclusions than union stewards upon reading our reports. This means that we remain reserved in regard to control theories with their claim to superior usefulness, to law-like theories with their attractive elegance, and to a metalanguage with its hermetic rhetoric. The usefulness of such highly glossed accounts remains open to question, too. Organizational actors are perfectly capable of producing simplifications and stylizations – action theories – themselves. They are constantly engaged in what Luhmann (1991) calls *Entparadoxierung,* or de-paradoxifying. We owe them a different type of assistance in tackling the irreducible complexity of organizational life, one we call *systematic reflection*, as a complement to action-induced simplifications.

In this chapter, we propose to complete familiar images of organizational change – as a series of planned moves from one state to another or as a continuum of reactive adaptations – with the image of materialization of ideas. This process (which might, but does not have to, become incorporated in some agent's attempt to achieve control) can be observed when, out of the myriads of ideas floating in the translocal organizational thought-worlds, certain ideas catch on and are subsequently translated into substance in a given organization, often barely touching the bureaucratic apparatus of planned change. More likely than not, it is the same ideas which materialize in similar organizations around the same time, indicating that mechanisms are at work which are best seen as something akin to fashion. This process is explored from a constructionist perspective, drawing in equal measure on narrative and scientific knowledge in organization theory and research (on the distinction between the two, see Lyotard, 1979, Bruner, 1986).

An Idea whose Time has Come

What made us interested in alternative conceptualizations of change? A phenomenon which can be called "travels of ideas". It has been repeatedly observed, for example, that many organizations introduce the same changes at about the same time (Zucker, 1977; March and Olsen, 1983; Forsell, 1989; Powell and DiMaggio, 1991). To explain this by saying that they do so hoping to gain strategic advantage is redundant: of course they do not introduce change to attract losses. But one would think that the ubiquity of a particular change would reduce its competitive value for a given organization and stimulate the search for unique novel solutions. Conventionality seems to have a competitive value of its own.

Why just this change and not any other? Why do ideas that have been with us for decades, if not for centuries, as not more than figments of vivid imagination, all of a sudden materialize in organizational action? Why do leaders come upon and implement certain ideas at a given time? Why is the environment seen as changing in a given way? Why didn't they implement what they had decided? Where did the "unintended consequences" come from? Traditional images of organizational change stop short of these questions, which we intend to take up by scrutinizing the inclusive, ongoing process of materialization of ideas, whereby ideas are turned into objects and actions and again into other ideas.

Before we start our inquiry, we shall introduce a series of examples of puzzling organizational changes to illustrate the issue.

Public Administration Reforms

In 1977, the local authorities in one Swedish municipality decided to decentralize their political decision-making and to do it in the form of Sub-Municipal Committees (Czarniawska-Joerges, 1988). Two other municipalities followed their example and in 1979 the Swedish Parliament introduced a Local Bodies Act, permitting and encouraging municipalities to experiment with various forms of local democracy. Sub-Municipal Committees (SMCs) were the most popular form and the original experimenters soon served as consultants to those who wanted to exploit their experience. In many such cases the potential followers, when asked why they wanted to introduce the reform, looked perplexed and answered: "Doesn't everybody?" As it turned out, this was not the case. Furthermore, when the Minister of Civil Affairs, who was enthusiastic about the changes and did much to propagate them, proposed a bill introducing the reform for all municipalities, Parliament said "no". By 1988, 25 municipalities had introduced SMCs, 65 rejected the proposal, 3 withdrew from change which was already well advanced, 26 were still experimenting, while 166 did not reveal any interest in the reform (Johansson 1988). The wave came, affected some places, and departed from others without leaving much of a trace.

However, this is only one possible version of the course of events (ours). When asked, the actors involved presented many other interpretations. One was that the whole process had been started already in the 1940s and was simply continuing, searching for optimal forms of local democracy – SMCs was just the most recent

201

form. Proponents of another version claimed that the reform was a reaction to defects in local democracy as a result of previous, administrative-type reforms (where the changes were ordered from above) which merged small municipalities into large administrative and political units. Still another attributed the reform to initiatives from a given party (there were at least three possible candidates). Yet another version would have it that the first municipality thrives on attracting attention and therefore always leads all possible experiments, which are then followed by other, like-minded opportunists. There were also suggestions that the whole idea came from the central government, and more specifically from the Ministry of Civil Affairs, whose Minister, ironically nicknamed "the Knight of Light", wanted to make it his contribution to posterity.

The only thing those interpretations had in common was that they all mentioned some *mechanism for idea spreading*: political response to societal need, imitation, subordination, fashion-following, or sometimes all of them together. In fact, when all such mechanisms seem to operate in the same direction, the interpretations can be combined. But who is right if some contradict others?

Beckman (1987) studied another public sector reform: introducing Research and Development units and other organizations at the regional level, with the aim of improving regional co-operation between research and higher education institutions on the one hand, and business companies on the other. The author suggested an interpretation according to which the new units were a result of a conscious central policy, based on a specific perception of the present situation (increased co-operation between the public and private sectors as one solution for a potential unemployment problem); a policy which followed a fashionable theory of regional industrial development (innovation and product cycle theory) and imitated international solutions.

The regional actors, however, did not see the developments as steered by central government. In their opinion, solutions emerged as a result of an organic, down-to-earth, anarchic and unstructured decision process. Beckman agreed that both processes took place and explained the difference in perceptions by the fact that what he called "value control" was not perceived as control. Administrative orders and check-ups are perceived as control, but not information spreading, idea-suggestions and persuasion.

We agree with Beckman that turning ideas into substance might take the form of a planned change. As it is now, however, organization studies tell us much more about planned change or "forced learning", and much less about materialization of ideas in general, or about unplanned change in particular. This might be interpreted as evidence that "ideas turning into substance" is a relatively recent way in which organizations change. More likely, though, it is because organization theory has never paid much attention to such mechanisms. Let us look at some other instances.

Development Projects and Technology Transfer

Speaking of turning ideas into substance inevitably brings technology issues to mind. Development projects and technology transfers to developing countries present particularly intricate cases of idea materialization (Joerges 1976). Ideas are turned into things, then things into ideas again, transferred from their time and place of origin and materialized again elsewhere. How does it happen and what are the mechanisms involved? Observing development projects, Hirschman (1967) noted something he called a "pseudo-imitation" technique: a method that is used to promote projects that would normally be discriminated against as too obviously replete with difficulties and uncertainties.

> One widely practised method consists in pretending that a project is nothing but a straightforward application of a well-known technique that has been used successfully elsewhere. For example, for a number of years after World War II, any river valley development scheme, whether it concerned the Sao Francisco River in Brazil, the Papaloapan River in Mexico, the Cauca in Colombia, the Dez in Iran, or the Damodarn in eastern India, was presented to a reassured public as a true copy – if possible, certified expressly by David Lilienthal – of the Tennessee Valley Authority. Although obviously two river valley development schemes wil differ vastly more from one another than two Coca Cola bottling plants, the impression was created by the appeal of the "TVA model", that clear sailing lay ahead for the proposed schemes. To be acceptable, it seems, a project must often be billed as a pure replica of a succesful venture in an advanced country (Hirschman, 1967, p.21).

This is a case where a set of actions is already in the offing and an idea is needed to legitimately trigger it. A technology arrives, first as a nebulous idea, something that only vaguely, in some minds, related to some actions, which then lands heavily on the ground, showing its nasty side, requiring still new investments and additional commitments. Hirschman was too optimistic about Coca Cola plants: when the holy drink was first imported to Poland in the 1970s, it turned out that there was no way of securing its required temperature when served. At worst, a new technology can break down a whole social system, as Trist and Bamforth's famous study of coal-mining documented (Trist and Bamforth 1951). At best, in the course of the fitting process, the idea and the set of actions will get adjusted to each other in a new, unique combination.

One could object that in all the above cases we are speaking about simple planned changes which can be satisfactorily interpreted in terms of leaders' ingenuity and/or environmental pressure. But what usually happens is that the materialization of a technical idea starts a chain-reaction of changes which are not only unplanned, but sometimes unpredictable and undesired as well. Nevertheless, such changes tend to go further than most planned changes ever plan to go. In the 1970s, Poland invested heavily in the production of refrigerators which, in light of the fact that its neighbors produced many such appliances cheaply, was not a clever move. Ensuing adaptive changes in other spheres of production, in imports and exports, distribution mechanisms and labor markets have continued until the present day (even though recently they have taken the form of winding-up operations).

Planned changes are often sets of ideas which never materialize; whereas materialized ideas go down like avalanches, rolling over almost all resistance, especially if they acquire the form of complicated machinery. But where do they come from? Where will they go? How can we follow them – with what metaphors – or vehicles?

Vehicles/Metaphors
On Ideas

Before we move any further, we will commit an act of reductionism and decide, for the purpose of this essay, how to conceive of "an idea".

Mitchell (1986), who faced a similar predicament, went back in etymology and observed that the word "idea" comes from the Greek word "to see" and is close to the noun "eidolon", central to Greek theories of physical perception. If we recall Rorty's interpretation of modern science as a mirror of nature (Rorty 1980), we will realize even more clearly how close the discourses related to mental phenomena and to physical optics are to each other. To understand is to see; to see is to understand; "the innocent eye is blind", and so on.

In agreement with Mitchell, we find it worthwhile "to give in to the temptation to see ideas as images, and to allow the recursive problem full play" (Mitchell 1986, p.5). Images can be classified, according to Mitchell, as graphic, optical, perceptual, verbal and mental. Ideas can be classified among the latter, together with dreams and memories. We admit having problems with the classification: how do we know that a mental image exists before it has taken the form of words or pictures? What is the difference between "optical" and "graphical"? Let us simplify this classification by saying that ideas are images which can take the form of pictures or sounds (words can be either one or another). They can then be materialized (turned into objects or actions) in many ways: pictures can be painted or written (like in stage-setting), sounds can be recorded or written down (like in a musical score) and so on and so forth. Their materialization causes change: unknown objects appear, known objects change their appearance, practices become transformed. This view accords with the pragmatist tradition:

> Ideas, in this [pragmatist] view, are instruments that not only can become true by doing their job in inquiry, but can also transform the environment to which they are applied (Hollinger 1980, p. 87)

The "application" of ideas takes place through acts of communication. Tracing repeated communication, we ask where ideas travel, and although this question is formulated in spatial terms, the movement of ideas involves of course both time and space.

Local and Global and their Relation to Time/Space; Particular/Universal, Micro/Macro

It has been pointed out many a time (e.g. Zey-Ferrell 1981) that much of organization theory is ahistorical. While macro-developments are plotted over historically long periods of time, organizational change studies invariably stress temporality. First there were losses, and then there was a plan of change, and then there was an implementation, which led to unexpected results... Or, in another variation of the same story: an organization was born, and then the environment changed, and then the organization adapted/failed to adapt and survived/died. Spatial considerations, in contrast, play a minor role: although the company executives might be traveling thousands of miles per day, "the organization" seems to be situated at one point, unless it expands.

On this score, organization theory remains fully in tune with modern music. "Did it start with Bergson or before?" asks Foucault. "Space was treated as the dead, the fixed, the undialectical, the immobile. Time, on the contrary was richness, fecundity, life, dialectic" (Foucault 1980, p.70). And he proceeds in his critique of modernism:

The great obsession of the nineteenth century was, as we know, history: with its themes of development and of suspension, of crisis and cycle, themes of the ever-accumulating past... The present epoch will perhaps be above all the epoch of space (Foucault 1980, p.22).

Sharing this sentiment, we insist on the travel metaphor – and yet we think that we can also explain why time is and remains so irreducibly important in all that is being said about social life. Time is sequentiality, the plot of every narrative, which remains our central mode of knowing (Bruner 1986; 1990), language games and postmodernist experiments nevertheless. Sequentiality implies causality – in terms of both objective causes and human intentions – and is the basic glue which holds together our narratives. On the other hand, all kinds of displacements in space and time are better captured using metaphors, this central element of the paradigmatic (i.e. scientific) mode of knowing. We therefore need notions which will allow us to grasp time *and* space simultaneously, like in *localized time* and, by contrast, in *globalized time*.[2] We will show that this is useful to conceive of these notions as

---

2   The everyday use prefers the essentialist adjectives "local" and "global". We shall mostly follow the common use for simplicity's sake, asking the reader to keep in mind that these are not ostensive but performative properties (Latour 1986): people *make* something into local or global; they localize or globalize.

space/time continua. In order to do this we shall first approach two other dichotomies which are closely related to the local/global distinction: cultural universals/particulars, and macro/micro.

Cultural universals much debated in anthropology since Kroeber (1923), seem to be taken for granted by mainstream anthropologists, even though they have come under attack by the discipline's "reflective" dissenters. It was perhaps Geertz's collection of essays *Local Knowledge* (1983) which firmly established the grounds for the position that there are no universals, only particulars, and that local knowledge is the only knowledge there is. Since then, this topic was taken up both in the Diltheyan tradition of romanticizing the unique, and in the more complex stance of "modernist anthropology" (Clifford and Marcus 1986; Marcus, 1992).

Closely related to this is a reformulation of the micro-macro problem undertaken by the French sociologists of knowledge, Callon and Latour (1981). In an article aptly named "Unscrewing the big Leviathan: how actors macro-structure reality and how sociologists help them to do so" they point out that no macro-actors exist: there are only micro-actors who associate with other micro-actors constructing networks that appear to be of a super-human size. What we call "global economy" is a network of many local economies, which thus acquire an unprecedented scale and scope of action.

But it is as important to say what "global" is not: it is not "total", in the sense including everybody on earth. It would be safe to guess that actually the majority of the inhabitants of the globe are not connected into this net, which does not mean that they are not infleunced by it, drectly or indirectly. In this last sense, though, "global" becomes trivialized and has nothing to do with the present era: acid rain was always global, whether produced by East German factories or by the outer space object which made the Yucatan crater and extinguished dinosaurs. Also, "global" is not an extra-entity, nothing "above" or "beyond" local: *it is a hugely extended network of localities*.

Taking our cue from these critiques of the mostly spatial metaphors of the universals/particulars and the macro/micro debates, we can now, carefully, introduce the notions of *localized time/space* and *globalized time/space* which should really be named "translocal", in the sense of interconnecting localized time/spaces. In this context, global and local do not form an irreducible dichotomy, but a continuum. Local time is a sequence of moments spent in a unique place, its antonym being not global time, but "momentary space" or "co-temporary space", an ensemble of places accessed at the same moment (e.g. the reach of your cable television). Similarly, the antonym of global time is "lasting space", or historic space, large ensembles of places permanently accessible – in reality, the Earth, in science-fiction, many other planets or satellites (see Figure 9.1 for an illustration).

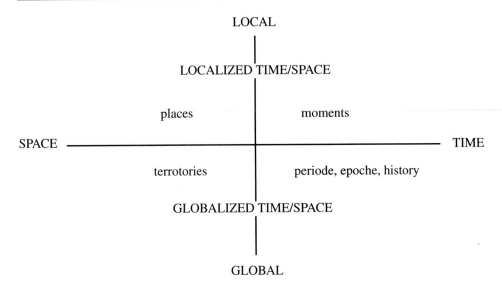

Figure 9.1

We begin by tracing ideas along the course of local time/space: how, at a given moment, do individuals and groups at a certain place happen to notice an idea? Of course, the beginning of the story is arbitrary, but we see a point in beginning just there, because it is a narrative, a yarn that we want to spin. We watch ideas become quasi-objects, transgressing the barriers of local time and entering translocal paths, and landing again and again in various localities, to be materialized in actions, and – although here we end – to occasion anew the generation of ideas.

Translation

How does one build a device mediating between local and global time/spaces so that "global" retains a sense which does not suggest a metaphysical idea of something beyond and above the localized time/space – a device that allows us to demonstrate how ideas can travel? How, in principle, should one conceive of idea-objects moving in space and time?

Idea-spreading is traditionally discussed in terms of "diffusion" (see, for example, Rogers 1962; for a recent review Levitt and March 1988). This seems a good example of how "metaphors of the field", employed for analytical purposes, can become misleading, and of how the play of recursivity falters somewhat. It is true that people speak about ideas as if they were objecs moving in time and space by virtue of some *inherent* properties. Like other field metaphors, this has an economic value, rendering the less known in terms of the more familiar, the

207

immaterial in material terms. But adopting the metaphor for our purposes takes us to an impasse. It may be plausible to say that ideas move from "more satiated" to "less satiated" environments, but by doing so we also suggest that the law of inertia applies to ideas as to physical objects. But does this offer a convincing interpretation of phenomena in question? If we look at phenomena such as the braindrain, we notice that the reverse is more apt: ideas travel from less satiated to more satiated environments, so that one has to save face by evoking another physical metaphor, that of "critical mass" which "attracts". Rather than adding new *physical* metaphors to defend one another (a very smart political move at times), we could replace them instead.

Latour (1986) has a suggestion:

> *[The] model of diffusion may be contrasted with another, that of the model of translation. According to the latter, the spread in time and space of anything – claims, orders, artefacts, goods – is in the hands of people; each of these people may act in many different ways, letting the token drop, or modifying it, or deflecting it, or betraying it, or adding to it, or appropriating it (p. 267).*

The translation model (see also Latour 1992; Callon 1986; 1992) can help us to reconcile the fact that a text is at the same time object-like and yet it can be read in differing ways. Also, it answers the question about the energy needed for traveling: it is the people, whether we see them as users or creators, who energize an idea any time they translate it for their own or somebody else's use. Ideas in books left on shelves do not travel, and no amount of satiation will help to diffuse ideas from closed libraries. Watching ideas travel, "[w]e observe a process of translation – not one of reception, rejection, resistance or acceptance" (Latour 1992, p.116).

It is important to stress, though, that the meaning of "translation" in this context surpasses the linguistic interpretation: it means "displacement, drift, invention, mediation, creation of a new link that did not exist before and modifies in part the two agents" (Latour 1993, p.6), that is, those who translated and that which is translated. This explains why the concept is so attractive to us: it comprises what exists *and* what is created; the relationship between humans and ideas, ideas and objects, and humans and objects – all needed in order to understand what in shorthand we call "organizational change".

But as presented above, translation sounds like a micro-process, something that happens between two people or maybe three: is that enough energy to send an idea all around the world? Basically, yes, but in the course of hundred years or so. However, we know that ideas travel at the speed of light-waves. Translation is speeded up, made continuous and magnified by technology: more specifically, by mass storage, mass reproduction and mass media technologies. It is this hybridized humans/technologies network which is the material basis for more complex translation mechanisms: fashion and institutionalization, which will be discussed at the place/moment where they are most visible. We begin our reconstruction of travels of ideas in a local place when some idea has been just noticed.

An Idea is Objectified

The circumstances in which an idea arose in the local time/space or, even more important, how and when it decisively came into the span of attention of a given group of organizational actors, are usually unknown. More likely than not, it was a meaningless event at that point in time/space. On the other hand, ideas do not arrive out of the blue: one can argue, as Merton did in *On the Shoulders of Giants* (1985), that all ideas circulate most of the time, at least in some places. Therefore it is more appropriate to discuss processes of *attention* rather than of information in relation to ideas that appeared in a given place/moment.

When the translation of ideas into actions is well advanced, the actors involved feel a need to mythologize by dramatizing origins. They say things like: "I remember when X went to Brussels for this special course and came back with that extraordinary idea..." or "When consultants came, they entranced us with an idea that we are living in a transition from the industrial to the information society..." But other actors quote other incidents or deny the initiating importance of this or that particular incident, which makes the observer wonder whether "the idea from Brussels" or the notion of "information society" were important as such. In his study of industrial policy in Sweden, Jacobsson (1989) found actors in the Ministry of Industry claiming that they had learned from experiences which, under scrutiny, had apparently never taken place. It might well be that, in the reconstruction of the past, an event is chosen or invented because it is rhetorically convenient (a "logical" starting point for a story that is being told).

Alternatively, the incidental and disruptive character of the initial events is stressed to demonstrate the incredible touch of luck in the idea's timely arrival. The idea fell on unprepared ground, as it were; but soon its effects were seen as it rapidly connected to important currents in organizational life.

Both types of memories serve the same purpose: to tie, meaningfully, the arrival of an idea to present problems experienced by people in organizations or attributed to the organizations themselves. Often there is an attempt to portray the process as functional: this particular idea was spotted and adopted because it served well in resolving a specific difficulty or in creating a new opportunity in situations of stagnation. The idea of attention as a social product serves well to tie together the variety of events constituting this process

209

Attention as a Social Product

Attention, or more properly speaking perceptual readiness (Bruner 1957) has been most frequently studied in the context of tangible objects and their attributes, where "objects" stand both for objects of perception and organs of perception, understood physiologically. Bruner's more general theory of perception shows a deep understanding of the social character. According to him, perception involves an act of categorization, that is, placing or giving an identity to an object, event or an idea. Such

> ... categorizing is often a "silent" or implicit process ... we do not experience a going-from-no-identity to an arrival-at-identity, but ... the first hallmark of any perception is some form of identity..." (Bruner 1957, p. 125)

It takes place against a system of categories, or, as Schütz would have put it, "typifications" built in the course of the life experience. This means that we cannot perceive something unless it somehow relates to what we already know. People reading the same texts see in them different ideas, depending, partly, on what they expect to see, and partly on what they are able to notice in terms of categories accessible to them. This explains why fresh and unique ideas take such a long time and so many repetitions to be observed. It also illustrates, in accordance with the postulates of hermeneutics, the initial requirement of translation: we cannot translate what is wholly unrecognizable.

When categories are all in place we focus attention on some, but not on others – why? Schütz' notion of "the purpose at hand" can be of use here.

> Man finds himself at any moment of his daily life in a biographically determined situation, that is, in a physical and socio-cultural environment as defined by him, within which he has his position, not merely his position in terms of physical space and outer time or of his status and role within the social system but also his moral and ideological position ... This biographically determined situation includes certain possibilities of future practical or theoretical activities which shall be briefly called "the purpose at hand." It is this purpose at hand which defines those elements among all the others contained in such a situation which are relevant for this purpose (Schütz 1953/1973, p.9).

Thus the managers of prosperous organizations look for something that seems different and exciting; those in crisis look for salvation; those who are already engaged in a program of action look for something that can be used as a "leading idea" (Czarniawska-Joerges 1990). What is more, organizational units in modern corporations are constantly fitted, as it were, with a "purpose" (goals, visions, business idea) which, especially in good times, changes them from slow ant-eaters into veritable idea-vacuum-cleaners: they will inhale everything that fits the tube

(Meyer 1990). If they see what they inhale as more of the same of what they already had, nothing happens; so many "changes" are just celebrations of the status quo. But certain encounters with ideas actually lead to a reformulation of the purpose at hand (Rorty 1991). This is why many practitioners consider evaluating the results of change in terms of its goals as superfluous: more often than not, the main achievement of a change program is the reformulation of its initial goals.

In such a context, Bruner (1961) speaks of a *discovery*, following the ideas of Vygotski, a Soviet psychologist and contemporary of Schütz. Discovery is not the act of finding out something which was previously unknown, but the act of obtaining knowledge for oneself by using one's own mind:

> It is rarely, on the frontier of knowledge or elsewhere, that new facts are "discovered" in the sense of being encountered as Newton suggested in the form of islands of truth in an unchartered sea of ignorance... [D]iscovery, whether by a schoolboy doing it on its own or by a scientist cultivating the growing edge of his field, is in its essence a matter of re-arranging or transforming evidence so reassembled to additional new insights (Bruner, 1961, p.22).

Similarly, Rorty (1991) writes of "reweaving our web of beliefs", or "recontextualization", whereas Latour (1992) writes of the change in the translator and in the translated. Thus a cognitive psychologist, a pragmatist philosopher and a sociologist of knowledge all agree in this account: we approach an idea in terms of what we already know, and sometimes the encounter barely confirms it; at other times, an idea re-arranges our beliefs and purposes as we translate it; the act of discovery creates a new idea and a new actor. This is the meaning of change on the phenomenological level.

However, even if a person or a group make a discovery, there are still many other people who have to participate in the process if the idea is to materialize. How can they be persuaded to continue the chain of translations?

Social Context

An obvious place to start looking for answers is the context of organizational decision making. Discussing this, we will do well by beginning with what is invisible: the influence of taken-for-granted political arrangements (call it structure if you must). Thus, gender studies[3] for instance tell us that in group-meetings ideas coming from a woman usually have to be re-proposed by a man in order to be noticed. If they are noticed at the first utterance, they are often incorrectly attributed to some man present at the gathering. Females who are tokens in all-male

---

3   And the life experience of one of us.

211

groups need external accounts for their ideas to gain influence (Taps and Martin 1988). The same phenomenon can be observed in most gatherings where high-status people are asked their opinions more often, talk more, receive more positive comments and are more likely to influence the group's decisions (Smith-Lovin and Brody 1989).

Such taken-for-granted political structures can be accompanied by taken-for-granted cultural ones. We use this term to cover what Bachrach and Baratz (1963) called "non-decisions" or "agenda setting". Certain issues will not appear on an agenda unless a serious disruption of taken-for-granted social reality takes place. A long experience within a certain type of cultural structure leads to cultural color-blindness. Thus managers are usually power-blind, men are gender-blind, and social scientists are ideology-blind.

But the fact that certain things are not consciously noticed does not mean that they are not pragmatically exploited. The greatest advantage of the taken-for-granted is, indeed, that it can be put to use without too much ado (Jansson 1989). For example, when the issue of power and politics in academia comes into the focus of a discussion, academics tend to deny its relevance (with honorable exceptions such as Sederberg 1986, or Agger 1991). This, however, does not prevent them from acting in ways which invite political interpretations. Hendriks and Kalishoek (1987), for instance, described the decision making on staff cut-backs at Dutch universities. A person or a group with an idea goes around and "anchors" it with potential allies. When the decision is formally taken, it only confirms what is already irreversible. But when a plan developed by one person or a small group is all of a sudden presented to a decision making body, it will be sent back for elaboration or accepted but simply left unimplemented, no matter how ingenious it was. In other words, an idea might strike an individual like the legendary apple which supposedly struck Newton's head[4], but not a group. One plants ideas into a group, one does not hit it with them.

The example also shows how one can create new structures through taken-for-granted processes. In the case of Dutch universities, the "lobbyists" did not, of course, try to anchor their ideas with those who would become potential victims of their plan. This weakened the latter's possibilities of fighting back and opposing the "decision" when it emerged. Similarly, Jansson (1989) described the way certain investment decisions are promoted through the skillful use of procedures which are taken-for-granted. Decision making seems to play a peculiar role in the materialization of ideas: it is mostly a legitimizing ritual. As Rorty puts it, "poetic, artistic, philosophical, scientific or political progress results from the accidental

---

4   This is a good example of how a folktale explains the phenomenon of inspiration by help of reification: an idea must be a thing if it "strikes."

coincidence of a private obsession with a public need" (1989, p.37), not from decisions made. Yet decision rituals need be performed, too.

Ideological Control

This is not to deny the role of intentional influence. We would like to emphasize the role of ideological control in this context – that is, control which takes place by influencing ideologies held by organizational actors, shaping their ideas about what reality is like, how it should be and how to achieve the desired state (Czarniawska-Joerges 1988). Teaching (organized learning) can be seen as one way of exerting such influence (other possible ways being public debate, straightforward offers of ideologies, rituals and so forth).

Bruner (1961) speaks of two teaching modes: *expository* and *hypothetical*. In the former mode, the relationship is unidirectional and all responsibility resides with the teacher. Truth is exposed to the "learner", whose only task is to assimilate it. In the hypothetical mode, the teacher and the learner go together through various "as if" states of affairs until the learner discovers the one that widens her or his understanding; it might or might not be a discovery already made by the teacher.

Ideological control in organizations tends to be of the expository kind: it is the authority of the "teacher-leader" and not the motivation of the "learner-follower" that gives weight to an idea. Ideas are noticed because that is what the leadership wishes; there are also official translations. But the ideas noticed by leaders often fail to materialize in practice. In many cases, though, the two modes blend into each other: an idea may be "rediscovered" by shop-floor actors and can thus be materialized "spontaneously", that is, by a series of non-official translations. We claim that discovery, either spontaneous or guided by a skillful teacher, is always important for the materialization of ideas. Exposing people to ready-made ideas preempts translation and therefore does not create the mobilization needed for action.

Another use of ideological control is the adoption of an idea already well entrenched, after the action has been carried out. Ideas are often appropriated and disowned as the process goes on. At the persuasion stage, it is convenient to present ideas as impersonally derived, from God, destiny or the *Zeitgeist* (on the assumption that ideas are greater than people). When an idea has caught on, those with control aspirations try to appropriate it for control purposes, or, in the event of failure, to get rid of it by attributing it to somebody else, as is often the case in unsuccessful technology transfers.

This discussion leads us to understanding how an event which takes place in a given time, is in fact related to many similar events taking place more or less simultaneously in other places, although the actors need not be conscious of it all the time. In fact, as Meyer points out, an excess of consciousness and reflection prevents the easy adoption of ideas and builds up a resistance to ideological control

(Meyer 1990). This may be why Beckman's (1987) interlocutors insisted on their disconnectedness, their independent discovery, as described in the section "Public Administration Reform". But nobody can deny at least one connection, the one created by mass media.

Public attention

Organizational actors are forced to pay attention to issues which arise not only in the marketplace but also in society at large. Politics is the proper arena for this, but the voices of modern politics would not be heard without amplifiers: politicians together with the mass-media construct the problems which demand attention. There seems to be a limit, however, to the number of issues people notice and react to, regardless of their acuity.

> The logic that explains official, public and media attention to political problems does not turn on their severity but rather upon their dramatic appeals. These, in turn, are vulnerable to satiation of attention and to novelty (Edelman 1988, p.28).

Similarly, Downs (1972) claimed that public reaction to problems is subject to "issue-attention cycles" where problems suddenly leap into prominence, remain in the center of attention for a short time, and then gradually fade from it. News is a form of entertainment, competing with other types of entertainment – especially in the United States, but also in other western countries. because of this, a problem must be dramatic and exciting in order to maintain public interest, that is, to survive in the translocal time/space.

As long as a problem is in the focus of attention, all the ideas which can be related to it have a greater chance of being realized. All already existing actions that can be represented as coupled to it have a greater chance of being legitimized. "Little wonder, then, that interest groups try to shape the content and the form of television and printed news, for to create a world dominated by a particular set of problems is at the same time to create support for specific courses of action" (Edelman 1988, p.29). The same reasoning can be transferred to the domain of organizational fashion, discussed later, where mass-media play an analogous role. It is thus time that we tried to conceptualize the ways in which ideas are made ready for travel.

Selected Ideas Translated into Objects

Ideas that have been selected and entered the chain of translations acquire almost physical, objective attributes; in other words, they become quasi-objects, and then objects.

The simplest way of objectifying ideas is by turning them into linguistic artefacts by using them repeatedly, as in the case of *labels, metaphors, platitudes*

(Czarniawska-Joerges and Joerges 1990). This represents a mechanical translation, intended to minimize displacement effects. Local labeling, for instance, is especially important in cases where ideas must be fitted into already existing action patterns, as they reflect the broader, societal categorizing. A river valley program fits any river (which has a valley), decentralization can be almost any change in organizational structure, but by labeling actions in such ways, desired associations are created to master-ideas (see below) such as modernity and community help in the former case, democracy and autonomy in the latter. Words are turned into labels by frequent repetition in an unquestioning mode in similar contexts, so that a possible "decentralization, why?" will give way to "decentralization, of course!" and therefore decentralization will become what we happen to be doing in our organization. Even intellectual progress (the development of ideas) depends on the literalization of certain metaphors, so that new ones are needed (Rorty 1989). The most successful labels turn into institutional categories themselves, like "decentralization" did.

Another way of turning ideas into things is design; putting images into a graphic form. Adrian Forty's book *Objects of Desire* (1986) develops this theme on various levels, but we shall take just one example out of his many. *Lucky Strike,* the ultra-American cigarette, originally had a packet showing the well known Lucky Strike sign against a green background, a different back of the packet and the word "cigarettes" in liberty-style lettering. Raymond Loewy redesigned it giving it a white background, repeating the pattern on the back and modernizing the lettering. The designer later suggested that by introducing "the impeccable whiteness", he managed to influence the way people thought of cigarettes ("Freshness of content and immaculate manufacturing"). Forty offers another interpretation, emphasizing the fact that the redesign took place in the 1940s, when cigarettes were not yet thought health-damaging:

> ... we can suggest two distinct factors as lying behind Lucky Strike Packet's success within a particular society at a particular point in history. The ideas of cleanliness and Americanness signified by the design belonged in the minds of all Americans and cannot in any way be said to have been an innovation of the designer. The other factor in the design's success was the way in which an association between ideas of whiteness, cleanliness and America was set up by the means of a single image. This image was a creation of the designer, and Loewy and his office certainly deserve credit for their skill in devising a form that conveyed the association so effectively.

No design works unless it embodies ideas that are held in common by the people for whom the object is intended (Forty 1986, p.245).

We linger on this example because it depicts a literal process of the materialization of an idea, revealing the complexity of the whole process, the mixture of chance, social mood and intention. Beyond this, we see that even after having become an object, the idea did not become entirely "objective" and unambiguous, as the difference of interpretations by Loewy and Forty indicates.

Ideas are *communicated images,* intersubjective creations, and therefore a "property" of a community rather than of a single person (although individuals tend to appropriate ideas that the narratives attribute them to heroes). It has been suggested that in place of the traditional image of subsequent generations standing "on the shoulders of giants", it is the giants who are standing "on a pyramid of midgets" (Merton 1985). Their collective character makes it possible to conceive of them as of things; everything that can be "seen" by more than one person acquires "objectivity"; this miracle of shared perception is in fact due to the already mentioned process of categorization according to the legitimate categories of a given time/space (Douglas 1986; Meyer 1990). The simultaneous collective and material character of ideas is especially interesting: we recognize an idea as "the same" or "different" because our social categorization tells us what to see, but at the same time we create a physical body to incorporate the idea, so that we know what to put into categories.

An Idea Travels

We can now depict a chain of translations, which gets speeded up as the ideas become more and more object-like and can be carried by modern transportation/communication technologies. And we shall try to say something more about travels: where from and where to?

Fashion was until recently a phenomenon treated with disdain and neglect in social theory and organization studies[5]. Part of the blame goes to critical theorists:

"Fashionability allows individuals who follow the imperatives of fashion to abandon the responsibility to make history and shape culture" (Finkelstein 1989, p.144). This is only one of the more recent examples of modern critique of fashion coming from that school. However, blame should be also directed to the masculine culture of the social sciences, where war, sport and technology are worth serious scrutiny and become a source of unproblematic metaphors; not so events and phenomena perceived as coming from feminine realms are denigrated and neglected.

To us, a metaphorical and literal understanding of fashion seems to be the key to understanding many puzzling developments in and between organizations. The concept can importantly complement another phenomenon which has attracted much more attention – institutionalization. We want then not only to redeem the

5   Although, following the inspiration of Mintzberg (1979), Eric Abrahamson's work among others announces increased interest in this issue (Abrahamson 1991).

importance of fashion, but we also want to put it together as the unseparable part of the "iron cage" of institutions, paradoxical as it may sound.

Fashion

In a classic article, Blumer (1969) postulated that fashion is a *competition mechanism* which influences the market and distorts the demand and supply curves, both using and serving the economic competition. Its important element is a collective choice among tastes, things, ideas; it is oriented towards finding but also towards creating what is typical of a given time. We tend to agree with Blumer in basic views, but want to add that fashion, together with a free market, operates at institutional fringes. On the one hand, its variety is limited by the "iron cage" of existing institutions, which fashion actually reproduces; on the other hand, fashion is engaged in a constant subversion of the existing institutional order, gnawing ant-like at its bars. This is the first paradox connected to fashion: its simultaneous unimportance and saliency.

The translation mechanism helps to understand the second paradox: fashion is created while it is followed. It is the subsequent translations which at the same time produce variations in fashion and reproduce it. Hence the third paradox: fashion followers act differently due to the attempt to act in the same way. But what makes people follow fashions?

Fashion is the expression of what is *modern,* of what the community to which one belongs recently chose as the most valuable or exciting. It is worth adding that "belonging" ceased to be determined by birth and even by a permanent location. In globalized worlds, where people mass commute to work or to marriage between Tokyo and San Francisco, the notion of "community" acquires a new ring (Gergen 1991).

For people in high organizational positions who perceive their mission as being that of bringing progress to organizations, to follow what is modern feels often like a duty (Forssell 1989). However, this obligation is only part of their mission. Their duty is, equally, to protect organizations from what might be just a passing fad. One of their tasks is therefore to keep a distance to "mere" fashion.

> One could say that the fashion's double nature – distance and interest – are the two constituents of self-awareness.
> Those who stay at fashion's frontlines and participate in fashion's competitions must, naturally, be especially self-aware. This concerns also some companies. They invest in the current image, a profile matching the times (Sellerberg 1987, p.66, translation BC).

Thus, following fashion can be, in a company, a way of keeping abreast of the competition, and in public administration a way of keeping up with the times in the

217

interest of the people by being in the forefront of novelty. But one other aspect must be emphasized as well. Fashion, as a collective translation process, also functions as a release from the responsibility of individual choice (Sellerberg 1987). To follow fashion is to be conformist *and* creative. In this sense fashion (like translation) stands for change, as opposed to tradition (literal imitation). But, as fashion is also repetitive, in a long range perspective it stands for tradition, too. Tarde, the classic imitation analyst, contrasted the control of the "timeless society" with the control of "times we live in", a time-collective, as Sellerberg (1987) interprets it. An interesting observation made in one of the early fashion studies was that fashion is not related to progress:

> In a real sense, fashion is evolution without destination. The world generally considers that progress in material things consists in changes that make them more useful, or better looking, or less expensive. In the long run fashion never attains these objectives. Its idea is slow, continuos change, unhampered by the restrictions of either aesthetics or practicality (Young 1937/1973, p. 109).

We would claim, then, that the concept of fashion concerns ways of changing, as an alternative to the notion of progress, and that it is descriptive rather than normative in character. Agnes Brook Young's observation makes the paradoxical character of change more obvious: fashion operates through dramatized "revolutions", but "... in a real sense, fashion is evolution...".

Fashion, then, transpires as a highly paradoxical process. Its constitutive paradoxes: creation *and* imitation, variation *and* uniformity, distance *and* interest, novelty *and* conservatism, unity *and* segregation, conformity *and* deviation, change *and* status quo, revolution *and* evolution are only variations on the basic duality of communal life: the collective construction of individuality *and* the individual construction of collectivity. Separately, the two processes are often tackled, even within organization theory. But as a whole, understanding the process of social construction in the Berger and Luckmann's (1966) perspective remains largely a theoretical claim. And yet it lies at the very heart of organizational life and action.

In organizations, the most important point is that fashion (together with other processes like control or negotiation) introduces order and uniformity into what might seem an overwhelming variety of possibilities. In this sense fashion helps to come to grips with the present. At the same time, it "serves to detach the grip of the past in the moving world. By placing a premium on being in the mode and derogating what developments have left behind, it frees actions for new movement" (Blumer 1969/1973, p.339). It also introduces some appearance of order and predictability into preparations for what is necessarily disorderly and uncertain: the future. Fashion, in its gradual emergence, eases up the surprises of the next fashion, tunes in the collective by making it known to itself, as reflected in the present fashion and in the rejection of past fashions.

Fashion Leaders

Blumer's eulogy of fashion (which is portrayed as an epitome of an egalitarian, free choice process) neglects the intentional influences – of a political and economic character – to which fashion is an easy prey. In a collective not everybody plays the same role. Some people's translations have more weight than others', and may become a gospel for others. In the world of fashion the role of opinion leaders is well known. Francesco Alberoni, an Italian sociologist, called them *Divi* (gods), the "powerless elite" (after Sellerberg 1987).

> They control nothing themselves and this is not only a question of a possible lack of political influence. It is important to notice that they are also powerless in the fashion process.. . .
>   Fashion does not stem from them. Members of this elite were, as a study showed, themselves interested in remaining up-to-date with fashion. If anybody, it was they who had to "hang on" (Sellerberg 1987, translation BC).

The collective choice also selects those, who are then admired, looked up at and imitated by the rest (or else, declared passé and forgotten).

But it is not only the fashion leaders who could be called "legislators in taste" or "taste makers" (Robinson 1960). Robinson's interesting analysis of a historical triad of taste makers – Winckelmann, Hamilton, and Wedgwood – may illustrate this point. He saw these three personages as mainly responsible for the greek revival in England in the secon half of the eighteenth century. Johann Joachim Winckelmann, A German scholar-aesthete, was the first to launch the absolute aesthgetic supremacy of the classical fifth century BC. Sir William Hamilton, a career diplomat, took up the hobby of studying and collecting Etruscan vases and the mission of propoagating the aesthetic message of Winckelmann. Josiah Wedgwood, under Winckelmann's influence, revolutionized English pottery for a long time to come. It is irrelevant although amusing, Robinson points out, that Winckelmann's "Greek statues" were actually Roman and Hamilton's "Etruscan vases" were Greek, and that there are many who would give a great deal to wipe Wedgwood's merits in developing a medieval craft into a modern industry, and he himself claimed most emphatically that the progress of the arts depended on people like Hamilton who, "by their rank and affluence are legislators in taste" (Robinson 1960/1973, pp. 29–30).

Individuals cannot create fashion, but they may try to influence it, and often successfully. Obviously, there are such fashion leaders, or market leaders in the organizational world as well. The study of municipal reforms revealed leading local governments who were accustomed to being first with any change in the local authority system. Hinings and Greenwood (1988) observed the same phenomenon in the British public sector. The leading local authorities popularized their translations via the Association of Local Authorities (the same in Sweden), by professional associations, and by the transfer of personnel through a career-system. DiMaggio and Powell (1983) speak, in this context, of "central organizations".

The market leaders are at their most powerful when they ally with political leaders or when political leaders decide to dictate taste. The Parisian fashion house of Rose Bertin, the outstanding *marchande de modes* of the late eighteenth century earned its position thanks to the assistance and consultation of Mari-Antoinette, whereas the Swedish Gustav II and the Polish Stanislaus August ordered the wearing of national costumes to aid their respective wool industries (Freudenberger 1963). Nowadays, some companies issue more or less explicit rules concerning the dress style of their employees, no doubt because they are concerned about the company image, but they nonetheless promote certain styles, like the "preppy" style in the United States in the early 1980s.

It is interesting that there seem to be "idea-bearing" organizations and professional roles which deal mainly with translations. This is, to an increasing extent, the role of professional consultants. Like traveling salesmen, they arrive at organizations and open their attaché-cases full of quasi-objects to be translated into localized ideas (Czarniawska-Joerges 1990). Often they bring in the whole equipment needed for the materialization of an idea, but almost always they spill some extra ideas which might then materialize through some local translation – or might not. They are designers and distributors, wholesalers and retailers in ideas-turned-into-things, which then locally once more can be turned into ideas-to-be-enacted.

Between Fashions and Institutions: Master Ideas

We want to advance the following argument:although fashionability and institutionalization appear to be opposites, the former standing for temporality and frivolousness and the other for stability and seriousness, it seems more fruitful to see them as interconnected and interdependent. Fashion is the fringe, the margin, the challenge to the institutionalized order of things, but its durability in time and mobility in space, indeed, its use of technologies which are required for that scope, depends on its firm institutionalization in the contemporary western world. Similarly, although fashion seems to sabotage and threaten established institutions, it is also an institutional playfield: new fashions can be tried out and disposed of – or institutionalized, thus revitalizing the existing institutional order. Although it has been tried many a time, it is hard to show a fashion that brought about a revolution; it would be easier to show that totalitarian systems suffocate fashion.

We can probably get the tentative agreement of our readers for this reasoning, only because it will permit them to ask the next question: which ideas brought about by fashion are institutionalized, and which are not? This is an honorable question that has produced many an answer. Mary Douglas, for instance, says that, "[to] acquire legitimacy, every kind of institution needs a formula that founds its rightness in reason and in nature" (1986, p.45). In the context of the invention of the camera, Mitchell concludes that: "What is natural is, evidently, what we can build a machine to do for us" (1986, p.37). In organizational thought-worlds almost all ideas are, or can be presented as based on reason and nature. Hence: those ideas which can be presented as natural (for example, by showing that they can be materialized into tangible machines), lend themselves to be institutionalized.

The answer to the question does not lie, in other words, in inherent properties of ideas, but in the success of their presentation. The same question can actually be put earlier on: which ideas become fashionable and which remain for ever local? We think that, on their way to become institutionalized practices, ideas are turned around and about, in this process acquiring object-like attributes, becoming quasi-objects, more like crawling ants than free-floating spirits. Organizational actors, like a collective ant-eater, catch many, spit out most, and savor some, presumably on the grounds of relevance to some organizational problem. But the match does not lie in the attributes of an idea or in the characteristics of the problem. It can hardly be claimed that the inventor of the camera did it to solve the problem of taking pictures. The perceived attributes of an idea, the perceived characteristics of a problem and the match between them are all created, negotiated or imposed during the collective translation process. All three are the results, not the antecedents of this process. With some exaggeration, one can claim that most ideas can be proven to fit most problems, assuming good will, creativity, and a tendency to consensus.

The final say in the selection of ideas, even for fashion, is often given to the *Zeitgeist* who, like all the holy spirits, has the double virtue of being invisible and all-encompassing, thus stopping the spiral of still further questions. We shall, however, try to be a bit more specific and speak instead about legitimating narratives, such as metanarratives of modernity (e.g., emancipation and progress, Lyotard 1979). Although they need not be evoked in their entirety, they give rise to a multitude of master-ideas, blueprints, paradigms which dominate a given period (with many other present, waiting for their turn). Therefore we agreed with Forty (1986) when he argued that, in a sense, an idea cannot catch on unless it already exists for some time in many people's minds, as a part of a master idea in a translocal space/time.

Master-ideas serve as foci for fashions and build a bridge between the passing fashion and a lasting institution. Where does a new set of master-ideas come from?

221

It seems that it comes from the narratives of the past (MacIntyre 1981), and are projected into the future, often in opposition to the present. Is not postmodernism building on the sophists and on Nietzsche? It is not that their ideas were nonexistent during all that time; but all the texts which are now industriously studied were meaningless to most social scientists, dedicated for so many years to what is now sweepingly called "positivism". Positivism, in its turn, came as a reaction to a certain kind of metaphysics, and so forth. What is important to understand is the sequential, step-by-step character of paradigm-forming and paradigm-dissolution. Kuhnian "paradigm-revolutions" are rather non-revolutionary (although in personal discovery they might incense the neophyte). As Rorty observes:

> *Europe did not decide to accept the idiom of Romantic poetry, or of socialist politics, or of Galilean mechanics. That sort of shift was no more an act of will than it was a result of argument. Rather, Europe gradually lost the habit of using certain words and gradually acquired the habit of using others" (1989, p.6).*

There is a loop-like relationship between the ideas of the past and of the present; between metanarratives and master-ideas; between the mainstream and the fringe. A paradigm is a product and a producer; and probably never more influential than at its end, when its master ideas enter the globalized time/space and therefore their capacity of endowing local events with unique meaning is exhausted. Hirschman (1977) pointed out that this phenomenon is well known in intellectual history, exemplifying his point with the acceptance of the concept of "interest". Once the notion of interest acquired paradigmatic status, most of human action was explained by self-interest, and nobody bothered to define the notion with any precision. The power of master-ideas resides in the fact that they are taken for granted, unproblematic and used for all possible purposes. At the beginning of the rule of a paradigm, it is its power to excite, to mobilize and to energize that is most noticeable; toward the end, it is its unquestionability, obviousness and taken-for-granted explanatory power.

Although our story is about change and therefore about ideas which succeed, it is worth mentioning here that a ruling paradigm has a deadly power to reject ideas which are perceived as challenging it. In their study of urban reform, Warren et al. (1974) described how what they called "an institutionalized thought structure" repelled any idea suggesting an innovation in the paradigm itself, even within a massive program of innovation. To understand how this is possible, we need to introduce the notion of organization fields.

Institutionalization

Not all organizational ideas which are in fashion at a given time are tried out by all organizations in a given space-frame; fashion has its niches, merchants of meaning cultivate their specialties. Yet organizations form time- and space-collectives, acquiring more or less ubiquitously and permanently similar practices. Fashion always operates against a background of seeming stability and unchangeability. The war of skirt-lengths presupposes the global practice of wearing skirts.

How do such collectives arise and delineate their boundaries? A useful concept here is that of the *structuration of organization fields* (Giddens 1979; DiMaggio and Powell 1983). Four elements constitute the process: an increase in interactions among organizations in a given field; the emergence of interorganizational structures of domination and coalition patterns; obligatory (and increasing) information exchange between the organizations of the field; and the development of a "field consciousness" – an awareness among participants that they belong together (DiMaggio and Powell 1983). Structuration may come as a consequence of economic competition, the influence of the state (or some other political authority), and the pressures cutting across professional networks. Once a field has been structured, forces arise which prompt the organizations in the field to become more alike. DiMaggio and Powell speak of *coercive isomorphism* (organizations are forced or encouraged to be alike by actors from outside the field), *mimetic isomorphism* (organizations imitate one another when faced with uncertainty) and *normative isomorphism,* related to professionalization.

One wonders, however, whether the implicit determinism of a concept such as "field forces" is at all necessary. After all, actors might want to segregate their organizations from those outside the field, and will call it "coercion" in an act of self-justification; and to link themselves with those inside the field (uncertainty is a human condition, too unspecified to serve as an explanation). Seen this way, the first two "forces of the field" are not extraneous to the actors and recall the functions of fashion described by Simmel (1904/1973): to unify a community by conforming to what is accepted and to separate by differentiating from all others.

The third "force", normative isomorphism, on the other hand, can be seen as a kind of mimesis itself, operating within different but partly overlapping fields (organizations versus professions), or else, as a conscious imitation based on value choice (this interpretation, however, collapses the difference between mimetic and normative isomorphisms).

From our point of view, a time-and-space collective constantly selects and de-selects among plans for action from a common repertoire of ideas, and the ideas repetitively selected then acquire *institutional status*. Fashions bring in a variety of ideas; organizations within a field try them out, creating fashion by following it, but also creating institutions by persevering in certain practices, by refusing to reject previous fashions, or by hailing a new fashion as the final solution. Generally, one might say that what remains unaffected, after one fashion has changed into another, acquires the status of institutionalized action, the more so the longer it survives. One aspect of this is an increased attractiveness at the local level. Local actions conforming to existing institutions gain in what is the gain of institutions: the economy of effort, stability, order and control, the source of identity for individuals and groups (Berger and Luckmann 1966; Douglas 1986).

Presented like this, institutions seem to be just the opposite of fashion. How can one claim that institutions arise from fashion, and that the two mechanisms are complementary? It might be easier to accept if we scrutinize the other side of institutionalization. The economy of effort provided by institutionalization creates room for new ideas, which will eventually upset old institutions; a strong identity provides a basis for innovative experiments and social control creates, among other effects, social unrest and disorder. Creativity grows out of routine. Rationality breeds irrationality.

So we claim that fashions give birth to institutions and institutions make room for other fashions. The meaning of both forms of change is equally vexing: a new local action means, of course, a change in practices existing in a given place and moment, even if it recreates an old institution at another time, elsewhere. What was imitative for Beckman (1987), was new and original to his respondents. But as the re-creation process was idea-mediated and then transplanted onto different material ground, the institution was indeed new – even when compared with its original. On the other hand, when an idea legitimizes an already existing practice, this is possible precisely because the idea already has the status of an institution carrier and therefore is expected to transfer this status to existing actions. Such processes, described here from the local perspective of organizational collectives, can be seen, then, (from the translocal view, if such is possible), as resulting in institutional isomorphisms within the organization field.

An Idea is Enacted

We began our story in local time/space – an idea is objectified at a given place and moment – and then followed it through different moments and places into a global time/space, speculating about the means by which it travels. Now we come again to a local time/space: an idea has been objectified, traveled, arrived at a new place ready to be translated into action. The journey approaches completion (before the idea will get on its way again) and we shall now watch the next stage of the story.

Ideas onto Actions

Many actions take place because they form a routine and nobody really remembers what their meaning originally was. Some were initially undertaken for ambiguous reasons and need to be legitimized by having commonly accepted motives ascribed to them. Others are expressions of an energy overload on the part of certain actors ("let's do something!") and, again, require ongoing legitimation. All can acquire respectable meanings by being successfully related to fashionable ideas. Celebrations and many technology transfers exemplify this. Giving a name to what is already being done is a major step in history-making: now we know what we have been doing all along and we will be able to tell the story. In the present, we "muddle through" hardly seeing the light, but we shall be able to acquire the appropriate distance, and a searchlight, once we discover an idea that suits our endeavors. Matching ideas to actions will change both, but this is a part of translation process.

A process of idea-materialization clearly operates in structuring future events and present happenings, as studies of large projects show (Sahlin-Andersson 1989; Spetz 1988). There seems to be a magic attraction to big projects, used as umbrellas for many actions already in existence, giving meaning and legitimacy to those about to begin, and providing a space for plans, dreams and designs. Big projects are in search for big ideas: Sahlin-Andersson's scrutiny of many such projects reveals a quantitative orientation of the search: with some exaggeration, it can be said that the idea does not seem to matter so much as its scale. Thus large buildings are more appreciated than small buildings, big research projects are more carefully considered by foundations than small projects, and long range plans appear as more serious than the short-term ones. Big is beautiful here, as we will also see later with reference to big events.

The same idea can be used in both ways: either to give a name to past and present action or to initiate a new set of actions. In Gherardi and Strati's (1988) example of introducing Computer Aided Design in two engineering companies, one company interpreted the concepts as one step in a long, ongoing process of the replacement g of manned by automated technology while the other chose to see it as a beginning of a change towards a new way of working. This example shows once again that neither the attributes of the idea nor those of the action are decisive for the way the two will be matched – the match is a result and not the cause of the translation process.

Ideas into Actions

How can ideas be put into action at all? Obviously, to be put into action an idea must be supplied with an *image of action*, a verbal of graphic picture of possible action. Ideas that have been for centuries considered unrealizable slowly acquire an action-image resulting from the changes in other ideas and in things (technology). But an image of action is not yet an action, a design for a machine is not yet a machine, and stage-set instructions are not yet a stage. How are they materialized? Not by decision as an act of choice, as Brunsson (1985) observes with insight: competing ideas paralyze action. Hamlet puts himself in a hopeless situation with his ill-formulated question. Rather, it is a decision as an act of will, prompted by positive expectations concerning the process itself ("let it be!"), its results, or both.

Indeed, the positive emotions concerning cognitive and material aspects of action must be taken for granted – why else should an idea be put into action at all? It must invoke an exciting, promising or aesthetically pleasing feeling. The cognitive process, prompted by acts of will, moves then toward calibrating "images of action" into something more like detailed "plans of action" (Miller et al. 1960) and then into deeds. "In places, all ready, run!" And they run. This magic moment when words become deeds is the one that truly deserves to be called materialization, whether performed by human actors or by material artefacts.

Sooner or later, a river valley project has to encounter the concrete river, the specific valley, the given groups of people and interests, the available machines and resources. Inevitably, it will turn into something different than expected and than planned. Sahlin-Andersson (1991) studied research parks which at present seem to be more popular than river valley projects. Constructing a research park, populating and running it does not end the chain of translation. Inevitably, discussions start whether the idea is still the same or a different one: is Lund's research park the same as Stanford's? If not, what remained from the original idea? The tangible fit is no less socially constructed than the political and cultural "matches" discussed so far; it is simply – and surprisingly – even less discussed in the context of organizational studies. And this is a drawback, because even if it is just one moment-place through which an idea must pass, it is a crucial one in producing change. Soon the new object will provoke new ideas or a resurgence of old ones. Most ideas always float in between time/spaces; it is their repetitive touch downs in local places/moments which make the difference. The idea of space travel is as old as humanity, but compare Icarus' chariot with the Apollo or Mir spaceships. Ideas into objects, and then into actions, and then into ideas again...

Exploiting Institutions: Big Events

Institutional theory concentrates on the making of institutions and their perseverance. Our image of of materializing ideas turns us toward yet another phenomenon: using the institutions already in existence as sources of ideas, as stimuli for action or both. Institutionalized celebrations are as concrete as any objects: take anniversaries, birthdays, centennials and millennia. Are they not objectively inscribed in the respective time/space?

A question like this one can provoke an extremely convoluted debate: how do we know when to celebrate the year 2000? According to what calendar? We claim, instead, that it is neither the date which is important (or global, for that matter) nor the particulars of the celebration. The date exists objectively only as temporal reference point, which seems to be quite malleable at that. It is said that the Dubliners decided to celebrate their millennium at very short notice and then chose a suitable date among several possible occasions. The Swedish city of Västerås (home of ABB) has repeated this highly successful operation in 1990 in spite of some locals claiming that no information exists reporting the alleged foundatory event. Neither the repertoire of rituals, nor the date's specific meaning are fixed. Many anniversaries, centennials and Common Europe occasions acquire their special significance by attracting a multitude of actions and ideas floating by, as it were.

The fascinating aspect of big events is that they are by definition transgressing the localized time and space, often both. It is an institution which permits the gathering of various unengaged ideas and actions (what about building a new sports arena? how about having a gala concert?) under one umbrella, giving them legitimacy and coherence. The actual celebration is a combination of a set of ideas, a set of actions, and the connection between the same which constitutes the meaning. One can start the coupling process from either end: existing actions which call for extra meaning or a date which promises such a meaning when coupled to some action. Even a completely fictitious date like the Orwellian *1984* (in fact, nonprophetically intended: Stalin's 1948), managed to produce a flood of intellectual debates and other cultural disturbances when that year came around. Daimler-Benz's celebration of 100 years of automobiles can be seen as a reverse example: here the date served as a pretext to emphasize what is actually being done.

Big events provoke enormous amounts of sense-making and lead to change (Joerges 1990). People's and organizations' time perspectives are turned around; courses of action are not (only) built on past events and experiences which have formed expectations about what is "normal", lawful, repetitive. Paradoxically, the unique, the unlikely, the unprecedented, even the impossible happen – or are anticipated and begin to guide action. Epochs are closed (and thereby defined), other futures are opened (and thereby tentatively defined) by coming clean with the past. This is the context for turning latent ideas into projects. It entails vast redefinition of situations, an extraordinary mobilization of resources and the unfreezing of institutionalized resource allocations.

But how and when is all that decided? The year 1993 was to be decisive for Europeans but as it went by, the expected grand opening of Fortress Europe somehow did not take place. Greece did not apply for the 1996 Olympic Games although everybody expected them to take this opportunity to celebrate the 100th return of the Games. Too many complications were in the picture to let the actions run smoothly, to glue the ideas into a coherent picture. Celebrations are institutions empty in content, but decisive in form; they are the ceremonies and rituals of modernity, like big projects are its totems. We know what to do when a big event comes along (or is created): summarize the past, imagine the future, celebrate the moment, and start doing things which otherwise were just in the air.

The Idea whose Time/Space has Come

Greater than the tread of mighty armies is an idea whose time has come... Victor Hugo
(after Kingdon 1984, p. 1.)

In our terms, Victor Hugo spoke of an idea whose time/space has come through many interconnected chains of translation. On its trajectory from an idea to an object, to an institution, to an action and to an idea again, ideas go through many transformations and passage points in the course of subsequent translations.

We started our narrative with ideas that take root in local knowledge (sometimes just in one head). As more and more people are persuaded to translate the idea for their own use, it can be materialized into a collective action. In order to become public knowledge, though, an idea must become objectified, made into a quasi-object: only then can it travel between local places and moments so as to move into translocal (global, collective-historical) time/spaces.

This process can be bolstered by willing political agents, but it is also shaped by contingent events and little controlled processes such as fashion. The actors involved, however, rarely see more than one or two stages of the entire process, framed as they are by the fictions created in local time/space. Thus in a given municipality, regional authority, city or government agency, some group of people "discover" an idea: having submunicipal committees, or a laboratory (R&D units), or millennial celebrations, or a river valley project. The idea may appear new, sometimes shocking, even revolutionary.

The idea is then enacted: other people are persuaded to join in, decisions are formally made, municipalities divided into subparts, laboratories called to life, celebrations planned and performed, licenses bought and applied. In order to solidify, to legitimize the idea-become-material, signals are sent to the wider community: dramatizing, justifying, marketing, selling, propagating. An idea, locally translated into action, is reified into a quasi-object that can travel: a book, a picture, a design, for purposes of non-local communication, recognizable in terms of a translocal frame of reference.

All these signals contribute to the creation of a wave, a fashion, which sometimes survives subsequent fashions and turns into an institution: public administration reforms, the ritual of Round Dates Celebration, the TVA developmental model. Such sedimented institutional patterns enable the next municipality, next region, next city, next river valley to notice easily idea-objects that have passed the tests of local action. Institutions are exchange networks through which properly packaged and blackboxed representations of ideas onto/into action are passed on constantly.

The limits of local vision obscure the fact that, if ideas are to be translated on/into a local action, all of this must already have happened. Global time/space operates spirally, and those stretches of local time/space which did not enter the spiral are replete with ideas whose time has not come. They are asynchronic. In the local parlance they are experienced, very appropriately, as a "waste of time".

The Swedish municipal reform, for instance, "caught on" to the degree it did because there were earlier decentralization episodes in the translocal history of municipalities, a new municipal law and a preceding public debate: it was "fashionable". Reform partly failed because the transition into institutionalization was not achieved (had been prevented by a legislatory body). Or take the difference of interpretations between Beckman (1987) and the actors in regional units. This too was a difference in time perspectives. Typically, researchers aim at reconstructing unfolding events in translocal time and space whereas the actors, naturally, are bound to their local place and time as their frame of reference.

Ideas and Change

The time has come to end the story-telling and come to a point, which in our genre comes usually in a form of a summarizing metaphor. Here is ours: a spiral of fashion constituting the globalized time/space by connecting localized time/ spaces. Figure 2 is animated by an ambition to keep the theoretical cake and to eat it, too; to point out the illusionary character of "choices" within dichotomies of modernism. Dichotomies are logical devices meant to de-paradoxify: they apport-ion in two what is known as a whole. Although many such apportionings can be made with great success, the ensuing privileging of the one part at the expense of the other raises our doubts. It cannot be done without paying a price, which has to be paid in anticipation of action; managers are expected to make up their minds whether to introduce a planned change or to wait for automatic adaptations to take place. No such decision is necessary in research, dedicated as it is to reflection. Therefore we propose to combine what is usually kept disjointed.

229

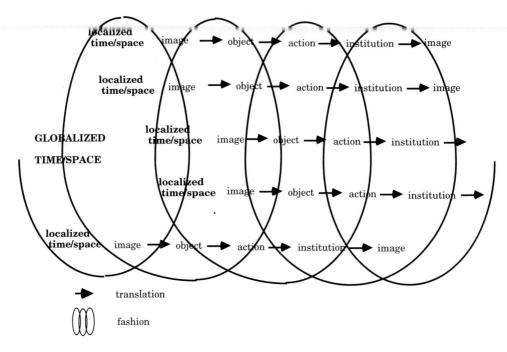

Figure 9.2

Contingency and Control

Does the image of organizational change as resulting from travels of ideas reconstruct change as a contingent process or the result of control processes? Both.

In the first place, planned organizational change, which is an attempt at controlled production of desired results, does not have to concern only the ideas which are the bestsellers on the translation lists. In most of our examples, organizational change happened as a result of some peripheral idea acquiring substance as a side-effect. In the case of Swedish municipalities, the leading idea was to decentralize political power, in the case of the Swedish regional boards, the idea was to experiment with new forms of industrial policy, in the case of TVA-like projects the ideas were many, ranging from political to technological to social, and in the case of Daimler-Benz the main idea was, presumably, to implement an effective form of publicity. Many of the translators may never have thought of contingent organizational changes (at least if one listens to what the rank-and-file employees have to say afterward). Each attempt at a "planned change", however, might have inadvertently provoked (caused, pulled, pushed, driven, occasioned) a string of changes: restructuring, introduction of new structures, reshuffling of responsibilities, and so on. In relation to planned change, idea-materialization processes are like avalanches compared to a stone thrown on the ground.

This leads to many surprises in situations where a seemingly new idea is adopted as a label for an already existing practice, the intention being precisely to maintain the status quo. But the result usually encompasses much more change and innovation than was desired. The materialization of ideas can be also spontaneous or random. The concept of translation is useful to the extent that it captures the coupling between arising contingencies and attempted control, created by actors in search for meaning.

This reasoning can be as well reversed. Actually, we show change as adaptation to the institutional requirements of the environment. But such an adaptation is far from unconscious or passive: it activates the intentional processes of the creation of meaning. Presenting those processes in a translocal view as populations in motion has a certain metaphorical value, but offers insights of a very little pragmatic value. Any intentional action originates on the phenomenological level and all pragmatic knowledge must concentrate on how individual action become collectivized and the other way around. Describing actions of collectives and individuals as separate realms is as futile as the common wish to build bridges between them afterwards. The picture we want to convey is not dualistic: it is an image of how contingency is made meaningful (sometimes downright functional) by interpretation.

Explanations and Interpretations

The mixture of intentional and contingent effects that ultimately shapes change in any and all organizations vexes many, if not all, students of organizations. Usually, an analyst chooses one of two paths to follow: the "positive" one of looking for "objective" explanations which should eventually lead to formulation of "universal laws", or the "hermeneutic" one of looking for "subjective" interpretations which will end with the celebration of the particular and the unique. We do not want to follow either road.

Instead, we shall follow a route, marked by many others before us, where narrative knowledge, this mainstay of everyday life, freely mixes explanations with interpretations, opening causality to negotiation (Bruner 1990). Planning to act at a distance requires the objectification of the target in order to produce strong explanations (Latour 1992). Being acted upon elicits interpretations in terms of intentions of those who are acting upon you. Acting upon the world, we expect to change it objectively, but the knowledge about both methods and results of change will always remain enclosed in language. The crucial point is the choice of vocabulary, and here we opt to be disloyal to the ideal of science in which we have been schooled because we find blurred genres (Geertz 1980) more receptive to a successful grasping of the complexity of organizational life.

231

Where is the place of the present attempt of blurring narrative and scientific genres in the processes we describe? Do our ideas stand any chance of going translocal? Reflexivity of the kind we endorse has become fashionable, but not institutionalized in social research. Our organization field turns ideas into publications which count as materialization. Will our ideas become translated into thers' publications? Will these be translated into other quasi-objects that can travel into other organization fields, for example outside the academia?

We have tried to cast a scientifically phrased issue in the narrative form. This is, in a sense, the opposite of what structuralists and formalists theorists are after. In fact it is very much what the transition from school to life, say from Business School to management, requires; thus there might already exist a need for stories like ours. But as the results of the translation process cannot be deduced from the idea itself, we will wait and see what happens next. The intentional part ends here.

References

Abrahamson, E. (1991) "Managerial Fads and Fashions: The Diffusion and Rejection of Innovations", *Academy of Management Review* 16(3): 586–612.

Agger, B. (1991) *The Decline of Discourse*. New York: The Falmer Press.

Bachrach, P. and Baratz, M.S. (1963) "Decisions and Non-decisions: An Analytical Framework", *American Political Science Review* 57: 632–42.

Beckman, B. (1987) *Att bilda EOU-organ*. Stockholm: ERU-rapport 51.

Berger, P.L. and Luckmann, T. (1966) *The Social Construction of Reality*. Harmondsworth, Middlesex: Penguin.

Blumer, H. (1969/1973) "Fashion: From Class Differentiation to Collective Selection", in G. Wills and D. Midgley (eds.) *Fashion Marketing*. London: Allen & Unwin.

Bruner, J.S. (1957) "On Perceptual Readiness", *Psychological Review* 64(2): 123–145.

_____. (1961) "The Act of Discovery", *Harvard Educational Review* 31: 21–32.

_____. (1986) *Actual Minds, Possible Worlds*. Cambridge, Mass.: Harvard University Press.

_____. (1990) *The Acts of Meaning*. Cambridge, Mass.: Harvard University Press.

Brunsson, N. (1985) *The Irrational Organization*. London: Wiley.

Callon, M. (1986) "Some Elements of a Sociology of Translation: Domestication of the Scallops and the Fishermen of St. Brieuc"s Bay", in J. Law (ed.) *Power, Action and Belief*, pp. 196–229. London: Routledge and Kegan Paul.

_____. (1992) "Technoeconomic Networks and Irreversibility", in J. Law (ed.) *A Sociology of Monsters: Essays on Power, Technology and Domination*, pp. 132–161. London: Routledge and Kegan Paul.

Callon, M. and Latour, B. (1981) "Unscrewing the Big Leviathan: How Actors Macro-structure Reality and How Sociologists Help Them To Do So", in K. Knorr-Cetina and A.V. Cicourel (eds.) *Advances in social theory and methodology,* pp. 277–303. London: Routledge and Kegan Paul.

Clifford, J. and Marcus, G. (1986) *Writing Culture. The Poetics and Politics of Ethnography.* Berkeley: University of California Press.

Cohen, M.D. and March, J.G. (1974) *Leadership and Ambiguity.* New York: McGraw-Hill.

Czarniawska-Joerges, B. (1988) *Ideological Control in Nonideological Organizations.* New York: Praeger.

_____. (1990) "Merchants of Meaning", in B. Turner (ed.) *Organizational Symbolism.* Berlin: de Gruyter.

Czarniawska-Joerges, B. and Joerges, B. (1990) "Linguistic Artifacts at Service of Organizational Control", in P. Gagliardi (ed.) *The Symbolics of Corporate Artifacts,* pp. 509–548. Berlin: de Gruyter.

DiMaggio, P.J. and Powell, W.W. (1983) "The Iron Cage Revisited: Institutional Isomorphism and Collective Rationality in Organizational Fields", *American Sociological Review* 48: 147–160.

Douglas, M. (1986) *How Institutions Think.* Syracuse, New York: Syracuse University Press.

Downs, A. (1972) "Up and Down with Ecology: The Issue-Attention Cycle", *The Public Interest* 28: 38–50.

Edelman, M. (1988) *Constructing the Political Spectacle.* Chicago: The University of Chicago Press.

Finkelstein, J. (1989) *Dining Out. A Sociology of Modern Manners.* Cambridge: Polity Press.

Forssell, A. (1989) "How to Become Modern and Businesslike: An Attempt to Understand the Modernization of Swedish Savings Banks", *International Studies of Management & Organization* 19(3): 32–46.

Forty, A. (1986) *Objects of Desire. Design and Society 1750–1980.* London: Cameron.

Foucault, M. (1980) "Questions on Geography", in C. Gordon (ed.) *Power/ Knowledge: Selected Interviews and Other Writings 1972–1977.* New York: Pantheon.

Freudenberger, H. (1963/1973) "Fashion, Sumptuary Laws, and Business", in G. Wills and D. Midgley (eds.) *Fashion Marketing.* London: Allen & Unwin.

Geertz, C. (1980) "Blurred Genres: The Refiguration of Social Thought", *American Scholar* 49: 165–179.

_____. (1983) *Local Knowledge.* New York: Basic Books.

Gergen, K.J. (1991) *The Saturated Self. Dilemmas of Identity in Contemporary Life.* New York: Basic Books.

Gherardi, S. and Strati, A. (1988) "The Temporal Dimension in Organizational Studies", *Organization Studies* 9(2): 149–164.

Giddens, A. (1979) *Central Problems in Social Theory: Action, Structure and Contradiction in Social Analysis.* Berkeley: University of California Press.

Hendriks, J. and Kalishoek, A. (1987) *Decision-making on Cutting Back of Staff at Dutch Universities*, paper presented at EGPA-conference, 6–9 May, Valencia (Spain)

Hinings, B. and. Greenwood, R. (1988) "The Normative Prescription of Organizations", in L.G. Zucker (ed.) *Institutional Patterns and Organizations: Culture and Environment.* Cambridge, Mass.: Ballinger.

Hirschman, A.O. (1967) *Development Projects Observed.* Washington, DC: The Brookings Institution.

_____. (1977/1981) *The Passions and the Interests.* Princeton, NJ: Princeton University Press.

Hollinger, D. (1980) "The Problem of Pragmatism in American History", *The Journal of American History* 67(1): 88–107.

Jacobsson, B. (1989) *Konsten att reagera.* Stockholm: Carlssons.

Jansson, D. (1989) "The Pragmatic Uses of What is Taken for Granted: Project Leaders" Applications of Investment Calculations", *International Studies of Management & Organization* 19(3): 47–62.

Joerges, B. (1976) *Beratung und Technologietransfer: Untersuchungen zur Professionalisierbarkeit gesellschaftsüberschreitender Beratung.* Baden-Baden: Nomos.

Joerges, B. (1990) "'Global 2000": Social Science, Ecology and the Bimillennium", *Futures* 1: 3–20

Johansson, J. (1988) *Kommundelsnämndsreformen i Sverige*, paper presented at Statensvetenskapliga Förbundets Årsmöte, Förvaltningskonferens, Mariehamn, Åland, 3–5 October.

Kingdon, J.W. (1984) *Agendas, Alternatives and Public Policies.* Boston: Little, Brown and Company.

Kroeber, A.L. (1923/1948) *Anthropology.* New York: Harcourt, Brace and Co.

Latour, B. (1986) "The Powers of Association", in J. Law (ed.) *Power, Action and Belief*, pp. 261–277. London: Routledge and Kegan Paul.

_____. (1992) "Technology is Society Made Durable", in J. Law (ed.) *A Sociology of Monsters: Essays on Power, Technology and Domination*, pp. 103–131. London: Routledge and Kegan Paul.

_____. (1993) *Messenger Talks.* Lund: The Institute of Economic Research. Working paper.

Levitt, B. and March, J.G. (1988) "Organizational Learning", *Annual Review of Sociology* 14: 319–340.

Luhmann, N. (1991) "Sthenographie und Euryalistik", in H.-U. Gumbrecht and K.-L. Pfeiffer (eds.) *Paradoxien, Dissonanzen, Zusammenbrüche. Situationen offener Eputemologie*, pp. 58–82. Frankfurt: Suhrkamp.

Lyotard, J.-F. (1979/1986) *The Postmodern Condition: A Report on Knowledge.* Manchester: The Manchester University Press.

MacIntyre, A. (1981/1990) *After Virtue.* London: Duckworth Press.

March, J.G. (1988) *Decisions and Organizations.* Oxford: Basil Blackwell.

March, J.G. and Olsen, J.P. (1976) *Ambiguity and Choice.* Bergen: Universitetsforlaget.

_____. (1983) "The New Institutionalism: Organizational Factors in Political Life", *The American Political Science Review* 78: 734–749.

_____. (1989) *Rediscovering Institutions. The Organizational Basis of Politics.* New York, The Free Press.

Marcus, G. (1992) "Past, Present and Emergent Identities: Requirements for Ethnographies of Late Twentieth-Century Modernity World-Wide", in S. Lash and J. Friedman (eds.) *Modernity & identity,* pp. 309–330. Oxford: Blackwell.

Maslow, A. (1966) *The Psychology of Science.* New York: Harper and Row.

McCloskey, D.N. (1990) *If You're So Smart. The Narrative of Economic Expertise.* Chicago: University of Chicago Press.

Merton, R.K. (1965/1985) *On the Shoulders of Giants.* New York: Harcourt and Jovanovich.

Meyer, J.W. (1990) Personal communication, May 16.

Miller, G.A., Galanter, E., and Pribram, K.H. (1960) *Plans and the Structure of Behaviour.* New York: Holt, Rinehart and Winston.

Mintzberg, H. (1979) *The Structuring of Organizations.* Englewood Cliffs, NJ: Prentice-Hall.

Mitchell, W.J.T. (1986) *Iconology. Image, Text, Ideology.* Chicago: The University of Chicago Press.

Powell, W. and DiMaggio, P.J. (eds.) (1991) *The New Institutionalism in Organizational Analysis.* Chicago: Chicago University Press.

Robinson, D.E. (1960/1973) "The Styling and Transmission of Fashions Historically Considered", in G. Wills and D. Midgley (eds.) *Fashion Marketing.* London: Allen & Unwin.

Rogers, E.M. (1962) *The Diffusion of Innovation.* New York: Free Press.

Rorty, R. (1980) *Philosophy and the Mirror of Nature.* Oxford: Basil Blackwell.

_____. (1982) *Consequences of Pragmatism.* Minneapolis: University of Minnesota Press.

_____. (1989) *Contingency, Irony and Solidarity.* Cambridge: Cambridge University Press.

_____. (1991) *Objectivity, Relativism and Truth. Philosophical Papers,* vol. I. New York: Cambridge University Press.

Sahlin-Andersson, K. (1989) *Oklarhetens strategi.* Lund: Studentlitteratur.

_____. (1991) *Science Parks as Organized Fields.* Stockholm: EFI Researeh Paper.

Schütz, A. (1953/1973) "Common-Sense and the Scientific Interpretation of Human Action", *Collected papers,* vol. I. The Hague: Martinus Nijhoff.

Sederberg, P.C. (1984) *The Politics o f Meaning.* Tucson: The University of Arizona Press.

Sellerberg, A.-M. (1987) *Avstånd och attraktion.* Stockholm: Carlssons.

Simmel, G. (1904/1973) "Fashion", in G. Wills and D. Midgley (eds.) *Fashion Marketing.* London: Allen & Unwin.

Smith-Lovin, L. and Brody, C. (1989) "Interruptions in Group Discussions", *American Sociological Review* 54(3): 424–435.

Spetz, G. (1988) *Vägen till nej. Anade och oanade konsekvenser av en OS-satsning.* Stockholm: EFI.

Taps, J. and Martin, P.Y. (1988) *Gender Composition and Attributional Accounts: Impact on Women's Influence and Likability in Task Groups*, paper presented at the Southern Sociological Society Meeting, March.

Trist, E. and Bamford, K.W. (1951) "Some Social and Psychological Consequences of the Longwall Method of Goal-getting", *Human Relations* 4: 3–38.

Warren, R., Rose, S. and Bergunder, A. (1974) *The Structure of Urban Reform.* Lexington, Mass.: Lexington Books.

Young, A.B. (1937/1973) "Recurring Cycles of Fashion", in G. Wills and D. Midgley (eds.) *Fashion Marketing.* London: Allen & Unwin.

Zey-Ferrel, M. (1981) "Criticisms of the Dominant Perspective on Organizations", *The Sociological Quarterly* 22: 181–205.

Zucker, L.G. (1977) "The Role of Institutionalization in Cultural Persistence", *American Sociological Review* 42: 726–743.

Chapter 10

Organizational Imitation in Identity Transformation

Guje Sevón

Western society applauds its winners. It is a competitive civilization in which the successful nation-states, firms and individuals are praised. Mary Douglas (1987) compares this society to a hierarchy that celebrates its patriarch, and the sect which commemorates its martyrs. Not only do Western people and organizations praise their heroes, they imitate them. The great popularity of books describing successful firms (see for example Peters and Waterman, 1982) is one indication of this trend. Firms imitate seemingly successful business strategies (going international), policies (applying strategic human resource management), organizational structure (divisionalizing organizations), technologies (adopting best practices, just-in-time-management), preferences (focusing on ecological management), and products. Products now routinely counterfeited include chemicals, computers, drugs, fertilizers, pesticides, medical devices, military hardware, and food, as well as parts for airplanes and automobiles. It is estimated that up to $600 billion in annual world trade is in fakes (*International Business Week*, December 16, 1985).

The intent of this chapter is to introduce and develop the notion of organizational imitation. The objective is to define and discuss imitation in such a way that multiple research questions become visible. A main argument is that organizations are socially transformed in a process of imitation. Organizations are defined as social constructions; they are sets of collective action. For the discussion it is however useful to metaphorically describe an organization as a legal person an actor in the modern institutional order. This actor will be seen as a superperson, borrowing the argument from Czarniawska-Joerges (1994) that organizations are often metaphorically seen and taken for granted as superpersons: decision makers, leaders, and sometimes management groups or collectives. Here, an organization will be treated as an actor which is capable of cognitive action (although the actor not necessarily reflects upon its own capability): to attend to the environment, to make comparisons and judgments, to reason about causality and to act according to desires. An actor (in this essay exemplified by a corporate organization, a work unit, and a nation-state) is also able to conceive of itself and others as having identities. Based on the assumption that imitation is principally described as action by organizations as superpersons, literature on human actors will be referred to along with literature on organizations as actors.

Ostensive and Performative Definitions of Imitation

Imitation can be defined and understood in different ways. Imitation in most current literature is seen as an equivalent term to copying, namely reproducing or transcribing an original product. This literature puts stress on the effort which goes into finding a good model to imitate. The remaining process becomes a mechanical adaptation; one simply imitates (see the discussion below about literature on diffusion of innovations).

Imitation, especially if it is seen as a product that is a copy of an original, has been and still is a frequent object of study, especially when the original is seen as an innovation. In many of these studies, the focus has been on the spread of innovations where imitation has been treated as a cause of diffusion, as the mechanism that facilitates a diffusion of a certain object or idea. Borrowing Latour's (1986) classification of definitions, this research tradition has applied an ostensive definition of imitation. It implies that what is to be imitated is seen as a *given* phenomenon, as something that is objectified. It is seen as something immutable born with some impetus that propels it across a social area or space with various degrees of resistance.

These traditional models emphasize three elements in the process of diffusion (Latour, 1986). The first element is the initial energy (initiative, order, quote command, instruction) which usually is connected to power and leadership and seen as coming from an individual source (Czarniawska-Joerges, 1994, p. 208). This energy is seen as a trigger of movement, and it constitutes the only energy for diffusion. The second element is the inertia that conserves this energy, and the third is the medium through which the something is diffused. From this ostensive perspective, what spurs research interest are questions of why some object, idea or behavior is not perfectly transmitted, and why there is resistance (like lack of communication, ill will, opposition of interests groups, perception errors, indifference, et cetera) which hinders the diffusion. Typical inquires into these studies look at how frequent, how fast, how accurately, and to whom something is transmitted.

Imitation as ostensively defined has been examined by scholars from many disciplines who often have given it different labels. Scholars in marketing (e.g. Rogers, 1962) traditionally have looked upon imitation as a process of diffusion by which consumer products or technologies (more seldom administrative technologies) are adopted within a community. A similar focus exists in early work of economists; Tarde (1902) suggested that the cumulative number of adopters of a new idea follows an S-shaped distribution over time. Contemporary economists mainly study speed, costs/time trade-off, and information spillover in diffusion processes of innovations (Mansfield et al., 1981; Reingaum, 1983; Dasgupta, 1988). Business strategy researchers (e.g. MacMillan et al., 1985) look at imitation response time of competitors. In developmental psychology there is an interest both in imitation as a cognitive skill (e.g. Piaget 1951) and in motoric imitation among neonatal children (e.g. Maratos, 1973). Among contemporary students of organization theory, imitation is a central notion in institutionalization and mimetic isomorphism (e.g. DiMaggio and Powell, 1983; Tolbert and Zucker, 1983). There is also an interest in imitation among students of anthropology (e.g. Durkheim, 1912; Linton, 1936; Douglas, 1987), and of psychoanalytic theory (Girard, 1977). Imitation as copying of original work is furthermore a popular object of study in the disciplines of literature, art history, and religion.

Contrary to most of the literature on imitation, which assumes that there is an immutable something which is carried by an autonomous impetus that diffuses across actors, I will see imitation as a process in which something is created and transformed by chains of translators. From this it follows that ideas or practices do not force themselves on organizations which then have to adopt them. The impetus for imitation must come from the imitators themselves, from their conception of situation, self-identity and others' identity, as well as from analogical reasoning by which these conceptions are combined. Imitation, hence performatively defined (Latour, 1986), becomes a process of translation with a specific focus on conceptualizing. This performative definition fosters description of an organization picking up an idea, translating it into something that fits its own context, and materializing it into action. The result of this action may or may not be similar to the idea that was originally conceptualized by the imitating organization. In other words, whatever is spread is not immutable; it may change in an on-going process of borrowing ideas or practices in a chain of actors. Latour states that.

> According to [the model of translation]..., the spread in time or space of anything claims, orders, artifacts, goods is in the hands of people; each of these people may act in many different ways, letting the token drop, or modifying it, or deflecting it, or betraying it, or adding to it, or appropriating it. The faithful transmission of, for instance an order by a large number of people is a rarity in such a model and if it occurs it requires explanation. (Latour, 1986, p.267)

The image of imitation as an ongoing translation of transforming organizations differs from the diffusion model: in a translation model the initial force of the first actor in the chain is no more important than the hundredths. Furthermore, it is not possible to know where or when the process concludes; parts of an idea that is spread in time and space may turn up in quite new circumstances. Furthermore, it becomes less meaningful to distinguish between new (discovery, original, innovation) and old (copy), as the model of diffusion does. The arbitrary labeling of action as either copying or discovery is less useful in discussion about imitation as translation (for an extensive discussion about what is an original and what is a copy, or a fake, see Eco, 1990) because in both copying and discovery one uses bits of one's own and others' experience: I may sometimes be copying what you are doing (presumably by using bits of actions I already know); or I may have recognized the whole pattern of yours as one I already know, or similar to one I already know. According to Margolis (1987), in the latter case, I am not really copying the outside. Rather I am navigating through a now-recognized pattern from my own repertoire in a new context. Alternatively, there may simply be some (chance or characteristic) feature made salient by the very encounter with this context that cues the novel use of a pattern already in the repertoire. Whether the product of this interaction should be called copying or discovery has to do with how much and how important own parts are and how much is borrowed from others. For this essay such a quantitative distinction is not important. I see imitation as a process of identity transformation that is neither solely a copy nor a totally new invention, but something between these ideal types.

Elements in the Imitation Process

To imitate is to act like someone else with the more or less conscious intent to achieve the same, or similar, consequences. It is a way of learning from others' experience of having done and achieved something. Imitation may be considered a good strategy both by individuals and organizations as a strategy that saves time and resources: one does not have to use a trial-and-error strategy, or one may even

240

avoid mistakes altogether. However, imitation as a strategy for saving resources and achieving desired identity may also be considered to have pitfalls. One of them is situated in the reasoning about connections between others' actions and identities. In situations of perceived uncertainty and uncomplete knowledge, organizations might feel that they do not know for sure what caused the desired states of others and whether the same magic will work once again, for themselves.

Imitation as a rationale for organizational change has been discussed by March (1981). This rationality which he calls the logic of appropriateness includes a judgment of what is a rational, or appropriate action. The judgment is based on comparison (matching) with others: *Who am I?, What situation is this?,* and consecutive action is based on the perceived action and achievements of other actors. Borrowing the main idea from this model, imitation will here be described as a process based on (1) matching of identifications and situations, (2) construction of desire to transform, and (3) institutionalized action.

A match is a judgment that something is similar to something else. In a process of matching questions and answers are posed and stated: *What am I like? (I am like X).* Identity transformation starts when the organization asks *What would I like to be?* and answers *(I would like to be like Xa).* In principal, as I see it, when an organization is positively matched in identity type and situation with another actor, it is possible to learn from this other's experience.

Identity is a modern institution, i.e. temporal and local (Meyer 1986; Czarniawska-Joerges, 1994). It is taken for granted that organizations, like individuals, have identities. Meyer points out that a modern identity includes self-respect, efficiency, autonomy, and flexibility. In a positive match with another actor Xa, who is seen as having a similar type of identity, but is still more successful, more efficient, more autonomous, et cetera, a desire to change own identity may arise. The match may trigger new questions: *How can I become more like Xa?, What situation is this?* and *What is the appropriate action for me in this situation?* The analogical reasoning which follows is: If I do as Xa does, I may become more like Xa. The subsequent action taken in consideration of the result of the matching (acting like Xa) is a legitimate, appropriate action in an effort to transform one's own identity. It is borrowing the experience of this other actor acting in an institutional manner.

As organizational imitation may aim at becoming similar to some other organization in identity, crucial for the discussion about organizational imitation is, therefore, a statement that organizational identity is not seen as a stable, essential feature but rather as a conception of a feature that develops in an ongoing and never-completed accomplishment: The identity of an organization is a description of an individual identity *emerging from interactions* between actors rather than existing as a form of an essence that is consequently exhibited (Czarniawska-Joerges, 1994, p.200).

241

Selective Attention in Organizational Imitation

Among modern organizations there is a taken-for-granted idea that it is desirable and possible to engineer social events in order to achieve features of modern identities, like self-respect, efficiency, autonomy, and flexibility. A firm with a good reputation (seen as having a desired identity) may become a model for imitation, and ideas about how to act be borrowed from this actor's repertoire. When there is uncertainty about what is proper action, information about what the majority of firms do may also serve a similar guiding function. A firm might search for a reliable recipe for good achievement when the context is changed for the firm, for example when the firm is newly established (new in the field), or when its performance is below average within the industry. Knowledge of others is not always available, though, and when there is a felt need to get ideas about action and practices from other firms, firms which are close, and therefore well-known, may also serve as models. Firms sometimes perceive market changes and changes among competitors that trigger changes in own strategy. These strategic action are often imitations of organizations which are seen as similar. Business strategy scholars (Porter, 1980; Huff, 1982; Rumelt, 1987) argue that key decision makers monitor rival organizations and formulate strategies to achieve desired competitive success. Outside the arena of competitive dynamics, organizations also nevertheless continuously monitor, perceive, and interpret what is going on in the environment; they pay attention to changes (Daft and Weick,1984).

An organization does not imitate every other organization, and neither does it imitate all the time. Let us focus on instances when an organization imitates a comparable entity, perhaps in similar surroundings, from which there seems to be something to be learned. This are instances where an organization imitates when it has more confidence in the history of others than in its own (the other knows better), that is, when it perceives uncertainty or ambiguity about how to act given its own experience. Examples of perceived uncertainty are discussed by Abrahamson. He points out (1991) that imitating organizations are uncertain about environmental impact, goals, or technical efficiency. He argues that imitation is therefore expected (in literature) to be more frequent in some areas than in other depending on this uncertainty: for example, as administrative technologies produce unclear output but certain production technologies output which is less so, imitation of administrative techniques should be more common (see also Meyer and Rowan, 1977).

An organization's span of attention also determines what can be imitated. How organizations come to attend to certain parts of their environment is not at all a trivial issue. Generally, we can expect firms to attend more to changes than to non-changes; movement attracts attention (Bateson, 1979). For example, a firm may perceive a change in its market share, but not know how large a market share it has. Not all changes are perceived, though. An organization has a span of attention; it cannot attend to everything that can be considered its whole environment. Imitation, seen as a result of matching focused on identity, is normally assumed to occur in organization fields (DiMaggio and Powell, 1983).[1] Within an organization field thoughts are shared[2] and diffused among organizations. That has to do with shared frames of meaning; an organization's attention to the environment is based on available interpretative frames that are constructed within the social space in which it operates. An organization field is for example an activity field which comprises organizations with a similar activity definition. These organizations have the same thought world. When imitation is the result of matching that is focused on identity transformation, the organizations attend to changes in the thought world. Let us assume that when imitation is a result of matching which is less focused on identities but more on desired outcomes (when it does not matter who I am, but only that I want the same outcome) we can assume that imitation occurs mainly in networks of action. These are organization fields which comprise organizations that usually interact. However, the distinction between a network of action and a thought world is blurred. Desired outcomes and desired identity are closely related, and it is evident that imitation also occurs across thought worlds in organization fields. Forssell and Jansson (1996) describe a case in which local governments want to act like the financial giants they meet in their organization field.

An organization mostly perceives changes in its organization field. Perceived changes in actions, practices and achievements may trigger imitation. As thoughts are shared within a field, one would expect many organizations to imitate the actions and practices of field members. This in turn might increase the homogeneity of the field. DiMaggio and Powell consequently argue that (large) organizations are likely to come to resemble one another. The process behind this, they claim, is the professionalization of managers that tends to create a particular world view of appropriate organizational behavior. In that sense, networks of action become also thought worlds. But, as professionalization is a socialization process that makes

---

1   A notion related to organization field appears in industrial economics (see, for example Fligstein (1985), who states that industries are good theoretical proxies for environment.

2   The idea of shared meaning within a social space, or a society is, however older than the notion of an organization field in institutional theory. Fleck (1935) introduced the concept thought collective (cf. collective group, Durkheim & Mauss, 1903; Durkheim 1912) and thought style (cf. Durkheim's collective representation) to describe what leads and exercises cognition and produces a stock of knowledge within a society.

actors perceive and act in a similar manner, how is it then possible that over time not all organizations in a field become clones of one organization with admired actions or practices? An answer to this question is available if we depart from the traditional perspective of institutional theory and look at imitative action from a performative perspective.

When organizational imitation is seen as translation rather than as copying of a stable feature, or as a spread of this feature within an area, the imitative action and the resulting outcome may as well vary between actors and change over time and space. As a result, thought worlds and networks of action may transform, too. The variation between actors comes from the fact that actors may differ in what they learn from others and how they learn. Thus, the professionalization of actors within an organization field is not perfect. Moreover, organizations often borrow only certain features from another organization, and not the whole pattern, and they modify the borrowed idea in order to adjust it to their own conditions. Organizations conceive of themselves not only as similar to others but also as exclusively different. Consequently, to some degree they sometimes act differently, and end up as partly different from one another. Therefore, the result of imitation as a process of translation is that the fields are to some degree heterogeneous, and to some degree homogeneous. Furthermore, new fields may appear as a result; both organizations and organization fields change over time as a result of processes of translation.

A very distinct example of imitation seen as translation is given by Westney (1987) who studied Japan during the Meiji period, 1868–1912, when it experienced a most remarkable social transformation. During this period, Japan emulated many organizations from Britain, France, the United States, Germany and Belgium. Japan developed its navy, army, postal system, primary school system, judicial system, police system, and more. The police system was an emulation of the French system, but also partly of Japan's own traditions. From Paris was borrowed the system of financing, the formal regulatory structure, the political role of the chief, and the functions, size, and formal roles of differentiation and specialization. Such borrowed ideas were emulated in concert with Japanese characteristics and experiences. Japanese traditions contributed with ideas concerning the control of individual performance, orientation to public education, vertical administrative unit differentiation, training and education, information, and weaponry. Instead of choosing the French police recruitment system, Japan choose to continue the tradition of the Samurai and the Satsuma, who performed functions similar to those of the police but who were outside of the society. Japanese policemen were therefore recruited heavily from areas outside the population in which they were to function. The system for education and training of policemen was also taken from old Samurai traditions. From this mixture of attributes of the French police system and their own traditions, some innovations were born: the upper-level career patterns, the spatial dispersion, and the utilization of new communication technology.

Westney claims that the most important factor in deliberate departures from the original organizational model is the social context into which the organization is introduced when it is transferred out of the institutional environment in which it developed. The differences between Japanese and French society made it natural to modify the French system when adopted by Japan. This reminds us that an accomplished imitation does not imply a true and total copying. When Westney argues that the successful imitation of foreign organizational patterns requires innovation, she implies that an organization has many different desires, related to its different attributes (and desired belongings), and in the ongoing transformation of the organization a blend of these desires guides both deliberate and unintended changes. This triggers another less common discussion about the premises of the variability between organizations: that organizations may have more than one identity that controls their attention, and that they may also possess the desire to acquire the identities of others. To this I will later return.

Organizational Self-Identification: What Am I Like?

Matching of identities demands self-identification, an answer to the question: *What am I like?* One cannot make a self-identification, i.e. a social labeling applied to oneself, without reference to others. It is possible to only label oneself in relation to others. This implies that self-identification also demands at least indirectly the social labeling of others´ identities. The question *What am I like?* becomes *Whom do I look like?* In cases of imitation, an organization may label itself with reference to and in comparison with, for example, high-reputation business firms. Such firms are, I suppose, most probably seen in the thought collective, to which the organization belongs. One reason for this is that the collective has a shared language for labeling and comparison, e.g. an organization might be seen as relatively high-reputational and, for example, small, progressive, and risk-seeking. The language and mental models of organizations is however not necessarily limited to business language. A thought collective can also offer language and mental images about a non-social world; in which case matching may also be made with non-human actors, as in: *What do I look like?*

The rhetorical strategy that organizations choose in order to present their identities seems to focus on three aspects: central character, temporal continuity, and distinctiveness (Albert and Whetten, 1985). A *central character* distinguishes the organization on the basis of something important and essential. *Temporal continuity* means that the identification includes features that exhibit some degree of sameness or continuity over time, and *distinctiveness* implies a classification that identifies the organization as recognizably different from others. Statements of ideology, management philosophy, culture, and rituals may be chosen in the rhetoric of an organization as a strategy to define its uniqueness. In those cases in which a distinctive identity is prized, a chosen strategy may be to select uncommon dimensions of interorganizational comparison as well as uncommon locations along more widely employed dimensions. Rhetorical statements may include habitual strategic propositions for example, a known willingness to take high risks, as may be the case for a company that is distinctively presented as entrepreneurial (Albert and Whetten, 1985). As imitation starts from the idea that there is something a similar entity has or shows which is worth taking on an as ideas for one's own action; we should expect firms that prefer to claim their distinctiveness to be less prone to imitate. Imitation is probably more common among firms that describe themselves by stating their central character.

As organizational self-identification is based on a process of matching with something else, the part of an identity which becomes salient therefore rests on what the organization compares itself with. A judgment of similarity is dynamic and context-dependent, and the perceived properties of an organization may vary as a function of what it is compared to (Medin, Goldstone and Gentner, 1993). It is easy to accept this statement in the case of individuals. For example, a manager may possess several unrelated self-identifications at the same time, and may refer to several social collectives simultaneously as well. Which of these identities and self-descriptions becomes salient depends however on the current context. A manager's identification and action may be more mother-like at home and more business-like at work. As a consequence, she may describe herself in reference to the class of women, the class of mothers, and the class of managers, but during working hours see herself mainly as a manager, or as a female manager (see also Elster, 1985; Leiser, Sevón & Lévy, 1990).

Likewise, an organization may identify itself in more than one way. A business firm may describe itself as a member of the class of international firms, the paper and pulp industry, family firms, and firms heavily burdened by debt.

Self-identification varies with reference group, and choice of reference group depends on the salient context at the moment. When the environment changes, the task at hand varies, the market situation turns, or the experience of the organization otherwise develops, the context may shift, which may in turn lead to a matching with entities different than those before, and, consequently, a reformulation of the identity. New labels may be added to earlier ones, because important features of an earlier identification persist in the structure, philosophy, strategy, et cetera. This is clearly shown by Westney (1987) in her description of Japan during the Meiji period. Sometimes, however, the identities form a hybrid organization, meaning an organization whose identity is composed of two or more types that would not normally go together. Examples include a bank which is operated by a religious organization (Albert and Whetten, 1985) and a state organization which is both the master of the public and the public servant (Czarniawska-Joerges, 1994).

Perhaps because few studies have until now focused on the process of organizational imitation from a performative perspective, there are barely any studies of implicit theories of how a business organization might answer the question of what it looks like, which classes of phenomena it belongs to. Neither are there many studies of changes in such self-descriptions. It seems as if such striving towards a consistent self-description is aimed less at finding «true» identity and values and more towards developing a suitable identity. Explicitly stated self-identity is also often the result of many years of self-assessment, often with help from outside, such as consulting firms.

Despite little research, and few known implicit and explicit self-labels, some examples of self-description are well known and widely shared. It is common to talk about firms as belonging to a certain industry. It is also popular to discriminate more specifically between international and domestic business and to differentiate firms according to products and services. Turnover is also a common feature of identification: «we are a large, international business firm in the paper and pulp industry». Self-identification may serve as a statement about the central character of the organization, important in a certain context. Sometimes, such a claim of identity may have another purpose, but it is generally meant to distinguish the organization from other organizations.

Imitation of Desires: What Would I Like to Be?

One prerequisite for organizational imitation is a self-identification like the type of self-identification experienced and broadcast by others. Perceived likeness of identity and/or context with an imitated model seems to be necessary, both for the attention to and the development of beliefs about what is correct, true and desired, and for judgment about whether it is possible to obtain a similar outcome. However, it would be meaningless to imitate an organization that is considered to be identical in all aspects, and in their rhetoric, organizations also state, in addition to their central characteristics, features of identity that make them distinctive.

The striving to be similar but also different is a dilemma that has been touched upon by scholars of organization theory. Institutionalists claim, on the one hand, that strong pressure exists to imitate organizations, or more specificly, organizational forms that have been successful (Hannan and Freeman, 1977; DiMaggio and Powell, 1983). But students of competitive dynamics, on the other hand, claim that the superiority of an organization comes from creating and sustaining attributes that are not easily imitated (Porter, 1980; Rumelt, 1984: Peteraf, 1993). However, this literature does not discuss the matter of what ends up being considered as successful achievement by an organization, and therefore desired. It is obvious that in organizational imitation, a constituent element of an organizational identity is its system of desires, the collection of values concerning what is beneficial and to be sincerely wished for.

Where do these desires come from? They are not deducible from needs. Organizational desires, like individual ones, are socially constructed. Howe (1994) claims that (individual) desires can be characterized as cognitive phenomena which are heavily influenced by social learning. He summarizes his view:

> Human desire is something which is ultimately directionless a mere force, a potential for action or movement (...) Direction must be given to it through learning, through being taught, implicitly, to place certain values on things. In some cases, such as eating, this is just a matter of being conditioned to identify food as being that which relieves the pain of hunger. In more interesting cases, it comes about by observing others and thereby learning what they value, which then seems to have a value in itself. (Howe, 1994, p.4)

Howe claims that one learns to desire something by adopting the desires of those around. Desires for a certain identity are also socially learned. One special case of imitating desires in order to obtain a closer likeness in identity is described by Girard (1977). He studied rivalry, specifically the imitation of the rival from a psychoanalytical perspective. His focus may also be relevant in the context of organizational imitation, because firms pay attention to and compare themselves with their competitors (Huff, 1990). Girard claims that rivalry does not arise because of the fortuitous convergence of two desires on a single object; rather, the subject desires the object because the rival desires it. Girard states that in desiring an object the rival alerts the subject to the desirability of the object. The rival, then, serves as a model for the subject, not only in regard to such secondary matters as style and opinion but also, and more essentially, in regard to desires. Girard writes:

> In human relationships words like sameness and similarity evoke an image of harmony. If we have the same taste, (...) surely we are bound to get along. But, the model, even if he has openly encouraged imitation, is surprised to find himself engaged in competition. (Girard, 1977, p. 146)

Girard concludes that the disciple has betrayed the confidence of the model by following in his or her footsteps. Simultaneously the disciple feels both rejected and humiliated, judged unworthy by the model of participating in the superior existence that the model enjoys. In business societies, unlike among people, similarity between firms may not be seen as a state of harmony. On the contrary, competitiveness between members of the society of firms is predominantly part of the formula; competitors are rivals, and they fight for the same objects. This is an important aspect of corporate action. Also, Fligstein (1985) claims that every theory of organizational change must take into account the fact that the leaders of organizations watch one another and adopt what they perceive as successful strategies for growth and organizational structure. Stories in business magazines tell about these successes, and appoint the winners in the competition among companies. The winners gain distinction, and the losers perhaps envy.

Reasoning about Appropriate Action: Analogical Thinking

Imitation is a process which begins with identification and results in transformation. A link between the two is causal reasoning: what is before causes what is after; what is visible should be coupled together; great outcomes are caused by great events; et cetera. Business life is full of causal reasoning; reasoning about causes and effects is seen as necessary in order to behave in a rational way. Business people think that setting goals makes sense only if supported by ideas about how it is possible to reach goals, and, that diagnosed problems can be dealt with only if there is knowledge about what caused the problems. Examples of causal reasoning in business are connections perceived between a risk-taking propensity and a technical innovation, between a divisionalized organizational form and growth in turnover, and between employing a certain consultant in quality management and a subsequent turn-around.

For causal reasoning about what is appropriate action, analogies may be used. What analogy is chosen for a matching with one's own situation then becomes a crucial issue concerning what is imitated. There are several aspects of analogies which are interesting: the domain that the analogical model describes and the form and place of this description.

Analogical reasoning enhances the interpretation of a new situation. Actors use analogies to map the set of transition rules from a known domain into one which is a new, thereby constructing a mental model that can generate inferences in the new domain. Any system whose transition rules are reasonably well-specified can serve as an analogical model for understanding a new system (Collins and Gentner, 1989). Douglas (1987) and Quinn and Holland (1989) claim that there is however an advantage with analogies from the physical world. This advantage rests on the nature of the physical world itself, and the manner in which physical properties and relations are comprehended by human beings.

Identifying with and imitating non-human actors

Organizations may consider themselves metaphorically in terms of non-human actors and organizations; it is well known that organizations are engaged in metaphorical thinking (Morgan, 1986). One example of the use of metaphors from the non-human world is delivered by semiotic scholars: in order to gain insights about its identity an organization may compare itself to an animal, such as a lion, or to a car, such as a Volvo. Although metaphorical thinking is an important element in identity construction (Czarniawska-Joerges, 1994), it is less important in the case of imitation. What I wish to instead take up are interesting cases of matching in which the reasoning looks metaphorical but is in fact analogical.

When an organization perceives a similarity between itself and the features of a structure or an object in the non-human world it is engaged in analogical reasoning. The power of analogical reasoning vis-à-vis the non-human world is shown in a field study of international joint R&D ventures (Sevón, forthcoming).

Some project managers' descriptions of their R&D organizations were not stated in traditional organization terminology. Rather, the organizations were described as similar to the product or the scientific process that was the concern of the daily R&D work. Not only were they described as cases parallel to a physical world; organizational structures and processes that seemed important to the project managers were also designed similarly to physical ones. The study shows that this reasoning was used for making sense of organizational structure and action and of important organizational features. Maybe it also illustrates an interplay between analogical models and designing of an organization. The field study was, however, not focussing on this aspect, so we have to leave this issue open to speculation. In any case, the study indicates that the identity description and formation of an organization may originate from inference about a physical entity rather than from project organizations. Let me illustrate this.

The aim of one project organization was to develop compound electrical component systems. The total project included many subprojects, and it involved 39 participating firms. These partners developed different components which were to become part of larger systems. Therefore, the success of the total project was seen as mostly contingent upon the ability to coordinate the participating firms.

The organization of this large project was complex, with many different relationships between the partners. For example, in one subproject one partner dominated, while in others all partners were equal. As the partners did not necessarily trust each other, in some projects the R&D work was smooth, while in others it experienced difficulties. The competitiveness in the electricity industry is hard; partners in the same subproject even hesitated to inform each other about the latest development in the work. Although these conditions for a joint venture seem very problematic for scholars of organization design, a project organization had been set up that was considered adequate and efficient. What then would an organization look like that can perform during such problematic circumstances, and how might it be described? The project manager of one partner gave the answer:

> The collaboration between the firms is organized by one of the partners, Coordina, whose only function is to control and support the collaboration. Coordina has a main role as transmitter of information and stimulator of the R&D work. This agency acts as a central junction, with a female engineer who also works as a secretary for all projects. We all get information from her about what is simultaneously going on in the other projects. This is important because the progress of all projects is relatively interrelated. Coordina scans the work of all partners; it makes sure that everybody keeps to their deadlines. Coordina also gives administrative support.

The project is interesting in the way its organization is conceived. The project manager, an engineer and himself a researcher in the project, uses a component system analogy to describe the project organization. It is described as a structure consisting of different components that fit together by a centrally-located coordination and control office. This constructed reality of the project organization matches its products; the whole project is organized analogously to the systems of components that it develops. The competitiveness between partners that implies a low level of trust is compensated by the design of a neutral organizing and controlling partner, Coordina, which has nothing else at stake but the success of the whole project.

The case illustrates how a model from the physical world can function as the model in an organizational transformation as it creates beliefs about what is proper and desirable. Although the engineer himself was not aware of his analogical reasoning, the case tells us how an engineer might utilize his acquaintance with a technical system to make sense of the organizational world. The engineer did not offer an alternative model that could be found in traditional management literature. It seems to me that he used well-known products as a parallel case that allowed him to generate predictions about what would happen in various situations in a complex project organization. The case illustrates how people may intuitively use a picture from the domain in which they are skilled to map onto the domain of organizational structure, which is less well-known to them. And, simultaneously, the organizational structure may become perceived as the structure of an electrical component system. We can imagine that the project manager as an R&D engineer had faith in the idea of a component system. I got the impression from the project manager's description that for him an ideal organization consists of subunits which contribute to the whole organization with information transmitted in accordance with fixed rules, and of a communication center acting as the agent responsible for the efficiency of the information flow.

The structures of other R&D project organizations studied were different from those in this case. One project aiming at developing chemical products consisted of only two partners. The project manager of one of the partners described the relation as trustful, very close and reciprocal. He stressed that the most salient attribute was the good chemistry between the researchers of the two partners. In addition to the R&D project, a friendship development subproject was developed. This project, that was taken very seriously, was aimed at entertaining the other partner and strengthening the ties between the two partners. The Finnish partner arranged smoke-sauna baths with sauna diplomas for survivors, the Danish partner arranged crayfish parties on a ship in the North Sea. This subproject of friendship development can be analogically described as a catalyst aimed at fostering the success of the work developing chemical compounds.

These two cases indicate that a comparison with non-human entities sometimes makes sense. It makes sense, for example, when an organization type is uncommon and it may be difficult to ascertain to which class of organization it belongs. Also, if the organization knows little about organization fields, it may be difficult to tell to which group of organizations it belongs. As for ad-hoc organizations, like project organizations, which are led by people who have little knowledge about the management of organizations and are not always likely to be able to use the language of managers, the use of images and language from a non-organizational world may be a rather feasible alternative. For a project manager in a high-technology project organization, which is usually run by natural scientists who do not have much experience in business management, the immediate source for making sense of the project organization may derive from the natural science paradigm that occupies its daily scientific work. By analogical reasoning appropriate in the thought collective, the organization may be understood as a case parallel to the non-human world; the organizational pattern and functioning may in this case be perceived as similar to the physical. For other organizations, as with business organizations led by professional managers, the use of images from this domain may however be less customary. The managers of these organizations may prefer to rely on analogies that describe social organizations, and consequently imitate social action and patterns.

Agents of organizational imitation

In business life, analogical reasoning often appears in the costume of narrative structures which are communicated in story-telling. Story-telling or gossiping has an entertainment value but it also focuses attention on organizational agents and actions, and on organizations' history, rules, values, and morals usually by pointing at failures to satisfy them (March and Sevón, 1984/1988). Also, Bruner (1990) adds that as good stories, which should have some exceptional features, narratives are often about dramatic phenomena, about the successful or unsuccessful actions and outcomes of members of the society of organizations. He refers to Brown (1973) who told how young children in their first speech already show that they especially notice human interaction: agent-and-action, action-and-object, agent-and-object, action-and-location, and possessor-and-possession. This interest in stories about agents and actions does not disappear with age. Adults in business organizations teach each other stories about agents and actions. This activity is considered important. Business firms observe and describe the behavior of other firms because their own existence depends on the competitors' achievements, but also because getting ideas from others may save energy and time and reduce uncertainty and ambiguity.

Story-telling contributes to institution maintenance and the maintenance of exclusivity (March and Sevón, 1984/1988). It states what the natural norms, rules, properties and contexts are. Narratives about organizational life teach us about how to interpret situations and the identity of others and oneself. Indirectly, they suggest answers to questions like *What kind of situation is this?*, *What am I like?*, *What would I like to be?*, and *What is appropriate for me in this situation?* The narratives may also suggest answers like *We are like X*, *We should want to be like Xa*, and *We should act like Xa*. The answers may be supplied by a recipe. An industrial recipe is grounded on taken-for-granted aspects that govern what are proper narrative themes, and it embodies shared believes about rational action for firms within an industry (Spender, 1989).

The channels for distributing recipes in narrative form are many. Newspapers print stories daily. Business consultants are influential agents as they construct and spread stories about organizational life (Huff, 1982; Czarniawska-Joerges, 1990; March, 1991). They use narratives to help define visionary statements for the identification of their clients. They also offer methods for organizational change, such as benchmarking, reengineering and adoption of best practice, that fully appreciate the usefulness of learning from others, and they write about them (for example, see Hammer, 1990). Business leaders write biographies. Some leaders who are judged successful write books to make their exclusivity publicly known (for example, Lee Iacocca, see Iacocca and Novac, 1984), and explain the problems they have experienced. Management training courses diffuse information about the experiences of various firms, and the social interaction during such courses is often an important occasion for gossiping. Also, communication networks among professionals from different organizations, and movement of personnel from one firm to another, as when there is a change of manager, promote the flow of narratives.

Concluding Remarks

To conclude, given the breadth of the topic of imitation so central to human and organizational action no work of the scope of the current piece can hope to be conclusive, but ideas and arguments have been introduced which should at least give pause for thought. The pivotal ideas presented have grown out of a perspective of imitation as a process in identity construction. When organizational imitation is viewed, as here, as learning from others, it means that imitating organizations answer the following questions: *What am I like?* (identification of one-self and others), *What would I like to be?* (a question about desire and the construction of desire), *What kind of situation is this like?* (analogical reasoning), and *What is appropriate for me in this situation?* (institutionalized action). The answers concern identification of oneself and others and how it is possible to become as one would desire. The organizational reasoning behind these answers is facilitated by analogical models borrowed from the human world, but also from the non-human. These models offer ideas about what is true and best. They are often shared among organizations in the same thought world or network of action. The models are often spread as narratives through the work of agents of different kinds.

Merton (1985) states that we live in a world where nothing is absolute new, where there are no absolute original ideas or actions. In such a world, every act is related to one's own and others' ideas, experiences and actions. At the same time, however, no idea or action is completely a copy from other organizations, as organizations pick up ideas and translate them into something that fits their own context. In this way, action, although imitated, may become different. Imitation is an ongoing and never-completed action. Through imitation, ideas, experiences and actions are constructed and spread over time and space thereby transforming ideas, mental models, actions, organizational forms, and organization fields.

I have stated that this perspective for discussing organizational imitation is rather uncommon. There are not many field studies which have so far focused on imitation from this viewpoint. A question of central interest concerns how an organization identifies itself, and therefore also with whom or what it compares itself. That means that studies of organizational attention and taxonomic mental models are needed, because these may tell from where an organization picks up ideas that it translates according to its own conditions. I have claimed that comparison with others is context-dependent, and therefore also variable. Field studies are needed to get illustrations of how identifications and perceived contexts change. Furthermore, the dynamic of an organization field is itself interesting to study. I have claimed that two processes occur in fields which are interesting results of organizational imitation: increases in homogeneity (see Abrahamson, (1996), for an extensive discussion) and increases in heterogeneity. The latter process has been less frequently focused upon in earlier literature, but is discussed at length in Røvik (1996) and Abrahamson (1996). For the discussion about organizational imitation it would be of great interest to learn more from field studies that focus on how organization fields are transformed and how this is connected to changes in organizational identifications.

References

Abrahamson, E. (1991) "Managerial fads and fashion: The diffusion and rejection of innovations", *Academy of Management Review* 16: 586–612.

Abrahamson, E. (1996) "Technical and astethic fashion", in B. Czarniawska and G. Sevón (eds.) *Translating organizational change*, pp. 117–137. Berlin: de Gruyter

Albert, S. and Whetten, D.A. (1985) "Organizational identity", *Research in Organizational Behavior* 7: 263–295.

Bateson, G. (1979) *Mind and nature*. Toronto: Bantam Books

Brown, R. (1973) *A first language: The early stages*. Cambridge, Mass.: Harvard University Press.

Bruner, J. (1990) *Acts of meaning*. Cambridge, Mass.: Harvard University Press.

Collins, A. and Gentner, D. (1989) "How people construct mental models", in D. Holland and N. Quinn (eds.) *Cultural models in language and thought*, pp. 243–265. Cambridge: Cambridge University Press.

Cyert, R.M. and March, J.G. (1983) *A behavioral theory of the firm*. New Jersey: Prentice-Hall.

Czarniawska-Joerges, B. (1988) *To coin a phrase. On organizational talk, organizational control and management consulting*. Stockholm: The study of Power and Democracy in Sweden.

_____. (1994) "Narratives of individual and organizational identities", in S. Deetz (ed.) *Communication Yearbook* 17: 193–221. Newbury Park: Sage.

Daft, R.L. and Weick, K.E. (1984) "Towards a model of organizations as interpretative systems", *Academy of Management Review* 9: 284–295.

Dasgupta, P. (1988) "Patents, priority and imitation or, the economics races and waiting games", *The Economic Journal* 98: 66–80.

DiMaggio, P.J. and Powell, W.W. (1983) "The iron cage revisited: Institutional isomorphism and collective rationality in organization fields", *American Sociological Review* 48: 147–160.

Douglas, M. (1987) *How institutions think*. London: Routledge and Kegan Paul.

Durkheim, E. (1912) *Les Formes Elementaries de la vie Religieuse: le systeme Totemique en Australie. Paris: Alcan. (Translation 1915)*

Durkheim, E. and Mauss, M. (1903) "De Quelques Formes Primitives de la Classification: Contribution à L'Etude des Représentations Collectives", *L'Année Sociologique* 6: 1–72.

Eco, U. (1990) "Fakes and forgeries", in U. Eco (ed.) *The limits of interpretation,* pp.174–292. Bloomington: Indiana University Press.

Elster, J. (1985) "Introduction", in J. Elster (ed.) *The multiple self. Studies in rationality and social change*, pp. 1–31. Cambridge: Cambridge University Press.

Fleck, L. (1935) *The genesis and development of a scientific fact.* Chicago: University of Chicago Press. (Translation, 1979).

Fligstein, N.J. (1985) "The spread of the multidivisional form among large firms, 1919–1979", *American Sociological Review* 50: 377–391.

Forsell, A. and Jansson, D. (1996) " The logic of organizational transformation: on the conversion of non-business organizations", in B. Czarniawska and G. Sevón (eds.) *Translating organizational change*, pp. 93–115. Berlin: de Gruyter

Girard, R. (1977) *Violence and the sacred.* Baltimore: The John Hopkins University Press.

Hammer, M. (1990) "Reengineering work: Don't automate, obliterate", *Harvard Business Review* 68(4): 104–112.

Hannan, M.T. and Freeman, J. (1977) "The population ecology of organizations", *American Journal of Sociology* 82: 929–64.

Howe, R.B.K. (1994) "A social-cognitive theory of desire", *Journal for the Theory of Social Behaviour* 24(1): 1–23.

Huff, A.S. (1982) "Industry influences on strategy reformulation", *Strategic Management Journal* 3: 119–131.

_____. (1990) *Mapping strategic thought.* Chichester: Wiley.

Iacocca, I. and Novac, W. (1984) *Iacocca, an autobiography.* New York: Bantam Books.

International Business Week (1985) "The counterfeit trade". Cover story. December 16: 48–53.

Latour, B. (1986) "The powers of association", in J. Law (ed.) *Power, action and belief. A new sociology of knowledge?*, pp. 261–277. London: Routledge and Kegan Paul.

Leiser, D., Sevón, G., and Lévy, D. (1990) "Children's economic socialization: Summarizing the cross-cultural comparison of ten countries", *Journal of Economic Psychology* 11: 591–614.

Linton, R. (1936) *The study of man.* New York: Appleton-Century-Crofts.

MacMillan, I., McCaffery, M.L. and van Wijk, G. (1985) "Competitor's responses to easily imitated new products – Exploring commercial banking product introductions", *Strategic Management Journal* 6: 75–86.

Mansfield, E., Schwartz, M.M. and Wagner, S. (1981) "Imitation costs and patents: An empirical study", *The Economic Journal* 91: 907–918.

Maratos, O. (1973) *The origin and development of imitation in the first six months of life.* Paper presented at the Annual Meeting of the British Psychological Society. Liverpool, UK.

March, J.G. (1981) "Decisions in organizations and theories of choice", in A. Van de Ven and W. Joyce (eds.) *Assessing Organizational Design and Performance*, pp. 205–244. New York: Wiley.

_____. (1991) "Organizational consultants and organizational research", *Journal of Applied Communications Research* 19: 20–31.

March, J.G. and Sevón, G. (1984/1988) "Gossip, information, and decision-making", in L.S. Sproull and P.D. Larkey (eds.) (1984) *Advances in information processing in organizations*, pp. 95–107. Greenwich: JAI Press. Also in J.G. March (ed.) (1988) *Decisions and Organizations*, pp. 429–442. Oxford: Basil Blackwell.

Margolis, H. (1987) *Patterns, thinking and cognition. A theory of judgment.* Chicago: The University of Chicago Press.

Medin, D.L., Goldstone, R.L. and Gentner, D. (1993) "Respects for similarity", *Psychological Review* 100: 254–278.

Merton, R. (1985) *On the shoulders of giants: A Shandean postscript.* San Diego: Harcourt Brace Jovanivich.

Meyer, J.W. (1986) "Myths of socialization and of personality", in T.C. Hellner, M. Sosna and D.E. Wellbery (eds.) *Reconstructing individualism*, pp. 208–221. Stanford, Calif.: Stanford University Press.

Meyer, J.W. and Rowan, B. (1977) "Institutionalized organizations: Formal structure as myth and ceremony", *American Journal of Sociology* 83: 340–363.

Morgan, G. (1986) *Images in organization.* London: Sage.

Peteraf, M.A. (1993) "The cornerstone of competitive advantage: A Resource-based view", *Strategic Management Journal* 14: 179–191.

Peters, T.J. and Waterman, R.H. (1982) *In search of excellence: Lessons from America's best run companies.* New York: Harper and Row.

Piaget, J.(1951) *Play, dreams and imitation in childhood.* New York: W.W. Norton. (Original French edition 1945).

Porter, M.E. (1980) *Competitive strategy.* New York: Free Press.

Quinn, N. and Holland, D. (1989) "Culture and cognition", in D. Holland and N. Quinn (eds.) *Cultural models in language and thought*, pp. 3–40. Cambridge: Cambridge University Press.

Reinganum, J.F. (1983) "Uncertain innovation and the persistence of monopoly", *The American Economic Review* 73: 741–747.

Rogers, E.M. (1962) *Diffusion of innovations*. New York: Free Press.

Rumelt, R.P. (1984) "Towards a strategic theory of the firm", in R.B. Lamb (ed.) *Competitive strategy management*, pp. 556–570. Englewood Cliffs, New Jersey: Prentice-Hall.

————. (1987) "Theory, strategy and entrepreneurship", in D.J. Teece (ed.) *The competitive challenge*, pp. 137–158. Cambridge, Mass.: Ballinger.

Røvik, K.A. (1996) "Deinstitutionalization and the logic of fashion", in B. Czarniawska and G. Sevón (eds.) *Translating organizational change*, pp. 139–172. Berlin: de Gruyter.

Sevón, G. (forthcoming) "The joints in joint R&D ventures", in K. Kreiner and G. Sevón (eds.) *Constructing R&D collaboration. The enactment of EUREKA*. Helsinki: Swedish School of Economics.

Spender, J.-S. (1989) *Industry recipes*. Oxford: Blackwell.

Tarde, G. (1902) *La Psychologie Economique*, 2 vols. Paris: Alcan.

Tolbert, P.S. and Zucker, L.G. (1983) "Institutional sources of change in organizational structure: The diffusion of civil service reform, 1880–1935", *Administrative Science Quarterly* 28: 22–39.

Westney, D.E. (1987) *Imitation and innovation. The transfer of Western organizational patterns to Meiji Japan*. Cambridge, Mass.: Harvard University Press.

Chapter 11

Homogeneity and Heterogeneity in Organizational Forms as the Result of Cropping-up Processes

Nils Brunsson

Large modern organizations tend to have fairly elaborate forms, i.e. formal structures, procedures and ideologies which are presented externally and internally as characteristics of the organization in question. Such forms are not usually unique to one organization but are shared_by many. Among organizations the patterns of homogeneity and heterogeneitv in these forms are often complex. Organizations that differ in many other respects may still exhibit very similar forms, while organizations that are essentially similar may exhibit forms that are quite different. There is often little homogeneity over time: many organizations change their forms with considerable frequency. The homogeneity and heterogeneity of organizational structures, procedures and ideologies can be explained in several ways.

Organizations may differ in their forms because they are undertaking different kinds of operations, or because they are working in different environments. But there can also be striking similarities in the forms adopted by organizations with very different kinds of operations or working in seemingly different environments. Similar forms have been observed in organizations involved in quite different kinds of production (Woodward, 1965). Organizations in different fields may exhibit similar forms: for instance, private organizations have adopted many of the forms of public organizations such as budgeting and strategic planning, while public organizations have borrowed from the private sector. And fashions in organizational forms spread rapidly among large companies located in different countries (Mintzberg, 1979; Abrahamson, 1996).

These similarities may arise because organizations actually do encounter similar environments and problems, and have found similar ways of handling them (Thompson. 1967). For instance, if employees acquire a stronger belief in, and claims to, their own individuality (Thomas *et al.,* 1987), many organizations may invent similar, more decentralized forms as a result. Or if a growing number of people begin to see themselves as customers rather than citizens in relation to their public organizations, then the organizations may start to adopt forms similar to those in private companies.

This kind of explanation builds on the assumption that formal structures, procedures and ideologies are important to the organization's operations and its ability to solve practical problems. But the relation between organizational form and organizational activities is often weak (Weick, 1969; Meyer and Rowan, 1977). The «de-coupling» of form and operations opens the way to other types of explanation. A key argument in institutional theories of organization is that organizational forms are strongly influenced by widely held norms and ideas about the kind of organizational forms that are natural, correct or desirable (Meyer and Rowan, 1977; Powell and DiMaggio, 1991). Norms and ideas held in common constitute a major impetus to homogeneity; they promote similarities in many organizations, even those which conduct quite different types of production but which operate within the same culture or the same field (DiMaggio and Powell, 1983).

But the existence of common conceptions is not enough to explain homogeneity in organizational forms. There is no guarantee that all organizations adhering to commonly held conceptions will have similar forms. There is often a combination of homogeneity and heterogeneity within a single culture or organizational field: even if some organizations introduce a fashionable form, others do not. So the argument that organizations are exposed to common norms about what makes a good organization, cannot fully explain their organizational forms. We need to explain the homogeneity and the heterogeneity that can arise among organizations which do in fact recognize similar ideas. One way of discovering such explanations involves examining the processes whereby general conceptions are transformed into local organizational forms.

In this chapter I will argue that processes giving raise to homogeneity are likely to differ when different kinds of ideas and norms obtain. I will pay particular attention to what I call informal norms. It is sometimes assumed that such norms give rise to homogeneity via a process of diffusion. I will argue that under some circumstances a diffusion model is not particularly useful for explaining homogeneity. As an alternative I will present a «cropping-up» model.

In the next section I will examine various kinds of ideas and norms. I will look at a diffusion model and consider its limitations. In the following section I will then present the basic concepts underlying a «cropping-up» model: forms, reforms and organizational discourse. This is followed by a section in which I describe how organizational forms are determined by the interaction between general discourse and local reform cycles. Finally, I will discuss the way local reforms may affect the norms expressed in the general discourse.

Processes Behind Homogeneity and Heterogeneity

Various conceptions about appropriate organizational forms are likely to affect organizations in different ways. Some of the conceptions have a constitutive character, i.e. they are necessary ingredients if an entity is to be regarded as an organization at all, or as a particular type of organization. For instance, it is hard to make people believe that an entity is a real organization if there is no accounting system and no responsible person at the top; likewise, a «real» company must have owners, or an association must have members.

Constitutive conceptions are contingent on the construction of organizations. They are relevant only when people consider an entity to be an organization or a special type of organization, but in such considerations these conceptions are a necessary ingredient. Constitutive features are similar in all organizations, or at least in all organizations of a specific kind, but it still needs to be explained why certain activities or entities come to be regarded as organizations, or as organizations of a different type than before. The existence of constitutive conceptions enables us to explain why a school that comes to be regarded as an organization will acquire a local leadership and a local accounting system, but it does not help us to explain why it came to be regarded as an organization in the first place. Processes leading to such redefinitions seem to have been little studied.

Other ideas about appropriate organizational forms are expressed in formal rules combined with sanctions. These may be part of the legal system or of professional codes. For instance, organizations of different types in different countries must use specific forms of accounting.

Formal rules create homogeneity through various mechanisms of coercion (DiMaggio and Powell, 1983), such as imposition, authorization or inducement (Scott, 1991). Heterogeneity can arise from variations actually stipulated in the rules themselves, or from non-compliance on the part of certain organizations.

But there are also norms of a less formal kind, which have much weaker links or even no links at all with national or professional codes and which are combined with weaker or more ambiguous sanctions. Examples include ideas about particular organizational forms that emerge as fashions in the organizational world, such as the matrix organization, total quality management or service-orientation. Ideas initiated or reinforced by business schools, such as budgeting or human resource management techniques, are further examples.

Informal norms are not a necessary part of the constituting of the organization; nor can they be forced upon it. There is no guarantee that they will always be familiar to local actors who are able to influence organizational forms, or that these actors will accept them. And yet they affect many organizations and help to create similarities between them. The exact outcome of this influence depends on the processes involved. It is the process whereby informal norms produce homogeneity and heterogeneity that I shall be discussing in this chapter.

A diffusion model

A possible tool for analysing how informal norms produce homogeneity and heterogeneity is a common one in social research, namely the diffusion model. Diffusion is a standard concept in the social sciences for explaining homogeneity (Strang and Meyer, 1993). The concept is often used to describe the end result of a process – the existence of similar forms and practices at different places at a certain point in time. But it is sometimes also understood as a description of a process whereby these similarities arise. Something diffuses from a centre to a periphery. Information about new ideas, things or practices is disseminated to ever more distant places, and this diffusion produces increasing homogeneity among such social entities as have the attributes to render them susceptible to it.

The process is somewhat similar to the process of contagion or infection (March, 1981); organizations or other entities in close contact with the centre of contagion or with other infected entities are likely to become infected themselves, that is to say they are likely to adopt whatever it is that is being diffused. Unlike an infection, however, «the object» of the diffusion cannot spread by itself – it must be actively adopted by some actor or other (Malinowski, 1927; Latour, 1986). Knowledge is often assumed to be a crucial scarce resource: before we have come into contact with others, we do not know about the new entity being diffused and cannot therefore adopt it. The diffusion process is thus a process in which actors learn from others.

Diffusion processes may well explain how some informal norms about organizational forms are adopted by organizations, thus producing homogeneity in the forms they use. For example, representatives of different organizations may meet one another and learn about each others' forms, after which they may try to introduce them into their own organizations. Professionals employed in organizations attend professional meetings and can be «infected» in this way. Management and leadership are increasingly coming to be regarded as professional skills, which can mean that managers – those who formally make decisions about organizational forms – meet each other in a similar way.

The individual organization may also be infected indirectly by a carrier or transmitter, the equvialent of the rat or mosquito in the transmission of disease. Management consultants, for instance, may spread the same form to one organization after another as they move among them offering their services. Many organizations can be infected at the same time by listening to the same experts at conferences.

The basic micro-process whereby organizations adopt the form that is being diffused is sometimes referred to in terms of imitation, i.e. people in one organization try to imitate what is being said about the forms in other organizations, either by representatives of these organizations or by other peopie (Westnes, 1987). The imitation may be far from perfect – it could perhaps be described as a translation ot the general idea adapted to local circumstances (Malinowski, 1927: Latour, 1986) or as a local edition of the general idea (Sahlin-Andersson, 1991).

Over time the process of diffusion produces increasing homogeneity. But the model also explains heterogeneity among organizations. Like the similarities, differences among organizations are dependent on time, distance and susceptibility. During the diffusion process there are differences between the organizations: some, which have not (yet) been infected, differ from those which have. Organizations with a limited contact network or located in the periphery are less likely to be infected early on or even at all. Some differences may persist because certain organizations are immune – perhaps they have internal characteristics which make them less apt to adopt a specific form, such as not being competent, rich or willing enough. They may be conservative and resistant to change. Or – if there is some connection between forms and operations – they may have a type of operation and a local environment that do not fit the new form.

The diffusion model is based on a physical metaphor. Contact with specific others who possess some particular knowledge is a key explanatory element. Traditionally the model has been used in explaining fairly slow processes whereby new practices in agriculture, for instance, spread to distant places and become dominant there (Smith *et al.,* 1927).

Limited applicability

The diffusion model described above may provide a good way of describing certain phenomena. But under modern conditions its applicability seems to be somewhat restricted: information on many issues spreads almost immediately and there are often an enormous number of entities which define themselves in the same way and therefore easily adopt new ideas said to concern their type of entity (Strang and Meyer, 1993). For instance, knowledge of organizational forms is not a very scarce resource in modern societies: ideas and information about organizational forms are often spread almost instantly and worldwide to an extremely large number of entities perceived as organizations. These are all «infected» at almost the same time. And yet by no means all of them adopt the new form, and the group of adopters may appear to have little else in common. Adoption may take place at about the same time almost everywhere, so adopting organizations have little chance of imitating each other.

More specifically, the diffusion model is less useful for explaining the kind of homogeneity that arises without any contact between similar organizations or contact with a common transmitter, or when knowledge is not a scarce resource. It is less useful when widespread knowledge of a certain form, or even its popularity, does not result in much homogeneity, i.e. when a form that is popular and fashionable in the public debate is not actually installed in many local organizations. The diffusion model is also less useful when the micro-process is one not of imitation but of innovation, i.e. when individual organizations introduce forms which no other organization has yet tried, or they invent a new form, and still they end up with forms that are similar to those of other organizations. Nor is the diffusion model very useful when organizations appear to lack any stable quality that could explain whether or not they are susceptible, for instance when organizations have very similar operations and local environments and still exhibit different forms, or when a certain organization resists a popular form on one occasion and on another is quick to adopt some other very similar form.

An empirical case in which the diffusion model seems to be of little use is provided by the changing forms that have been adopted by Swedish municipalities over the last few decades. In the public debate new ideas about organizational forms have popped up at intervals of a few years (Johansson and Johnsson, 1994). The public debate was familiar to municipal managers (Fernler, 1996) and it can be assumed that they learnt about the new ideas at about the same time. A new form was often adopted by many municipalities during the short period when the form in question was popular in the public debate (Johansson and Johnsson, 1994): most adopting organizations had no other organization to imitate. However, most forms were taken up by a minority of the municipalities only: the extent to which municipalities adopted any one specific fashionable form varied between 6 and 70 % (Johansson and Johnsson, 1995). Further, it was difficult to find any strong correlation between the forms adopted, or any specific qualities of the municipalities concerned such as size or the identity of the political party in power (*ibid.*). Some of the new forms arose at about the same time in other countries, in the public debate as well as in municipalities there (Hood, 1991; Reichard, 1995). Some forms seem to have been invented in several municipalities at about the same time (Fernler, 1996).

In order to explain such processes we need a model which differs in several respects from the diffusion model. The one we require should be able to explain homogeneity arising through processes other than imitation among organizations which lack contact with one another or a common transmitter. It should be possible to use the model for explaining not only homogeneity but also heterogeneity, i.e. why some organizations do not adopt a particular common form. All in all the model should explain something that we could call «cropping up» as opposed to diffusion, that is to say the scattered and seemingly random appearance of similar forms in many but far from all organizations at the same time. In the next section I will describe one version of such a cropping-up model.

A Cropping-up Model of Organizational forms

The model to be outlined below contains three basic components: organizational forms, reforms and discourse. The model contains specific assumptions on the nature and dynamics of these components. It is based on the assumption that, fundamentally, organizational forms are not things or practices, like the items often described as spreading in the diffusion model: rather, they are presentations. They must therefore follow the rules regarding the way we can talk about organizations. The reform processes whereby these forms are introduced require even closer adaptation to the rules. They also require attempts at implementing the talk in practice – attempts which are often time-consuming and frustrating. The common component that makes homogeneity possible is assumed to be a broad societal discourse on organizations. Here some forms are more popular or fashionable than others. But popularity or fashion does not necessarily lead to homogeneity. Very popular fashions in the discourse may not be reflected in a high degree of homogeneity in organizational forms (just as a *haute couture* fashion may not be reflected in many people's way of dressing). The model will describe the mechanisms whereby popular forms are, or are not, translated into local forms.

Organizational forms

Organizational forms are part of the way organizations are presented to the external world or to their own members by authorized people such as managers. Organizational structures are often displayed in organization charts, while procedures appear in documents containing rules and ideology in established and documented policies. These written sources are normally confirmed by oral presentations by management and by labels denoting entities, practices or ideas. The forms are presented as descriptions of the way the organization actually works, or the way it will be working in the near future. The forms also tend to be highly rationalized, being typically presented as means to legitimate ends or as solutions to important problems. Or at least rationalizations are readily available upon request (Meyer and Rowan, 1977).

The extent to which forms describe actual practices and the extent to which practices and forms affect each other, will differ from one form, organization or practice to another; they will also differ over time. As noted in the introduction above, forms and operations are often «de-coupled» and are not very consistent. Practice tends to be less affected by the form than the presentations suggest, or to be affected differently. And the efficacy of the forms in achieving the ends and solutions presented tends to be weaker, rarer and more uncertain than described in standard rationalizations (March and Olsen, 1989. ch. 5).

So if we adopt the basic distinction between organizational talk and action (Brunsson, 1989), then we can assign organizational forms to «talk». Just as there are norms and rules for action that restrict our freedom to act, so there are norms for talk that restrict the way we can talk, at least if we are to be believed or taken seriously (Brunsson, 1995). In the model it is assumed that this is true of talk about organizations, and thus of organizational forms. Organizations cannot then be presented just anyhow: the presentation must be adapted to ideas about what an organization can and should be. The forms must be such that they can be regarded as possible organizational forms; they should be adapted to what people consider good or at least acceptable. In addition, they should be understandable: excessively complex or ambiguous forms are not likely to be understood.

Reforms

The processes whereby new forms are launched will be referred to below as reforms. Reforms as defined here consist of two basic activities: attempts at convincing people that the new forms should be installed and attempts at getting them implemented. Studies of many such reforms in a variety of organizations (Brunsson and Olsen, 1993) revealed a certain pattern, which will be used here in formulating some assumptions about the reform component in the model.

The extent and intensity of talk differed as between existing forms and new ones. Reforms required much more mobilization and talk than existing forms. Typically reforms produced a lot of elaborate talk about the forms-to-be, and a good deal of rationalizing argument. Reforms were well adapted to general, aesthetic norms of talk, such as those referring to logic, consistency and clarity. Reforms were also adapted to what was generally considered to be a good organization. They promised major improvements in the way the organization functioned.

At the outset, the reforms were described as a set of simple, general and seemingly very sensible not to say beautiful principles; for instance, the organizations were to become more goal-oriented, everybody's tasks should be clearer and should not overlap with the tasks of others, everyone's freedom to act efficiently should be increased, better planning and evaluation processes should be installed, etc. The principles contained elements which were popular and not controversial at the time of their introduction, such as decentralization or management by objectives. The situation before the implementation of the reform was described in a less favourable way: it was said to be complicated, tasks were unclear, there were inefficiencies, lack of local freedom, etc.

In sum, it seemed that reforms not only produced more talk than existing forms, but they also followed the norms for talk more closely. This can be explained by the fact that reforms are future-oriented and intentional. The way we can talk about existing forms may be limited to some extent not only by the rules for talk, but also by practice. It may be necessary to adapt talk somewhat to what people actually do, in particular if the talk is directed at the doers themselves. Reforms, on the other hand, can be more easily adapted to the norms geared exclusively for talk, since they are not meant to reflect current practices. Reforms include descriptions of practice; their implementation and their effect on practice is the standard argument in their favour. But this practice is still in the future, and can thus easily be adapted to the new forms instead of the other way around. But reforms not only *can* but *must* be well adapted to norms for talk about organizations. Reforms contain intentions; the forms presented are those we intend, and they are to lead to the effects we intend. The norms regarding the intentions which we can present are generally stricter than those applying to our presentations; for instance, we may admit to bad results but we are less likely to say that we intended them. This may be true of reforms as well; we may present current organizational forms as less than perfect, but it is more difficult not to intend to be as near to perfect as possible.

It is not being claimed that all empirical reforms are like those described here, but the model includes this type of reform. It will be assumed that organizations are attracted by such reforms. Since these reforms can be much more beautiful than possible presentations of today's practice, most reform proposals will prevail over the defence of most old forms. But it is still assumed that there is one major obstacle to reforms, namely previous reforms.

Reforms are supposed to be implemented, i.e. the principles of the reform should be turned into detailed instructions and should affect organizational behaviour, and even results; and this takes time. It is hard to argue for a new reform until the previous one has been given a serious try, particularly if the reforms concern the same activities.

However, this obstacle is only temporary. When the new forms become existing forms, they have to be adapted somewhat to current practices, and they are therefore likely to become less attractive; a new form will easily appear more attractive. And a new reform does not necessarily have to wait for the full implementation – or, even less, for the results – of the old reform; the old reform can become relatively unattractive at a much earlier stage. This is because implementation is assumed to be an important threat to reforms. When the beautiful principles are turned into more detailed instructions and are adapted to the special practical conditions of the specific organization, the new forms soon become less beautiful and more like the old ones, thus losing much of their attraction. Their promises do not seem to be being fulfilled. The new forms may also become more controversial. Further, principles adapted to norms for talk are not necessarily feasible or favourable in practice. This may become obvious long before the reform is regarded as fully implemented – or, even more, before it has given rise to any intended effects on daily practice. So, after a serious attempt at implementation, the reform may fall into disrepute and may well be interrupted by a new reform (Brunsson and Olsen, 1993. ch. 3).

When reform processes look as described here, and when there is no lack of new reform ideas, a specific pattern of reform can be established. A reform starts when the previous reform has been in the process of implementation long enough, and it ends when its own implementation has been under way for a while. The organization is almost continuously in the throes of some stage of a reform, but reforms can only be launched at intervals.

The assumption of implementation as a threat to reform and the resulting pattern of reform also reflected the empirical situation in the reforms studied. Reforms easily prevailed over older forms, often over those still being implemented. A common way of ending a reform was to start a new one. In some large organizations reforms were a standard recurring activity. Major reforms occurred often but not constantly – generally at intervals of a few years. A study of the 125-year history of one large organization showed that major reorganizations took place at intervals of 3-15 years, and that the intervals had been shrinking more recently (Brunsson *et al.*, 1989).

Although it is assumed that reforms easily win over existing forms, a specific reform proposal may meet competition from other reform proposals which also contain attractive principles. It is assumed that such competition will be won by reforms which fit better at a more detailed level with the norms for talk about intended forms, and for which more favourable and less critical arguments are available. Such norms and arguments are largely produced and reproduced in an arena other than the individual organization, namely in a general public discourse.

Organizational discourse

It is not only people in individual organizations who talk about the present and future forms in their own case; there is also a more general discourse in modern society about these things. Organizational forms in general are a popular topic in higher education where it touches on organizations, as well as among the relevant commentators – not least in business magazines and management books – and among those involved in helping organizations to reform. such as management consultants (Alvarez, 1991). Although the discourse varies somewhat from one organizational field or country to another, much of it is very general and treats large groups of organizations as though they were in need of the same forms (Furusten, 1995). The discourse is to a large extent international, i.e. national borders are not thought to be important and much of the discussion takes place across such borders. Organizational problems and solutions are both discussed. The discourse produces ideas and norms about possible and desirable organizational forms.

Although the forms discussed are likely to be based on some common basic conceptions of organizations, they differ when it comes to more detailed aspects. For example, all the forms discussed may be based on the assumption that organizations should be controlled from the top, but they may still differ greatly about the form that is best for bringing this about.

In this discourse only a limited set of ideas can be attended to at one time. The ideas attended to can be variously controversial, and the level of controversy may change over time. Ideas can also differ in their level of abstraction. Very specific organizational forms are sometimes suggested as the «right» ones. Zero-based budgeting might be an example of this. In other instances the suggested forms are of a more principled and abstract character, more in the nature of slogans than recipes. «Back to basics» – concentrating on the «core» business – and decentralization are cases in point. At an even higher level of abstraction the discourse may concern problems but no specific solutions; there may be a large measure of agreement in identifying the important and urgent problems, without any suggestion being made about specific forms that could perhaps provide a solution. The attention paid to problems varies just as much as the attention paid to solutions. In the Seventies the lack of internal democracy in organizations was a popular problem; later, inadequate customer orientation and cost-efficiency were among the problems in vogue.

Knowledge of this general discourse is not «outside» the organizations; people working on the managing and reforming of organizations are aware of the discourse and may even take part in it. In the cropping-up model, unlike the diffusion model, it is not assumed that knowledge is a scarce resource. Rather, it is assumed that people interested in organizational issues will hear very quickly about any new arguments, regardless of where these originated; they will all be reported widely in the media.

This kind of discourse is thus added to our model. We assume that a set of organizations is connected to a common discourse. The discourse provides norms and arguments regarding what are acceptable or good organizational forms, about forms that should be striven for and problems that require solutions. In addition, people participating in the discourse may have an authority that can be referred to in arguing for reforms in the right direction. The norms and arguments in the discourse help to explain which reforms are chosen by individual organizations; they may serve as an important inspiration for reformers who are designing a new reform, and they can determine which of several reform proposals is accepted by an organization.

It is assumed that the discourse evolves continually. New ideas are attended to, others become uninteresting. A basic mechanism behind changes in attention may be a focus on novelty; when no further descriptions and arguments can be added to the discourse, there is not much left to discuss and attention can be directed towards a new idea.

Some ideas move from commanding general agreement to becoming highly controversial. Others move in the opposite direction or retain a fairly stable element of controversy. Finally, some ideas even become generally regarded as bad. The discourse can move towards greater specification, i.e. abstract principles are given a more detailed, concrete content; problems are given solutions, or concrete cases are quoted in which principles are said to have been transformed into practice. Or the discourse may move towards more conflict, as counterarguments are proposed. These two tendencies may be interrelated as they were in the reform processes in individual organizations described above, so that more specification produces more controversy. Specification and controversy may be replaced by new abstract ideas or by compromise, and perhaps by abstraction again.

Model Dynamics

The cropping-up model is thus based on specific assumptions about organizational forms, local reforms and a general discourse. Organizational forms are ways of talking about organizations. Reforms, the presentation of new forms and attempts at implementing them, have to be adapted to the norms for talking about organizations, and particularly to talking about organizational intentions. Some of these norms are provided by a general and continually evolving discourse about organizational forms. But due to their connection with talk and discourse, reforms are apt to lead to disappointment when it comes to implementation; what is considered good talk does not necessarily correspond to good or even possible local practice. Moreover, what is good generally may not be good for the individual organization. The result of all this is recurring reforms in a continually evolving discourse.

There is thus a certain dynamic. At any one moment we have a set of organizations ripe for reform, i.e. organizations which have gone so far in implementing previously popular forms as to create frustration and an interest in new forms. At every such moment all these organizations are exposed to the same discourse, with its specific set of more or less controversial and more or less specific ideas.

From the discourse it is possible to gather ideas about forms currently attracting attention there, and to find arguments and support for them. Reform proposals implying fairly uncontroversial forms will have the advantage over reform proposals along other lines. The level of attention and of controversy affects not only the organizations' choice of forms, but also to some extent the area – organizational structure, perhaps, or budget procedure – in which they reform, since not all areas are necessarily being attended to or are sparking uncontroversial ideas at every point in time. Since the discourse is continually evolving – creating new ideas, new controversies and new specifications – the set of organizations which go in for reform during the next period, will not introduce the same set of forms.

Processes such as these could explain both homogeneity and heterogeneity between organizations. The explanation refers to no attributes of the individual organization apart from the timing of its reform cycles. Organizational reforms are similar in organizations reforming at the same time, and different in organizations reformed at different times.

If the implementation process differs somewhat in length in different organizations, perhaps due to some random external variables, organizations which have embarked on a certain reform simultaneously, will not be ripe for a new reform at quite the same time. It is then slightly less likely that these organizations will choose the same reform as the others in the second round. This makes for variation over time as regards the organizations which any specific organization is likely to resemble. In other words it impedes any order among organizations on a cohort basis, and confirms a picture of great variability and randomness.

The model explains how popular ideas in the general discourse are translated into local organizational forms. It also demonstrates why popular forms are not necessarily very common in organizations; they are adopted only by organizations which happen to be ripe for reform during the period when the forms are popular.

Processes producing homogeneity

The processes whereby forms are transferred from the general discourse into the local organization should also be specified. One of these processes can be called adoption. In diffusion models (and in my description of such models above), the term «adoption» generally refers to the outcome of a process. In our present model, instead, adoption describes a specific process whereby the local organization takes over a form described in the discourse.

Another possible process involves invention, whereby a form is constructed locally. If the uncontroversial ideas in the discourse are fairly abstract and do not define any particular forms, the individual organization has to invent its own. But even if the ideas are abstract, they may contain problems and ideas about the present situation or about organizations in general which are specific enough to make most reformers in most organizations come to very similar conclusions regarding what form to introduce. The forms are invented locally, but are still very similar. There is a parallel here with certain inventions and discoveries in science; oxygen, for example, was discovered by at least two scientists simultaneously (Kuhn, 1962). Similarities arising from inventions are particularly likely when there is a strong consensus about what problems are important, but no agreement on specific solutions.

Organization members may well see their own invented form as something unique at first, only to learn later that it is in fact quite common. In this case they may perceive themselves as the first to introduce it, and perhaps develop a theory about how they have influenced other organizations. When such forms enter the general discourse they have to be generalized to some extent. Talk of a more detailed kind in the individual local organizations may vary somewhat, but can still lend itself to a common description at the discourse level.

In the adoption case, reformers advocate the same relatively specific forms as those attended to in the discourse. Even though the forms here are more specific than in the invention case, they are seldom so specific that they cannot be interpreted a little differently and adapted to local conditions and taste, just as in the case of diffusion. Again this allows some scope for slightly different local versions, without disturbing the impression that the local reform ideas are in fact the same as those being generally discussed.

The adoption process can follow different routes. It may be a question of inspiration, whereby local reformers gather their ideas from the general discourse. Or it may be a question of labelling (Czarniawska-Joerges, 1988), whereby reformers adapt their ideas (regardless of their source), as well as their talk about their ideas, to the forms currently appearing in the general discourse. Inspiration often involves a process of specification in which general forms are translated into a local version; labelling normally involves a process of generalization, in which specific local ideas are given more general labels.

Frequency of forms

Given the processes described above, the number of organizations using a particular form will depend mainly on the length of time during which a particular form is comparatively uncontroversial in the discourse. The longer a form or a problem is considered to be the right one in the discourse or the greater the frequency of its being so considered, the greater will be the number of organizations which will have embarked upon a reform period during this particular discourse, and the greater the number which will have adopted the form or invented similar forms. In this way (length of) time translates into (width of) space.

The frequency of a particular form also depends on whether or not competing forms appear. If new forms do compete, the old ones are ultimately likely to be erased. For instance, an old principle for structuring the whole organization cannot normally be retained when a new such principle is installed. It is hard to be basically centralized *and* basically decentralized. When the competitive aspect is weaker, an old form can be retained together with new ones, so long as it does not fall into disrepute for other reasons.

A form becomes very common if it is attractive and remains uncontroversial for a long time, and if competitive ideas do not appear for a considerable time after the attention giving rise to the reform has faded away. Budgeting can provide a relevant example here. It became popular for use in the private sector in the Sixties, and generated a great deal of literature over a long period. It has proved possible to combine budgeting with various other organizational forms, including other management accounting procedures, and it has not so far fallen into serious disrepute. Thus most organizations still present budgets, although budgeting is no longer receiving much attention in the discourse. Budgeting has even become highly institutionalized, almost a constitutive norm; having formed the basis for special departments etc. in many organizations it is now taken for granted and could not be easily questioned in the discourse – or such questioning would not affect organizations very much anyway (Wallander, 1994). Similarly, organizations may maintain that they hold «development talks» with their employees long after everybody except a few specialists have ceased to refer to the technique as important. In this way forms which may once have appeared quite suddenly can become sedimental, continuing to exist although they are no longer paid much attention (Danielsson, 1983).

Cropping-up explained

The cropping-up model is not intended for use in explaining all homogeneity or heterogeneity in organizational forms. But it can sometimes help to clarify certain phenomena which the diffusion model, or the model mentioned in the introduction which relates operations, environments and forms, cannot altogether explain. The cropping-up model provides a possible or partial explanation of the more or less simultaneous appearance of similar forms among organizations which have no contact with each other and which lack a common transmitter. And when we use this model for explaining homogeneity and heterogeneity, we do not need to know any specific characteristics of any individual organizations apart from their position in the reform cycle. Further, the model can explain instances of homogeneity arising from processes other than imitation.

Interaction Between Reforms and Discourse

In the cropping-up model it is assumed that the general discourse affects local reforms. But in reality influence may also work in the opposite direction. Local reforms may influence organizational discourse; experience of local reforms may be generally discussed. Local organizations may in fact reinforce the popularity of certain forms, by reporting their own reforms and proclaiming their success.

But local reforms in line with the current discourse may also introduce controversy about a particular form, or even engender agreement on its negative aspects. The form may then be abandoned, leaving room for a new idea. As in the individual organizations, attempts at implementing reform may make general principles seem less attractive. There may be several reasons for this.

First, reforms can lead the discourse towards a higher level of specification. As has been noted, local reform generally calls for a more specified version of a general form, or a general problem must be met by a specific form. The specifications may vary from one organization to another; if these different specifications appear in the general discourse, there will be a higher risk of controversy than before. Different people may advocate different specifications, which can reduce confidence in any specifications. But this process depends on the way the specifications are reported back in the general discourse. The more general the terms in which they are described, the less impact they have on the discourse. If the discourse is dominated by top managers possessing little information about details or consultants or researchers skilled in generalization, then controversy is less likely than if the discourse is joined by people who possess more detailed information and who are less prone to generalize.

Secondly, information about local attempts at implementing reform can be expected to produce a more mixed discourse on implementation and results. Without empirical evidence, agreement on any particular form is based on the expectation of its relatively easy implementation and its positive results. If empirical observations are included in the discussions, there is a greater risk that information about difficulties and negative results will emerge, thus producing a less favourable picture which may then increase controversy and produce many arguments against that particular form. Difficulties in implementation can be expected to be more threatening than negative results. Assessments of results tend to be more ambiguous, and hence less obviously negative. On the other hand, in periods of general decline and difficulty, ambiguity about the results of reform may turn reforms into scapegoats, thereby producing agreement on how «bad» they are, and making room for new ideas.

Thirdly, reforms in the same direction in a large number of organizations may change perceptions of the form in question among organizational actors and in the discourse. When the news spreads that this form is being implemented in many organizations of different kinds, the invention process is no longer possible, and the ways in which the form can be introduced become limited. But, what is more, the form may now come to be perceived in some cases as a «fashion» rather than a rational solution; its adoption may be criticized as an instance of imitation, which is difficult to combine with the standard conception of the organization and its management as rational problem-solvers (Abrahamson, 1996). Fashions are also difficult to combine with the basic idea that organizations have strong identities of their own, with particular or even unique characteristics and tasks. Such a view of an organizational form involves negative arguments in the discourse, making it more difficult to implement that form locally. Fashions are more powerful when actors do not perceive them as fashions (Røvik, 1993).

These mechanisms do not always work: in some cases the high frequency of an organizational form has the opposite effect of reinforcing agreement that it is a good one. On the other hand, it is not likely that attention will be paid to such a form in the discourse for much longer.

Fourthly, the discourse may be affected by an active local demand for new forms. After a while there will be a number of organizations which have failed in the implementing of a specific reform, or which have recognized the absence of results and which therefore enter upon a phase of new reform. To borrow a term from the diffusion model, we could say that previous reforms may make organizations immune to the form in question. It will be difficult for reformers to produce the same reform again, so they will look for another area of agreement in order to be able to launch a new reform.

In most of these cases local reforms create, or help to create, changes in the content of the general discourse. This in turn provides a basis for new reforms, which in turn tend to change the discourse again, and so on. In most of the circumstances described above, the system as a whole becomes very dynamic and highly diversified; the discourse changes at a great rate and individual forms are therefore chosen by few organizations only, which in turn gives rise to diversity.

Some Additional Questions

In this chapter I have mentioned three ways of explaining homogeneity and heterogeneity in organizational forms; by referring to operations and environments, to diffusion processes and to cropping-up processes. The first explanation builds on the assumption that forms and operations are closely connected, the other two on the assumption that forms and operations may be fairly independent of each other. Some homogeneity and heterogeneitv among organizations can be explained by versions of one of these models only. Other cases can only be explained with the help of more than one of the models. Detailed empirical studies of reform processes can give us insights into the way the conditions and processes described in the models interact in practice.

All three models explain homogeneity by referring to a common element among the organizations concerned. They work under similar operational conditions, they have been infected by the same idea or they share a common discourse. But the models do not explain much about the way these common underlying elements arise or develop; rather, they indicate that this is an urgent topic for research. In the first model it is important to investigate how similar conditions come about. In the diffusion model it is important to explain why something «diffuses» at all, and why it affects a particular population of social entities. In the cropping-up model, it becomes important to explain how the organizational discourse evolves over time and how its perceived relevance for various organizations develops. All these questions call for empirical studies at a higher level than that of the individual organization.

References

Abrahamson, E. (1996) "Management fashion", *Academy of Management Review* 21: 254–285.

Alvarez, J.-L. (1991) *The international diffusion and institutionalization of the new entrepreneurship movement. A study in the sociology of knowledge.* Boston: Harvard University, dissertation.

Brunsson, N. (1989) *The Organization of Hypocrisy, Talk, Decisions and Actions in Organizations.* Chichester: Wiley.

_____. (1995) "Ideas and action. Justification and hypocrisy as alternatives to control", *Research in the Sociology of Organizations* 13: 211–235.

Brunsson, N., Forssell., A. and Winberg, H. (1989) *Reform som tradition, administrativa reformer i statens järnvägar.* Stockholm: EFI.

Brunsson, N. and Olsen, J.P. (1993) *The Reforming Organization.* London: Routledge.

Czarniawska-Joerges, B. (1988) *To Coin a Phrase.* Stockholm: The Study of Power and Democracy in Sweden.

Danielsson, A. (1983) *Företagsekonomi – en översikt.* Lund: Studentlitteratur.

DiMaggio, P.J. and Powell, W.W. (1983) "The iron cage revisited: institutional isomorphism and collective rationality in organizational fields", *American Sociological Review* 48: 147–160.

Fernler, K. (1996) *Mångfald eller likriktning. Effekter av en avreglering*. Stockholm: Nerenius and Santerus.

Furusten, S. (1995) *The Managerial Discourse – a Study of the Creation and Diffusion of Popular Management Knowledge*. Uppsala: Företagsekonomiska institutionen.

Hood, C. (1991) "A public management for all seasons?", *Public Administration* 69: 3–19.

Johansson, P. and Johnsson, M. (1994) *Är kommunerna slavar under motetrenderna?* Göteborgs Universitet, Förvaltningshögskolan, Göteborg.

_____. (1995) *Kommunernas sökande i reformernas labyrint*. Göteborgs Universitet, Förvaltningshögskolan, Göteborg.

Kuhn, T. (1962) *The Structure of Scientific Revolutions*. Chicago: The University of Chicago Press.

Latour, B. (1986) "The powers of association", in J. Law (ed.) *Power, Action and Belief: A New Sociology of Knowledge?* London: Routledge and Kegan.

Malinowski, B. (1927) "The life of culture", in G.E. Smith, B. Malinowski, H. Spinden and A. Goldenweiser (eds.) *Culture, The Diffusion Controversy*. New York: W.W. Norton.

March, J.G. (1981) "Footnotes to organizational change", *Administrative Science Quarterly* 26: 563–577.

March, J.G. and Olsen, J.P. (1989) *Rediscovering Institutions: The Organizational Basis of Politics*. New York: The Free Press.

Meyer, J. and Rowan, B. (1977) "Institutionalized organizations: formal structure as myth and ceremony", *American Journal of Sociology* 83: 364–385.

Mintzberg, H. (1979) *The Structuring of Organizations*. Englewood Cliffs: Prentice-Hall.

Powell, W.W. and DiMaggio, P.J. (eds.) (1991) *The New Institutionalism in Organizational Analysis*. Chicago: The University of Chicago Press.

Reichard, C. (1995) *"New steering models" as the German variant of new public management concepts*, paper presented at the EGPA Conference, Rotterdam.

Røvik, K.A. (1993) *De-institutionalization and the Fashion Mechanism*. Tromsø: University of Tromsø.

Sahlin-Andersson, K. (1991) *Imitating and Editing Success. Public agencies shifting organizational field*. Stockholm: EFI.

Scott, R. (1991) "Unpacking institutional arguments", in W.W. Powell and P.J. DiMaggio (eds.) *The New Institutionalism in Organizational Analysis*. Chicago: The University of Chicago Press.

Smith, G.E., Malinowski, B., Spinden, H. and Goldenweiser, A. (1927) *Culture. The Diffusion Controversy*. New York: W.W. Norton.

Strang, D. and Meyer, J. (1993) "Institutional conditions for diffusion", *Theory and Society* 22: 487–511.

Thomas, G., Meyer, J.M., Ramirez, J.W. and Boli, J. (1987) *Institutional Structure: Constituting State, Society and the Individual*. Beverly Hills: Sage.

Thompson, J. (1967) *Organizations in Action*. New York: McGraw-Hill.

Wallander, J. (1994) *Budgeten – ett onödigt ont*. Stockholm: SNS Förlag.

Weick, K.E. (1969) *The Social Psychology of organizing*. Reading, Mass..: Addison-Wesley.

Westney, D.E. (1987) *Imitation and Innovation: The Transfer of Western Organizational Patterns to Meiji, Japan*. Cambridge: Harvard University Press.

Woodward, J. (1965) *Industrial Organization: Theory and Practice*. Oxford: Oxford University Press.

Chapter 12

Institutionalization of Municipal Accounting – A Comparative Study Between Sweden and Norway

Lars-Eric Bergevärn, Frode Mellemvik
and Olov Olson

The public sector has been experiencing a period of many changes, and as part of this the reconstruction of accounting and accountability represents a topic of particular interest (Humphrey *et al.*, 1993). As a result of the changes new research tasks have arisen, but most of the them are geared to developments at the present time (Humphrey *et al.*, 1993; Hood, 1994). It is thus interesting and important to look back a little, and to try to understand how accounting has become a construction at all – something which is taken for granted in the new public sector. The purpose of the present paper is to examine this problem by using ideas from institutional theory, which deals with questions of how organizations adapt to ideologies and rules in their institutional environments (Meyer and Scott, 1983).

This is a comparative and historical study of municipal accounting, in two countries, Sweden and Norway, which in many respects are very similar. These countries were chosen on the assumption that in general similarities minimize possible variations in the institutionalization of accounting. An expected finding of the study could thus have been that the institutionalization of municipal accounting in the two countries was very similar. We seek to understand how accounting is becoming institutionalized, and what kind of legitimacy underpins this institutionalization. The historical perspective has been adopted in order to bring out the idea of a long process based on past tradition but with implications in the present.

Frame of Reference

The frame of reference has evolved over the years during which the authors have been engaged in the study. It is presented below in some detail, as this may help the reader to understand the results, as well as the assumptions on which they are based.

Institutionalist perspectives

Institutional visions are characteristic of various trends – in political science (see March and Olsen, 1989), in economics (see Williamson, 1975), and in sociology (see DiMaggio and Powell, 1983; Meyer and Scott, 1983). Political, economic and social institutions have evolved over time, becoming increasingly complex and exerting an influence on collective daily life, where many of the most important actors are formal organizations. Scott (1987) distinguishes four sociological research directions and definitions of institutional theory which occur in the analysis of organizations.

The first is based on the work of Philip Selznick. According to Selznick, the structure of the organization is adaptive, the result of individual and environmental influences and/or constraints (Selznick, 1957). Institutionalization refers to this adaptive process. This view links institutionalization with the adaptive process, claiming that *values are instilled*, not how it is done (Scott, 1987, p. 493). The second approach, which sees institutionalization as a process of creating reality, is based on the idea of a shared reality, a construction created in interaction between people (Berger and Luckman, 1967). Institutionalization is here viewed as the *process* where by actions are repeated over time, and are assigned similar meanings by the subject and by others. In this process separate individuals come to accept and share a definition of reality (Scott, 1987, p. 495). The third research direction also has its roots in the work of Berger and Luckman, but this time institutionalization is seen not as a process but as a set of elements (Scott, 1987, p. 497). Meyer and Rowan (1977) propose that organizations adapt to myths of the environment, or the wider culture, in order to gain legitimacy, resources, stability and the possibility of survival. An organization can gain legitimacy by turning to experts in some special field, for instance in accounting. The external symbolic, rhetorical and/or political order is ascribed a major influence on the internal structural order.

DiMaggio and Powell (1983) propose three major ways in which an organization conforms to the symbolic order: by coercive, mimetic, and/or normative processes. In each of these processes the symbolic form is spread by diffusion through the organization as a result of the latter's adaptability. The meaning of the fourth and final definition, whereby institutions are seen as distinct societal spheres, is that there are both symbolic and behavioural systems but that these differ in different institutional spheres (Scott, 1987, p. 499).

In this chapter we are concerned primarily with the content of the third formulation, according to which a diffusion of symbolic elements occurs between institutions and organizations, both within a certain society and from one society to another. Scott (1987) points out the diversity of institutional sources, such as regulatory structures, governmental requirements, laws, ideologies, educational systems and professions. Consequently, the institutional environment is of a complex and multiple character (DiMaggio and Powell, 1983; Meyer and Scott, 1983). Oliver (1991) argues that to deal with the institutions, organizations may use a variety of strategies ranging from passive conformity, compromise and avoidance, to defiance and finally to proactive manipulation. In other words organizations do not invariably conform to their institutions or institutional environments. Rather, organizations respond in a variety of ways to the normative, regulatory structures and so on, depending on the situation and its possible consequences for themselves. In the present chapter "institutionalization" refers to the processes whereby organizational action is adapted to the ideologies or regulatory structures of the institutions. This third definition of institutional theory has been chosen because it clearly shows the difference between accounting norms and accounting action, which is discussed further in the next section.

The accounting norm system, the accounting action system and their environment

In order to understand how municipal accounting in Sweden and Norway have become institutionalized it is necessary to make a distinction between the accounting action system and the accounting norm system. The accounting action system comprises the instrumental accounting activities. It operates within single organizations, and it can be clearly divided into separate but interrelated procedures, e.g. the daily registration of transactions and annual reporting.

The accounting norm system consists of the institutional environment of the accounting action system, and it is "characterized by the elaboration of rules and requirements to which individual organizations must conform if they are to receive support and legitimacy from the environment" (Scott and Meyer, 1983, p. 140). However, the accounting norm system should not be understood as a system acting in perfect harmony. Different interests are represented within the norm system, which often consists of many individuals and organizational actors (Mezias, 1990). The norm system can be said to comprise the multiple institutional environment of the accounting action system. The accounting norm system is involved in many activities, most of which can be designated as "talk", both as a process and an output. The articulation of the rhetoric of accounting is one of its main activities. The rhetoric of accounting emphasizes its role in reducing the uncertainty in processes of decision-making and accountability (Mellemvik *et al.*, 1988; Miller and O'Leary, 1990), and constitutes the basis for most normative and positive accounting theory (American Accounting Association, 1977; Watts and Zimmerman, 1986). It is also deeply rooted in the establishment of accounting as an organizational and societal activity (Birnberg, 1980; Jönsson, 1988). Rhetoric is important to the accounting norm system in its processes of regulating (Puxty *et al.*, 1987; Jönsson, 1988), generating and, finally, legitimizing norms – this being another important activity in which the accounting norm system is involved. Another type of activity is auditing, i.e. the evaluation of accounting procedures in relation to the existing norms. From the perspective of the single organization there can be two types of norm system – one external and one internal. Whereas an external norm system acts in order to coordinate accounting action in the organizations within its domain, an internal norm system acts mainly in order to adapt accounting action to the local context.

In theory the accounting norms are supposed to control the accounting action. Even though there may be a firm linkage between norms and action, the latter may generate more organizational and societal qualities than are included in the rhetoric of accounting.[1] The main reason is that an implemented accounting procedure always confronts its context (Birnberg *et al.*, 1983; Boland and Pondy, 1983; Hopwood, 1983, 1987; Roberts and Scapens, 1985; Swieringa and Weick, 1987; Nahapiet, 1988). Various stakeholders therefore want their interests to be represented in the processes of regulation (Mezias, 1990; Watts and Zimmerman, 1990). The use of accounting, in whatever dimension it can be discussed, can only to some extent be regulated by the norms. The consequences of norms will therefore be different from the intentions, even though accounting action may be totally controlled by the norms.

It is possible to separate the norm system, the action system and the accounting environment from each other, even though norms are supposed to control action. The idea of separating the organization, or an organizational activity, from its environment is basic to institutional literature (Meyer and Scott, 1983), and not only there:

---

1 Concepts used in the literature in order to discuss the same phenomena are *roles* in Hayes (1983), and Samuelson (1986), or *functions* in Mellemvik et al. (1988).

it is also basic to accounting itself. Accounting is in fact supposed to report on the financial transactions which an organization or a sub-unit has with its environment.

The focus of this chapter will be on the processes in two countries in which municipal accounting has been institutionalized. An understanding of these processes requires first that the relations between norms and action be described and analyzed, likewise the relations between the norms and the environment, and between action and the environment.

Learning by one's own experience and learning from the experience of others

We have noted that accounting can be decomposed into an accounting norm system and an accounting action system, and that this can help us to understand how accounting is becoming institutionalized. But how have the relations between these two systems evolved over time? This section will be devoted to answering that question, and will do so from the perspective of organizational learning, which in turn is concerned with the understanding of organizational behaviour and change. The arguments presented by Levitt and March (1988) are interesting here. These authors view organizations as social constructions in which "action stems from a logic of appropriateness or legitimacy more than from a logic of consequentiality or intention" (p. 320). They also claim that present action is history-dependent and that organizations are oriented towards targets; "organizations are seen as learning by encoding inferences from history into routines that guide behavior" (Levitt and March, 1988, p. 320). The authors have given the concept of routine a very broad meaning, stating that "routines are independent of the individual actors who execute them and are capable of surviving considerable turnover in individual actors" (p. 320). They further point out that organizational learning may be more or less intentional. In their terms both accounting norms and accounting action can be seen as routines, an idea that could be useful to our attempt to understand the changes in accounting norms and accounting action over time.

Levitt and March specify two different types of organizational learning: learning from one's own experience and learning from the experience of others. The authors discuss learning primarily in terms of people's own experience in the shape of experimentation involving trial-and-error and organizational search. Inspired by DiMaggio and Powell (1983), they argue further that, in principle there are three ways in which an organization can learn from the experience of other organizations: coercive, mimetic and normative. In processes of learning by coercion an organization has to adapt its routines to external routines. In processes of mimetic learning it imitates another organization's routines more or less intentionally. This kind of diffusion process may be the result of a search process, or of another organization's will to spread its routines, i.e. a standard solution created by a consulting firm to deal with a specific problem. Processes of normative diffusion occur primarily by way of professional education, whereby knowledge is transmitted to a wide audience by educational institutions.

An institutional learning model of accounting

Starting from the above discussion a model can be made, combining the traditional institutional view interpreted as a distinction between the accounting norm system and the accounting action system, with the two main ways of learning from one's own experience or from the experience of others. Accounting norms are seen in the model as a system capable of learning from the experience of others, i.e. from experiences in the system's environment and/or in the action system, or from its own experience. The same possibilities regarding the variety of learning modes also apply in discussing the action system. Finally, the environment can learn from both the norm system and the action system. This means that at the theoretical level several relations may occur in the institutionalization of accounting (see Fig. 1), even though the institutional argument says that the norm system learns only from the experience of the environment, while the action system learns only from the experience of the norm system.

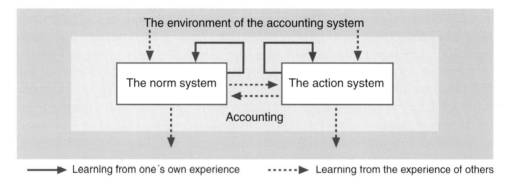

Figure 12.1 An illustration of all possible relations in the institutionalization of accounting.

Background and a Note on Method

Our interest in seeking to understand the processes whereby municipal accounting is becoming institutionalized was sparked by the institutional reactions we observed in the course of two longitudinal action-research projects in accounting, first in a Swedish municipality (see Olson, 1983, 1990; Polesie, 1981) and later in a Norwegian municipality (see Høgheim, 1987, 1990; Høgheim *et al.*, 1989, 1992; Mellemvik, 1987a, 1987b, 1989a, 1989b; Mellemvik *et al.*, 1988; Monsen, 1987, 1989; Olsen, 1987, 1990; Olson, 1993). The two action-research projects were concerned with the implementation of new perspectives on and new techniques in municipal accounting. The institutional reactions alerted us to the historical traditions that had shaped existing relations between the national accounting norm system and the local action system in the two countries. To promote a clearer understanding of these relations, two historical studies were made. The first was started in 1985, i.e. after the end of the action-research project in the Swedish municipality, and is reported in detail in Bergevärn and Olson (1987) and in the form of a summary in English in Bergevärn and Olson (1989). This study was made when the action-research project in the Norwegian municipality was under way. The similar institutional reactions in Sweden and Norway suggested that it would also be interesting to make a historical study of municipal accounting in Norway. This study is partly reported in Bergevärn and Olson (1987), and in Mellemvik (1987a, 1987b, 1989b).

The knowledge generated in the two action-research projects has been valuable in guiding our interest and has helped us to interpret the archival data in the historical studies reported here. The action experience was also useful to our presentation of the institutional learning model of accounting above. Thus the model has been used primarily to structure and analyze data rather than to seek it.. The search for data in the earlier historical studies was guided instead by a genealogical method, based on our own experience of action.

The Two Studies

The Swedish study[2]

The first Swedish Local Municipalities Acts for towns and rural municipalities respectively, were passed in 1862. At the beginning of the 20th century the municipalities in Sweden organized themselves into voluntary federations. The federations have subsequently acted primarily as advocates of the municipalities in their relations with the state, but also as guardians of the municipalities' interests in negotiations about salaries for employees. The Swedish Federation of Municipalities (est. 1968), like its predecessors the Federation of Towns (est. 1908) and the Federation of Rural Municipalities (est. 1919), is also responsible for the development of municipal accounting norms. The first Swedish national

---

2   The empirical material in this section is based on Bergevärn and Olson (1987, 1989), where it is described in detail.

municipal accounting norms were formulated in 1912 and have since been revised five times in 1930, 1956, 1962, 1987 and 1989.[3] These norms are only recommendations, however, which might suggest that Swedish municipal accounting is subject to relatively little regulation. But Swedish municipalities have always had, and still do have to report to the Swedish Central Bureau of Statistics according to the norms.

Up to 1912 the 1862 Local Municipalities Acts, which stipulated that a municipality had to make a budget and that it had to keep accounts of its expenditures and revenues, and the Swedish Central Bureau of Statistics (SCB), which since 1883 has requested financial information from the municipalities every year, were the only instruments for affecting the structure of municipal accounting. However, the information which SCB was able to collect from the municipalities was of such a poor quality as to be considered useless – a view shared by many. The Swedish Federation of Towns consequently organized a committee consisting of four representatives from the municipal accounting profession. This committee, which in the course of its work remained in contact with the SCB, presented its recommendation as regards norms in 1912. But the norms had no impact on municipal accounting practice, and SCB was still dissatisfied since the underlying purpose of creating order and uniformity in the municipalities' accounting had not been achieved. This, it was said, was of the utmost importance, as it would make it possible to compare the expenditures and revenues of the various municipalities.

In the early 1920s many cases of embezzlement and criminal transactions in Swedish municipalities were revealed. To prevent swindle, some municipalities went so far as to demand cash guarantees from people who were to be employed as accountants. During the same period a new Local Municipalities Act was discussed, and the question of common national accounting norms was also debated. The legislative body was of the opinion that the municipalities had had their chance, but that they should be given one final opportunity to create national norms on their own.

The reaction of the Federation of Towns was to contact the Swedish Association of Town Accountants, and to ask them to make a proposal. The following debate within the profession led to the fundamental proposition that not only should municipal accounting be uniform to allow comparisons, but it should also satisfy the requirement that the citizens in a given municipality should receive fair

---

3　For details regarding the content of the different norms, see Svenska Stadsförbundet, 1912; Svenska Stadsförbundet, 1930; Landkommunernas Förbund, 1956; Svenska Stadsförbundet, 1962; Svenska Kommunförbundet, 1987; Svenska Kommunförbundet, 1989.

treatment and justice. Under this last heading two themes in particular were discussed: first, that no generation should be allowed to consume the wealth which an earlier generation had built up, and secondly that taxpayers should not finance services which ought to be financed by fees paid by the users, and vice versa.

To meet the demands of fair treatment and justice it had to be possible to account for the wealth of a municipality, and the full cost of the various services it provided, and such accounting was to be based on advanced accounting principles regarding the depreciation of investments and the distribution of interest. At this time, i.e. the late 1920s, these questions were also being discussed in private companies in commerce and industry in Sweden. Some of the ideas initiated in the private sector were transferred to the municipal sector. Lastly, the practical formulation of the norms came to be based on the accounting practice of a model that had already been developed and was being implemented in the city of Malmö. The 1930 norms, elaborated and recommended by the Federation of Towns, had largely adopted this alternative as the prototype for its norms. These new national, central norms were very advanced, but also highly ambiguous.

Even though some cities tried to implement the 1930 norms, their inherent ambiguity meant that municipal accounting remained very heterogeneous well into the 1940s (Holmberg, 1938; Lundberg, 1942). Parliament still kept out of the regulation of municipal accounting, even though the new Local Municipalities Act of 1953 was altered to make it possible to monitor the wealth of the municipalities, i.e. the fair treatment and justice between generations.

At the beginning of the 1950s Parliament once again compelled the Federation of Towns to revise the norms, and again used the tacit threat of legislation if nothing was done. The Federation responded by organizing a committee responsible for revising the national norms. The city of Stockholm, however, had already been experimenting with its accounting system, and some of the ideas and experiences generated there became important elements in the model for the new norms produced under the auspices of the Federation, which had also started to cooperate with one of the most prominent accounting scholars in Sweden at that time. His task was to structure the ideas and experiences into a theoretical framework. The result of this process, presented in the 1956 norms, was that the ideas from the 1930 norms were elaborated and presented as a complete, logical and theoretical system, focusing on the valuation of wealth and full cost.

The next round of reforms resulted in the 1962 norms. The main object was to introduce cost accounting within the framework of the 1956 norms. Once again an experimenting municipality, this time the city of Gothenburg, served as a prototype for the Federation. However, the project in Gothenburg represented one small part of a larger diffusion process. The model for cost accounting in the city of Gothenburg's different administrative bodies was originally based on the standard chart of accounts for the Swedish mechanical engineering industry. This was certainly no coincidence. One of the leading spirits behind the making of this chart of accounts was Albert ter Vehn, professor of accounting at the Gothenburg Business School, born in Germany and educated in business economics there. By adapting the standard chart of accounts for the mechanical engineering industry to the requirements of the city of Gothenburg and later to the requirement for a national chart, municipal cost accounting became part of the diffusion of ideas originating in German accounting traditions of the 1920s. However, the 1962 norms were not an exact copy of the charts of accounts used in the administration in the city of Gothenburg, since some changes were made. As things turned out, the city of Gothenburg never did adapt its accounting to the new national norms for cost accounting in municipalities.

Even though the Federation of Towns was unable to control municipal behaviour by coercion, the 1956 and 1962 norms did mean that municipal accounting moved from a heterogeneous to a more homogeneous situation. A contributory factor here was that the number of municipalities in Sweden was reduced dramatically after World War II. In 1951 there were 2,500 municipalities, in 1971 about 450, and today there are about 280. This successive reduction in the number of municipalities made it a lot easier for the Federation to disseminate the norms successfully. One of their methods consisted of adapting the rhetoric of municipal accounting to the ideology of uniformity and justice, which was currently being discussed in society. Another method was to commission books and articles, and to arrange courses in the new municipal accounting. A third was to act as consultants to the municipalities in accounting and auditing. A fourth method involved supplying municipalities with accounting software adapted to the new norms, and with computer power from a company organized and owned by the Federation. A fifth method was to support the introduction of the norms into the basic education of students at schools of public administration and business, i.e. the places where potential municipal officers were to be found. The 1956 and 1962 norms were implemented in most municipalities and were regarded as a success, at least by the Federation. The norms were practical in application, but were well grounded in theory and incorporated into the relevant educational courses.

At the end of the 1970s and in the early 1980s the norms were subject to increasing criticism, mainly as a result of the new ideology of "businessification" that was invading the public sector in Sweden in full force. At the same time many people considered the very core of the norms, i.e. the principles for monitoring wealth, to be too complex as well as oversimplified. One reason for this was that inflation reduced wealth, which was recorded at historical values. Another was that the municipalities had organized some of their activities – particularly those which were financed by fees – into companies, partly as a way of avoiding control related to the concept of wealth.

The absence of consolidated statements made monitoring very difficult. Actors of many different kinds joined in the criticism, including members of Parliament, municipal politicians and accounting scholars at business schools. The lack of any means of coercion meant that the Swedish Federation of Municipalities could not stop those municipalities which wanted to experiment by adapting their accounting to the models used by private companies in commerce and industry. Indeed, the new ideology of businessification implied that this would be an appropriate solution. Accounting scholars at the business schools were engaged in some of these experiments, which were also often supported by local politicians because they were said to give the public greater insight into the activities of the municipality.

In the 1980s Parliament again entered the municipal accounting arena, arguing that the Swedish Federation of Municipalities must revise its norms. In contrast to earlier occasions, Parliament was now referring both to the experiments in some municipalities and to the norms used by private companies. The ideological debate in Sweden was changing. The efficiency of the public sector was being criticized, and the ideology of businessification was acquiring more and more supporters, even within the dominant Social Democratic Party. Because, like their precursors, the existing norms had been legitimized and accepted in an open and often ideological debate about accounting, the new criticism was disseminated in the same way. The criticism was public, and was spread in books, articles and seminars as by various descriptions of experiments made in the municipalities. The common denominator in the experiments was to view the municipality as a company and to reflect it in terms of the aggregated accounting models (primarily balance sheets, profit and loss statements and cash-flow analyses) used by companies in commerce and industry. These changes did not cause any great technical problems, since all the data needed was already in the 1956 norm system.

In the face of harsh criticism and the existence of the new models, the Swedish Federation of Municipalities soon stopped defending the old norms and its own ideology of uniformity and justice. Instead the Federation began to cooperate with various experimenting municipalities, and with the accounting scholars who had participated in the experiments. This cooperation resulted in the 1987 norms, which to a great extent were a copy of the accounting law controlling accounting practice in the private business sector in Sweden. In 1989 the 1987 norms were extended to include consolidated statements. As a consequence, Swedish municipalities are now structuring their accounting reporting in almost the same way as organizations in the Swedish private sector.

The Norwegian study[4]

The first Local Municipalities Act in Norway was passed in 1837. At that time, and since 1814, Norway had been joined in a union with Sweden – a result of the peace treaty after the Napoleonic Wars. Each country had its own Parliament but shared the same king, namely the sovereign ruler of Sweden. Norway was granted independence as late as 1905. Nonetheless, the Local Municipalities Act in Norway, declared that the municipalities were independent organizations, i.e. independent of the Swedish monarch and the officers of the Crown.[5] In this way the Norwegian municipalities became independent not only of the Norwegian state but also of the Swedish. This last was certainly the main purpose of the reform.

As in Sweden, the municipalities in Norway organized themselves into voluntary federations. There is one important difference between the two countries in this respect, however. Norwegian federations have not been responsible for developing the municipal accounting norms, as they were in Sweden. The Norwegian accounting norm system has evolved in a completely different way.

In the Swedish study we have noted that Parliament did extremely little to regulate municipal accounting practice, and the same goes for Norway. But whereas the Swedish Parliament delegated this task to the Federation of Municipalities, the Norwegian Parliament delegated it to certain ministries. The first Norwegian national norms were presented in 1883 and have subsequently been revised six times, in 1924, 1942, 1957, 1971, 1990 and 1993.[6] All municipalities have to adapt their accounting procedures to the norms, which have the force of law. The Norwegian municipalities have therefore had much more experience of regulated accounting procedures than their Swedish counterparts.

The first national norms for municipal accounting in modern times, apart from some paragraphs in the Local Municipalities Act of 1837, were promulgated in

---

4 The empirical material in this section is based on Mellemvik (1987a, 1987b, 1989b), where it is described in detail.

5 In 1833 and again in 1836 the Norwegian Parliament had passed proposals for a law declaring the independence of Norwegian municipalities (Sejersted, 1978). The Swedish king prevented implementation of the Local Municipalities Act, using his right of veto. According to the constitution a bill could only be stopped twice by the king's right of veto. Thus, after the decision of the Norwegian Parliament in 1837, the king had to accept the bill and sign the law.

6 For details regarding the content of the different norms, see Departementet for det Indre, 1883; Justisdepartementet, 1924; Innenriksdepartementet, 1942; Kommunal- og arbeidsdepartementet, 1958; Kommunal- og arbeidsdepartementet, 1971; Kommunal- og arbeidsdepartementet, 1990; Kommunal- og arbeidsdepartementet, 1993

1883 by the Ministry of the Interior. At this time Norway was still in union with Sweden. In these norms the state regarded the municipalities as independent organizations, as already established in the Local Municipalities Act. This was reflected in the norms in different ways. Each municipality was allowed to design its own accounting reports, except for a few required by the state to support the politicians in their work. The idea of local independence has persisted ever since, and is still very much alive in Norway today. However, it has also had to compete with a much stronger organizational ideology which arose in the early years of the 20th century.

At that time, in the 1910s and 1920s, these relatively independent municipalities were making big investments in electrical energy plants, and the investments were financed by loans taken up by the municipalities. However, in the depression following World War I unemployment rose, with a consequent drop in the municipalities' income tax revenues. As a result many municipalities had difficulty in amortizing their loans (Seip, 1949). The state intervened, guaranteeing that the municipal loans from banks and other lenders would be repaid.

The intervention of the state in the 1920s dramatically changed the relationship between state and municipalities, which now came to be seen as agents of the state. This situation was clearly expressed in the 1924 norms. The main objective underlying the norms was to give the state a way of monitoring the economies of the municipalities. The norms reflected the new order and the new hierarchy, when they were adapted to meet the supervisory requirements of the state. This also meant that from now on the legitimacy of the norms was based on the need of the state to monitor the municipalities rather than on the independence of the municipalities.

Ever since, at least the 14th century and into the present century, the Norwegian state has known recurring instability. Norway was occupied by German forces between 1940 and 1945, and it was this period that saw the next change in the norms. The occupying forces wanted to strengthen their control and supervision of the municipalities. For this reason in 1942 they introduced the most radical reform ever to be made in Norwegian municipal accounting, and it was the previously established hierarchy, whereby the municipalities were seen as agents of the state, which made such a rapid and radical change possible.

Postwar independence brought a period of euphoria. There was renewed discussion about municipal independence, and a debate on new accounting norms started at the same time. A committee of three municipal officers was appointed by the Ministry of Law and Justice to work out a proposal. However, the Association of Municipal Auditors insisted on a seat for themselves on the committee and went on to argue that the existing norms were excellent and there was no need for any change. The municipal officers argued that a change was necessary, to support the municipalities in their management control processes. These two conflicting views resulted in two proposals, one by the municipal officers and one by the auditor member. The proposals were submitted to various organizations for comment. The Norwegian Federation of Municipalities supported the officers' proposal, and the Association of Municipal Auditors supported the proposal of the single auditor. The Ministry of Finance and the Norwegian Central Bureau of Statistics argued that the 1942 norms had increased the uniformity of the collected material, and had made it useful to the work on the state budget. They wanted to see greater correspondence between the municipal and the state accounting. In the end no change was made in the 1942 norms as a result of these discussions.

In the mid 1950s the Ministry of Municipalities set up a new committee, which concluded that the current national norms would also do for the future. For this reason the 1957 norms were basically a copy of the 1942 version, except that some parts were made even more detailed to satisfy various demands from the ministries.

The next reform process began just as computers were coming into use in organizations. The new committee was preoccupied with the idea of adapting the 1957 norms to the opportunities provided by computers. Once again the tradition which saw the municipalities as agents of the state determined the process with the result that the 1971 norms represented no major changes but simply a few minor adjustments to make it easier to use computer technology. Once again the 1942 norms had served as the foundation for a new set.

In 1979 the Ministry of Municipalities declared that the existing norms had to be changed (Kommunal- og arbeidsdepartementet, 1979), but there was still no reform until 1990. The new set of norms that finally emerged could be regarded as the state's response to the municipalities' criticism of the earlier norms. In the mid 1980s many municipalities started to design their own annual reports (Mellemvik and Monsen, 1994). In the atmosphere of criticism and local initiative in redesigning accounting reports, the following passage appeared in a circular issued by the Ministry of Municipalities in 1987:

> The Ministry of Municipalities regards it as important that accounting reports are regarded as part of local government's management control system. The Ministry has observed that a growing number of local governments are producing locally designed annual reports and it sees this local initiative and experimentation as very desirable (Kommunal- og arbeidsdepartementet, 1987, p. 1; our translation).

According to the 1990 norms every municipality was allowed to use whatever accounting system it liked, but all accounting transactions had to be convertible to the system required by the norms. According to the norms only four accounting statements were explicitly required, but these were quite different from the locally

292

designed annual reports, showing that the new norms had not emerged from the action system. Many similarities could be found between the 1990 norms and the earlier norms; three of the required statements were virtually copies of statements prescribed by earlier norms (Mellemvik and Monsen, 1994). So even though the 1990 norms were more liberal than their predecessors, the norm system had again derived new norms mostly from its own history, rather than from practices in the action system. The present norms, formulated in 1993 and including technical adjustments to the 1992 Local Municipalities Act, are very much a carbon copy of the 1990 norms.

An instrumental similarity between Sweden and Norway

These descriptions have shown that the influence of the accounting norm system on the accounting action system can vary very much. It has also been pointed out that the norm system influences the action system much more strongly in Norway than in Sweden. In discussing the action side we have referred to the use of a standardized chart of accounts, which is used to classify transactions into different types (e.g. cost items such as salaries and activities such as education), and to the aggregation of the various types of transactions in standardized accounting reports as prescribed by the norm system. We have not focused on the *quality* of the classifying or reporting of transactions. In the course of the action-research projects in Sweden and Norway, however, we have come up against the difficulty of making comparisons. For instance, there are problems when it comes to comparing expenditures between single municipalities, different years in one municipality, and even budgets and actual outcomes for a single year. What happens is that, although action is formally controlled by the norms, a small but steady trickle of change occurs – changes that are made possible by the inherent complexity and ambiguity of the norms. This means that municipalities are able to make their own interpretations of the norms, and consequently to make small adjustments and changes which are accepted or sometimes not even noticed by the auditors. However, we have also observed some greater deviations from the norms in Norway. Mellemvik (1987b), for example, reported that one studied municipality repeatedly borrowed for investments, but then postponed the investments and used the borrowed funds to finance operating expenditures. This procedure is certainly not in line with the intentions of the national norms, but there has been no comment from the auditors. The accounting systems in Sweden and Norway are thus alike in that the norms do not control the substance of action in any of the studied cases, even though formal control is much more coercive in the Norwegian case. The learning processes studied can therefore be described as consisting of loosely coupled systems (Weick, 1979), which conforms with ideas in Oliver (1991) on different organizational action strategies.

Analysis and Conclusion

The national municipal accounting systems in the two countries have been involved in two quite different types of learning process. The Swedish accounting system has been developed primarily in an ideological learning process, while the Norwegian accounting system has been developed primarily in a process of hierarchic learning.

The ideological learning process

The state has had virtually no part in creating the Swedish norm system. It has been involved only by threatening the norm system with legislation on municipal accounting. These threats have clearly been very powerful, since they have all forced the norm system to do something. But this system has been pretty powerless, because it has not been in a position to coerce municipalities to follow the elaborate accounting norms by punishing deviant behaviour. The only way the norm system could act was by promoting the diffusion of its norms, and in this it has become increasingly successful. Swedish municipal accounting has thus largely been a municipal and local affair, which has given the municipalities the opportunity to conduct major experiments on their own and to learn from practices in the private sector. Paradoxically it is some of the experiments deviating most obviously from existing norms which have been used as prototypes in new reform processes initiated by the norm system. The possible reactions of the norm system to the experiments of the action system (which included both criticism of and alternatives to the existing national norms) have been to defend the norms or to start a reform process. The norm system also has to react to the threats from the state. But all these processes had one important consequence: they improved the norm system's ability to argue.

Societal ideologies have played an important role in these processes giving municipal accounting a meaning – a meaning which was and still is used to evaluate the existing norms and their alternatives. Uniformity and justice comprised the dominating ideology between the 1920s and the end of the 1970s. Since the 1980s the ideology of businessification has been predominating. It has been in these periods, when a conflict has surfaced between new and old ideologies, that experiments have been made and new radical reform processes have been launched. The learning process in the Swedish municipal accounting system is thus strongly related to ideologies in the environment of the accounting system. It is when misfits arise between the existing ideology and the existing norms, that experiments are viewed as an appropriate activity. The experience gained from these experiments is then diffused not only within the accounting action system but also to the norm system; that is to say, mimetic learning occurs in the norm system.

When an experiment is regarded as fitting the ideology, it may be adopted as a prototype in a national reform process. By entering into alliances with some of the leading actors involved in the experiments such as municipalities and scholars, the Federation – i.e. the central norm system – acquires access to the kind of knowledge that is usually only obtainable by direct experience. When the municipalities perceive a correspondence between the new accounting norms and the dominating ideology they then follow the norms and the national municipal accounting gradually becomes more homogeneous.

The institutionalization of municipal accounting in Sweden seems to include all the possible learning relations which were discussed in theoretical terms above and summarized in Figure 12.1. However, the situation in Sweden has been changed dramatically by the latest national reforms which were guided by the ideology of businessification. As a result of these reforms municipal accounting has become firmly coupled with national and international accounting norms in the private sector. This in term means that Swedish municipalities are now using the same form of accounting as organizations which are regarded as agents of the market. This kind of diffusion has in fact gone further in Sweden than in most counties. One of the most important organizations of the norm system in the private sector, the Swedish Association of Chartered Accountants, is now more involved in municipal accounting than ever before. The members of this association do audits in the municipalities, and they discuss municipal accounting. The Association arranges seminars and regularly publishes updates of a book entitled "Norms of accounting and auditing in the public sector" (Föreningen Auktoriserade Revisorer, 1992, 1994). The municipal accounting system has become involved in a much wider process of diffusion, whereby the Swedish norm system in the private sector is a recipient of accounting discourse and accounting norms from the international arena, as determined by the International Accounting Standards Committee or the Financial Accounting Standards Board. The learning process has thus changed radically over the last decade. One probable result of this change is that accounting activities in Swedish municipalities will be more closely related in future to international politics and the economy of the private sector than to experiments undertaken in individual Swedish municipalities. The question is whether any change in Swedish societal ideologies in the future will have any effect at all on municipal accounting. The genuinely municipal character of municipal accounting seems to have been lost, while at the same time the learning process in which it is involved is becoming more coercive than before, when normative diffusion was used. Let us now discuss a more hierarchical and coercive learning process by focusing upon the Norwegian study.

The hierarchic learning process

There is a clear difference between Sweden and Norway. Swedish municipalities are not seen as agents of the state to the same extent that they are in Norway. Even though the norm system can act coercively in Sweden, the Swedish accounting norms are not so far the result of hierarchical relations between the state and the municipalities, and the norm system cannot punish deviating behaviour. This is an important difference which may affect the direction of change in the future. The Norwegian central norm system has always been in the hands of the state. It was during the depression of the 1920s, however, that the state first started to regard the municipalities as state agents, and this was reflected in the 1924 norms. The norms were to be followed by the municipalities, primarily because they had the force of law. The ideology of municipalities as state agents and the coercive type of learning by action together formed a hierarchical basis for the accounting system, and the legitimacy of this system was difficult to question. In fact it took the Germans during the occupation in World War II to make any radical change in the norms, i.e. by coercion. The reason the Germans were able to change the accounting system was that it had had a hierarchical basis ever since the 1920s, whereby the central norm system, directed by the state, possessed the sole power to alter accounting norms and, consequently, municipal or local accounting action. It was thus enough for the Germans to control the norm system in order to change the whole municipal accounting system. It is astonishing, however, that the system was never adapted to the new postwar context. The main reason seems to be that actors of the norm system had learnt to use the accounting reports by then and had no incentive to unlearn the procedures. Meanwhile the municipalities were obliged to follow them.

The accounting system in Norway has become a closed and hierarchical system, in which the main mode of learning is coercive. Because the norm system acts at a great distance from the accounting action in the municipalities, the central norm system cannot easily learn from the experiences of the action system. Further, because of the strong one-way linkage between the state and the municipalities, the accounting system operates as a network of procedures in state ministries and in the departments of the municipalities. This means that a change in one part of the overall system has implications for the other part as well. The Norwegian national municipal accounting norm system thus has a tradition of learning from its own experience. It seems likely that this tradition can only be changed by the entry of a new strong actor or by a change in the ideology on which the accounting system is based. Maybe there will be an ideological change in Norway soon. As in Sweden the ideology of businessification is growing stronger. But so far there has been very little in the way of varied learning in the process of institutionalizing municipal accounting in Norway.

Theoretical contribution

The institutionalization of accounting may take the form of ideological or hierarchic learning processes. In an ideological learning process there is no clear relation between agents and principal; as a consequence, the norm system is not linked to a principal. The norm system cannot, therefore, base its legitimacy on the sovereignty of the principal. Instead it has to link its rhetoric to the existing societal ideologies to exploit accounting norms. The norm system is highly dependent on the action system to explore new accounting norms, i.e. by mimetic learning, and experiments in new types of action occur in periods of conflict, either between ideologies or between current norms and a dominating ideology. In such periods it is just as legitimate to experiment as it is to follow the existing norms. Various modes of action thus appear, some of which may gain supporters and generate demands for a national reform. Thus, experiments within the accounting action system may generate at least one alternative which the norm system could adopt as the prototype for a new reform process. This means that reform processes end up by formulating norms based on existing action but underpinned by a rhetoric linked to the new dominating ideology. This combination promotes the diffusion of the new norms into municipal action. There is no clear hierarchy in the ideological learning process, with the norm system controlling things from the top. Rather, it is the action system, on its own initiative, which generates learning processes; the norm system then has to react to these.

In the hierarchic learning process there is an ideology which emphasizes the existence of a strong relation between a principal and its agents. Here the norm system is linked to a principal. This structure primarily is best suited to the coercive diffusion of accounting norms to the accounting action system. However, the norm system has great difficulty in exploring new ideas, even though it is in a position to exploit them. It is not that it lacks ideas about theoretical alternatives or norms in other contexts; the main problem is that it lacks experience of alternative actions on the part of the agents it controls – which is ultimately the result of its own coercive mode. Its effective exploitation thus traps exploration. In such a hierarchic learning process exploration can only occur if there is a change in the hierarchy or the ideology.

The two learning processes studied here differ from one another in various ways, but they also reveal one important similarity, which concerns the influence of the environment of the accounting system. What characterizes hierarchic learning in our present context is the stability of the accounting norms, and the fact that the norm system becomes involved in learning when someone takes command of it or when the ideology changes. In the ideological learning mode, the accounting system is assessed on a basis of the ideologies in its environment, and radical reforms occur when these ideologies change. This means that, irrespective of the learning mode, the accounting norms are closely associated with the environment of the accounting system. In the hierarchic mode this linkage is effected by way of the norm system, and in the ideological mode by way of the action system. The existence of this environmental impacts makes it difficult to assert that either individual organizations or the norm system "choose" accounting norms. Rather, they appear to adapt their systems to whatever fits the prevailing ideology. Thus the foundation of accounting is extrinsic to accounting itself. However, depending on how firmly the norm system controls the accounting action system, there will be greater or less variety in the learning process.

We have thus found that the institutionalization processes studied above are different. This conclusion is surprising, because according to the institutional argument we would expect to find very similar processes in these two countries. Instead, we have found them to be very different. These have been conceptualized as different forms of institutionalization, involving ideological or hierarchic learning. Studies of institutionalization in other countries may generate other results. Such studies are obviously important today, when the public sector is putting so much effort into the reconstruction of accounting and accountability. The present study shows that the ideas associated with a new accountable public sector are being diffused in very different ways in two very similar countries. This difference depends to a large extent on the different institutionalization processes in which the two countries have been involved in the past. In the Norwegian case municipalities are accountable to the state, and the state therefore decides how the accounting is to be done. In the Swedish case the municipalities are more independent, which means that there is no obvious principal to decide on accounting matters. The municipalities and municipal accounting have consequently been closely linked to changes in ideology, so that accounting action and accounting norms have been influenced by the "new" ideas.

References

American Accounting Association (1977) *Statement on Accounting Theory and Theory Acceptance*. American Accounting Association Committee on concepts and standards for external financial reports. Sarasota.

Berger, P. and Luckman, T. (1967) *The social construction of reality*. New York: Doubleday.

Bergevärn, L.-E. and Olson, O. (1987) *Kommunal redovisning då och nu. Längtan efter likformighet, rättvisa och affärsmässighet*. Lund: Doxa.

_____. (1989) "Reforms and myths – A history of Swedish municipal accounting", *Accounting, Auditing and Accountability Journal* 2(3): 22–39.

Birnberg, J.G. (1980) "The role of accounting in financial disclosure", *Accounting, Organizations and Society* 5(1): 71–86.

Birnberg, J.G., Turopolec, L. and Young, S.M.(1983) "The organizational context of accounting", *Accounting, Organizations and Society* 8(2/3): 111–129.

Boland, R.J. and Pondy, L.R. (1983) "Accounting in organizations: A union of natural and rational perspectives", *Accounting, Organizations and Society* 8 (2/3): 223–234.

Departementet for det Indre (1883) Cirkulære af 15de November. Kristiania.

DiMaggio, P.J. and Powell, W.W. (1983) "The iron cage revisited: Institutional isomorphism and collective rationality in organizational fields", *American Sociological Review* 48: 147–160.

Föreningen Auktoriserade Revisorer (1992) *Normer för redovisning och revision i den offentliga sektorn*. Stockholm: Föreningen Auktoriserade Revisorer.

_____. (1994) *Normer för redovisning och revision i den offentliga sektorn*. Stockholm: Föreningen Auktoriserade Revisorer.

Hayes, D.C. (1983) "Accounting for accounting: A story about managerial accounting", *Accounting, Organizations and Society* 8(2/3): 241–249.

Holmberg, S. (1938) Inför tjugofemårsminnet, Sveriges Stadskamerala Förenings Handlingar, pp. 52–58.

Hood, C. (1995) "The "new public management" in the 1980s: Variations on a theme", *Accounting, Organizations and Society* 20(2/3): 93–110.

Hopwood, A.G. (1983) "On trying to study accounting in the context in which it operates", *Accounting, Organizations and Society* 8(2/3): 287–305.

_____. (1987) "The archaeology of accounting systems", *Accounting, Organizations and Society* 12(3): 207–234.

Humphrey, C., Miller, P. and Scapens, R.W. (1993) "Accountability and accountable management in the UK public sector", *Accounting, Auditing and Accountability Journal* 6(3): 7–29.

Høgheim, S. (1987) *Søkelys på årsrapporten*. Bergen: Center for Applied Research, at the Norwegian School of Economics, Repport 87: 8.

_____. (1990) *Rekneskapen i bruk. Frå talstabling til økonomisk informasjon i ein kommunal organisasjon*. Ph.D. thesis. Bergen: Norwegian School of Economics and Business Administration.

Høgheim S., Monsen, N., Olsen, R. and Olson, O. (1989) "The two worlds of management control", *Financial Accountability and Management in government, public services and charities* 5(3): 163–178.

_____. (1992) *Experience of action-research*, Working paper, Gothenburg University.

Innenriksdepartementet (1942) *Forskrifter for kommunale budsjett og regnskap*. Oslo: Grøndahl & Søns.

Justisdepartementet (1924) "Forskrifter for budgetoppstilling og regnskaps-avleggelse i bykommuner", *Norsk Lovtidende*, 2. avdeling: 98–148.

Jönsson, S. (1988) *Accounting regulation and the elite structures. Driving forces in the development of accounting policy*. New York: John Wiley.

Kommunal- og arbeidsdepartementet (1958) *Forskrifter og veiledning for budsjettoppstilling og regnskapsføring i kommunene*. Mysen: Indre Smaalenenes Trykkeri.

_____. (1971) *Forskrifter og veiledning for budsjettoppstilling og regnskapsføring i kommunene*, med senere tilleggsforskrifter. Oslo: Engers Boktrykkeri.

_____. (1979) Rundskriv nr. H 29/79, tillegg til forskriftene av 1971.

_____. (1987) Rundskriv nr. H 9/87.

Kommunal- og arbeidsdepartementet (1990) *Nye forskrifter for kommunale og fylkeskommunale budsjetter og regnskaper*. Rundskriv nr. H 14/90.Oslo: Akademika.

_____. (1993) *Nye forskrifter for kommunale og fylkeskomunale budsjetter og regnskap*.Oslo: Akademika.

Landskommunernas Förbund (1956) *Kommunernas kapitalredovisning*. Stockholm: Landskommunernas Förbunds förlag.

Levitt, B. and March, J.G. (1988) "Organizational learning", *Annual Review of Sociology* 14: 319-340.

Lundberg, G. (1942) Vad bör redogörelsen för ett kommunalt bokslut innehålla? Sveriges Stadskamerala Förenings Handlingar 1942, pp. 27–38.

March, J.G. and Olsen, J.P. (1989) *Rediscovering institutions. The organizational basis of politics*. New York: Free Press.

Mellemvik, F. (1987a) "Det standardiserte kommuneregnskapet", in O. Olson (ed.) *Kommunal Årsrapportering – om utviklingen til nå, og et alternativ*. Oslo: Bedriftsøkonomens Forlag.

_____. (1987b) *Kommunens lån – et regnskapsmessig problem?* Oslo: Universitetsforlaget.

_____. (1989a) *Kommuneregnskapets rikdom – Om regnskapets funksjoner i samspillet mellom en kommune og dens finansielle institusjoner*. Ph.D. thesis. Bergen: Norwegian School of Economics and Business Administration.

_____. (1989b) *Utvikling av de kommunale regnskapsforeskrifter sett uti fra et historiskt perspektiv*. Trial lecture for the Ph.D. Bergen: Norwegian School of Economics and Business Administration.

Mellemvik, F. and Monsen, N. (1994) *Divergence, exploration and exploitation: Development of annual reports in Norwegian local governments*, in review.

Mellemvik, F., Monsen, N. and Olson, O. (1988) "Functions of accounting – A discussion", *Scandinavian Journal of Management* 4(3/4): 101–119.

Meyer, J.W. and Rowan, B. (1977) Institutionalized organizations: Formal structure as myth and ceremony, *American Journal of Sociology* 83(2): 340–363.

Meyer, J.W. and Scott, W.R. (eds.) (1983) *Organizational environments. Ritual and rationality* Beverly Hills: Sage Publications.

Mezias, S.J. (1990) "An Institutional Model of Organizational Practice: Financial Reporting at the Fortune 200", *Administrative Science Quarterly* 35: 431–457.

Miller, P. and O'Leary, T. (1990) "Making accountancy practical", *Accounting, Organizations and Society* 15(5): 479–498.

Monsen, N. (1987) *Behandling av anleggsmidler og avskrivninger i kommunale regnskaper.* Oslo: Universitetsforlaget.

_____. (1989) *Regnskap i politikken? – om årsrapportens funksjoner for en kommune og dens toppledelse.* Ph.D. thesis. Bergen: Norwegian School of Economics and Business Administration.

Nahapiet, J. (1988) "The rhetoric and reality of an accounting change: A study of resource allocation", *Accounting, Organizations and Society* 13(4): 333–358.

Oliver, C. (1991) "Strategic responses to institutional processes", *Academy of Management Review* 16(1): 145–179.

Olsen, R. (1987) *Regnskap i "Maktsenteret" – om kommunalråders holdning til det tradisjonelle kommunale årsoppgjøret.* Oslo: Universitetsforlaget.

_____. (1990) *Årsrapportering og politikk. Konsekvenser av brukerorientert forandring av årsrapportering i Bergen kommune.* Ph.D. thesis. Bergen: Norwegian School of Economics and Business Administration.

Olson, O. (1983) *Ansvar och ändamål – om utveckling och användning av ett kommunalt ekonomisystem.* Ph.D.-thesis. Lund: Doxa.

_____. (1990) "Qualities of the programme concept in municipal budgeting", *Scandinavian Journal of Management* 6(1): 13–29.

_____. (1993) *Context bounded accounting,* Working paper, Gothenburg University.

Polesie, T. (1981) "Action and reaction: Decisive factors in developing accounting practice", *Accounting, Organizations and Society* 6(2): 167–174.

Puxty, A.G., Willmott, H.C., Cooper, D.J. and Lowe, T. (1987) "Modes of regulation in advanced capitalism: Locating accountancy in four countries", *Accounting, Organizations and Society* 12(3): 273–291.

Roberts, J. and Scapens, R. (1985) "Accounting systems and systems of accountability – Understanding accounting practices in their organizational contexts", *Accounting, Organizations and Society* 10(4): 443–456.

Samuelson, L.A. (1986) "Discrepancies between the roles of budgeting", *Accounting, Organizations and Society* 11(1): 35–45.

Scott, W.R. (1987) "The adolescence of institutional theory", *Administrative Science Quarterly 32:* 493–511.

Scott, W.R. and Meyer, J.W. (1983) "The organization of societal sectors", in J.W. Meyer and W.R. Scott (eds.) *Organizational environments. Ritual and rationality*. Beverly Hills: Sage Publications.

Seip, H. (1949) *Kommunenes økonomi*. Oslo: Tiden Norske Forlag.

Sejerstad, F. (1978) *Den vanskelige frihet 1814–1850*. Norges Historie bind 10. Oslo: Cappelens Forlag.

Selznick, P. (1957) *Leadership in administration*. New York: Harper & Row.

Svenska Kommunförbundet (1987) *Redovisning för kommuner och landsting*. Stockholm.

————. (1989) *Koncernredovisning för kommuner. Teori och praktik* .

Svenska Stadsförbundet (1912) "Förslag angående likformig bokföring för Sveriges stadskommuner", *Svenska Stadsförbundets skriftserie*, no. 7. Stockholm.

————. (1930) *Betänkande angående enhetligt budget- och räkenskapsväsen för städerna*. Kommunalbokföringskommitté 1927. Stockholm.

————. (1962) Kommunernas budget och räkenskaper. Stockholm.

Swieringa, R. J. and Weick, K.E. (1987) "Management accounting and action", *Accounting, Organizations and Society* 12(3): 293–308.

Watts, R.L. and Zimmerman, J.L. (1986) *Positive Accounting Theory*. Englewood Cliffs, New Jersey: Prentice-Hall, Inc.

————. (1990) "Positive Accounting Theory: A Ten Year Perspective", *The Accounting Review* 65: 131–156.

Weick, K. (1979) *The social psychology of organizing*. (2nd edition.) Reading, Mass.: Addison-Wesley.

Williamson, O.E. (1975) *Markets and hierarchies: Analysis and antitrust implications*. New York: Free Press.

Chapter 13

Changing Managerial Competitive Practices in the Context of Growth and Decline in the Finnish Banking Sector

Risto Tainio, Kari Lilja and Timo Santalainen

In this chapter we examine changes in managerial competitive practices in Finnish banks during the period of deregulation in the 1980s and 1990s. "Deregulation" here refers to the process of removing various institutional barriers, namely protective banking regulations.

In Finland it is widely argued that "deregulation increased banking competition" during the 1980s. Although it is not quite clear what "increased competition" means, it seems evident that the removal of institutional barriers extended competitive space and created a new type of competitive practice. This change coincided with an unusually strong economic boom of long duration in Finland during the 1980s.

In late 1989 banking competition changed again. The Finnish economy plunged into a deep recession, now under the conditions of the deregulated financial markets and liberalized exchange controls. For banking, this meant the start of an intense struggle for survival.

This chapter explores these changes in managerial competitive practices. Previously they have been explained mainly from the external forces and processes. For example, the emergence of new competitive practices in the mid-1980s period of growth has usually been explained in terms of the impact of deregulation. The destructive consequences in the Finnish banking sector in the 1990s, and the related competitive practices have, on the other hand, been explained mainly by the economic recession, decreased demand, persistence of the overvalued mark, high interest rates, and other macro economic indicators.

These explanations are powerful and obvious, and they demonstrate important insights into the competitive dynamics in the Finnish banking sector. However, they have their limitations. Especially the role of the banks themselves in the changing nature of competition needs more attention and elaboration. This may be described as an internal perspective.

From this internal perspective it can be shown that the changes of competitive practices in the period of growth were not, in fact, activated by major institutional reforms, but rather by the banks' own initiatives and small-scale experiments with new businesses. The banks altered the nature of competition between themselves by engaging in new activities, which were later on accentuated by new institutional rules and structures, that is,"deregulation."

The managerial struggles to find a new paradigm of competitive practices encouraged mimetic behaviour, and resulted in "managerial traps". These traps locked managers into certain practices which made it difficult for them to adapt and change when the Finnish banking sector moved from growth to decline.

Competitive Practices

In the previous literature the most common view of competitive practices is a "stylized" one. Competitive action is described as intentional, rational moves and countermoves by major actors in existing market structures. In general, these moves and countermoves are hypothesized to follow a certain behavioral principle. Both contemporary neoclassical analyses and early visions of strategic management were built upon "calculated rationality" in order to exploit competitive advantages and opportunities (Levinthal and March 1993).

More recent strategic management literature increasingly views competitive practices from the perspective of intentional, offensive action. Attention focuses mainly on "creative" competitive management, where management develops its capabilities and competencies to create new sources of competitive advantage. By learning from experience, management improves its competitive strategies and their implementation and is therefore able to dominate other players and affect the institutional rules of the competitive game. This "offensive approach" mostly assumes a strong agency perspective on management; management is a self-sufficient strategic agent in national and international competitive arenas (Ansoff, 1991). Competitors are mostly seen as "opponents", and the major managerial challenge is to dominate these opponents in the markets with distinct competitive strategies (Porter, 1980) and related resources and competencies (for example Bourgeois and Brodwin, 1984).

Another, equally important but often-neglected side of competitive practice is that of defence. Intentional efforts to avoid losses and failures become the central focus of the description. Attention turns to the ways management can renew and strengthen its agency character under deteriorating conditions (Weitzel and Jonsson,1989). Management seeks to identify ways out of crisis and to change its organization and often management itself in order to effect a turnaround. In reality, these defensive practices exist simultaneously with offensive ones in the same competitive arenas.

Both of these characterizations of competitive practices build heavily on the intentional side of managerial action. They pay little attention to the unintentional aspects of competitive dynamics and practice. These "irrational" features, or unanticipated outcomes, of competition include phenomena like vicious and virtuous circles, unpredictable side effects (i.e. surprises), and contradictory tendencies producing outcomes that are not intended by anyone (for example, March,1981; Masuch,1985). These unintentional appearances and outcomes seem, however, to be inherent in any competitive dynamics.

Managerial practices are:

> on the one hand, a result of a piece of past history and, on the other hand, an attempt to deal with a situation that is sure to change presently – an attempt by those firms to keep on their feet, on ground that is slipping away under them" (Schumpeter, 1942, p.84).

In this chapter we do not discuss the notion of rationality, but we do deal with the intentional and unintentional, as well as the offensive and defensive aspects of the competitive practices. We examine how competition as "creative destruction" actually occurs in the Finnish banking context. How does the institutional environment make new managerial practices possible and how do these new competitive practices further activate possible changes in institutional structures?

Finnish Financial System and its Institutional Development

The Finnish financial system can be characterized as predominantly credit-based (Zysman, 1983). Bank credit plays a central role in social and economic development. The banks pool resources from the public and allocate these resources to firms on a long-term basis. Since most investment credit is provided by banks, firms tend to become dependent on particular banks, and the banks tend to become dependent on the success of their major borrowers. Thus the industrial firms and bank groups in Finland are firmly interlinked on long-term basis, as are their counterparts in Germany. A credit-based system also enables state agencies to play a major role in controlling the allocation of financial resources and in directing firms' choices (Whitley, 1992). In Finland the major state institutions controlling and coordinating financial operations have long been the Bank of Finland and Bank Inspection.

Until the 1980s the Finnish banking sector consisted of six major banks: two large commercial banks (KOP and SYP), one medium sized commercial bank (HOP), the state-owned Postipankki Ltd, OKOBANK Group (co-operative banks), and SKOPBANK Group (savings banks). All these major Finnish banks have their own historical roots and customer groups. The closest rivals have traditionally been the two major commercial banks KOP and SYP. They form the hard core of "Finnish" and "Swedish-speaking" industrial groups in the country. OKO and SKOPBANK have been another competitive pair. They have specialized in retail banking and have been dominant in the rural areas of the country. In the mid-1980s SYP took over HOP. In 1993, most of the savings banks were split and liquidated by the four other banks, and finally in 1995 SYP and KOP were merged. In 1995 there were three major financial blocs to the Finnish economy; the commercial bank bloc the agricapital bloc, and the state bloc.

For over 60 years, until the mid-1980s, the Finnish banking sector had been sheltered by several protective and regulatory barriers. Bank competition in interest rates was eliminated already in Finland in the early 1930s by the Bank of Finland under the Tax Relief Act. Deposits obtained tax-exempt status as a condition for a uniform deposit rate. The Bank of Finland also imposed strict regulations on lending. The banks borrowed money from the Bank of Finland, which determined their lending rates. Foreign financing was also subject to the Bank of Finland's prior approval. Regulated interest rates provided the banks moderate but steady margins and "automatic" profits. Under these regulated conditions there was also a constant excess demand for credit in the economy. This made the banks powerful organizations, as their customers became dependent on them for credit.

Under these conditions, the competitive leverage of the banks was a direct function of their market shares. They offered products and services on almost identical terms. The competition between banks was largely superficial. Competitive practices appeared mainly in building up dense branch office networks to reach new depositors, in careful rationing and monitoring loans in order to minimize losses, and in improving the internal efficiency of bank organizations.

From 1970, new trends emerged which changed the nature of competition. In 1970 new banking legislation was passed under which all the banks received equal rights to operate and compete in consumer, commercial, and investment banking.

In the late 70s and early 80s short-term interfirm money markets emerged in Finland. The biggest corporations started to lend their excess cash to each other at daily rates. These "grey markets" were to a large extent due to the increased financial operations and high share of exports of the largest Finnish companies. Also the favourable prepayments obtained from the bilateral trade between Finland and Soviet Union catalyzed this stage of development in the Finnish financial markets.

The emergence of the disintermediation and new "industrial bankers" created pressure to reform the financial system. Banks became worried about their future role when the largest companies could lend and borrow directly from money markets. The Bank of Finland became concerned about the functioning of two separate and simultaneous markets. Gradually steps were taken to remove some of the protective barriers in the "official" banking system and at the same time to allow banks to compete more effectively in the new arenas. The first foreign banks started operations in Finland in 1982, and two years later Finnish banks were allowed to establish foreign subsidiaries. In 1984, remaining foreign exchange controls were also liberalized, and Finnish banks started to operate in international credit markets. New investment companies and other financial service firms entered the financial markets.

The major step in deregulation occurred, however, in 1986. The Bank of Finland stopped regulating loan rates. Now banks had abundant domestic and foreign funding sources. Interest rates started to balance demand and supply in the banks' loan markets. There was a shift away from competition for depositors, which was a consequence of interest rate regulation, towards competition in interest rates and in the pricing of services. Markets for certificates of deposit were created rapidly in the same year, and short-term interbank markets emerged and became institutionalized.

In 1987, stock options and futures markets were created and they expanded rapidly. In 1989, a new stock exchange law adjusting Finnish practice to international norms and legislation was passed. However, no compulsory debt to equity ratios were applied to money markets at that time.

The impact of deregulation on the Finnish banking sector, especially after 1986, was strong and indisputable. Old bank competition, based on regulated pricing and homogeneous "products", gave way to new dynamic forms of competition based on more flexible manoeuvring in the loan market. The formerly stable and bureaucratic bank organizations rapidly became competitive agents with an aggressive market approach with no restraints as to their equity requirements. Similar changes and tendencies in the 1980s have also been observed in Norway and Sweden (cf. Reve1990; Engwall 1994).

Change in Competitive Practices:
The Extended Competition

Viewed from the banks themselves, the new era in Finnish banking competition had in fact already started in 1985, before the major deregulation steps in 1986. The change culminated in a battle over HOP, the medium-sized commercial bank (Saari, 1990; Repo, 1992; Lassila, 1993; Hakkarainen,1993). The impact of this battle on competitive relations and practices in Finnish banks was immediate and far-reaching.

The instigator of that battle was SKOPBBANK, which had just obtained a new, young, and ambitious Board in late 1984.

> "In the beginning of 1985 SKOPBANK and one of the new venture capital companies began gradually acquiring HOP shares, which looked cheap considering their substance value. In the spring of 1985 rumours spread that HOP had made a 50 mFIN loss on its currency business. More and more HOP shares came onto the market. In October the two big commercial banks saw the real danger in SKOPBANK's takeover attempt; the emergence of a new, sizeable merchant bank in Finland. During the last week of October the battle became fierce. The prices of HOP stocks skyrocketed, when SYP and KOP also started buying them. During the last days of October KOP abandoned the struggle, and SKOPBANK sold its shares to SYP. The President of SYP described the deal as "historical"." (Saari, 1992)

The old system of bank competition was soon left behind by these events and a new competitive game was opened. Formerly bureaucratic banks, which were used to following rules and regulations, suddenly started to act in new ways. Stability was further undermined as competition shifted to the spheres of investment banking and corporate finance, where speculative and risky activities abounded. Competition in these spheres started to dominate overall bank competition and to affect both the structures of the banks and their institutional context.

The HOP battle was fought with relatively small stakes, but when the flows of funds were really opened in the summer of 1986 the scale of competitive operations increased rapidly. All the major banks started to compete openly in developing their securities business, expanding their international activities, engaging in corporate takeovers and venture capital operations, and in reorganizing the whole industrial structure of Finland.

Institutional control of these operations was difficult because there were only a few laws and regulations to follow and those that existed were easy to elude or reinterpret. A good example was the law that banks can own only 10 per cent of the shares of industrial companies. This was easily circumvented by establishing subsidiaries, using "loyal" companies of the finance group, or, as in the case of SKOPBANK, with the help of hundreds of independent savings banks.

In some new business areas there was simply no legislation. In securitization, for example, norms and behavioral principles were created through practice. Although the legislation implemented later on is commonly related to the process of "deregulation" it would be more appropriate to link it to "regulation." It finally brought practices which had previously been unregulated and uncontrolled in Finland under internationally established regulations and standards (for example, in the sphere of insider trading).

From the bank perspective it can therefore be argued that change in the competitive practices of the Finnish banking sector was not activated by major institutional reforms, but rather by small-scale experiments with new businesses. The banks altered their competition themselves by engaging in new activities, which were eventually accentuated by "deregulation." New competitive practices quickly created their own morals and ethics, generating tension between new and old bankers, and between new bankers and state authorities. This created pressure to bring these new, secret, and speculative practices under institutional control.

The battle for HOP permanently transformed the competitive scene in banking (Lassila,1993). It was not only that competition was extended by the emergence of new forms and arenas of competition. The results of the battle also activated some other processes which diffused new practices rapidly and eventually changed the competitive positions of the banks.

First, the results of the HOP battle unintentionally trapped managers into new ways of acting.

The most notable example of this is the emergence of what may be termed a "competence traps." The process can, to some extent, be identified in all Finnish banks in the late 1980s, but was especially obvious in SKOPBANK.

The competence trap occurs when favorable performance in one domain is rewarding in the short run. Management accumulates experience from this and the organization learns to specialize in niches where its competencies yield immediate advantage (Levitt and March, 1988).

309

In this case, the HOP takeover operation proved highly profitable for SKOPBANK, despite the fact that it did not achieve its ostensible object of taking over HOP (Saari, 1990). The bank had played aggressively. Although it did not have the strength for the final victory it was able to retreat and collect – much to its surprise and avid plaudits for its efforts – large profits.

The whole process raised expectations of fast profits and new business opportunities in the SKOPBANK Board. The chief executive officer became convinced that this was the way they would have to operate in the future. "Strike unexpectedly, stay calm, capitalize, and withdraw" (Saari, 1992, p.72). The success of this strategy occurred during his first year in office, and it was his first major personal accomplishment. The same type of manoeuvring continued, and was generally a success. During 1987–1988 SKOPBANK's profits from investment banking were five times bigger than its net interest income. The facts seemed to support the contention that the "success recipe" was working. This, together with public praise, created a strong athmosphere of self-sufficiency and complacency in the SKOPBANK Board. As the CEO expressed it, "Our competence had produced exceptional success, and that competence is a long-lasting property" (Saari, 1992). The bank had also become a long-lasting prisoner of that competence.

This process is a classical example of the ways in which learning is self-limiting. The effectiveness of learning in the short run and from current experience interferes with learning in the long run and at a distance (Levinthal and March, 1993). The management of SKOPBANK experienced its first takeover attempt as a success, sought to repeat this success and specializing in this type of manoeuvre. In doing so it standardized and routinized its actions. Management became increasingly removed from other bases of experience and strategy, and unconsciously "trapped" in the existing routines. When the environment changed, as it did eventually in Finland, the trap became obvious to management, but by this time its successes had driven the bank "beyond the limits of return". It was too strongly committed to its own view of its competence to be able to adapt and change in different circumstances. Some other banks (for example, Postipankki Ltd and OKOBANK) avoided this trap by experiencing losses early enough in the period and therefore did not commit themselves in the way SKOPBANK did.

The emergence of success-related competence traps does not prevent, but instead accelerates diffusion of new competitive practices. The "winner" sets the standards of performance and becomes an example of how to achieve them. This tends to force competitors to follow, and, despite possible doubts, to further imitation. The major Finnish banks responded to deregulation – new business opportunities and increased funding possibilities – with similar strategies. They diversified their business operations and extended their presence in investment banking, international businesses, and corporate banking and consulting. They decentralized their organizations and decision-making to become more "market"- or "consumer-oriented", and started to rationalize their dense branch networks and cut their operating costs.

Second, the battle over HOP also raised and personalized bank competition to the highest level of top management – managing directors and their key investment bankers. In former times competition was mainly a matter for a bank's branch office. Now it became significant for the entire organization. Critical to this extension of competition was how the final result of the HOP battle was interpreted. In public SYP was declared the winner. It won openly with the help of SKOPBANK. This changed the balance of power between SYP and KOP and became especially obvious in some of their jointly governed financial organizations. It created mistrust and cooled personal relations between the leaders of SYP and KOP (Lassila, 1993). When cooperation between SYP and SKOPBANK in investment banking continued, the mistrust between SYP and KOP deepened. This led to increased suspicions of each other's moves and to a need for self-protective measures. The time of gentlemen's agreements at the top level of Finnish banking was over and the competition became aggressive in spirit: "the end justifies the means." This meant that even deceptive strategies were acceptable, if circumstances so required. The two leading banks became worried about their own independence, their very existence. They attempted to take each other over. These secret takeover attempts came to light in 1988. Fights over the bank ownership were also extended to battles over their major industrial customers.

The aggressive destruction of HOP had therefore activated another process, where resources were exhausted to guarantee the independence of the major banks. The independence meant, however, isolation, from which it was not easy to break out. Structures are usually easier to build up than to break down and therefore they have more far-reaching and long-term consequences than initially thought.

In this case the ownership arrangements were protective moves which "froze" the new banking reality. The new businesses had resulted in great losses, but there was no return to the old banking practices. The way out could instead be expected to lie in these new practices, new competencies and the insights provided by them. Thus it can be claimed that under extended competition the new competitive fields and new practices rapidly destroyed the old competition. The first offensive moves were initiated from within and accentuated by institutional reforms. New practices had unexpected and unhealthy consequences, which activated re-regulation of these new practices. Extended competition tends to create internally generated processes which overheat development. Short-term success accelerates the destruction of old practices and institutional control; in the long run this tends to lead to self-isolating or even self-destroying effects.

Change in Competitive Practices:
The Retrenched Competition

The banks' new and expansive competitive practices together with the state's expansive fiscal and monetary policy overheated the Finnish economy by 1989. The Bank of Finland tried to cool the economy by imposing credit regulations on the banks, but was not entirely successful any more. In 1990, the Finnish economy entered a recession. This was due to both external and internal factors. The simultaneous slowdown in Western economies and the collapse of the Soviet Union were the major external factors. The Soviet trade, which had at best accounted for about 25 per cent of Finnish exports, practically disappeared. The decreased demand, the persistence of the overvalued Finnish mark, and the related high interest rates created a wave of corporate bankruptcies. The Helsinki Stock Exchange became sluggish. The property markets fell and interest rates stayed high. The whole banking sector drifted into a deep crisis. All the major banks started to fight for survival under these deteriorating conditions. The banks desperately sought leeway for their organizations, to identify their own solutions to problems, and to find new ways to exploit their remaining competitive resources.

In this new phase the banks found they had trapped themselves into practices which were no longer relevant. When the external conditions changed, these traps became visible and "real". "Success breeds failure," as organizational life has widely shown. Breaking out of these successes traps became a major managerial challenge and the seed for a new set of competitive practices. In addition to springing internally generated traps externally generated traps also emerged as economic conditions changed. What previously appeared as "new" and "successful" managerial practices now become increasingly problematic and questionable. Moreover, what had been earlier labelled "old" suddenly became more respected and desired again.

In the late 1980s Finnish banks were slow to recognize the existence of internally generated traps, but they were quick to experience and respond to the unfavorable external conditions and their imprisoning nature. A good example of this kind of externally generated trap is the "interest rate trap." The removal of interest rate regulation did not have an equal impact on the lending and funding sides of banking operations. Most lending, especially long-term housing loans, was still tied to the low base rate which remained regulated. In contrast, the rates for funds acquired on the markets were unregulated and were increasingly expensive. This "twin interest rate" problem eroded the profitability of all the banks since they had to lend at low rates whilst borrowing at high rates.

The difference between the market rate and the base rate exceeded 10 per cent in 1989–90 for several months. The banks tried jointly to persuade the Bank of

Finland to raise the base rate, but Parliament, which determines the level of the base rate, refused. The losses sustained by the banks at that time were estimated at 4–5 bFIN a year (Lassila,1993).

The interest rate trap can be described as external but unintentional. It was not "planned" by anyone; it merely emerged as a result of the different rates of fluidity in various parts of the financial system and the different prospects and "rhythms" of reforms made in them. At the outset this external trap was experienced as a common threat by the banks. It therefore encouraged them to increase their cooperation, but when these joint efforts were not successful, even more intense competition arose. This competition strikingly favored the financially strongest banks. They could best resist the strain of the trap and the related problems.

In the phase of retrenched competition it is not only that "the fittest survive," but that under these conditions the fittest are able to build on their existing advantage. The contracting economic space leads to intentional competitive maneuvering to take advantage of the situation. This is where the relative strength and resources matter most. Opportunities to capitalize on the relative weaknesses of competitors arise frequently, and various intentional efforts to trap weaker players are also likely to occur. In this case too, the strongest banks started to take advantage of the deteriorating position of the weakest in the early 1990s. Especially illustrative in this respect are the last years of SKOPBANK.

Competitors knew about SKOPBANK's emerging problems by late 1989. Its major venture capital company went bankrupt in June. It did not obey the orders of the Bank of Finland to limit lending in August. Its Managing Director committed suicide in December. All this spread rumours and mistrust about SKOPBANK's performance, but competitors did not take any action until early 1990. The other banks refused to buy SKOPBANK's certificates of deposit, or did so at a high price, thereby creating acute funding problems for SKOPBANK. Its overnight debt increased to almost 5 bFIMs and also created problems in international funding (Saari, 1992, p. 200). At SKOPBANK this was interpreted as revenge for their earlier successes and undeniably arrogant behavior. In the other banks all this could be regarded as normal, cautious business operations. The competitors also became active in spreading rumours about the critical situation of SKOPBANK once its survival was openly threatened. This eroded the public image of SKOPBANK and made it look like a failure well before the final disaster had actually occurred. The Board had to use its time and energy in combating negative publicity. "A retreating competitor can really be tortured," was how the Chief Executive Officer of SKOPBANK later summarized his experience. In the light of our evidence, retrenched competition can be characterized as the simultaneous presence of externally and internally generated traps; it is characterized by fierce struggle for survival and well-designed competitive moves by the strongest. The failure of the

313

weaker players can be aggravated by the small, even unnoticeable moves of competitors, which facilitate entrapment or at least hinder escape. It is very difficult to distinguish condition-driven entrapment from competitor-driven entrapment in retrenched competition. Both processes work in the same direction. Their combined effect, however, is clear. They tend to lead towards an endless cycle of loss and failure in the weakest, often the trapped, organization. These failures escalate pressure to withdraw from the "new" banking areas and tighten institutional control. SKOPBANK was brought under the control of the Bank of Finland in the autumn of 1990. A stabilization programme was proposed and accepted by the authorities, who monitored its implementation closely. The authorities were worried not only about SKOPBANK, but also about the Finnish banking system as a whole, especially its international reputation.

In 1991 the Bank of Finland had to take over SKOPBANK. As there was a danger that the Finnish banks would drop below minimum statutory capital-adequacy standards, the government was forced to give equity injections and state guarantees to all banks. A new agency, the State Guarantee Fund, was established to support the whole Finnish financial system. In 1992 the biggest savings banks merged and formed the Savings Bank of Finland. In October 1993 this bank was split and liquidated by the four other major banks.

Retrenched competition tends to create externally generated traps which "freeze" development and encourage exploitation of known alternatives, recruitment of risk-avoiders, and other conservative practices. This leads, however, to a paradox, since the new structures remain. Banking still takes place in the deregulated environment. The global financial markets, liberalized exchange controls, and the internationalization of corporations create continuous pressure in the opposite direction; a search for new fields of specialization, new combinations of services, and new forms of competitive alliances between banks across national borders.

Conclusions

There is an obvious asymmetry in how management practices evolve in extended and retrenched competition. During extended competition "new practices seem to destroy old ones" and "new organizations arise to challenge old institutions and institutional structures". During retrenched competition, on the other hand, "old practices seem to destroy new ones" and "old institutions, with some new elements, seem to modify what used to be "new" managerial practices" (March 1991). During the extended competitiveness phase emphasis is mainly on the exploration of new possibilities, and during the contracting phase on the exploitation of old certainties. In the extended competition period bank initiatives, combined with old and weak institutions catalyzed the emergence of new competitive practices. These were diffused by institutional reforms and self-reinforcing busi-

314

ness practices until the disturbances required new regulations and gradual institutional restructuring.

In the period of retrenched competition reduced demand alone was not decisive in changing managerial practices, but together with inherited success traps, it had the consequence of shaking out competitors. This shakeout of the whole banking sector activated new reforms in the institutions, that is, building up rescue structures and new control procedures. The changes in the competitive practices in the Finnish banking sector were indisputable and clear under regulation, deregulated growth, and deregulated decline.

Our examination suggests that internal impulses are significant in understanding these changes in competitive practices. These impulses are constantly "testing" the strength of institutional regulations. If regulations are relatively weak they are not destroyed, but left intact until the tensions and paradoxes created by new practices initiate institutional renewal processes. If regulations are relatively strong, exploitation of old certainties prevails or impulses are modified.

The interplay between external and internal developments and their relative strengths is conceptualized here by the various forms of managerial traps and their generative processes. The following types of traps could be identified from the development of the Finnish banking sector in the 1980s and 1990s.

Exhibit 1. Types of managerial traps in the Finnish banking sector

	Internally produced	Externally producent
Unintentional	i.e. competence trap	i.e. interest rate trap
Intentional	i.e. trap of self-isolation	i.e. competitors' trap

The traps illustrate the limits of managerial action and the turning points in the competitive dynamics. During extended competition internally generated traps are likely to occur. Experimentation with new competitive practices dominates and successes lead to entrapment, which further diffuses new practices. The longer this lasts the more vulnerable the winners become and the more drastic the changes that can be expected in competitive positions if the environment changes. In retrenched competition, on the other hand, externally generated traps become more likely and the pressures to return to the old competitive practices increase. The formation of external traps tends to change the relative positions of competitors in favour of the financially strongest. This change is easily extended to intentional "failure traps", to vicious circles where deteriorating conditions are aggravated by the intentional efforts of competitors to tighten the trap and to propel the victims towards failure. The formation of these traps sets the tone and rhythm for the institutional renewal of the Finnish banking sector. Institutional reforms dealt primarily with the consequences of earlier managerial practices. They regulated "history," while the managerial practices moulded the present.

Epilogue

After the full circle, boom and recession, who were the winners and losers in the Finnish banking competition? In public the losers seem to be the original innovators, and the "winners" those who remained conservative. From our perspective, however, the competitive victory went to those who balanced the "creative" and "conservative" competitive practices appropriately, and matched their changes to the pace of change in the wider social context. The losers were those who concentrated either mainly on the exploration of new possibilities or mainly on the exploitation of old certainties. And our guess is that this will happen again when the next boom occurs. Attraction to "one truth", which "fits" the conditions, may again prevent management from creating a balance between exploration and exploitation. It is difficult to create synthesis, if antithesis is absent, and if managerial learning itself contributes to this absence.

References

Ansoff, H.I. (1991) "Strategic management in a historical perspective", *International Review of Strategic Management* 2: 3–69.

Bourgeois, L.J. and Brodwin, D.R. (1984) "Strategic implementation: five approaches to elusive phenomena", *Strategic Management Journal* 5: 241–264.

Engwall, L. (1994) "Bridge, poker and banking", in D. Fair and R. Raymond (eds.) *The competiveness of financial institutions and centers in Europe*. Amsterdam: Kluwer.

Hakkarainen, N. (1993) *Oravanppyörässä*. WSOY: Juva.

Lassila, J. (1993) *Markka ja ääni*. Kirjayhtymä: Hämeenlinna.

Levinthal, D.A. and March, J.G. (1993) "The myopia of learning", *Strategic Management Journal* 14: 95–112.

Levitt, B. and March, J.G. (1988) "Organizational learning", *Annual Review of Sociology* 14: 319–340.

March, J.G. (1981) "Footnotes to organizational change", *Administrative Science Quarterly* 17: 563–577.

———. (1991) "Exploration and exploitation in organizational learning", *Organization Science* 2: 71–87.

Masuch, M. (1985) "Vicious circles in organizations", *Administrative Science Quarterly* 30: 14–33.

Porter, M. (1980) *Competitive Strategy*. New York: Free Press.

Repo, E. (1992) *Vallan havittelijat*. Gummerus: Jyväskylä.

Reve, T. (1990) *Mimetic strategic behavior in banking*, Working paper, 48. Bergen: Norwegian School of Economics and Business Administration.

Saari, M. (1992) *Minä, Christopher Wegelius*. Gummerus: Jyväskylä.

Schumpeter, J.A. (1942) *Capitalism, Socialism and Democracy*. New York: Harper & Brothers.

Weitzel, W. and Jonsson, E. (1989) "Decline in organizations: a literature integration and extension", *Administrative Science Quarterly* 34: 91–109.

Whitley, R. (1992) "Societies, firms and markets: the social structuring of business systems", in R. Whitley (ed.) *European Business Systems: firms and their markets in their national context*. London: Sage.

Zysman, J. (1983) *Governments, Markets and Growth: Financial Systems and the Politics of Industrial Change*. Ithaca, New York: Cornell University Press.

Chapter 14

Institutional Design in Democratic Contexts

Johan P. Olsen

Transcending Existing Institutions

This chapter considers the design and redesign of political institutions. Specifically, it discusses how the significance of design may be affected by key institutional features of contemporary democratic polities. The first question is: To what degree do democratic contexts create a viable space for institutional design – making design necessary, politically feasible and legitimate? The second question is: What kind of processes tend to make designers able to exploit the available space of design?[1]

---

1   A first draft of this chapter was presented at the Institutional Design Workshop, Research School of Social Sciences, Australian National University, Canberra. Since then, the key ideas have been discussed in workshops and seminars at The Stockholm Center of Organizational Research, The Norwegian Research Centre in Organization and Management, Bergen and Europäisches Zentrum für Staatswissenschaften und Staatspraxis, Berlin. I want to thank Peggy Simcic Brønn, Tom Christensen, Morten Egeberg, Andreas Føllesdal, Ian Marsh, Ketil Moen, Claus Offe, Janne Haaland Matlary, and the participants in the workshops and seminars. A special thanks to Robert E. Goodin and James G. March for constructive comments.

The chapter aims at going beyond the idea that design can best be understood as a process of problem-solving or power-struggle over policy-benefits in terms of pre-defined preferences and powers. It argues that design is more likely when designers exploit shifting political attention and the confluence of temporary, favorable circumstances; when they stabilize attention over extended periods; and when they trigger self-driving processes that make design independent of one-shot, grand decisions that change an institutional arrangement at once. Design is, furthermore, more likely when political actors evoke aspects other than an institution's instrumental value – in particular deontological concerns. Finally, design is more likely when political actors take into account how the working of institutions depends on properties of the citizens, not only rules and incentives; and when they take into account how institutions fashion, not only regulate, citizens.

Theoretical aspirations

John Stuart Mill thought that a proper understanding of how political institutions are constituted, sustained and transformed would require reconciliation of two old traditions. One was interpreting change instrumentally, as a matter of social engineering and choice between alternative arrangements. The other was viewing change as the outcome of organic, evolutionary processes (Mill 1861/1962:3). He underestimated the complexity. A well-developed theory of institutional dynamics would require the reconciliation of several logics of development and include processes like war, coercion, competitive selection, diffusion, evolution, chance, deliberate choice and design.

A somewhat less complex challenge is to specify to what extent and under which conditions humans are capable of establishing political institutions from reflection and choice, rather than being the victims of accident and force.[2] Much effort has been devoted to that task. Still, it has turned out to be difficult to specify a stable set of conditions under which design is a major factor in institutional change.[3] A more realistic aspiration is to specify how a restricted set of factors limits or expands the scope of institutional design in specific historical-cultural contexts.

The ideology of popular sovereignty suggests that developing political institutions of self-governance is a first-order political process and that human will, reason and power play a key role in institutional change (March and Olsen 1995). "Design" usually suggests a type of explanation that focusses on changes in the purposes, reasoning and power of identifiable political agents. A structure is created and

---

2   Hamilton, Jay and Madison 1964:1, Mill 1962:1.
3   Nystrom and Starbuck 1981, March and Olsen 1983, 1989,1995, Brunsson and Olsen 1993, Goodin 1995.

changes as a result of problem solving and conflict resolution among purposeful actors. A structure represents a solution to a shared problem in a consensus system, or an imposed, coerced solution from a winning coalition or a conqueror. In all cases, a structure arises and is maintained or transformed as a function of the degree to which it serves the purposes of relevant actors. The task is to identify the sources of political pressure for change and who is opposed (Olsen 1996:249).

Still, in "ideal" democracies, popular sovereignty, active participation and public debate are intended to secure continuous learning and adaptation and therefore reduce the need for major (re)design. In addition, constitutive rules delimit the space of legitimate design, in particular in fragmented societies. In real-life democracies, however, there is substantial room for design precisely because ordinary processes of learning and adaptation are inefficient, constitutive rules of legitimate change are ambiguous, contested and changing, and governments have limited capability of governance. In such contexts, design depends on the ability of prospective designers to exploit the imperfections and ambiguities that create a viable space of design.

These are the themes to be further elaborated. Focus is on "living institutions" and behavioral practices, and not formal-legal aspects alone. It is on factors that impinge upon the significance of the design of key governmental institutions and their interrelations with other institutions. Political institutions will refer to any institution that can be affected by, or can affect, a democratically-elected government and those deriving their authority and power from elected organs (Goodin and Pettit 1993:2). Finally, we are interested in radical changes in an existing political order, rather than revolutionary transformations, incremental modifications of a single aspect of specific institutions, or routine flexibility between existing standard operating procedures.[4] Much, however, depends on what is meant by "design".

Design

Institutional design refers, firstly, to a process aimed at producing prescriptions, organization charts and plans, usually with some adaptive rules for coping with unforeseen circumstances (Nystrom and Starbuck 1981:xx). In this meaning

---

4   *Revolutionary* change signifies fast and major change inconsistent with the identity of an existing institutional arrangement or order (Kuhn 1962). *Radical* change means fast and major changes in institutional configurations that in significant ways redefine the terms of governance, yet do not break with an existing order. *Incremental* change refers to slow and gradual changes, processes which are consistent with an existing order, but which in the long run may make existing institutions disappear or new ones emerge.

design is commonplace, in many organizations almost a matter of routine (Brunsson and Olsen 1993.Ch.3). Secondly, design is sometimes, although not completely correctly, used for a pattern or plan which can be detected, or imagined, in existing institutional structures without any reference to the processes that produced the pattern.

Design involves how institutions might be, and ought to be, constructed – how they are adapted to human purposes in order to function well and create improvement (Simon 1970). Designers try to make institutions more efficient or rational, more humane, representative, responsive, transparent or accountable. They also try to make them more useful to societies, more profitable for owners, more submissive to top managers, more stable and robust, or more flexible and able to learn (Nystrom and Starbuck 1981:xiii, Goodin 1995:39).

Students of institutions are interested in design behavior, in structural designs, in the effects of various designs, and in the criteria of improvement, independent of whether these aspects are tightly or loosely connected. Here, however, design signifies purposeful and deliberate intervention that succeeds in establishing new institutional structures and processes, or rearranging existing ones, thereby achieving intended outcomes and improvements. That is, design is understood in terms of a chain of effects from human purpose to desired results.

It is easy to imagine that such chains are less than perfect.

The general criticism of "constructivism", rationalism, social engineering and political utopias is well known.[5] In addition, students of organizational decision making observe that reforms often fail. Change takes place without explicit decisions and decisions to change follow after change has already occurred. Decisions to change often do not lead to change, or they lead to further unanticipated or unintended change. Intitutional reforms breed new demands for reforms rather than making reforms redundant.[6] Additionally, organizational sociologists show that the discretion and choice of institutional designers are constrained by institutional environments collective moral and causal beliefs providing organizational "templates" and "scripts." They also observe that participants over time ascribe value to organizational structures and processes beyond their technical-instrumental qualities, making change more difficult.[7] Still, these studies may underrate the role of choice and design (Heller 1995:707,711). Human actors are occasionally successful. They

---

5 Popper 1945, Hayek 1990, Hirschman 1991.
6 March and Olsen 1975, 1976,1983,1984,1989,1995; March 1981,1988; Brunsson 1985,1989; Olsen 1991,1992, Brunsson and Olsen 1993.
7 Selznick 1957, Eisenstadt 1964, Meyer and Rowan 1977, Thomas et al. 1987, Zucker 1988, Powell and DiMaggio 1991, Scott and Meyer 1994, Scott 1995.

are not always captives of forces they cannot comprehend or control. Or at least, that is what democratic ideology tells us to believe.

Democratic Contexts
An open political order

Democracy is a distinct political order that provides a distinct historical-institutional context for governance and design (March and Olsen 1995:2). Democracy signifies a set of historically evolving ideas – ideals, visions, principles, identities, allegiances and causal beliefs. Democracy also refers to a changing collection of accumulated institutional practices, rules and procedures, all of which are believed to have proven their worth in advancing democratic ideals. Finally, democracy implies a distribution of resources, rights and liberties which to some degree counteract the skewed distribution of economic and social resources and make individuals and institutions capable of functioning according to democratic ideals.

Yet, democracy is also an open-ended project (Bobbio 1987:17) and a "theme for development" (Broderick 1970: xvii). Its ideals are difficult to reach in practice and no polity has ever come close to the democratic vision. Taking it seriously would induce considerable change even in the most developed "democracies." Democratic ideals are also contested. They have been challenged by religious leaders, military people, the well-born, the rich, the experts, the proletariat, and others. The role of ordinary citizens in politics has been questioned, and so has the role of democratic politics in society. Finally, democracies live with tensions and contradictions among institutions, principles and ordering ideas (Lepsius 1990:256). Many aspects of political and social life are regulated by several institutions based on different logics, and tensions or contradictions between these logics are an important source of change in a democratic order.

Contemporary contexts

Historically, democracies have gone through periods of stasis and change. While criticism of political institutions has to a large extent focussed on institutional inertia and rigidity, political developments since the Second World War in most democracies have been characterized by radical change. In the European context, the first three decades of the post WWII period were dominated by the *centralized welfare state-project* – a large-scale experiment based on a belief in the ability of national democratic politics and strong state institutions to plan and improve society. Aspirations included taking collective responsibility for the well-being of all citizens, and reducing inequality by controlling or compensating for the social perversities of competitive markets. This was to be done by providing universal

323

high quality public services, and by redistributing resources between social groups and districts. Democratic citizenship was supposed to include economic and social rights and economic and social democracy (Allardt 1981, Ringen 1987).

Currently, institutional "choice" and "design" are again high on the political agenda. There is a search for new institutional arrangements (Wright 1994) and many governments have tried to give direction and structure to political life by constructing political institutions, roles and relationships (March and Olsen 1995:244). There is a possible reconceptualization of the state and citizenship – what it means to be a state and a member of a state – and how state-society-citizen relations can be most appropriately organized (Hesse and Johnson 1995). In particular, democracies need to rethink what "democracy" means in an increasingly international or global context (Held 1995).

At least four major, partly overlapping challenges to the leading role of a centralized welfare state have been discerned over the last two to three decades. Each challenge, represented by a project, portrays the centralized welfare state as too interventionist, powerful, bureaucratic, static and oppressive. First is a *democratic decentralization project* that criticizes the centralization of public power. A main aim is to move political decisions and public service production closer to those affected. Strengthening the institutions of local government is supposed to produce more democracy as well as functional efficiency (Schmidt 1990, Baldersheim and Ståhlberg 1994).

Second is a *civil society project* that claims that the welfare state project has lost much of its emancipatory effects and that it is increasingly producing negative ones. The civil society project is positive to decentralization, and it aspires to reduce the discretionary role of public authorities in general. The aim is to strengthen citizens' self-mobilization and civil society institutions in terms of legal rights, free debate and criticism, voluntary associations and collective citizen initiatives (Offe 1984, Cohen and Arato 1992).

Third is a *market society project* which, in addition to decentralization and anti-statism, also emphasizes economic individualism. Often labeled neo-liberal or New Right, the project represents a return to early nineteenth century ideas about the primacy of economic and social institutions over politics. Focus is on commercialism and the institutional prerequisites for a flourishing economy. The aim is to create a new political and social order with the competitive market, rather than have democratic politics and the welfare state as the institutional centerpiece. The market is supposed to discipline government, not the other way around. Free enterprise, private property, self-interest, the profit motive and economic rewards are key components. It is assumed that individuals want to be left alone and take individual responsibility for their lives. Dynamics and the improvement of human conditions are produced by entrepreneurs in economic and social spheres of life, not by government. The market is also assumed to improve the human character by contributing to a spirit of self-reliance, entrepreneurship and commerce (Thompson 1990).

Fourth is a *European integration project* that makes nation-states face the possibility of major changes in the division of tasks, powers and responsibilities between the national and the European level. The four projects of the welfare state, democratic decentralization, civil society and market society, all compete in the context of the development of the European Union, as well as the reconstitution of polities and societies in Central and Eastern Europe after the collapse of Communist regimes.[8] So far, the market society project, with its emphasis on the economic and technological necessities of global, capitalist competition, is the primary engine of change. Yet, the long-run success of each project is not obvious.

The aspiration of the major reform programs is nothing less than a major rearrangement of the relations among key institutions, with possible profound implications for the working of society. What then is the viable space of institutional design in a context of democratic institutions, their current dynamics and competing reform programs?

We focus on the impact of three key characteristics of democratic order which may affect the significance of design. Firstly, final authority and responsibility lie with free and equal citizens organized as a sovereign political community (Wolin 1981:31). Representative and accountable governance is majority governance driven by public opinion. The legitimacy of policy-making is contingent on the ability to secure support and commitment, or at least acquiescence among ordinary citizens. Secondly, democratic governance is enlightened. Democracies institutionalize reasoned debate and deliberation, legitimate opposition and criticism. Publicity, transparency and an active civil society are supposed to secure informed citizens and officials. Thirdly, democratic governance is rule-constrained. Constitutional rules and institutions constrain majority power and secure inalienable freedoms and liberties.

Such properties tend to constrain the viable space of radical design. In real-life, however, ambiguities and imperfections delay decisions, accumulate tensions, and therefore increase the legitimate space of design. Consider, first, how the viable space for design depends on how routine processes of institutional learning and adaptation are working, making design more or less necessary.

---

8   Offe 1991,1995; Hesse 1993, Bryant and Mokrzycki 1994, Elster, Offe and Preuss 1996.

Is Design Necessary?

All institutions develop experience-based standard responses for dealing with changing circumstances (March 1981). As a result, institutions are often transformed through mundane processes of learning and incremental adaptation. At other times, transformations are radical or revolutionary and characterized by conflict, crisis and break-downs. Change *in* a system can fail so badly that it generates change *of* the system itself (Kochanek 1971:319).

When it comes to understanding the relative importance of design, what then is the significance of variations in institutional ability to learn routinely from experience and adapt to changing circumstances? Even with fairly simple designs, it is difficult to predict in any detail how a specific organization of components will behave. Such knowledge requires observing behavior in practice (Simon 1970:16,21). While there may be no easy recipes for institutional design in a democratic context (Held 1986:6), design efforts themselves can provide important insight into how an institution actually works (Nystrom and Starbuck 1981:xii). Therefore, learning is sometimes seen as a precondition for institutional design (Metcalfe 1981:506). A supplementing or competing hypothesis is that *imperfect* learning routines are a precondition for radical design. The more efficient ordinary processes of learning and adaptation are, the less likely is accumulation of tensions and conflicts and radical change by design or breakdowns.

Trust in learning and adaptation

As the limitations of forecasting in uncertain, complex and dynamic contexts have become obvious, more interest has been focussed on experiential learning as a key organizational process (Levitt and March 1988). Learning aspirations are generally high in modern democracies. The expectation is that experience will improve the intelligence, effectiveness and adaptability of governance. Experiential learning is supposed to enable governments to detect and counteract failures, and to improve their performance record as well as the polity's fitness for the future (March and Olsen 1995, Olsen and Peters 1996).

The democratic challenge is not necessarily to make great designs and big leaps possible, but to foster the continuous learning and adaptation that make such leaps unnecessary. A well-functioning democracy – based on representative, responsive and accountable government and a well-developed civil society – is in particular supposed to facilitate continuous learning and adaptation. Democratic institutions are assumed to work as safety valves and as guarantors of incremental adjustments. Informed citizens and officials are supposed to learn realistic expectations when it comes to what different institutions can and can not do. Officials are expected to learn which actions, processes and structures are likely to achieve support or acquiescence among citizens. Therefore, in an ideal democracy, equilibrium institutional solutions are assumed to be common. That is, no actors are likely to act so as to challenge radically existing institutions.

Impediments to learning and adaptation

Practice is different from such ideals. "Inefficiencies" in institutional learning and adaptation are integral parts of governance in constitutional democracies. In addition, it is difficult for democracies to live up to the norms, expectations and claims of experiential learning. Policy-makers do not necessarily search for lessons. Their ability or willingness to learn from experience is often limited. Causal and normative beliefs, behavioral patterns and institutional designs do not easily change in light of experience.[9]

Actually, all the current reform projects include some attempt to improve institutional learning capabilities. For instance, replacing the state by markets and introducing market-like arrangements in the public sector are (among other things) based on trust in the market as a self-designing, self-regulating, self-correcting institution (Klein 1995). The basic idea is to use competitive pressures to compel institutional learning and adaptiveness. Institutions incapable of rapid adjustment to changing circumstances and opportunities are assumed to be eliminated by competition. Democratic authority is only to be used in a transformation phase to design institutional arrangements that minimize or eliminate the future need for central control and coercion. When market arrangements are in place, learning and adaptation capabilities will be improved, and there is no place for radical design.

Market mechanisms, however, are unlikely to be a panacea in a world dominated by large-scale formal organizations. The vision of an ideal self-regulating market society has to be held together with a practice of more or less perfect markets and with public and private organizations more or less able and willing to adapt to their environments (Nystrom and Starbuck 1981). Limited ability to learn and adapt is not a property of democratic politics and government alone. There is no guarantee that competitition will drive out inefficient institutions or firms (North 1990). Bounded rationality, sequential attention to tasks and goals, division of labor, and local rationality, are phenomena present in all formal organizations, including private firms operating in competitive markets (Cyert and March 1963, Nelson and Winter 1982). Experiential learning is usually complicated by limited experience, limited capability to make inferences from experience, limited ability to act on the basis of new knowledge, and limited memory and capability of retaining information (March and Olsen 1995:206–223). In addition, a major problem is that often

---

9   March and Olsen 1989,1995; Rose 1993, Olsen and Peters 1996.

many actors are learning simultaneously (March 1991,1994). As each part of a system adapts to its immediate task environment in a more or less myopic manner, the system as a whole may become incoherent and ineffective (Levinthal and March 1993).

Such impediments to learning are in particular relevant in the context of major reform programs that aim at changing complex institutional configurations comprising several levels and sectors of governance. One implication is that ordinary processes of experiential learning and adaptation can not *a priori* be assumed to make institutional design superfluous. It can not be taken as given that key democratic institutions, or other societal institutions, including market arrangements, are well organized and function well. Therefore, in order to identify needs and possibilities for institutional design, it is necessary to specify in some detail the main sources of inefficiency in mundane institutional processes of learning and adaptation, as well as those in forecasting. It is also necessary to specify to what degree democratic actors are able to act upon new knowledge and implement new designs.

Is Design Feasible?

While institutional design is often presented as a problem of finding the one optimal solution to a collective problem, new designs are resisted because those affected see reform proposals not as improvements and progress, but as disruptive, resource-demanding, painful and threatening in terms of status, power and policy consequences (Olsen 1991:130). In complex and heterogeneous polities in particular, radical designs are unlikely to generate consensus, except under extraordinary circumstances. The support for specific designs or a coherent policy of institutional design can not be taken as given. It has to be created, and the problem of political support or acquiescence cannot be assumed away by reference to some omnipotent or sovereign authority, as is sometimes done in political and organizational theory.[10] In contemporary democracies, governance takes place in polycentric policy networks of public and private actors,[11] and elected governments have to convince citizens and organized interests that design is possible and desirable.

---

10 For example, in *Discourses*, Machiavelli (1950:138) concludes that, "To found a new Republic, or to reform entirely the old institutions of an existing one, must be the work of one man only." More recently, Haberstroh (1965:1171) claims that, "The use of the word design implies a focus on aspects of structure that are prescribed by or at least acceptable to the formal authority of the organization." In contrast, Child and Kieser (1981: 55) argue that it is self defeating "to launch a design project without explicit attention to the power-setting."

11 Marin and Mayntz 1991, Mayntz 1993, Jachtenfuchs and Kohler-Koch 1996.

In a public opinion-driven system, building a majority for radical design may be hampered by traditional perceptions and attitudes in the population, as well as conflicting preferences, causal and moral beliefs. Properties of electoral systems and systems of governance may make design more or less likely. For instance, parliamentary systems of the Westminster model, based on disciplined majority parties tend to be more able to implement reforms than are federative systems with well-developed checks and balances, and based on less disciplined minority parties (Castles, Gerritsen and Vowles 1996, Olsen and Peters 1996).

Governments may face institutional resistance. Changes consistent with an institution's (or network's) identity, tradition and dynamics are likely to be continuous and incremental. Changes in opposition to existing identities, traditions and dynamics are likely to be episodic and problematic and create conflict (March and Olsen 1989,1995). This is even more so if an institution is integrated into a larger political and social order so that change in one institution requires changes in several others (Hernes 1976, Krasner 1988).

What governments can do also depends on organized interests in society. Winning elections give uncertain influence (Rokkan 1966). While political theorists have worried that democracy will allow the poor to plunder the rich, in reality democracies are characterized by substantial differences in the distribution of politically relevant economic, social and organizational resources. Possibly, the distribution is so skewed, and the political regulation of the use of private resources so inadequate, that political democracy can not work if society and in particular the economy are not further democratized (Dahl 1985).

Sometimes broad political mobilization makes change possible, yet it can also constrain the government's control of the process. For instance, the development of the welfare state in the Scandinavian countries, which involved a growing public agenda as well as new institutions, came together with expanded representation and integration of organized interests into public policy making (Olsen 1981). Likewise, an extended European agenda and new institutions have come together with increased participation of national actors at all stages of EU policy-making processes. The higher the intensity of European integration and the more new areas of policy are included, the more the affected parties have been involved, and the more discretion has been transferred to institutions in which member states are directly represented.[12]

In practice, democratic governments under normal circumstances have a limited capability for radical design. Political institutions are usually set up in a piecemeal way. Institutional developments are seldom driven by over-arching conceptions of

---

12 Kassim and Wright 1991:841, Dehousse et al. 1992:49, Schuppert 1995:341.

the preferred design of the polity as such. There is typically no single design or designer, but rather a process involving several competing designers and localized attempts at partial design (Goodin 1995:28). For instance, the European Union "has evolved incrementally into a labyrinthine set of political institutions serving a variety of discrete policy purposes" (Marks, Hooghe and Blank 1995:7). A similar observation is made at the nation-state level (March and Olsen 1983). In addition, design is constrained by rules of legitimacy.

Is Design Legitimate?

Political life most of the time functions according to relatively stable, historically evolved practices and rules embedded in institutions. Institutionalization signifies a slow process of accumulation and transformation of practices and rules. It involves structuralization and routinization of behavior; standardization, homogenization and authorization of codes of meaning and ways of reasoning; and it means linking resources to values and world-views. Authority and power are depersonalized, and resource mobilization and principles of resource allocations are routinized (March and Olsen 1995; Olsen 1995:10–11).

In particular, constitutional-liberal democracy is "the art of separation" (Walzer 1984). Constitutive rules specify agencies and agents, and their proper jurisdictions, responsibilities and relations. They create procedural reliability and predictability. They regulate the use of arbitrary power. They protect inalienable liberties and freedoms and specify partly autonomous institutional spheres outside the immediate reach of majority government. The emphasis is on "government of laws, and not of men", deliberately limiting the legitimate discretion of shifting majorities in order to avoid majority tyranny (Berg 1965).

Consequently, constitutive rules also limit the legitimate space of institutional design. The constitution is assumed to prevent, complicate or delay change that a current majority wants (Elster and Slagstad 1988). Some types of design that imply sudden, comprehensive or coercive change, are illegitimate; others demand cumbersome procedures and qualified majorities. Order and predictability are as important as adaptation and change. Slowing down change may make it possible for individuals to adjust their plans and to retain their sense of dignity (Deutsch 1966:131–132, Shklar 1990:90,120). Institutional rigidity and resistance to change may express institutional identity and integrity and a defense of legitimate concerns. This is an aspect of democratic governance that may be of special relevance in periods, like the current one, characterized by rapid economic and technological modernization and a tendency to make economics the new *prima philosophia*, that is, the type of reasoning used as a measuring stick for all aspects of human life (Koslowski 1985:6–8).

Heterogeneous societies in particular demand strongly qualified majorities to change the power of different branches and levels of government or the relative power of public authorities and citizens (Weaver and Rockman 1993:464). In contrast, cultural homogeneity, a history of compromise and peaceful co-existence, socio-economic equality, and growing resources, may help develop a comparatively high acceptance of majority government and institutional design. The Scandinavian countries during the post-war buildup of the welfare state may be an example of this (Ringen 1987, Olsen 1990).

Constitutional rules, however, also create a dynamic element. They institutionalize orderly change and reconcile adaptiveness and institutional identity and integrity. The rules maintain institutions that survive and flourish in the face of changing environments, while maintaining a basic commitment to the primacy of democratic values (March and Olsen 1995:192). Therefore, they reduce conflict and opposition and legitimatize design.

Constitutive rules are more or less permissive towards rapid and radical change. Yet they are hardly unambiguous and constant. Rules are open for competing interpretations. What is a democratically justifiable balance between competing ideas and institutions, and what is the legitimate space and speed for institutional design, are major themes for political discourse and struggle.

For instance, currently there is fairly widespread agreement that democratic designs can not include changing certain aspects of the existing order, like universal suffrage.[13] In contrast, there is widespread disagreement over other issues of institutional continuity and change. Major ideologies disagree as to whether political, legal, economic, social and cultural institutions should be tightly or loosely coupled, i.e. separated or integrated. They disagree on which institutions and institutional spheres should be the most central and powerful. They give different answers when it comes to what a democratic government can legitimately change at will, how quickly it can do it, and in what ways existing institutions and traditions can be transformed. The answers reflect disagreement concerning how institutions function, how they could function, what it means to function well, and

---

13 However, as late as between the two world wars, results from intelligence tests that showed low scores for many of the tested were used for attacks on universal voting rights. For instance, in a Presidential address delivered before the American Political Science Association's annual meeting, it was argued that "... the dogma of universal suffrage must give way to a system of educational and other tests which will exclude the ignorant, the uninformed, and the anti-social elements which hitherto have so frequently controlled elections" (Shephard 1935: 18–19). The appeal was: "Seize the torch, men of brains" (ibid. p.20).

to what degree human conditions can be improved through deliberate political intervention, social engineering and institutional design.

Democratic polities are "mixed orders." They function on the basis of a shifting balance between institutions with different concerns, logics, histories, dynamics and resources. The major ideologies and institutions of democracies have developed in interaction, and as reactions to each other. Long-term historical changes in their content and relative importance have reflected, as well as influenced, shifts in power in society (Hirschman 1991). Yet, political, legal, economic, social and cultural institutions are assumed to be able simultaneously to absorb or respond to changes in their environments, and to protect their identity and integrity. They are assumed to be able to maintain their different characteristics even when challenged by institutional spheres with hegemonic aspirations – be they democratic politics, state bureaucracies, corporative bargaining systems, competitive markets, organized religion, organized science, or others. If a single value, like order, utility, liberty, or community, and its institutional expression, achieves a hegemonic role, the effects are likely to be undesirable and the order likely to be challenged.[14]

In addition to long-term trends, there are short-term cycles resulting from sequential attention to values and institutional arrangements. Shifts from a focus on market failure to a focus on state failure, and from political governance to laissez-faire and competitive markets, can be interpreted in this perspective. Such shifts are then not seen (only) as an inevitable and irreversible reflection of technological changes. They are also not seen (only) as a necessary consequence of an increasingly differentiated society, moving towards more individualism and therefore making collective policies and institutions less likely.[15] Instead, the shift can be interpreted as (also) being part of a balancing process where no order or institutional mix is very durable.

In this perspective, the centralized welfare state project has triggered competing alternatives. The more successful any of these projects are, the more likely they, in turn, are to produce claims for a new balance. That is, yesterday's solutions have become today's problems, and today's solutions will eventually become tomorrow's problems. For instance, like the institutional designs of the welfare state project (Ringen 1987:vii), the designs of the market society project have been based on a mix of knowledge, beliefs, guesses, suggestions and hopes. It remains to be seen how the designs of the market society project will perform under varying conditions. What is fairly certain is that "living institutions" will never be able to match their ideal counterparts used in rhetorical struggles. This tends to create disappointment and legitimizes future (re)designs.

---

14 For an unconventional discussion, see Lukes 1995.
15 Polanyi 1944, Helleiner 1995, Notermans 1995.

Resistance to change that produces new social and economic inequalities may depend on the perceived causal process producing them, and changes seen as created by market forces may activate less resistance than those seen as caused by political decisions (Elster 1983:90). Still, a purified market society with no social purpose and responsibility may be socially unsustainable. It may generate so severe ecological imbalances and so much social exclusion and marginalization, injustice and exploitation, instability and upheavals, that there will be counter-reactions, as suggested by the "society-hits-back" hypothesis formulated by Polanyi (Polanyi 1944, Glasman 1994). Michels similarily argued that all institutions would eventually turn into self-interested oligarchies and generate reactions (Michels 1968). In this spirit, the "new social movements" are seen as part of a cyclical historical pattern of social criticism in the name of the general public (Dalton and Kuechler 1990).

To conclude, constitutive rules delimit the kinds of design that are legitimate, in particular in heterogeneous democracies. The rules stabilize and legitimize behavioral practices, ways of reasoning and making accounts, as well as resource distributions. They prevent some designs and complicate and delay others. Still, constitutive rules do not make design impossible. The rules routinize and legitimize some changes. In addition, the rules themselves are interpreted, reinterpreted and changed as part of political processes and the viable space for design depends on both how permissive and ambiguous the rules are.

The intricacies of institutional design are partly due to the fact that the same properties of democratic polities which create a space for design, also constrain the possibilities for exploiting that space. Theories of democratic design must recognize that often constitutional rules are ambiguous, the ability to learn and adapt is limited, and the political system is only able to digest incremental change. Therefore, theories of design can not assume design to refer to a single act or a discrete decision or reform, except under very special conditions. The conception of a constitutive convention where the best and brightest come together and formulate the basic principles and enduring rules for the organization of politics and society, is most of the time unlikely to capture the complexities of institutional design.

Facilitating Design

While contemporary democracies have a limited capability of deliberate intervention in existing institutional arrangements, political actors are not impotent. They do not act under circumstances of their own choosing, but they can under special conditions change institutions and make history (Marx 1963). Therefore, it may be worthwhile to identify some processes and conditions that make it more, rather than less likely that design will be a major process in the development of political institutions. Here, it is suggested that success in contemporary democracies may depend on *when* prospective designers act, *how* they proceed and *what* they try to achieve.

The organization of attention

Concepts like timely intervention, windows of opportunity, formative events, and breaking points in history suggest that there are time periods and situations where a confluence of events makes design efforts more likely to succeed than in others. Yet, it is problematic to specify under what conditions such phenomena are likely to occur. We suggest that design may depend on the ability to exploit inattention and mobilize attention. That is, we distinguish between situations in which design is possible because of the inattention of others and situations in which design is possible because attention is focussed to an unusual degree on an issue of great common concern. In addition, design may depend on the ability to exploit shifts in the general ideological climate or *Zeitgeist*.

Success as a result of the inattention of others is illustrated by cases where a new design is having something like a honeymoon period. When other actors discover what is going on, and realize what the implications are, it is difficult to reverse the process, at least in the short run (Blichner 1995). A possible implication is that prospective designers are most likely to be successful in relatively new, institution-free and actor-free policy areas. Generally, the founding, or birth period of an institution is of special importance. After some formative years, there is inertia and rigidity, making it more difficult to reform established patterns.[16]

Sudden surprises and major external shocks – great victories, shared trauma of war or natural disasters, financial crises, and situations of great urgency – also make design more likely. This is because such situations create drama. They focus collective attention on common destiny and shared concerns and sentiments, rather than on what divides people under normal circumstances. Therefore, they make constitutive acts in the name of "We the People" possible (Ackerman 1991). Institutional "crisis" may signify a temporary agreement on the inadequacies of inherited institutions in terms of shared conceptions of success criteria (Elias 1982, 1988; Herzog 1989). Sudden system breakdown, like in the former communist countries in Central and East Europe, especially creates a feeling of urgency. If the agreed perception is that there is no time for incremental learning and slow evolution, it may be easier to get support for radical redesigns (Offe 1991:871). However, as time goes on, the contingency of the consensus becomes evident and

---

16 Michels 1915, Simon 1953, Stinchcombe 1965.

the support is likely to decline. The question of reversability then becomes salient, an issue of obvious relevance in Central and East Europe.

Reformers, therefore, are more likely to succeed if they exploit existing sentiments of crises and opportunities, and try to change institutions in ways consistent with long-term trends or current institutional fashions. Generally, it is easier to row with the tide than against it. To create support and allegiance in opposition to existing sentiments requires major resource mobilization and long-term commitment. For instance, since the 1980s, it has been easier in all Western democracies to advocate market solutions, cuts in the public sector and "new public management" techniques, than to promote new governmental interventions, expanded welfare services and (Weberian) bureaucratic organization. It has also been easier to mobilize support for the market society project in countries where this ideology traditionally has been comparatively strong compared to the welfare state ideology, e.g. Anglo-American countries, than in countries where it has been relatively weak, e.g. the Scandinavian countries.[17]

Design without grand decisions

An alternative to exploiting favorable situations or periods is to expand the time horizon of design by stabilizing attention, energy and resources (March and Olsen 1983). Design then is more a question of keeping a developmental process alive, than creating a stable solution (Nystrom and Starbuck 1981:xx). A standard argument is that democracies are too myopic to give priority to long-term projects. Yet, it can also be argued that democratic institutions offer a long time horizon for political action. For instance, they make it possible to focus attention on the possibility of future victories rather than on the defeats of the day (Przeworski 1991:19).

Therefore, actors who know that democracies have limited capacity for digesting comprehensive design can try to combine the incremental improvements possible in everyday politics with a commitment to political visions and basic principles, and a general sense of direction towards an imagined good society and government. In this way, it may over time be possible to create coherent and enduring transformations in the basic institutional pattern of a political order and thereby change the map of political power and the mode of governance. One implication is that there is a role for patience in institutional design. Another is that design is more likely when political leaders have long tenure. Examples would be polities dominated by a single well-disciplined majority party over long time periods and

---

17 Wright 1994, Olsen and Peters 1996, Castles, Gerritsen and Vowles 1996.

polities where two competing parties replace each other in government only at long intervals.

An alternative way of achieving grand designs without grand decisions, is when a small timely intervention triggers a process which keeps itself going and over time leads to radical change. "Chain-reaction," "avalanche" or "slippery-slope" types of processes, all indicate a causally connected sequence of actions (or events) and outcomes. The process may be started by an insignificant decision. Yet, because it mobilizes enthusiasm or hatred, releases energy, or creates imbalances which "logically" lead to new behavior, the direction and outcome of the unfolding process are determined.

In the European context such processes have often been believed to play a key role. A tradition from Monnet to Delors has assumed that European integration and cooperation can be rejuvenated by creating situations of "dynamic disequilibrium" which in turn produce "spill over" effects and new dynamics. The key idea is that modest functional cooperation and economic integration among former enemies over time will (more or less by necessity) lead to expanded functional cooperation and political integration (Haas 1958). Similar ideas are also known from other attempts to develop international cooperation. Cooperation on non-controversial issues is supposed to develop trust among nations and then gradually lead to more cooperation (Luard 1990).

Yet, as is well known from natural processes, a chain reaction is easily upset by various inhabitants. Probably, this is even more the case in social and political processes. For instance, tensions and conflicts from big issues may be transfered to smaller, uncontroversial issues (Luard 1990). Or, attention may be detracted by events and decisions completely "unconnected" to the process in focus (Cohen, March and Olsen 1972). For example, conflicts over "mad cow-disease" (the BSE beef crisis) could for some time overshadow the preparation of the 1996 European Intergovernmental Conference and stall European cooperation for an extended period.

In sum, chain reactions may facilitate design, but it remains to develop a better understanding of the conditions under which such processes can be initiated at will and kept alive for extended time periods, and the conditions under which they will produce desired results. One challenge is to clarify the possible importance of existing institutional and group networks as carriers of chain reactions. Another is to clarify how success may depend on what designers are trying to do. For instance, it may be more difficult to secure a chain process that leads to a precise policy outcome than to a desired structural development, for instance that the introduction of one democratic institution increases the likelihood of more democratic institutions. This raises the issue of the role of deontological designs in institutional transformations.

Deontological designs

A political institution can be assessed instrumentally on the basis of its contribution to immediate substantive results. Or a structural arrangement can be evaluated deontologically, i.e. on the basis of specific properties of the institution itself. The test then is not an issue of precise calculation of the effectiveness and efficiency of alternative designs in specific situations. Instead, it is whether the institution is seen as the appropriate way of coping with certain classes of tasks and situations. The key issue is whether institutional practices and rules are consistent with basic principles of reason and morality in a culture – possibly involving general conceptions of good/evil, just/unjust, right/wrong, legal/illegal, true/false – so that it becomes a duty for citizens to follow its rules and prescriptions (Tyler 1990). For instance, support for representative institutions is a commitment to a long-term institutional arrangement, not to a specific outcome (Pitkin 1972:234). Likewise, the rule of law, the prohibition of retroactive laws, and recruitment based on merit, exemplify legitimizing principles not linked to the immediate substantive outcome of specific decisions. Such principles and institutions encourage some types of behavior and inhibit others. They create a "bias" in political life (Schattschneider 1960), yet they do not determine precise outcomes.

In an instrumental perspective, political institutions are conceptualized as malleable instruments, "consciously planned, deliberately constructed and restructured." (Etzioni 1964:3) The basic idea is to secure a tight coupling between structure and improved performance. Design is a search for the organizational tool most suited to serve a given set of pre-specified goals in a cost-effective way. Form follows strategy (Chandler 1962). Design depends on what the entrepreneurs want from an organization and whose interests are to be served (Hammond 1996:167).

Within this perspective, lack of exact causal knowledge is a serious problem. A growing empirical literature shows that institutions have an impact. They focus attention and resources and create a capability for action. They keep issues apart or coordinated, and they influence contact networks and communication, as well as policy making and outcomes (Egeberg 1987,1994; Weaver and Rockman 1993). Yet, it is often argued that existing empirical knowledge is not adequate for an explicit policy of institutional design. There are intuitions and strong beliefs in institutional forms, but existing knowledge "leaves a broad margin for disagreements about institutional design." (Przeworski 1991:35) Furthermore, more information does not necessarily make design easier. Disagreement on facts is often a consequence rather than a cause of political conflict (Wildavsky and Tenenbaum 1981).

Within a deontological perspective – where institutions are seen as part of a political order making it possible to live peacefully together with enduring tensions and conflicts, more than an organizational tool for the policy achievements of one

337

group of actors – the problem of exact causal knowledge is less acute. It may even be argued that in pluralistic polities design may be easier when structural arrangements are loosely coupled with substantive outcomes. That is, when institutions are wrapped in *a veil of vagueness*,[18] so that the actors have modest exact knowledge about the policy implications for different groups of alternative designs.

For instance, Preuss has argued that the relative openness of institutions to different outcomes tends to create acceptance. Durability and stability is secured because institutions provide a space for the maneuvers of the uncertainties of the political process (Preuss 1991:117,118). Impartiality, neutrality and other Rechtsstaat principles imply that institutional forms are not designed for achieving a specific outcome in single cases. The principle of separating law-making, implementation and control into different branches of government, tends to make the connection between legislative intent and final outcomes less certain, but it also tends to reduce the level of conflict. Likewise, constitutions are easier to establish when their immediate implications are somewhat uncertain, than in periods where constitutional rules and highly conflictual substantive issues have to be dealt with simultaneously. Finally, Offe suggests that prospective designers are more likely to have success if they copy institutional arrangements with a high status and good record elsewhere, or if they present designs as such copies rather than as instruments for achieving substantive goals. Imitation acts to play down conflicts and reduces the likelihood that designers will be suspected of favoring their own interests (Offe 1995:211–214).

To sum up, the argument is that in pluralistic polities, it may be easier to build support and commitment for robust deontological designs that constrain political processes in somewhat uncertain and ambiguous ways and allow different substantive outcomes, than for instrumental designs that dictate precise policy outcomes. In very heterogenous and conflictual societies deontological designs may also be the only achievable solution. Compared to the huge number of problems institutions are supposed to cope with, there seems to be a limited number of viable institutional options (Goodin 1993:157). An implication is that design processes will often be driven by available, legitimate institutional building-blocks rather than substantive problems (Cyert and March 1963). If so, prospective designers will be more successful if they start out studying the viability of alternative structures, rather than aiming at tailor-made designs for achieving immediate policy goals. Democratic processes, however, will not necessarily formulate design tasks for which there is an institutional solution. Possibly design,

---

18 This Rawlsian-inspired term was suggested to me by Diane Gibson.

and a viable polity in general, depend as much on the character of citizens as on institutional arrangements.

Beyond the worst case scenario

Can democratic designers be successful independent of properties of the population? Can they succeed with uninformed and corrupt citizens, as well as with citizens who are informed and competent, virtuous and civic minded? Is it possible to design democratic institutions without democrats, or a European polity without Europeans, so that the legitimacy of institutional arrangements is based solely on a continuous proof of their functional efficiency?

What may be called the worst case scenario of institutional design makes no assumptions about friendship, solidarity, shared collective identity or democratic attitudes among citizens. A standard position is that if only external incentives are right, good government is guaranteed whatever the character of individuals. Human nature is portrayed as universal and stable, self-interested and calculative. Institutional arrangements are supposed to compensate for the lack of human virtue and intelligence and compel individuals to act in ways that do not seriously hurt society (Hamilton, Jay and Madison 1964:19).

An older view is that the quality of a polity depends not only on external rules and incentive structures, but also on properties of its citizens (Aristotle 1985). Without citizens and officials who are well informed, active, civic minded and self-restrained, good government is impossible.[19] Consequently, institutions are required to help in the formation of personality characteristics and competences which sustain a civil society and democratic polity.[20] The ultimate democratic criterion of institutional design is the degree to which alternative arrangements facilitate or hinder a sustainable democratic culture and a demos of informed and politically capable citizens.

This older conception has not had an easy time recently (Putnam 1993). Standard arguments have been that it belongs to traditional society more than modern society, and to small (city) states more than modern, large-scale, multicultural states. Common advice is that one should not expect too much community, collective interests and shared culture in highly differentiated democracies (Goodin 1988,1992). It is also common to argue that a nation-state strategy of cultural homogenization is no longer viable. Instead, the answer is constitutional

---

19 Mill 1962:30, Viroli 1992, Kymlicka 1995:175.

20 For instance, Mill argued that, "The first question in respect to any political institution is, how far they tend to foster in the members of the community the various desirable qualities, moral and intellectual...." (Mill 1962:32).

patriotism, emphasizing identification with political institutions and rules as a way of coping with unresolved tensions and conflicts.[21]

If, however, well-functioning democratic institutions require democrats, how and where do individuals learn to become citizens? How and where do they learn self-restraint and to follow obligatory, common rules of political life? Becoming a citizen is a demanding project (Offe 1997), and the problematic democratic legitimacy for forming human character, moral and causal beliefs and expectations by political means are well known. Such forming is usually seen as part of totalitarian, not democratic, societies (Friedrich 1939). A caveat is that *all* institutions potentially contribute to forming individual and collective identity. Families, markets and the institutions of science, religion, and art, together with the mass media, the movie industry, public relations agencies, and multinational companies, may all have an effect. There is no guarantee that any arbitrary mix of institutions will help develop democratic citizens and a democratic culture if only democratic politics are not involved.

Political actors may shape a design and a design process (Simon 1970:76,83), and the latter role may be more legitimate in democracies. An appropriate task for democratic design may be to influence the mix of institutional structures and processes fashioning citizens in order to avoid democratic perversions (March and Olsen 1995). One example is to establish and protect institutional configurations which provide good settings for reflective processes where participants critically can examine their own preferences (Offe 1997). Another is to influence the access of issues and participants to arenas for collective interpretation and decision-making (Cohen, March and Olsen 1972, March and Olsen 1976).

In the short run, individuals have to be taken as given. In the long run, it is possible to construct institutional frameworks that help bring about new citizens (Boli 1989, Tønnessen 1992). For example, children's role as future citizens gives the state a legitimate concern for their education (Rawls 1988:268), and the construction of compulsory mass educational systems during the nineteenth century throughout Europe illustrates how a new type of socialization may be created and institutionalized (Soysal and Strang 1989).

The argument is that the design of political institutions can not be seen in isolation from properties of the citizens. Doing so is likely to produce failure for prospective designers. In particular, it is easier to construct workable democratic institutions in a polity of devoted democrats than in a polity without democrats, i.e. individuals driven solely by external incentives and private benefits, or by non-democratic norms.

---

21 Habermas 1992, Rawls 1993, Kymlicka 1995

Therefore, design may be more likely if political actors go beyond the assumptions of the worst case scenario. That is, if they, first, take more interest in how the working of institutions is influenced by properties of citizens, and, second, how different institutional arrangements form the mentality, character and identity of individuals and collectivities, including their sense of being part of a democratic community. An implication is that design may become a more significant part of institutional transformations if political actors concentrate less one-sidedly on the design of institutions of policy making and implementation and take more interest in the design of institutions of education and socialization.

Changing the Existing Order

Much remains to be seen: What will be the ideals and projects that generate major new designs? What will be the factors that trigger such projects? Who will be able to succeed in institutional design? What can and will be the role of ordinary citizens in the transformation of political institutions? Indeed, it remains to be seen how the meaning of "democracy" may be modified, and how the relative importance of democratic criteria of institutional assessment may change as part of current transformations in democratic polities.

This chapter has presented a fairly long list of factors involved in understanding the possibilities of design, rather than a precise specification of the conditions under which a democratic polity is susceptible to one kind of intervention rather than another. This outcome may disappoint prospective designers. Yet, it reflects the state of the discipline and the intricacies of contemporary democratic orders. Designers are unlikely to eliminate competitive selection, incremental adaptation, slow processes of institutionalization, chance, coercion, breakdowns, and a variety of other processes in the development of political institutions. Still, by deftly deploying their reason, experience and resources, actors operating in contemporary democratic contexts can to some degree influence how those institutions are constituted, sustained, and transformed. A better theoretical understanding of how key features of democratic institutions influence the relative importance of design in institutional change, requires ideas beyond those portraying design as a question of finding the most cost-effective tool for achieving immediate policy benefits. The main purpose of this chapter has been to make a modest contribution towards such a development.

References

Ackerman, B. (1991) *We, the People*. Cambridge, Mass.: Harvard University Press.

Allardt, E. (ed.) (1981) *Nordic Democracy*. København: Det Danske Selskab.

Aristotle (384–322 B.C.) (1985) *Nichomachean Ethics* (transl. by Terence Irwin). Indianapolis, IN: Hacket.

Baldersheim, H. and Ståhlberg, K. (1994) "From top-down to bottom- up: free communes and the politics of administrative modernization", in H. Baldersheim and K. Ståhlberg (eds.) *Toward the Self-Regulating Municipality*, pp. 3–18. Darthmouth: Aldershot.

Berg, E. (1965) *Democracy and the Majority Principle*. Stockholm: Ivar Heggströms Tryckeri.

Blichner, L.C. (1995) *Radical Change and Experiential Learning*. Ph.D. thesis. Report no. 37/95. Bergen: University of Bergen, Department of Administration and Organizational Theory.

Bobbio, N. (1987) *The Future of Democracy*. Minneapolis: University of Minnesota Press.

Boli, J. (1989) *New Citizens for a New Society. The Institutional Origins of Mass Schooling in Sweden*. Oxford: Pergamon.

Broderick, A. (1970) "Preface", in A. Broderick (ed.) *The French Institutionalists: Maurice Hauriou, Georges Renard, Joseph T. Delos*, xiii–xxv. Cambridge, Mass.: Harvard University Press.

Brunsson, N. (1985) *The Irrational Organization*. Chichester: Wiley.

————. (1989) *The Organisation of Hypocrisy*. Chichester: Wiley.

Brunsson, N. and Olsen, J.P. (1993) *The Reforming Organization*. London: Routledge. New edition 1997 by Fagbokforlaget, Bergen.

Bryant, C.G.A. and Mokrzycki, E. (eds.) (1994) *The New Great Transformation?* London: Routledge.

Castles, F., Gerritsen, R. and Vowles, J. (eds.) (1996) *The Great Experiment. Labor Parties and Public Policy Transformation in Australia and New Zealand*. Auckland: Auckland University Press.

Chandler, A.D.Jr. (1962) *Strategy and Structure*. Cambridge, Mass.: MIT Press.

Child, J. and Kieser, A. (1981) "Development of organizations over time", in P.C. Nystrom and W.H. Starbuck (eds.) *Handbook of Organizational Design* 1: 28–64. Oxford: Oxford University Press.

Cohen, J.L. and Arato, A. (1992) *Civil Society and Political Theory*. Cambridge, Mass.: MIT Press.

Cohen, M.D., March, J.D. and Olsen, J.P. (1972) "A garbage can model of organizational choice", *Administrative Science Quarterly* 17: 1–25.

Cyert, R.M. and March, J.G. (1963) *A Behavioral Theory of the Firm*. Englewood Cliffs NJ: Prentice Hall.

Dahl, R.A. (1985) *A Preface to Economic Democracy*. Cambridge: Polity Press.

Dalton, R.J. and Kuechler, M. (1990) *Challenging the Political Order: New Social and Political Movements in Western Democracies*. New York: Oxford University Press.

Dehousse, R. et al. (1992) *Europe after 1992: New Regulatory Strategies*. Florence: European University Institute, EUI working papers no. 92/31.

Deutsch, K.W. (1966) *The Nerves of Government*. New York: Free Press.

Egeberg, M. (1987) "Designing public organizations", in J. Kooiman and K.A. Eliassen (eds.) *Managing Public Organizations*, pp. 142–157. London: Sage.

Egeberg, M. (1994) "Bridging the gap between theory and practice: The case of administrative policy", *Governance* 7(1): 83–98.

Eisenstadt, S.N. (1964) "Institutionalization and change", *American Sociological Review* 29: 235–47.

Elias, N. (1939/1982) *The Civilizing Process: State Formation and Civilization*. Oxford: Basil Blackwell.

_____. (1988) "Violence and civilization: The state monopoly of physical violence and its infringement", in J. Keane (ed.) *Civil Society and the State*, pp. 177–198. London: Verso.

Elster, J. (1983) *Sour Grapes: Studies in the Subversion of Rationality*. Cambridge: Cambridge University Press.

Elster, J. and Slagstad, R. (eds.) (1988) *Constitutionalism and Democracy*. Cambridge/Oslo: Cambridge University Press/ Norwegian University Press.

Elster, J., Offe, C. and Preuss, U. (1997) *Repairing the Boat in the Open Sea: Constitutional Politics and Economic Transformation in Post-communist Societies*. Cambridge: Cambridge University Press (forthcoming).

Etzioni, A. (1964) *Modern Organizations*. Englewood Cliffs, New Jersey: Prentice-Hall.

Friedrich, C.J. (1939) "Democracy and dissent", *Political Quarterly* (October–December): 571–582.

Glasman, M. (1994) "The great deformation: Polanyi, Poland and the terrors of planned spontaneity", in C.G.A. Bryant and E. Mokrzycki (eds.) *The New Great Transformation?*, pp. 191–217. London: Routledge.

Goodin, R.E. (1988) *Reasons for Welfare*. Princeton, New Jersey: Princeton University Press.

_____. (1992) *Motivating Political Morality*. Cambridge, Mass.: Blackwell.

_____. (1993) "The contribution of political science", in R.E. Goodin and P. Pettit (eds.) *A Companion to Contemporary Political Philosophy*, pp. 157–182. Oxford: Blackwell.

_____. (1995) "Institutions and their design", in R.E. Goodin (ed.) *The Theory of Institutional Design*, pp. 1–53. Cambridge: Cambridge University Press.

Goodin, R.E. and Pettit, P. (1993) "Introduction", in R.E. Goodin and P. Pettit (eds.) *A Companion to Contemporary Political Philosophy*, pp. 1–4. Oxford: Blackwell.

Haas, E. (1958) *The Uniting of Europe*. Stanford, Calif.: Stanford University Press.

Habermas, J. (1992) "Citizenship and national identity: Some reflections on the future of Europe", *Praxis International* 12(1): 1–19.

Haberstroh, C.J. (1965) "Organizational design and system analysis", in J.G. March (ed.) *Handbook of Organizations*, pp. 1171–1211. Chicago: Rand McNally.

Hamilton, A., Jay, J. and Madison, J. (1787/1964) *The Federalist Papers*. New York: Pocket Books.

Hammond, T.H. (1996) "Formal theory and the institutions of governance", *Governance* 9 (2): 107–185.

Hayek, F.A. (1990) "The errors of constructivism", in F.A. Hayek *New Studies in Philosophy, Politics, Economics and the History of Ideas*, pp. 3–22. London: Routledge (Paperback ed.).

Held, D. (1986) "Introduction: New forms of democracy?", in D. Held and C. Pollitt (eds.) *New Forms of Democracy:*, pp.1–50. London: Sage.

_____. (1995) *Democracy and the Global Order. From the Modern State to Cosmopolitan Governance*. Cambridge: Polity Press.

Helleiner, E. (1995) "Great transformations: A Polanyian perspective on the contemporary global financial order", *Studies in Political Economy* 48: 149–164.

Heller, F. (1995) "Review of N. Brunsson and J.P. Olsen: The Reforming Organization", *Organizational Studies* 16(4): 707–711.

Hernes, G. (1976) "Structural change in social processes", *American Journal of Sociology* 82 (3): 513–547.

Herzog, D. (1989) *Happy Slaves: A Critique of Consent Theory*. Chicago: University of Chicago Press.

Hesse, J.J. (ed.) (1993) *Administrative Transformation in Central and Eastern Europe. Towards Public Sector Reform in Post-Communist Societies*. Oxford: Blackwell.

Hesse, J.J. and Johnson, N. (eds.) (1995) *Constitutional Policy and Change in Europe*. Oxford: Oxford University Press.

Hirschman, A.O. (1991) *The Rhetoric of Reaction, Perversity, Futility, Jeopardy*. Cambridge, Mass.: Belknap.

Jachtenfuchs, M. and Kohler-Koch, B. (eds.) (1996) *Europäische Integration*. Opladen: Leske & Budrich.

Kassim, H. and Wright, V. (1991) "The role of national administrations in the decision-making processes of the European Community", *Estratto*: 832–850. Rome: Rivista trimestrale di diritto pubblico.

Klein, R. (1995) "Self-inventing institutions: Institutional design and the U.K. welfare state", in R.E. Goodin (ed.) *The Theory of Institutional Design*, pp. 240–253. Cambridge: Cambridge University Press.

Kochanek, S.A. (1971) "Perspectives on the study of revolution and social change", *Comparative Politics* 5(3): 313–319.

Koslowski, P. (1985) "Philosophy and economics. An introduction", in P. Koslowski (ed.) *Economics and Philosophy*, pp. 1–16. Tübingen: J.C.B. Mohr (Paul Siebeck).

Krasner, S.D. (1988) "Sovereignty: An institutional perspective", *Comparative Political Studies* 21: 66–94.

Kuhn, T.S. (1962) *The Structure of Scientific Revolutions*. Chicago: The University of Chicago Press.

Kymlicka, W. (1995) *Multicultural Citizenship*. Oxford: Claredon Press.

Lepsius, M.R. (1990) *Interessen, Ideen und Institutionen*. Opladen: Westdeutsche Verlag.

Levinthal, D.A. and March, J.G. (1993) "The myopia of learning", *Strategic Management Journal* 14: 95–112.

Levitt, B. and March, J.G. (1988) "Organizational Learning", *Annual Review of Sociology* 14: 319–340.

Luard, E. (1990) *The Globalization of Politics. The Changed Focus of Political Action in the Modern World*. New York: New York University Press.

Lukes, S. (1995) *The Curious Enlightenment of Professor Caritat*. London: Verso.

Machiavelli, N. (1950) *The Prince and The Discourses* (intro. by M. Lerner). New York: Random House, The Modern Library.

March, J.G. (1981) "Footnotes to organizational change", *Administrative Science Quarterly* 26: 563–577.

_____. (1988) *Decisions and Organizations*. Oxford: Blackwell.

_____. (1991) "Exploration and exploitation in organizational learning", *Organization Science* 2: 71–87.

_____. (1994) "The evolution of evolution", in J. Baum and J. Singh (eds.) *The Evolutionary Dynamics of Organizations*, pp. 39–49. New York: Oxford University Press.

March, J.G. and Olsen, J.P. (1975) "The uncertainty of the past: organizational learning under ambiguity", *European Journal of Political Research* 3: 147–171.

_____. (1976) *Ambiguity and Choice in Organizations*. Bergen: Universitetsforlaget.

_____. (1983) "Organizing political life: what administrative reorganization tells us about government", *American Political Science Review* 77: 281–96.

_____. (1984) "The new institutionalism: organizational factors in political life", *American Political Science Review* 78: 734–749.

_____. (1989) *Rediscovering Institutions*. New York: Free Press.

_____. (1995) *Democratic Governance*. New York: Free Press.

Marin, B. and Mayntz, R. (eds.) (1991) *Policy Networks*. Frankfurt am Main: Campus.

Marks, G., Hooghe, L. and Blank, K. (1995) *European integration and the state*. Florence, European University Institute: Working paper RSC No. 95/7.

Marx, K. (1852/1963) *The Eighteenth Brumaire of Louis Bonaparte*. New York: International Publishers.

Mayntz, R. (1993) "Governing failures and the problem of governability: some comments on a theoretical paradigm", in J. Kooiman (ed.)*Modern Governance: New Government-Society Interactions*: 9–21. London: Sage.

Metcalfe, L. (1981) "Designing precarious partnerships", in P.C. Nystrom and W.H. Starbuck (eds.) *Handbook of Organizational Design*, Volume 1: 503–530. Oxford: Oxford University Press.

Meyer, J. and Rowan, B. (1977) "Institutionalized organizations: Formal structure as myth and ceremony", *American Journal of Sociology* 83: 340–363.

Michels, R. (1915/1968) *Political Parties*. New York: Free Press.

Mill, J.S. (1861/1962) *Considerations on Representative Government*. South Bend, IN: Gateway editions.

Nelson, R.R. and Winter, S.G. (1982) *An Evolutionary Theory of Economic Change*. Cambridge, Mass.: Harvard University Press.

North, D.C. (1990) *Institutions, Institutional Change and Economic Performance. Cambridge:* Cambridge University Press.

Notermans, T. (1995) *Social democracy and external constraints*. Oslo, ARENA-programme: Working paper No. 15 1995.

Nystrom, P.C. and Starbuck, W.H. (1981) "Designing and understanding organizations", in P.C. Nystrom and W.H. Starbuck (eds.) *Handbook of Organizational Design* Vol.1: Adapting Organizations to their Environments: IX-XXII. Oxford: Oxford University Press.

Offe, C. (1984) *Contradictions of the Welfare State*. Cambridge, Mass.: MIT Press.

_____. (1991) "Capitalism by democratic design? Democratic theory facing the triple transition in East and Central Europe", *Social Research* 58 (4): 864–892.

_____. (1995) "Designing institutions in East European transitions", in R.E. Goodin (ed.) *The Theory of Institutional Design*, pp. 199–226. Cambridge: Cambridge University Press.

_____. (1997) "Micro-aspects of democratic theory: what makes for the deliberative competence of citizens?", in A. Hadenius (ed.) *Democracy's Victory and Crisis*. Cambridge: Cambridge University Press.

Olsen, J.P. (1981) "Integrated organizational participation in government", in P.C. Nystrom and W.H. Starbuck (eds.) *Handbook of Organizational Design*. Vol. 2: Remodeling Organizations and their Environments: 492–516. Oxford: Oxford University Press.

_____. (1990) *Demokrati på svenska*. Stockholm: Carlssons.

_____. (1991) "Modernization programs in perspective: Institutional analysis of organizational change", *Governance* 4 (2): 125–149.

_____. (1992) "Analyzing institutional dynamics", *Statswissenschaften und Staatspraxis* 2: 247–271.

_____. (1995) European Challenges to the nation-state, in Seeking a New Paradigm of Public Administration in Democratic Society: 5–53. Seoul: Proceedings, The Korean Association for Public Administration.

_____. (1996) "Europeanization and nation-state dynamics", in S. Gustavsson and L. Lewin (eds.) *The Future of the Nation-State*, pp. 245–285. London: Routledge.

Olsen, J.P. and Peters, B.G. (1996) *Lessons from Experience: Experiential Learning in Administrative Reforms in Eight Democracies*. Oslo: Scandinavian University Press.

Pitkin, H.F. (1967/1972) *The Concept of Representation*. Berkeley: University of California Press.

Polanyi, K. (1944) *The Great Transformation*. Boston: Beacon Press.

Popper, K.R. (1945) *The Open Society and Its Enemies*. London: Routledge & Kegan Paul.

Powell W.W. and DiMaggio, P.J. (eds.) (1991) *The New Institutionalism in Organizational Analysis*. Chicago: University of Chicago Press.

Preuss, U.K. (1991) "The politics of constitution making: Transforming politics into constitutions", *Law and Policy* 13 (2): 107–123.

Przeworski, A. (1991) *Democracy and the Market*. Cambridge/Oslo: Cambridge University Press/Norwegian University Press.

Putnam, R.D. (1993) *Making Democracy Work: Civic Traditions in Modern Italy*. Princeton, New Jersey: Princeton University Press.

Rawls, J. (1988) "The priority of right and the ideas of the good", *Philosophy and Public Affairs* 17: 251–276.

_____. (1993) *Political Liberalism*. New York: Columbia University Press.

Ringen, S. (1987) *The Possibility of Politics: A Study in the Political Economy of the Welfare State*. Oxford: Claredon.

Rokkan, S. (1966) "Norway: numerical democracy and corporate pluralism", in R.A. Dahl (ed.) *Political Oppositions in Western Democracies*, pp. 70–116. New Haven: Yale University Press.

Rose, R. (1993) *Lesson-drawing in Public Policy*. Chatham, New Jersey: Chatham House.

Schattschneider, E.E. (1960) *The Semi-Sovereign People*. New York: Holt, Rinehard and Winston.

Schmidt, V.A. (1990) *Democratizing France: The Political and Administrative History of Decentralization*. Cambridge: Cambridge University Press.

Schuppert, G.F. (1995) "On the evolution of a European state: Reflections on the conditions for and the prospects for a European constitution", in J.J. Hesse and N. Johnson (eds.) *Constitutional Policy and Change in Europe*, pp. 329–368. Oxford: Oxford University Press.

Scott, W.R. (1995) *Institutions and Organizations*. Thousand Oaks, Calif.: Sage.

Scott, W.R. and Meyer, J.W. et al. (1994) *Institutional Environments and Organizations*. Thousand Oaks, Calif.: Sage.

Selznick, P. (1957) *Leadership in Administration*. New York: Harper & Row.

Shephard, W.J. (1935) "Democracy in transition", *The American Political Science Review*, 29 (1): 1–20.

Shklar, J.N. (1990) *The Faces of Injustice*. New Haven, New Jersey: Yale University Press.

Simon, H.A. (1953) "Birth of an organization: the economic cooperation administration", *Public Administration Review* 13: 227–236.

————. (1970) (paperback ed.) *The Sciences of the Artificial*. Cambridge Mass.: MIT Press.

Soysal, Y.N. and Strang, D. (1989) "Construction of the first mass education systems in nineteenth century Europe", *Sociology of Education* 62 (October): 277–288.

Stinchcombe, A.L. (1965) "Social Structure and Organizations", in J.G. March (ed) *Handbook of Organizations*, pp. 142–193. Chicago: Rand McNally.

Thomas, G.M. et al. (1987) *Institutional Structure*. Newbury Park, Calif.: Sage.

Thompson, G. (1990) *The Political Economy of the New Right*. Boston: Twayne Publishers.

Tønnessen, R.T. (1992) *Demokratisk dannelse i tysk perspektiv. 20 års diskusjon om Hermann Gieseckes syn på den politiske oppdragelsen*. Oslo: Universitets-forlaget.

Tyler, T. (1990) *Why People Obey the Law*. New Haven, New Jersey: Yale University Press.

Viroli, M. (1992) *From Politics to Reason of State*. Cambridge: Cambridge University Press.

Walzer, M. (1984) "The resources of American liberalism: Liberalism and the art of separation", *Political Theory* 12 (3): 315–330.

Weaver, R.K. and Rockman, B.A. (1993) "Institutional reform and constitutional design", in R.K. Weaver and B.A. Rockman (eds.) *Do Institutions Matter*, pp. 462–481. Washington D.C.: Brookings.

Wildavsky, A. and Tenenbaum, E. (1981) *The Politics of Mistrust*. Beverly Hills, Calif.: Sage.

Wolin, S. (1981) "The new public philosophy", *Democracy* 1(4): 23–36.

Wright, V. (1994) "Reshaping the state: the implications for public administration", *West European Politics* 17 (3): 102–137.

Zucker, L.G. (ed.) (1988) *Institutional Patterns and Organizations: Culture and Environment*. Cambridge, Mass.: Ballinger.

Contributors

NILS BRUNSSON, professor of management, Stockholm School of Economics and the chairman of Stockholm Center for Organizational Research.

JOHAN P. OLSEN, director of the Norwegian Research Council's programme ARENA (Advanced Research on the Europeanisation of the Nation-State) and adjunct professor of political science, University of Oslo.

LARS-ERIK BERGEVÄRN, PhD-student in accounting, School of Economics and Commercial Law, Gothenburg University.

LARS BLICHNER, associate professor, Department of Administration and Organization Theory, University of Bergen.

SØREN CHRISTENSEN, professor, Department of Organization and Industrial Sociology, Copenhagen Business School.

TOM CHRISTENSEN, professor, Department of Political Science, University of Oslo.

BARBARA CZARNIAWSKA, Chair in management, Gothenburg Research Institute, School of Economics and Commercial Law, Gothenburg University.

MORTEN EGEBERG, professor, Department of Political Science, University of Oslo.

HÅKAN HÅKANSSON, professor of business administration, Uppsala University.

BERNWARD JOERGES, professor of sociology, Technical University, Berlin.

JAN JOHANSON, professor of business administration, Uppsala University.

KRISTIAN KREINER, professor, Department of Organization and Industrial Sociology, Copenhagen Business School.

KARI LILJA, professor, Organization and Management, Helsinki School of Economics and Business Administration.

PER LÆGREID, professor, Department of Administration and Organization Theory, University of Bergen and Norwegian Centre in Organization and Management, Bergen.

FRODE MELLEMVIK, professor in accounting, Bodø Graduate School of Business, Bodø College.

JAN MOLIN, associate professor, Department of Organization and Industrial Sociology, Copenhagen Business School.

OLOV OLSON, professor in accounting, School of Economics and Commercial Law, Gothenburg University.

KERSTIN SAHLIN-ANDERSSON, professor of management, Stockholm University and director of Stockholm Center for Organizational Research.

LINDA SANGOLT, associate professor, Department of Administration and Organization Theory, University of Bergen.

TIMO SANTALAINEN, docent, Organization and Management, and MANNET, Director of Strategic Development, Switzerland.

MAJKEN SCHULTZ, professor, Department of Intercultural Communication and Management, Copenhagen Business School.

GUJE SEVÓN, professor, Department of Management, Politics, and Philosophy, Copenhagen Business School.

RISTO TAINO, professor, Organization and Management, Helsinki School of Economics and Business Administration.